THE NATIONAL RECOVERY ADMINISTRATION

Volume I

A Da Capo Press Reprint Series

FRANKLIN D. ROOSEVELT
AND THE ERA OF THE NEW DEAL

GENERAL EDITOR : FRANK FREIDEL

Harvard University

THE NATIONAL RECOVERY ADMINISTRATION

An Analysis and Appraisal

BY

LEVERETT S. LYON

PAUL T. HOMAN   LEWIS L. LORWIN

GEORGE TERBORGH   CHARLES L. DEARING

LEON C. MARSHALL

Volume I

DA CAPO PRESS • NEW YORK • 1972

Library of Congress Cataloging in Publication Data

Lyon, Leverett Samuel, 1885-
  The National Recovery Administration.
  (Franklin D. Roosevelt and the era of the New Deal)
  Reprint of the 1935 ed., which was issued in one volume as
Publication no. 60 of the Institute of Economics of the Brookings
Institution.
    1. U.S. National Recovery Administration.
  I. Series: Brookings Institution, Washington, D.C.
  Institute of Economics. Publication no. 60. II. Series: Franklin D.
  Roosevelt and the era of the New Deal.
  HD3616.U46L8   1972   330.973   71-171386
  ISBN 0-306-70385-8

338. 0973
A995N1

This Da Capo Press edition of *The National Recovery Adminis-tration* is an unabridged republication in two volumes of the one-volume first edition published in Washington, D.C., in 1935 as Publication No. 60 of The Institute of Economics of the Brookings Institution.

Published by Da Capo Press, Inc.
A Subsidiary of Plenum Publishing Corporation
227 West 17th Street, New York, New York 10011

THE NATIONAL RECOVERY ADMINISTRATION

THE NATIONAL RECOVERY ADMINISTRATION

An Analysis and Appraisal

BY

LEVERETT S. LYON

PAUL T. HOMAN   LEWIS L. LORWIN

GEORGE TERBORGH   CHARLES L. DEARING

LEON C. MARSHALL

WASHINGTON, D.C.

THE BROOKINGS INSTITUTION

1935

COPYRIGHT, 1935, BY
THE BROOKINGS INSTITUTION

Set up and printed
Published April 1935

Printed in the United States of America
George Banta Publishing Company
Menasha, Wisconsin

DIRECTOR'S PREFACE

This is the fifth of a series of studies of the NRA undertaken by the Institute of Economics under the immediate direction of Leverett S. Lyon. Of the earlier studies in the series, one presented a general preliminary analysis of the Recovery Administration, another dealt with a specific controversial trade practice, and two others surveyed the regulatory action of the NRA in certain fields. The present volume is a general analysis and appraisal of the NRA as a whole.

The National Recovery Administration was given a central place in the President's recovery program. Now that the two-year period for which the National Industrial Recovery Act was enacted has almost run, Congress and the country are engaged in an appraisal of the work of the Recovery Administration and in an effort to decide whether it should be allowed to disappear with the expiration of the law upon which it is based or whether it should be continued in its present or in some modified form. To the consideration of this problem the present volume contributes a painstaking and objective analysis of the NRA. The study deals with its organization and operation as an administrative mechanism and with the substantive output in the form of code law as this relates to wages and hours and to trade practices. It analyzes the work of the NRA in industrial relations and appraises the effects of its work on recovery. The publication of this work at the moment when Congressional consideration of the NRA is active makes it particularly appropriate to the Institute's purpose of ascertaining and interpreting the facts concerning current economic problems.

Various members of the group directly concerned have acted as committees on the separate parts of the study. The responsibility of the several authors is indicated in the Acknowledgments. Harold G. Moulton has acted as a committee member in passing on the volume as a whole, as has Charles O. Hardy in connection with Part VI. We have also had the aid of an advisory committee of the Social Science Research Council.

EDWIN G. NOURSE
Director

Institute of Economics
April 1935

ACKNOWLEDGMENTS

The somewhat unusual conditions under which this book has been written make appropriate a brief statement in connection with acknowledgments. This study began almost with the inception of the Recovery Administration itself. It hardly needs to be said that there were no data, no record of activities, not even a basis for forecasting with certainty the direction which NRA developments would take. On the other hand, there began almost immediately explosive activity of kaleidoscopic type. In part this activity was directed to the formation and re-formation of the NRA itself. Its structure was recast and again recast almost before any form was sufficiently determined for observation and description. No less shifting and varied were its other activities. The initiation of the code-making process, the emotionalism of the Blue Eagle campaign, and early enforcement efforts, followed one another and were in turn succeeded by other dramatic actions with a feverish haste which offered a minimum of opportunity for careful scrutiny and appraisal.

Even when the early phases of NRA history were passed the problem of calm study was sufficiently difficult. The NRA expended its energies upon problems of organization, code making and enforcement, and in coping with the political pressures under which it operated. It at no time made available to the public any full record of its operations.

The prosecution of the study under these peculiar circumstances has led to a wider and more varied range of

personal obligations than is usually the case at the conclusion of even so extended an investigation. They are
indeed too many and too varied to be given in detail.
Issues involved in various aspects of the study have been
the subject of discussions with many professional students of economics and government administration and
with government officials generally. Of no less assistance have been conferences with members of code authorities, individual business men, and labor leaders, and
the helpful co-operation of the members and staffs of
the various national labor boards.

At the beginning of the study the Administrator
granted access to NRA materials. While in practice this
grant was not and perhaps could not be fully carried out,
the NRA has made available, in addition to its official
publications and releases, many other types of documents which have been of great value. Following its organization the National Industrial Recovery Board initiated a practice of making material available to research
organizations. This practice greatly facilitated the securing of factual data. The Brookings Institution has
in turn given certain material and made certain suggestions to the Recovery Board. The compilations of hours
and wages used in Part III were planned by members
of the Brookings staff, while in making the counts extensive assistance was given by the NRA staff. Similarly,
members of the Brookings group collaborated with the
Research and Planning Division of the NRA in making
the general analysis which constituted the basis for the
tables dealing with provisions relating to minimum
prices and cost methods, machine- and plant-hour limitations, production quotas, productive capacity, and inventory control. These tables appear in Chapters XXIII
and XXIV. The making of the count for these tables is,

however, entirely the work of the Research and Planning Division of the NRA. On other particular aspects of the work important assistance has been given by the members of the Recovery Administration staff; the Labor, Industrial, and Consumer Advisory Boards; and members of the Research and Planning and Legal Divisions.

The form and content of this study have been materially affected by the fact that certain members of the group have been, for various periods, integral parts of the NRA organization. Charles Dearing was for a period of nine months an assistant deputy administrator in charge of the preparation and administration of the trucking code. Paul T. Homan was for several weeks a member of the advisory committee to the office of the Deputy Assistant Administrator for Code Administration and Classification Problems. Leverett S. Lyon was deputy assistant administrator for trade practices from the origin of that office in April 1934 until the organization of the National Industrial Recovery Board in September of the same year. It goes without saying that these contacts contributed to an understanding of the tremendous responsibilities with which the NRA was struggling and of the techniques created to deal with these responsibilities. They also contributed greatly by affording acquaintanceship with NRA personnel and the opportunity for discussion of all aspects of the NRA experiment with those most directly concerned and directly responsible.

Assistants to the major authors have made substantial contributions to the volume. Elva Marquard and Frank Coe in the study of wages and hours provisions, Arthur Wubnig in the work on industrial relations, Robert Beall and Hugo Bezdek in working with the statistics relevant to recovery, Helen Wheeler and Victor Abramson in connection with the analysis and interpretation of trade practices, have all rendered aid of high quality.

The general relationship of responsibility as among the authors should also be specially noted. The study was conducted as a unified project to cover the various major aspects of the Recovery Administration. The work of each author has been so planned and handled as to avoid unnecessary overlapping and duplication. Moreover, as the various authors have been associated as a group, and as the subject matter of the book has been under more or less continuous discussion, it is impossible to allocate credit for every idea or item of evidence which appears. Each author is, however, directly responsible only for the particular part of the work for which credit is assigned to him below. There has been no effort to strive for unanimity on points of detail, and since each author was alone in possession of all of the data out of which his specific judgments arose, the primary interpretation is necessarily his.

Mr. Lyon and Mr. Homan are responsible for the writing of Part I. Mr. Dearing is responsible for Chapters IV and V, Mr. Homan for Chapters VI-IX, and Mr. Dearing and Mr. Homan jointly for Chapter X. Mr. Lorwin is responsible for Part IV, Mr. Lyon for Part V, and Mr. Terborgh for Part VI. The factual content of the analysis of wages and hour provisions of codes appearing in Part III is the work of Mr. Marshall, who before his appointment to the National Industrial Recovery Board was a member of the staff working on the study. Mr. Marshall, however, is not responsible for the expressions of judgment and appraisal which accompany the factual text.

Leverett S. Lyon

CONTENTS

xiii

CONTENTS

CHAPTER VIII

CONTENTS

CONTENTS

CONTENTS

APPENDIXES

PART I
THE UNDERLYING LAW

CHAPTER I

THE BACKGROUND OF THE
RECOVERY ACT

The spring of 1933 found the United States in the fourth year of the most serious economic depression which the nation had ever experienced. It was in this situation that a new Administration, skeptical of the individualism of the past, expressing confidence in a greater degree of collective action, and heralding a "New Deal" in terms of this belief, came into office. This new Administration quickly spread upon the federal statute books a number of laws designed to restore prosperity and to effect those reforms which the "New Deal" implied.

Of all this legislation the President of the United States appraised the National Recovery Act as of outstanding significance. When affixing his signature to this law on June 16, 1933, he declared:

> History probably will record the National Industrial Recovery Act as the most important and far-reaching legislation ever enacted by the American Congress.
>
> It represents a supreme effort to stabilize for all time the many factors which make for the prosperity of the nation and the preservation of American standards.
>
> Its goal is the assurance of a reasonable profit to industry and living wages for labor, with the elimination of the piratical methods and practices which have not only harassed honest business but also contributed to the ills of labor.

He thus indicated his opinion of the predominant importance of the NIRA in the legislation which had been passed under his direct influence, the magnitude of the problems to which the law was directed, and the deviation

3

from past lines of economic policy which it represented.

The public mind was receptive to action of a heroic cast. Deflationary developments had carried economic maladjustments to a point where the experience of earlier depressions appeared to many observers to furnish no guidance. Faith in the "self-generating" forces of recovery had almost completely vanished. The widespread belief that the government must intervene to rout the forces of depression, in a more comprehensive way than had ever before been attempted, opened the way for new and unconventional experiments in economic policy.

While the Recovery Act grew from a situation calling for prompt action and was devised to meet immediate needs, it was not wholly without precedent in the ideas of the past. The Interstate Commerce Commission, the various public utility commissions, labor laws, trade practice conference agreements under the Federal Trade Commission, and the corporate bodies of war time had all established patterns of thought, in terms of which it was easy to conceive of new regulation. Familiar also to the American mind was the idea of collective action. The working man was experienced with trade unions; the farmer with co-operatives; the business man with trade associations. The attempt to extend economic power through group action had already a long history and objectives which had found expression in proposals for legislative action.

Several lines of thought prominent during the depression gave support to the idea that the national government should attempt actively to promote industrial recovery. Most general in nature was the much discussed concept of economic planning. This was a broad phrase under which were included numerous proposals to increase the amount of collective economic control. Such proposals had the common ground of distrusting individualism as the guiding principle of economic life. They varied widely in the extent to which they envisaged a departure from the capitalistic structure of economic society, ranging from modest suggestions for setting up an advisory economic council to proposals for reorganizing American industry into vast monopolistic trusts under close government regulation.

Many who were unsympathetic with economic planning in general terms or to whom the idea was even abhorrent, found it appealing in certain limited areas. Planning on an industry basis found support in a popularly prevailing view that there existed an excess of producing capacity, and that it was desirable to "balance production and consumption" by direct means of control. The so-called "lack of balance" was believed to be an important factor in continuing the depression. Even before the depression there was much talk of so-called "sick industries"—those which had experienced a rapid expansion during and immediately after the war and which found unusual difficulty in adjusting themselves to a contracting market. That "industry planning" with government assistance could aid in this situation was widely believed.

There was further the view that much competition is "predatory." This view, held in more prosperous days chiefly by business men in regard to the actions of their competitors, was nourished by widespread business failures and the price and wage reductions which always accompany depressions. Thus nourished, the notion of predatory competition was expanded into a doctrine, accepted by many, that the degree of competition to which we were accustomed was itself an evil, essentially "destructive," and both a cause of the depression and a factor in its continuance. The prevalence of this point of view gave support to business men's proposals for modifying the anti-trust laws in quarters which heretofore had supported these laws as a bulwark against monopoly.

Still another strain of thought was the idea of technological unemployment. A realization of the fact that the introduction of machines causes at least temporary unemployment is at least as old as the Industrial Revolution; but the rapid technological advance of recent years, striking instances of displacement of men by machinery, and the advancing "rationalization" of American industry between 1922 and 1929 had given the idea of technological unemployment a new interest and had made large numbers of persons susceptible to proposals which seemed to show a way toward spreading the available work.

Vaguely, but none the less effectively, these strains of thought made contact with another somewhat related economic idea. This was that current income in the hands of the masses was insufficient to carry from the market the potential output of the highly productive industrial system. The correlative of this proposition was that economic stability could be promoted through larger current distribution of income to the working population. During the depression this idea was re-enforced by the absence of income in the hands of the unemployed and the loss of income of those whose wages had been cut. There developed a wide popular belief that escape from the depression was through "an increase in mass purchasing power."

These various strains of thought, in one form or another, were all actively present in the discussion of means of escape from the depression, and each has some relevancy to the history of the National Industrial Recovery Act.[1]

[1] It is perhaps unnecessary to state that these theories are mentioned

The immediate origins of the act were very complex and will furnish a fascinating and perplexing study for some legislative historian. The suggestions of many persons and groups for ending the depression were consulted. There were proposals for a government guarantee against loss to private construction enterprises as an inducement to stimulate activity in capital goods industries. There were suggestions for a more general use of the principle of government insurance against loss as a means of encouraging private business expansion. A third kind of proposal was that government leadership should sponsor voluntary agreements among the leading establishments of the most important industries to expand their schedules of production simultaneously for a period of months and also to set minimum wages and prices.

These and other suggested plans when thrown into the arena of official discussion were brought into contact with many proposals then before Congress, for eliminating "unfair and excessive" competition by amendment of the anti-trust laws and for limiting working hours in the interest of re-employment. A curious combination of support was engendered among reform groups, business groups, and labor groups, each seeing in the developing bill an opportunity to promote ends of its own. In the outcome a law was passed which was highly inexplicit in its terms but vastly comprehensive in its powers. It allocated to the President unprecedented lines of economic authority.[2]

---

merely as those prevalent. No implication of their validity or invalidity is intended. Some of them are appraised in later chapters.

[2] This chapter and the one which follows are in some considerable degree summaries of the Introduction and Chapter I of the *ABC of the NRA,* published by The Brookings Institution.

CHAPTER II

PROVISIONS OF THE ACT

The National Industrial Recovery Act is made up of three titles. The heading of Title I is Industrial Recovery; of Title II, Public Works and Construction Projects; and of Title III, Amendments to Emergency Relief and Construction Act and Miscellaneous Provisions. The contents of Title III need no consideration in a discussion of the law. Title II authorizes an appropriation of 3.3 billion dollars for the financing of public works. Although strongly supplemental to the purposes of Title I, it may be regarded as a separate piece of legislation. In this book Title I only will be in the foreground of attention.[1]

The law opens with a declaration of policy.[2] The second section of Title I is essentially an empowering paragraph. This section authorizes the President, as he may find necessary, to establish agencies; to accept voluntary services; to appoint officers and employees without regard to the civil service laws; and to utilize federal officers and employees, and, with the consent of the state, state and local officers. Any or all of his functions and powers under the act, he is authorized to delegate to such agents as he may designate or appoint. It is on this authorization of power that the establishment of the National Recovery Administration—the NRA—is based. From the same source is drawn the extensive authority delegated to and exercised first by the Administrator,

---

[1] For text of Title I, see Appendix A.
[2] The content of this declaration is discussed in Chap. III.

General Hugh S. Johnson, and now by the National Industrial Recovery Board (NIRB).

Section 2 also limits the operation of the act to two years and authorizes the President to end it sooner by a proclamation, or the Congress to end it by a joint resolution declaring that the emergency recognized by the opening sentences of the act has ceased to exist.

It is with Section 3 that the real content of the law begins. Section 3(a) provides for codes of fair competition and lays down the basic procedure by which codes have up to the present been formed. Under this section the initiative is taken by "trade or industrial associations or groups," which may place before the President for approval codes of fair competition for their respective trades or industries. The President is authorized to approve such codes, if he finds: (1) that the applicants for a code impose no inequitable restrictions to membership in the groups represented; (2) that the applicants are truly representative of the trades or industries for which they speak; (3) that such proposed codes are not designed to promote monopolies or to eliminate or oppress small enterprises and will not operate to discriminate against the latter; and (4) that the proposed codes will, in his judgment, tend to effectuate the policy of the law.

Section 3(a) also specifically provides that codes shall not permit monopolies or monopolistic practices and makes mention of the right to be heard. This right, however, is guaranteed only to "persons engaged in other steps of the economic process" covered by a particular code, if their welfare stands to be affected by the operation of such code. The President may impose as a condition of his approval such requirements as he believes necessary for the protection of consumers, competitors, employees, and others, and he may make such exceptions to and exemptions from the provisions of codes as he deems necessary.

Under Section 3(b) codes approved by the President become legally binding. The approval of a code makes any violation of its provisions an "unfair method of competition" within the meaning of the Federal Trade Commission Act and its amendments. Violations of the terms of a code may, therefore, be proceeded against by the Federal Trade Commission. Section 3(c) invests the district courts of the United States with jurisdiction to prevent and restrain violations of the codes, and directs United States district attorneys to institute equity proceedings to restrain violations. Section 3(f) makes any violation of code provisions a misdemeanor punishable by a fine of not more than $500 for each offense, and each day such violation continues is deemed a separate offense.

If trade groups fail to take the initiative in code making, the President may do so. This power, given in Section 3(d) of the law, permits the President either upon his own initiative or upon complaints which he believes to justify the action, after such public notice and public hearings as he shall specify, to prescribe a code of fair competition for any trade or industry for which a code has not already been approved. Such codes have the same status as those initiated by trade groups under the provisions of Section 3(a).

Section 3(e) of the law gives the President regulatory powers over imports when, on the basis of an investigation by the Tariff Commission, he believes such regulation necessary to render effective the purposes of codes and agreements made under the act. He is empowered to lay down conditions upon which goods may be imported, to prescribe fees, and to limit the quantity of imports. Importers may be forbidden to import without first obtaining a federal license.

Section 4(a) authorizes the President to enter into agreements with and approve voluntary agreements among persons engaged in trade or industry, labor organizations, and trade and industrial groups, if in his judgment such agreements will aid in accomplishing the purposes of the law. It is under this section that the President promulgated the President's Re-employment Agreement (PRA) urging employers to agree with him to maintain certain conditions, particularly regarding wages and employment. It was these general agreements which were popularly called "the blanket code," and for which the Blue Eagle was first invented.

The possibilities under this sub-section are very extensive. Almost any type of agreement (between employers and employees, between members of trade groups, between one labor union and another, between one trade group and another, and so on) which is deemed to effectuate the purposes of the law and to which the President wishes to give the sanction of his approval may be comprehended within its sweeping terms. Its purpose appears to be to facilitate any sort of agreement which may be deemed a desirable supplement to the provisions of codes. Separate codes are entered into by the members of particular trade groups, whereas individuals, different trade groups, and different labor groups may severally or jointly enter into agreements. No penalties are specified for violation of such agreements.

Section 4(b) of the act, which was limited to one year's duration and expired June 16, 1934, further expanded the President's powers. It authorized him, whenever he should find that destructive wage or price cutting or other activities contrary to the purpose of the law were being practiced in any trade or industry, after public notice and hearing, to license business enterprises if he deemed it essential to make effective a code of fair competition or agreement. The licensing provision, giving the President the power of life or death over business enterprises, was the ultimate weapon of enforcement and the capstone of the powers granted to the President. Recognized as the most extraordinary extension of Presidential power in American history, this section was bitterly attacked in Congress.

Section 5 provides that codes, agreements, or licenses, approved or prescribed, and all actions complying with the provisions of codes or agreements, shall be exempt from the provisions of the anti-trust laws of the United States. Section 5 also includes a declaration that nothing in the act shall prevent an individual from pursuing the vocation of manual labor or selling the products thereof and that the act and its regulations shall not prevent any one from marketing or trading the produce of his farm.

Section 6 makes it necessary for a group, as a qualification of eligibility, to file such information concerning its activities as the President shall prescribe. It also empowers the President to prescribe such rules as shall insure that any organization availing itself of the benefits of the law shall be actually representative of the industry which it purports to represent. The President is authorized to use the investigatory powers of the Federal Trade Commission to carry out this and other provisions of Title I.

Section 7(a) contains a mandatory prescription to be included in each code adopted. This mandate, comprising three clauses, is designed in the interests of labor. Every code shall contain the conditions: (1) that employees shall have the right to organize and bargain collectively and shall be free from interference by employers in the designation of their representatives or in other concerted activities; (2) that no employee and no one seeking employment shall be required as a condition of employment to join any company union or to refrain from joining or assisting a labor organization of his own choosing; and (3) that employers shall comply with the maximum hours, rates of pay, and other conditions of employment approved or prescribed by the President.

Following the mandatory provision described, Section 7(b) goes on to prescribe that where employers and employees have by mutual agreement established the standards of hours, rates of pay, and such other conditions of employment as may be necessary to effectuate the purposes of the act, these standards may, upon approval by the President, have the same effect as a code of fair competition. The President is to "afford every opportunity" to employers and employees to arrive at such mutual agreements. Where no such agreement is arrived at or approved, under Section 7(c) the President may investigate the situation and prescribe a limited code of fair competition fixing such maximum hours of labor, minimum rates of pay, and other conditions of employment as he finds necessary to effectuate the policy of the law. The agreement provision of Section 7(b) appears to be a special application of Section 4(a), giving the force of a code to a particular kind of agreement. The power of the President to prescribe a "limited code" likewise appears to be a special application of Section 3(d), under which he may prescribe a comprehensive code.

Final sections of Title I of the act (Sections 8, 9, and 10) deal with its relationships to the Agricultural Adjustment Act, with a special provision concerning oil regulation, and with authorizations to the President for making the law effective. Section 10 gives the President power "from time to time to cancel or modify any order, approval, license, rule, or regulation issued under this title," and requires that every code issued under the law shall contain an express provision to that effect. The President, it appears, is thus authorized to remake in any way any code at any time during the life of the law.

Viewed as a whole, the National Industrial Recovery Act is primarily a piece of enabling legislation. Giving the President unprecedented peace-time powers, it requires nothing of him. He need not promulgate or approve any code. If a code is approved, the only positive requirement, as above stated, is that it include the labor provisions stated in Section 7(a). Negatively there are the requirements stated in Section 3 concerning the representative character of trade groups, the prohibition of monopolistic practices, and the interests of small enterprises. Except in the case of tariff investigations, procedural requirements are limited to the vague specification of public notice and hearing.

CHAPTER III

OBJECTIVES OF THE ACT

Concerning the purpose of Title II, providing for public works, there is no ambiguity. It was designed to stimulate recovery through the expenditure of public loan funds upon useful public works, and correlatively to provide additional work for the unemployed. Its primary stimulative effect was expected to operate in the fields of construction and capital goods where the unemployment of men and equipment was most marked.

No such simplicity of statement is possible with respect to the purposes of Title I. A little space may therefore be used profitably in examining the evidence. The official name of the whole act, including three titles, is "an act to encourage national industrial recovery, to foster fair competition, and to provide for the construction of certain useful public works, and for other purposes." The declaration of policy with which Title I begins reads as follows:

A national emergency productive of widespread unemployment and disorganization of industry, which burdens interstate and foreign commerce, affects the public welfare, and undermines the standards of living of the American people, is hereby declared to exist. It is hereby declared to be the policy of Congress

[1] to remove obstructions to the free flow of interstate and foreign commerce which tend to diminish the amount thereof; and

[2] to provide for the general welfare by promoting the organization of industry for the purpose of co-operative action among trade groups,

[3] to induce and maintain united action of labor and man-

15

agement under adequate governmental sanctions and supervision,

[4] to eliminate unfair competitive practices,

[5] to promote the fullest possible utilization of the present productive capacity of industries,

[6] to avoid undue restriction of production (except as may be temporarily required),

[7] to increase the consumption of industrial and agricultural products by increasing purchasing power,

[8] to reduce and relieve unemployment,

[9] to improve standards of labor, and otherwise

[10] to rehabilitate industry and to conserve natural resources.

Several clauses, it will be observed, imply the truism that larger production and fuller employment are desired. No indication is given of the degree to which "unfair competitive practices" implies more than does "unfair methods of competition" under the Federal Trade Commission Act. "Promoting the organization of industry for the purpose of co-operative action among trade groups" indicates an intended form of implementation without disclosing the intended lines of action. "United action of labor and management" means nothing until elaborated. The same may be said of "to improve standards of labor." The declaration, in short, exhibits merely general economic objectives, disclosing nothing concerning the more explicit lines of action contemplated.[1]

Turning to the body of the act, one finds that Section 3, providing for submittal and approval of voluntary codes of fair competition and for the imposition of codes, makes no mention of the intended content of such codes. Sec-

[1] The Supreme Court has characterized Section 1 of the act as "a broad outline" which "is simply an introduction of the act, leaving the legislative policy as to particular subjects to be declared and defined, if at all, by the subsequent sections." Supreme Court of the United States, Nos. 135 and 260, October Term, 1934. 293 U.S. 388.

tion 4(b) is less barren. The grant of licensing power to the President is prefaced by the clause, "whenever the President shall find that destructive wage or price cutting or other activities contrary to the policy of this title are being practiced in any trade or industry or any subdivision thereof, and . . . shall find it essential to license business enterprises in order to make effective a code of fair competition or an agreement." This may be interpreted to mean that a primary purpose of codes is to eliminate business conduct which may be characterized as "destructive wage or price cutting."

Some positive content is also found in Section 7. The President is instructed to encourage employers and employees "to establish by mutual agreement the standards as to the maximum hours of labor, minimum rates of pay, and such other conditions of employment." (Section 7-b.) But, "where no such mutual agreement has been approved by the President, . . . he is authorized to prescribe a limited code of fair competition, fixing such maximum hours of labor, minimum rates of pay, and other conditions of employment." (Section 7-c.) These provisions make it clear that wage and hour standards are primary objectives under the act. There is, however, no indication as to whether or not it was intended that protective labor provisions be initiated by trade or industrial groups under Section 3(a), or otherwise. The ambiguity on this point has been serious, since it at once raised a controversial situation inimical to "united action of labor and management," which was one of the stated purposes of the act. Though on the surface merely a procedural point, the ambiguity really relates to a rather fundamental matter of policy concerning the intended relationship between employer and employee groups.

Section 7(a) also states policy to the extent of indicating an intention to facilitate labor organization and to protect labor groups in certain rights of action. Both the rights of labor groups and the responsibilities of the government relative thereto are stated in such general terms that all concrete meaning depends upon later administrative interpretation.

The only positive guides to policy to be found in the act are those that have been mentioned. If they all be interpreted as applying to the purposes of voluntary codes under Section 3(a), codes were expected to include the somewhat overlapping categories of (a) provisions covering minimum wages, maximum hours, and "other conditions of employment"; (b) measures to prevent "destructive" wage cutting and price cutting; (c) fair trade practice provisions; and (d) provisions protecting certain labor rights of collective bargaining.

The provision in Section 5 placing what is done under the act outside the scope of the anti-trust laws, had it stood unlimited, would have been a tremendous grant of policy-making power. By amendment in the Senate, limitations were placed upon it, proscribing monopolies, monopolistic practices, and oppression of small enterprises, and protecting individuals in "pursuing the vocation of manual labor and selling or trading the products thereof." These limitations introduce a new ambiguity. The Sherman Act has been interpreted by the Supreme Court to forbid "unreasonable restraint of trade," and the content of the phrase has been organically connected with the concept of monopolization as it has been juristically developed. The Recovery Act in effect authorizes agreements "in restraint of trade" (else the stay of the anti-trust law provisions was unnecessary), but only such agreements as are free from "monopolistic practices."

How the court will resolve this issue, there is no way of knowing. Is the President's finding of fact that codes or agreements further the purposes of the act sufficient to establish the "reasonableness" of a "restraint of trade," or are the courts to have resort to external criteria by which to overrule his finding? And if so, what criteria? In either event the extent, or even the character, of the relief from the anti-trust laws is left in doubt.

The hearings on the bill before committees of the Senate and House of Representatives are equally vague. The evidence of Senator Wagner and Mr. Richberg, who were nearest to occupying the role of official sponsorship, centered on the idea of price stabilization by stopping competitive undercutting of labor standards. Thus Mr. Richberg, after saying "It has been the desire of the trade associations . . . to be permitted to get together and make agreements . . . for the purpose of eliminating unfair practices, and also, let us say, for the purpose of establishing price levels on which the industry felt it could survive," shortly thereafter in the same connected statement continued that the act provides "the most tremendous experiment in the way of governmental activity that has been undertaken by this government in connection with business; and that is the experiment of encouraging business organizations to get together to establish agreements that will promote fair competition, and primarily, from my point of view, fair competition as to labor; fair competition in wages and working conditions."[2] More vaguely, these sponsors used such terms as "destructive competition" and "civilizing competition." Both insisted that the bill supplemented, rather than did away with the anti-trust laws; that it was to

[2] 73 Cong. 1 sess., *National Industrial Recovery*, Hearings on H.R. 5664 before House Committee on Ways and Means, pp. 68 and 69.

purify rather than suppress competition. At one point Senator Wagner said, "This is supplemental to the anti-trust laws; it is not destructive of them. We are going to retain competition. We are simply going to put competition on a high standard of efficiency rather than on a low standard of exploitation of labor. That is the only difference."[3] At another point he said that he did not anticipate price fixing.[4] On the other hand he mentioned the making of agreements on production as a possible line of action.[5] In reply to a question by Senator King, "Is your bill drawn largely from the philosophy of the old German cartel system?" he replied, "Not at all." He went on to refer to it as a plan for "a nationally planned economy," but immediately limited the significance of this phrase to "a rationalization of competition" based on eliminating "exploitation of labor."[6]

When Representative Knutson asked, ". . . it is proposed to allow them to regulate their outputs, to have trade agreements as to prices, as to territory, and as to production?" Mr. Richberg gave the noncommittal answer that, "I see no limitation on the agreement or code which could be adopted except the limitations that are fixed in the act."[7] Shortly thereafter this colloquy occurred:

Mr. Knutson. Under this legislation, would it be permissible for industries which are competitors to get together and form cartels such as they have in Europe?
Mr. Richberg. I do not wish to compare this too broadly with the European cartel, Mr. Knutson.

[3] The same, p. 105.
[4] 73 Cong. 1 sess., *National Industrial Recovery*, Hearings on S. 1712 before Committee on Finance, p. 19.
[5] Hearings on H.R. 5664, p. 96.
[6] Hearings on S. 1712, p. 6.
[7] Hearings on H.R. 5664, p. 71.

Mr. Knutson. I am in thorough sympathy with your aim; but I consider this the most important section of the whole bill which we are dealing with right now.

Mr. Richberg. I think it of very vital importance.

Mr. Knutson. And I think we ought to understand it as fully as our limited power of understanding will permit us.

Mr. Richberg. I do not want to make too much of an analogy and that is the reason I do not want to simply say that this is the cartel type of operation.

Mr. Knutson. Oh, no.

Mr. Richberg. But in a general way it has that tendency.

Mr. Knutson. In a general way it encourages manufacturers to do the same things that the cartels are doing in Europe?

Mr. Richberg. I think, in a general way, that may be true; yes.

Mr. Knutson. And they couldn't be prosecuted for getting together and fixing prices?

Mr. Richberg. Assuming that the prices themselves have a reasonable relationship to the costs and so forth; yes.

Mr. Knutson. Of course, they would be subject to regulation by the government; but it would not be necessary, would it, for the steel industry, under this legislation, to get specific permission from the government to fix prices of steel products, and to limit production.

Mr. Richberg. I would say that depended entirely upon the regulations that were enforced by the Administration, which would be suited to the needs of a particular industry. . . .[8]

In response to a further question, "Do the provisions of the bill cover the wholesaler and the retailer where they employ labor?" Mr. Richberg replied, "It appears to me to cover all forms of trade and industry."[9]

All that such statements really showed was that powers of an extensive character were being granted, and not what use was expected to be made of them. A rather striking difference of view did, however, appear between Senator Wagner and Mr. Richberg concerning the prospects of cartel-like developments. Both seem to

[8] The same, pp. 71-72.   [9] The same, p. 83.

have been primarily interested in the public works and labor phases of the bill, and to have given little thought to its other aspects.

Discussion on the floor of the House and Senate elicited no new light. In answer to questions by Senator Borah and others, the sponsors of the bill tended to play down the intended degree of deviation from the anti-trust laws, even to the extent of appearing to suggest that agreements to support labor standards were the only important outcome to be expected. The acceptance by both houses of the Borah amendment against monopolistic practices indicated an intention of Congress not to authorize extensive deviation from the anti-trust laws.

The argument presented to the committees of the House and Senate, and to the House and Senate themselves, was that it was necessary in the emergency to grant sweeping powers to the President without being able to foresee in what ways they were to be used, beyond propping up labor standards. From all that can be learned of the legislative history of the act, Congress may be said to have been essentially uninformed upon what lines of action were to be anticipated under the act, and upon whether, or to what degree, it was seriously impairing the policy of the anti-trust laws.

The opinions of persons who had some early relationship to the bill are no more helpful in clarifying the underlying policy. Some of them certainly thought its primary function was to support labor standards, with possibly some spreading of work, more active policing of the sort of competitive practices which was already illegal, and the extension of accredited trade association practices. Their underlying thought in this connection— quite apart from any consideration of the direct creation of "purchasing power"—was that the competitive cutting of wages and other labor standards had reached a stage where a progressively "destructive" degree of price competition was feeding upon it. It was felt that if "labor standards" could be "stabilized" at "reasonable" levels business men could go forward with business commitments in a renewed state of confidence. The central thought, in more general form, was that the important elements in business costs needed to be brought to a degree of stability to permit reasonable adjustment of business plans to future market prospects.

To the range of action indicated in the preceding paragraph some persons added special treatment of "sick" industries, a phrase limited in its current meaning to a very few fields especially affected by dynamic industrial changes. Coal and textiles were the usual illustrations. Fairly thoroughgoing forms of government guardianship were thought of in this connection, particularly with respect to the natural resource industries.

Some persons, especially the sponsors of certain early proposals which had been influential in leading up to the framing of the act, conceived that agreements to step up the current rate of industrial production would be promoted, possibly in conjunction with some allocation of production quotas.

Others, including important members of the business community, envisaged the power of industrial groups to enter into cartel-like price and production agreements. This is at least hinted in the statement of Mr. H. I. Harriman, president of the United States Chamber of Commerce, at the hearings on the House bill. In response to a question, "Is there anything in this bill to assist industries to get back on their feet?" he replied, "Yes, sir;

because in this bill they can fix a fair price for their products with the consent of the President."[10] He further stated "a fair price," "fair wages," and "a fair dividend" as a trilogy of objectives.[11] But even he conceived that "the first codes that will be submitted will cover nothing, or practically nothing, but the matter of wages and hours, and so forth, and those can go into effect very promptly. Then . . . the refinements of the codes can be developed later."[12] The nature of the "refinements" is not made clear.

The diversity of ideas upon price and production control was very great, ranging from mild measures against collapsing prices to thoroughgoing forced cartels. Views of business men concerning the bill were so varied as to reach from one extreme of those who thought the object to raise labor costs, spread work, and hand American industry over in bonds to organized labor, to the other extreme of those who came in full cry on the scent of price and production control.

There were other persons who thought the act was meant primarily to implement certain advantages, both for recovery and for long-range business stabilization, which were supposed to derive from redistributing income more heavily toward the lower income brackets. These in some degree coincided with those who thought the bill to be among other things a charter of liberties to labor unions. And finally, not to attempt to display all shades or combinations of opinion, others of a more radical turn of mind took the invoking of group action and the granting of coercive powers to the President to mean that the New Deal was on the road toward dismantling economic individualism.

[10] Hearings on H.R. 5664, p. 154.
[11] The same, p. 134.   [12] The same, p. 153.

When one has canvassed the sources of information, the conviction grows that those most closely concerned with drafting or sponsoring the act had themselves vague ideas of what was to be done, and not to be done, under it; and what administrative organization and procedure could effect its purposes while observing its limitations. In some degree all the viewpoints noted above seem to have touched the inner circle. There was doubtless substantial agreement that the lowest wages were to be raised, that the total wage bill was to be increased, and that available work was to be spread among more workers. Beyond that, each person had his own ideas of what should be done. There is some evidence of an official view that when industrial groups had come in and displayed their troubles it would be soon enough to determine what should be done. So far as can be learned, even the Administration had no idea to what extent it was fostering a modification or impairment of the familiar outlines of the system of free private enterprise.

All these unfocused views make impossible any explicit answer to the question, What was the "theory" underlying the act? The theories were as numerous as the expectations of persons concerning the use which would be made of the powers. The powers were so great that there was no means of prognosticating in what particular directions they would be used.

In the most general sense, there seems to have been a more or less official recovery theory based upon three hypotheses: (1) That an increase in total payrolls would add to net current spending; (2) that raising the lowest wages would both promote spending, as just stated, and in addition restore a proper balance between occupations which the depression had broken down; and (3) that measures which prevented further price declines, or in some cases raised prices, would create a state of business confidence favorable to forward commitments. There was a more or less official view—that is to say, a view entertained by at least some officials—that the primary lift to recovery lay in Title II, providing funds for public works, and that Title I was to insure that the benefits therefrom were not neutralized by the deflationary effects of desperate competition.

With respect to a longer run, there were presumably three related ideas which impressed the President and his advisers: first, that the method of collective action of groups was important for stabilization of business activity; second, that this involved a higher degree of organization of both business and labor groups than existed; and third, that instability could be mitigated by measures directed to producing less inequality in the distribution of income.

In the light of all the foregoing considerations, little is to be gained by extensive exposition of the objectives of the act, as evidenced by the bill itself, by its legislative history, or by external reaction to it. The circumstances under which it was passed and the powers which it conferred are significant developments in the processes of American government. But, since it was an act under which diverse lines of policy and action were possible, its primary significance must be sought concretely through an examination of what has been done and is being done under its terms.

PART II

ADMINISTRATIVE ORGANIZATION
AND PROCEDURE

CHAPTER IV

ADMINISTRATIVE ORGANIZATION

Within a period of less than two years the National
Recovery Administration has developed into a sprawling
administrative colossus. In volume and scope its product
probably has never been equalled by any peace-time government agency. In its pursuit of the objectives of the
Recovery Act, as it interpreted those objectives, the NRA
has fixed into law a body of wage and hour legislation
for a large portion of the country's employers, controls
over production and prices affecting all consumers of
commodities, and detailed rules of business ethics and
practice.

Employers who, by pre-depression estimates, are the
source of employment for some 22 million workers have
been made directly subject to its operations. Its jurisdiction runs the full range of industrial and trade activity
from the animal soft hair industry code, covering 45
workers, to the retail trade code, holding legal jurisdiction over nearly 3.5 million employees. This has come
about through the formulation and approval of 546 codes
of fair competition and 185 supplemental codes, filling
18 volumes and 13,000 pages; through the approval of
685 amendments and modifications to these codes;
through the issuance of over 11,000 administrative
orders interpreting, granting exemptions from, and establishing classifications under the provisions of individual codes;[1] through the issuance of 139 administrative

[1] The preceding figures are taken from NRA Research and Planning
Division, *Report on the Operation of the National Industrial Recovery
Act, February 1935.*

orders bearing generally upon the administrative procedure of NRA; and through the promulgation by the
President of some 70 executive orders dealing specifically
with rights, procedure, and privileges under the NIRA.
The bulk of these orders and rulings have the full force
and effect of law.

Only the broad outline of NRA law-making activity is
furnished by this recital. As a means of implementing its
legislative acts the NRA has approved the establishment
of 585 agencies of industrial self-government (code
authorities) under which there are several thousand regional and divisional subordinate agencies. Most of the
approved code agencies have been granted the power
to levy legally compulsory assessments. Budgets covering estimated costs of code authority operation and ag-
gregating 41 million dollars have been scrutinized or
approved by the NRA.[2]

Supplementary to its major law-making activities the
NRA early in its career negotiated some 2.3 million
agreements between industrial and trade employers and
the President of the United States. The working conditions of about 16 million employees were temporarily
controlled by the provisions of these bilateral contracts
—officially termed President's Re-employment Agreements. In contrast with codes of fair competition, these
agreements were not enforceable at law. Public opinion
was supposed to furnish the persuasive force for compliance.

This is a bare sketch of NRA's work product. Its accomplishment has required the services of a staff ranging
from about 400 in August 1933 to a high of 4,500 in
February 1935, divided between the Washington office
and field agencies. Through February first 1935 the

[2] The same.

administrative expenses of the NRA have amounted to $13,566,000, ranging from a monthly expenditure of $393,000 in August 1933 to $1,054,000 in January 1935.[3]

The sweeping activity outlined above has taken the definite form of a tremendous and complex body of administrative law, and a greater and more complex body of detailed administrative interpretations and decisions which must be consulted by the bulk of active and potential business concerns of the country in the daily conduct of ordinary business.

Briefly stated the NRA has been interpreting a legislative act—the NIRA—and out of this interpretation has been formulating policies on the basis of which numerous codes having full force and effect of law have been negotiated and approved. It has been administering its own legislative acts, and to some extent adjudicating its own administrative decisions. In short, it is one single machine performing administrative, legislative, and judicial functions.

THE DEVELOPMENT OF ADMINISTRATIVE LAW

Viewed merely as an administrative agency performing law-making functions in combination with other activities, the NRA represents no unique development in the field of government. Administrative law making has been developing rapidly during the past generation. Indeed it may be regarded as the most significant aspect of recent legal history, in both national and state and European and American law making. Under the Roosevelt Administration, the activities of such agencies as the Securities and Exchange Commission, the Agricultural Adjustment Administration, and various other so-called

---

[3] The same.

"alphabetical" organizations have made extensive additions to the already substantial body of federal administrative law. It has been found that between 50 and 60 federal administrative agencies are exercising quasi-legislative powers in some important degree.[4] This plethora of new agencies reflects not merely a series of measures for coping with the economic depression, but an important redefinition of American ideas concerning the responsibilities of the federal government.

In the realm of administrative law the traditional distinction between legislative, judicial, and executive branches of government is being severely impaired. This impairment is inherent in the attempt of governments to regulate those detailed phases of human conduct which cannot be written into general rules of law. Developments of this sort are commonly explained on the grounds that social organization, especially in its economic aspects, has become so complex that legislative bodies are no longer technically competent to exercise the types of legislative control which the situation demands. Justification or criticism of this movement cannot be made in general terms. The particular circumstances of each case are of controlling significance.

The general characteristic of administrative legislation is that, while the legislative body lays down a line of policy, the specific detailed content of the law derives from the rules and regulations promulgated by some administrative body or official. Such an agency therefore exercises in some degree what is really legislative power, the degree depending upon how narrowly or broadly its powers are defined by the legislature. Very commonly, also, administrative agencies have the *de facto*

[4] See Frederick F. Blachly and Miriam E. Oatman, *Administrative Legislation and Adjudication*, p. 10.

power to interpret the rules and to settle disputes arising under them, thereby exercising what, strictly speaking, are judicial powers. This trend in law making covers the great extension of the activities of governments to regulation and control in many fields, such as public health, industrial safety, transportation, local utilities, banking, and insurance.

While the law-making activities of the NRA represent only an extension of previously established trends in the field of government regulation, there are distinct points of difference between the controls which the legislature has ordinarily attached to delegations of legislative powers and those set up to control the administration of the NIRA. The simplest way to bring these contrasts into clear relief is to compare the statutory controls provided in NRA with the type of general control retained by the legislative branch of government in the past when delegating legislative functions to a so-called administrative agency charged with the exercise of regulatory controls similar to those which have grown out of the activities of NRA.

The statutes controlling the operations of the Interstate Commerce Commission perhaps furnish the most comparable conditions for such a comparison.[5] In this

[5] In various aspects of its operations the NRA strongly resembles the ICC and similar agencies: (1) The powers exercised depend upon and represent a vast extension of the idea "business affected with public interest," and involve resort to the same general concepts of "fair," "reasonable," "inimical to the public interest," and so on. (2) The approved acts, rules, and regulations have the full force and effect of law, and the processes of action in effect possess the combined characteristics of administrative, legislative, and judicial acts. (3) It has made its authority felt over practically the whole area of trade and industry potentially subject to it. (4) Its powers derive from federal authority over interstate commerce, and its operations extend the concept of interstate commerce into fields of regulation heretofore thought to be occupied by the several states.

case the legislative body launched a vast program of regulation of transportation agencies designed to protect them from their own ruinous competition, and to protect the public interest. Inasmuch as methods of achieving the objectives sought were highly technical in character, involving control over such matters as rates, safety regulations, and capital investment, the legislature admitted its incompetence for exercising the degree of regulation required, and set up an independent agent to carry out the expressed legislative policy. But at the same time it exercised its constitutional right to adapt the administrative machine to the type of work to be done,[6] as well as its constitutional duty to define policy and standards.

Congress, however, realized that a high degree of discretionary power would of necessity be exercised by the agent; that its decisions would inevitably be reasoned from such vague and varying concepts as "the public interest," "fairness," "justness," and "reasonableness." In recognition of this fact it established by mandate the type of administrative agency which would be as far as possible removed from the importunings of special interests, from the influences of swiftly changing party politics, and from the even more disturbing influences of rapidly shifting internal policies and methods. In short, it specified the commission form of administrative agency and defined both its relationship to the legislature and its composition. In the first place the legislature provided that the Commission should derive its power and duties di-

[6] Established by Supreme Court in *Kendall* v. *United States,* which stated in part: ". . . But it would be an alarming doctrine that Congress cannot impose upon any executive officer any duty they may think proper, which is not repugnant to any rights secured and protected by the Constitution and in such cases, the duty and responsibility grow out of and are subject to the control of the law and not to the direction of the President."

rectly from the legislature and be subject to immediate discipline for its acts only by the legislature. Second, Congress provided that the Commission should be composed of a rotating membership serving in seven-year terms, thereby making it amenable to executive control only through appointment. The appointing power was conditioned by the statutory requirement of Senate concurrence. The line of direct authority and responsibility was therefore from the legislature to the administrative agency.

In thus removing its administrative agent as far as reasonably possible from the influences of the interests which it was established to control and from the immediate control of the executive branch of government, the legislature took cognizance of the vast implications of its act.[7] These were (1) that the agency created would not only hold life and death power over transportation companies themselves, but would exercise similar power over a property ownership related to transportation agencies only through its dependence upon transportation services; (2) that it would of necessity make incursions upon regulatory jurisdiction previously exercised and jealously guarded by the various states; (3) that in carrying out legislative policy it would of necessity perform functions possessing all the characteristics of, and overlapping far into the field of, legislative and judicial action.

The illustration furnished by the statutes controlling the Interstate Commerce Commission could be multiplied and extended into other regulatory and administra-

[7] The present control exercised by the Interstate Commerce Commission over transportation agencies of course represents a long evolution of regulatory technique applied to a particular set of service agencies over a long period since the creation of the Commission in 1887.

tive fields, both federal and state. All of these regulatory fields have several common characteristics: they deal with highly technical phenomena where the very nature of the controls exercised require the delegation of a large degree of discretionary powers to the designated administrative agency; they deal with operations which directly and indirectly affect widespread interests; and they deal with the types of interests which by virtue of financial strength are in position to exercise powerfully persuasive influences on the regulatory body. It is no accident that, except in rare cases, regulatory authority designed to exercise control of these types of economic activity has been delegated only to agencies removed as far as possible from shifting policies and from the reach of pressure groups—that is, to the general character of regulatory body typified by the Interstate Commerce Commission.

The calculated attempt has been to achieve a structure rigid enough to preserve continuity of policy; sufficiently thorough in its operation to afford reasonable protection to individual interest and to the broad public interest; and finally, flexible enough in its operating structure to insure reasonable administrative expedition. Needless to say the history of regulatory activity discloses varying degrees of success in attaining these objectives, all falling short of complete realization of the ideal. This history, however, shows a sufficiently uniform approach, and extends over a long enough period, to command attention in any discussion of the administrative organization and procedure set up to guide the operations of an agency designed to exercise the type of controls characteristic of a public utility regulatory body.

In comparing the controls imposed upon executive and administrative discretion under the provisions of the

NIRA with those characteristic of past delegations of legislative power (as illustrated above), we find several points of striking difference. Chief among these is the extent to which all phases of the NRA organization and operation have been founded upon executive and administrative discretion rather than upon legislative mandate.

With reference to the creation of an administrative agency the Recovery Act has very little to say. The President is

... authorized to establish such agencies, to accept and utilize such voluntary and uncompensated services, to appoint, without regard to the provisions of the civil service laws, such officers and employees and to utilize such federal officers and employees, and with the consent of the state, such state and local officers and employees, as he may find necessary, ...[8]

And the President may, under authority of the act, redelegate any of the powers delegated to him by Congress to whatever agency or agent he chooses. The law therefore imposes no restrictions on the freedom of choice which the President may exercise in setting up an agency to administer, and, as experience has indicated, actually to interpret the act. As a matter of fact he could have chosen to nullify the entire act merely by failing to establish an administrative agency.

In other words, the legislative branch of government lodged with the executive branch the function of general direction, supervision, and control over the administrative agency; that is, the function of deciding by what type of organization, by whom, and by what general methods the requirements of the laws were to be carried out. The lines of authority over NRA activities, in contrast to those of the ICC, run directly to the

[8] National Industrial Recovery Act, Title I, Sec. 2(a).

President; and the forms of the administrative organization and procedure depend entirely upon executive discretion rather than upon legislative determination. Moreover, executive discretion bears almost the whole responsibility for NRA policy determination; whereas in the case of the ICC an independent agency created by the legislature and relatively free from executive control is charged with general policy determination in so far as it has not been defined by the legislature, and with the promulgation of administrative policy (internal operating organization, procedural rules and regulations, etc.).

We therefore have to look to the actions of the President to discover the general pattern of administrative control created for NRA, as well as for a statement of specific objectives and of methods to be used in attaining those objectives. Such an inquiry will obviously not furnish material for a final evaluation of NRA administrative procedure, since ultimate evaluation of the operating effectiveness of any administrative agency must of course be made in terms of its net accomplishment. There are no immutable laws which guarantee that given substantive results will emerge from one or another combination of legislative controls, structural organizations, and administrative method. An understanding of the administrative pattern and specific objectives of the Recovery Administration may, however, be expected to lay a foundation for an eventual answer to the query as to whether or not the NRA as organized and operated is properly constituted to exercise the vast administrative and legislative powers over which Congress has given it control.

In the subsequent analysis of the administrative organization and operation of NRA it will be helpful to the reader to keep in mind three major topics: (1) the considerations which have conditioned the choice of administrative machinery and methods which have been used in attempting to effectuate the provisions of NIRA; (2) the forces which have dictated the development of the organizational structure and procedural rules of NRA, and (3) the manner in which these various factors have been combined to produce the NRA work product.

The discussion immediately following will deal only with the first two of these items. Detailed analysis of the NRA product will occur later under such headings as: code making; code administration; trade practice provisions; industrial relations; and wage and hour regulations.

CHOICE OF ADMINISTRATIVE MACHINERY AND METHOD

In the practical exercise of the power of general direction and control which the legislature had delegated to him under the NIRA, the President at the outset made two important decisions. First, from among the several possible types of action provided for in the law (see page 10), the President chose to rely mainly on the co-operative method of formulating voluntary codes of fair competition. The coercive powers, to impose codes and to license, did not thereupon drop out of sight, but remained as a sort of whip to drive business groups into "voluntary" commitments which they might otherwise not have agreed to. On the whole, however, the story of developments under the act is that of the making, the administering, the content, and the consequences of voluntary codes.

At the outset major industries were invited to submit basic codes covering hour and wage provisions without delaying to work out elaborate trade practice devices designed to control various business relationships.[9] The adoption of this limited immediate goal did not debar some attention to the elimination of trade abuses in so far as this was possible without slowing down the drive for re-employment. It did, however, imply the postponement for later consideration of the more comprehensive devices for the regulation of business procedure. Industry was advised that "additions, modifications, and refinements of such basic codes will be considered later upon application by such association or groups."[10]

These statements clearly indicate that at the outset the Administration looked upon the code-making task as one which could be separated into two administrative phases—the first, re-employment, and the second, basic reform.[11] Speed was the characteristic feature of the entire administrative method adopted to achieve the goal. The general method followed, the machinery established, and the specific rules and regulations prescribed to govern code making all reflect the calculated desire to create a product designed to serve an immediate and limited purpose, rather than one to accommodate long-term objectives.

[9] Upon signing the act the President announced that the National Recovery Administration ". . . is now prepared to receive proposed codes and to conduct prompt hearings looking toward their submission to me for approval. While acceptable proposals of no trade group will be delayed, it is my hope that the ten major industries which control the bulk of industrial employment can submit their simple basic codes at once and that the country can look forward to the month of July as the beginning of our great national movement back to work." *NRA Bulletin No. 1*, June 16, 1933.

[10] *NRA Bulletin No. 2*, June 19, 1933.

[11] In the official statement outlining the policies of the NRA the President said: "This task is in two stages—first, to get many hundreds of thousands of the unemployed back on the payroll by snowfall and second, to plan for a better future for the longer pull. While we shall not neglect the second, the first state is an emergency job. It has the right of way." *NRA Bulletin No. 1*, June 16, 1933.

The second important decision of the President is found in his choice of a single administrator form of control in preference to an impartial commission or board. On June 16 the President by executive order[12] named an avowed man of action as Administrator for Industrial Recovery. Under this executive order the Administrator was given temporary powers to appoint personnel, to conduct hearings, and to take various other administrative actions—all subject to the general approval of the special Industrial Recovery Board.[13] But by a subsequent order

[12] Executive Order No. 6173.

[13] The law governing the personnel administration of the National Recovery Administration is contained in Section 2(a) of the NIRA. See Appendix A.

In the personnel procedure of NRA a practice, popularly called "political clearance," was instituted from the outset. Many applicants for appointment filed with their applications letters of endorsement from their senators or representatives, or both. In some cases persons applied without presenting any political endorsements. If they possessed qualifications or connections that seemed to the officials of the Recovery Administration desirable, they were often told that it would be highly advantageous, if not absolutely essential, that they get political endorsements so that there would be no difficulty in getting them "cleared politically." This practice was generally, or customarily, followed with respect to the large clerical personnel. For upper administrative positions and for scientific and professional positions the practice appears to have been less general, but many persons appointed to these positions had political endorsements which were considered in making selections for appointment.

The NRA issued no announcements to the public regarding positions in that organization, nor did it issue public instructions as to how one should proceed in applying for a position. Specifically, it did not issue circulars describing the duties to be performed in a specific class of positions and qualification standards that would be applied in making selections.

Although the applicant was asked to give three references it was not the general practice to correspond with former employers or with colleges, universities, or schools at which the applicant had studied or with former teachers of the applicant. Such correspondence was conducted only in isolated cases.

The NRA made no use of the examining facilities that have been developed in the Civil Service Commission. It gave its own tests for (1) stenographers, (2) typists, and (3) other machine operators.

For many scientific and professional workers it is obvious that high

of July 15, 1933 the President delegated to the Administrator continuing and sweeping powers:

> . . . to appoint the necessary personnel on a permanent basis, to fix their compensation, and to conduct such hearings and to exercise such other functions as are vested in me by Title I of said act, except the approval of codes, or making of agreements, or issuance of licenses, or exercise of powers conferred in Section 3(e), Section 6(c), Section 8(b), Section 9, and Section 10.[14]

Neither in the executive order creating the office of Administrator for Industrial Recovery nor in any subsequent executive order is any mention made even of the broad organizational outline of the administrative machine to be used in effectuating the act. The President prescribed directly only one important organizational feature in providing for three advisory boards to represent the interests of consumer, industrial, and labor groups in the code-making process. Apparently the authority, or mandate as the case may be, for the establishment of these boards is found in a statement made by the President on June 16, 1934, the date on which he signed the Recovery Act. The entire statement was issued on June 16 as *National Recovery Administration Bulletin No. 1*,[15] marking the first appearance of the official title "National Recovery Administration." It outlines the broad policies and objectives of the act and indicates the

---

standards of education, experience, and professional reputation were applied. Persons were secured who would have qualified under any reasonable civil service examination based on education, experience, and professional standing. It is equally obvious that some purely political appointments were made of the kind that the civil service system was designed to prevent.

[14] Executive Order No. 6205-A. See Appendix A for sections of the act referred to in this order.

[15] Full title of *Bulletin No. 1* is "Statement of the President of the United States of America Outlining Policies of the National Recovery Administration."

general method to be used in formulating codes of fair competition.

The "machinery" referred to in the following statement of the Administrator is presumably composed of the Administrator for Industrial Recovery, the three advisory boards, and the Special Industrial Recovery Board:

The machinery the President has set up is a balanced sort of executive-legislative-judicial tribunal. It is not a bureau and it will not become one. It is rather a forum for co-operation. It will duplicate no existing government machinery. It has the active and vital guidance, co-operation, and support of every government department, and on its board of directors sits every Cabinet officer whose department is affected or can help.[16]

The "board of directors" referred to in the Administrator's statement was created by executive order and given the title of Special Industrial Recovery Board.[17] Although presumably created to serve as a general policy board, the executive order establishing it failed to define its duties and made no provisions for an administrative staff. Being composed entirely of high government officials, each with his own multiplicity of duties and harassments, it never functioned effectively as a general policy board. Its official acts were largely limited to approval of three NRA bulletins, outlining to the public the Administration's policy relative to voluntary codes of fair competition, and the President's re-employment program.[18] During the early months of code negotiations

[16] *NRA Release No. 11*, June 25, 1933.

[17] The Secretary of Commerce, chairman; the Attorney General; the Secretary of Interior; the Secretary of Agriculture; the Secretary of Labor; the Director of the Budget; the Administrator for Industrial Recovery; and the Chairman of the Federal Trade Commission.

[18] "Basic Codes of Fair Competition," *NRA Bulletin No. 2*, June 19, 1933; "The President's Re-employment Agreement Program," *NRA Bulletin No. 3*, July 20, 1933; "Regulations on Procedure for local NRA Compliance Boards," *NRA Bulletin No. 5*, Sept. 12, 1933.

the special board did, however, conduct a series of price studies designed to formulate NRA policy relative to price-control devices in codes. No policies were arrived at or promulgated, however, and the Board was soon lost in the fast-shifting NRA scene.

On November 17, 1933 the President created the National Emergency Council[19] and by order of December 18, 1933 transferred to it the functions of the Special Industrial Recovery Board.[20] This action had the effect of removing the Recovery Administrator even further from the control of any supervisory or policy-making board. The Emergency Council was created "for the purpose of co-ordinating and making more efficient and productive the work of the numerous field agencies of the government established under, and for the purpose of carrying into effect the provisions" of the National Industrial Recovery Act, the Agricultural Adjustment Act, and the Federal Emergency Relief Act. In contrast with the Special Industrial Recovery Board, it was implemented with an executive staff, its powers and duties were defined, and it was furnished with operating funds. But it also failed to function as an effective stabilizer of NRA policies and methods.[21]

From time to time the President expanded the powers of the Administrator[22] and by executive order imposed certain rules and regulations defining procedure and interpreting orders issued by the NRA.

[19] Executive Order No. 6433-A.

[20] Executive Order No. 6513.

[21] For a detailed discussion of the evolution of policy and administrative procedures, see pp. 47-67.

[22] By Executive Order No. 6543-A of Dec. 30, 1933, the President delegated to the Administrator the power to approve all codes of fair competition except those for major industries (in general those employing in excess of 50,000 workers) and to approve all amendments to, modifications of, exemptions from, and eliminations of any one or more provisions of approved codes of fair competition.

Thus between June 16, 1933 and the creation of the National Industrial Recovery Board on September 27, 1934 the Administrator exercised a control over the policies and operations of the Recovery Administration limited in effect only by orders from the Chief Executive, which for the most part were highly generalized.[23]

In reviewing the general character of the administrative aspects set forth above, it is apparent that so far as administrative patterns are concerned the NRA represents a distinct break with the past. In determining the exercise of the general function of administrative policy making and direction, neither the legislature nor the President made any appreciable use of administrative patterns ordinarily adopted for the types of regulatory activity which the NRA has been exercising.

It should not be assumed, however, that the NRA administrative organization was devised without reference to past experience or without a calculated attempt to adapt the administrative machinery to the requirements of the recovery program; and for that matter, not without some misgivings as to its adequacy.[24] Regulatory forms such as those found in the operations of the Federal Trade Commission and in public utility commissions were considered and discarded for one reason or another. In general those in charge of the NRA experiment

[23] These orders, some 70 in all, dealt with such matters as the administrative organization of NRA; the assurance to members of codes that no constitutional rights had been forfeited by code provisions; the suspension of certain code provisions for service trades and industries; the establishment of the National Labor Board; and the establishment of labor boards for various specified industries.

[24] "Its trial by the American people is a great adventure. The economic theories underlying may be wrong. But that will be hard to prove. The mechanism provided for in the law and set up by the Recovery Administration may prove to be inadequate or impractical. The sponsors and administrators of the law claim neither genius nor divine inspiration." See *NRA Release No. 628*, dated Sept. 6, 1933; address of NRA General Counsel.

thought that the administration of NIRA required a less rigid and faster functioning machine than that developed in public utility regulation,[25] as well as one adapted to the industrial self-government method of regulation.

The nature of the issues considered in selecting administrative procedures is indicated in the following statement made by the Recovery Administrator:

There were two ways to go about the NRA job, one was to precede definite recovery action by a slow academic study of all the complications and contingencies to be met in code drafting punctuated by expert testimony and oriented in the long-term effects of those changes in economic balance that would inevitably result from the new recovery set-up—that is, in the opinion of men who, however rich in academic learning, never knew the weight of a business responsibility in their whole lives.

The other was to get the codes in, meeting the unemployment situation after some fashion, cleaning up the work of the economic abuses, putting first things first, letting the minor maladjustments fall where they might, and dealing with the long-term effects as they became evident.

The choice was between academic conjecture and action and the decision was for action. Now according to plan, NRA stops to take stock of its shortcomings, to deal with the complaints. The work of refinement begins.[26]

Out of these concepts came the declaration of administrative method dedicated to action. It was conditioned in the early stages only by the extremely vague objectives defined by statute and by a few mandates imposed by Congress; and it was controlled in its later stages by the application of the so-called experimental

[25] "Recognizing the weaknesses in our methods of regulating public utilities, and the utter impracticability of applying these methods in any co-operative program of government aid in establishing industrial self-government, it was necessary to plan the procedure for the making and administration of codes of fair competition along new lines. . . ." *NRA Release No. 1381*, Oct. 12, 1933; address of NRA General Counsel.

[26] *NRA Release No. 2993*, Jan. 25, 1934; address of Recovery Administrator.

method. This experimentation involved relatively simple concepts and amounted in effect to the trial and error method.[27] The order of the day was to get codes approved by any administrative method found to be consonant with speed—and then as abuses, whether of limited application or of general public concern, came to light, immediately to make the required adjustment of policy and method. (For a discussion of the manner in which the trial and error method actually operated see Chapter V.

As already stated, the mere fact that an organization breaks with traditional patterns and methods furnishes in itself no final basis for an evaluation of its operating effectiveness. The following section is designed to build a foundation for an evaluation of the NRA as an operating mechanism by giving a picture of the development of machinery and method as occasioned by the changing volume and character of work done, and by the appearance of glaring deficiencies.

DEVELOPMENT OF ADMINISTRATIVE MACHINERY AND METHOD

For convenience in the discussion, the history of NRA administrative development and activity may be divided into three broad phases:[28] (1) the period of intense code-making activity, (2) re-organization for code administration and policy making, and (3) general administrative reorganization and reorientation of policy. There is

---

[27] "Not only we in the government but the leaders of these industries were working in the dark. We had no guide, no definite economic rules; we put the code through almost by the old try and error method. We hammered. Sometimes we hit the nail, sometimes the thumb." *NRA Release No. 5889*, June 21, 1934; address of Recovery Administrator.

[28] For a more detailed discussion of organizational features of the NRA during its first six months of operation, together with the relationship existing between NRA and other government agencies, see *The ABC of the NRA*, The Brookings Institution, 1934.

no sharply marked line between the periods, for the characteristic activity of each blends into that of the next, and the minor activity of one period may become the major point of emphasis during the following period.

The Code-Making Period

Driving speed and administrative confusion, at times approaching hysteria, marked the period of major code-making activity, extending approximately from June 1933 to March 1934. (See the chart on page 49 for the administrative organization utilized during this period.) In the first six months of activity the NRA negotiated and approved codes of fair competition covering the major portion of American industry and trade. As a supplementary activity it supervised a nation-wide campaign for the President's re-employment program[29] (generally known as the Blue Eagle Drive). Whatever one may think of the product or of the administrative method used, admiration is compelled by the tremendous energy and devotion with which both the NRA personnel and industry representatives applied themselves to the task of code negotiations. As a matter of fact, such was the general atmosphere of the code-making scene that a casual observer might well have assumed that all parties involved had taken serious counsel from Santayana's comment that "Vitality even if expressed in pure fancy will prevail at times when reason would despair." In reviewing the achievement of this period the Recovery Administrator commented with characteristic enthusiasm:

The Recovery Act was passed on June 16, 1933. With one of the most remarkable demonstrations of administrative speed in history over 80 per cent of all industries has been codified

---

[29] Discussed on p. 52.

EARLY ADMINISTRATIVE ORGANIZATION OF THE NRA

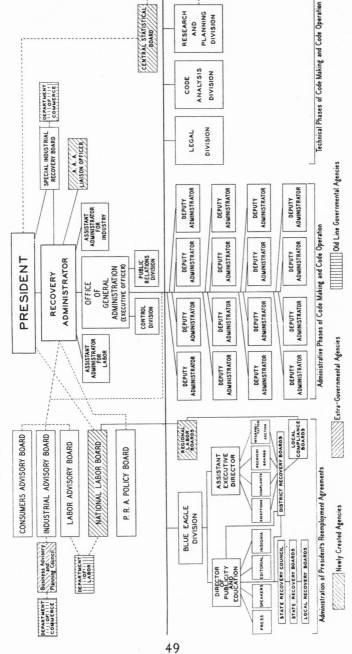

49

since that date. Practically 100 per cent of industry has now submitted codes and the popular acceptance of NRA is almost universal.[30]

The NRA code-making program, it will be recalled, originally called for carrying on code negotiations with a limited number of large industries. The immediate task was to get codes through the mill. To facilitate this process the simplest and presumably the most expeditious administrative set-up was adopted; that is, the wheel type of organization in which lines of authority and responsibility run direct from the operating personnel to the supervising head. During the early code-making period, each deputy administrator in charge of the actual work of code negotiating reported directly to the Administrator for approval of his actions and received direct from the Administrator instructions as to policy and procedure. In this way all impediments to speedy administrative action were supposed to be removed, since the one with powers of decision was expected to be familiar with the details of all negotiations being carried on by each of his deputies. By this method one individual attempted not only to perform the function of general supervision and control, including policy making, but at the same time to assume responsibility for a tremendous volume of administrative detail.

The impossibility of following this procedure soon became evident. Some delegation of authority was required in order to avert the virtual stoppage of administrative action. This started unofficially with the increase in the degree of discretionary power exercised by the deputies. In October 1933 four administrative divisions were created. Each was headed by a division administrator, to

[30] *NRA Release No. 2993*, Jan. 25, 1934; address of Recovery Administrator.

whom a group of deputies reported. An operating staff of advisers was assigned to each division in an attempt to create an integral operating unit.[31]

This reorganization alleviated but did not remove the congestion. The relative isolation of the deputies continued, and the division administrators inherited the same sort of ineffective command of their bailiwicks which had overtaken the Administrator. This was in part due to the mere pressure of infinite detail, but in part also to the character of the assignments. A casual glance at the assignment of codes to each division will indicate that the rationalization of structure unfortunately was not accompanied by a rationalization of function.[32] Administrative control over public utilities and automobile manufacturing, for example, was placed under one division administrator. Another had placed in his hands such diverse business activities as motion pictures, trucking, theaters, and freight forwarding.[33] In requiring a single administrator's approval of a multiplicity of administrative actions dealing with wholly unrelated industries, one of two results was inevitable: either the approval was

[31] The advisory staff consisted of representatives of the Legal Division and Research and Planning Division, and of the Industrial, Labor, and Consumers' Advisory Boards. The functions of these agencies are discussed at a later point.

[32] The principal codes handled in each division as of Feb. 15, 1934, were as follows:
Division   I. Public utilities, mining, shipping, iron and steel, automobile manufacture, rubber.
Division   II. Machinery, lumber, and metals.
Division III. Chemicals, construction, shoes, leather, and miscellaneous small manufactures.
Division   IV. Trades and services, textiles, and clothing.
Division   V. Amusements and transportation.
Division   VI. AAA codes.
Division VII. Publications and graphic arts.

[33] This situation was not corrected until late in 1934, with the creation of twelve industry divisions and reassignment of codes according to basic character.

rubber stamped, and consequently of no value; or an administrative bottle-neck was created. Somewhat similar difficulties attended the assignment of miscellaneous codes to deputies.

In spite of all efforts to expedite the process, the code mill ground slowly at first. Although many code proposals were presented, the progress of negotiation to completion was slow. The approval of Code No. 1 (cotton textile industry) required a full month of negotiations; and at the end of the second month only eight codes had been approved out of the hundreds pending. It was apparent to officials that something had to be done if the NRA was to make any rapid impression upon the unemployment situation. Of even greater urgency was the creation of some device to prevent a collapse of employment upon the recession of the early summer speculative activity which had grown out of the anticipation of higher costs under NRA. Clearly, the solution was not to be found in the code program.

Out of this near-desperate situation the President's Re-employment Agreement was conceived. It was a simple plan designed to spread work and increase payrolls. The work of "selling" it to the country brought into play demonstrations of emotionalism, pageantry, and oratorical appeals usually associated with war-time propaganda rather than with the ordinary functioning of peace-time government.[34] The Herculean task of making the country Blue Eagle conscious did not, however, seriously divert the NRA from its code-making work. In fact, various circumstances associated with the Blue Eagle Drive worked together materially to speed the final approval of many code proposals.

[34] For a more extended discussion of the PRA and the Blue Eagle Campaign, see *The ABC of the NRA*.

As a means of enticing some of the more hesitant industrial groups into the NRA fold, the Administration had found it expedient to grant to early code-seeking groups various inducements in the way of price-control devices and other important trade practice powers. In the meantime the Blue Eagle Drive had blanketed the country with re-employment agreements which dealt only with labor conditions. These gave employers higher labor costs, but no gains excepting whatever satisfaction was obtained from participating in what many no doubt regarded as a patriotic movement. In areas where the extra-legal coercive force of the Blue Eagle was made effective, the employers' sense of patriotism was reinforced by his natural instinct for business survival. Under the bargaining facilities set up by NRA the advantage to employers clearly appeared to lie on the side of cooperative efforts to secure separate codes. It was a good gamble, with the possibility of securing special advantages in compensation for higher wage payments and other restrictive labor provisions. Thus the way was cleared for a period of intense activity in code making which diminished only with the emergence of the vexing problem of administering the complex of laws which the code mill had ground out.

Adjustment to Changing Functions

During the six or seven months of intense code making little time and thought were given to the problem of organizing and educating industry for the task of industrial self-government. But, during the next phase of the NRA career, attention shifted largely to this task, particularly to the work of implementing codes with administrative and enforcement machinery. In connection therewith policy questions were forced upon the Administration by the attempt of various industrial and trade groups to operate the machinery of industrial self-government.

Throughout the second period, extending roughly from March 1934 to September 1934, the basic organization of Administrator, division administrators, and deputy administrators remained unchanged. In part, it continued to function for code making, but increasingly it was transformed into a means for facilitating the organization of code authorities and supervising their operations. This change of function involved additions to the mechanism. (See the chart on page 55 for the administrative organization characteristic of this period.) Detailed comment on these developments is not required here since they are dealt with in later sections dealing with code administration, trade practices, and labor. Brief reference, however, may be made to the three distinct alterations in procedure and organization which were affected in order to accommodate the shift in administrative emphasis. Administrative machinery was set up to supervise code authority organization; compliance and enforcement procedure was renovated; and for the first time recognition was given to policy making as a function distinct from administrative execution.

Code administration. As early as November 1933 a Code Authority Organization Committee was created to "consider and advise on plans proposed for code authority and trade association organization for industrial self-government." The active chairman was the head of the Trade Association Division which had been set up with special reference to the adaptation of trade associations to code functions. This committee devoted the greater portion of its time to formulating general principles and procedures to govern code authority organization, and

ADMINISTRATIVE ORGANIZATION OF THE NRA—INTERMEDIATE PERIOD

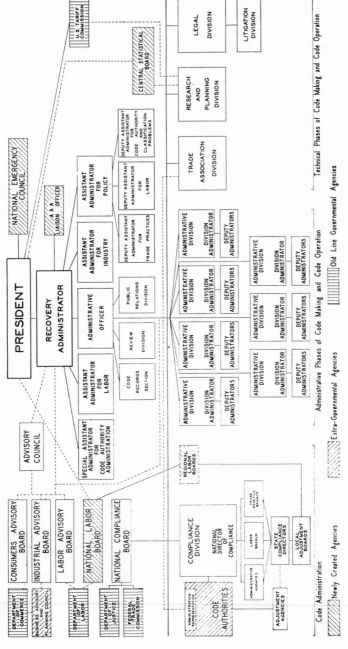

Newly Created Agencies   Extra-Governmental Agencies   Old Line Governmental Agencies

Code Administration   Administrative Phases of Code Making and Code Operation   Technical Phases of Code Making and Code Operation

to drawing up plans for the code authority conference held early in March 1934. This conference was designed by NRA to instruct code authority members in their obligations as governing bodies of industry. It resulted, however, chiefly in complaints that the uncertainty in NRA policy was creating "jumpiness" among business men; that the NRA procedure slowed down approval of code authority organization plans; and that effective enforcement of code provisions was not being obtained. All three counts were no doubt true, but industry's united indictment of government's failure to breathe life into the industrial government machine must have struck an ironical note for some NRA officials. For during the code-making process there were not a few advisers and other officials who maintained that many of the provisions most sought after by industry were non-administrable. The general effect of the conference was to impress NRA with its own deficiencies.

Late in March the NRA made adjustments in its internal operating procedure along lines designed to promote more effective organization for the work of code administration. A Special Assistant Administrator[35] was named "to co-ordinate the reorganization and functioning of NRA for code administration." The Code Authority Organization Committee was abolished, and the administrative functions previously performed by it with regard to code authority organization were transferred to the office of the Special Assistant Administrator. Each divisional administrator was directed to appoint an assistant for code authority organization with instructions to speed up approval of administrative organiza-

[35] Originally designated First Assistant Administrator, and later changed to Special Assistant Administrator.

tions for all codes under his supervision. Assistants were also provided for code administration and compliance. Under this plan the NRA was able to secure more uniform procedure in facilitating code authority organization, and to exercise more effective scrutiny of industry's requests for approval of by-laws, code authority membership, and budgets. It was discovered that most such proposals, particularly by-laws and budgets, needed material alteration before approval could be granted. Code authority organization was therefore delayed in the first instance by inaction; and then by NRA's realization that "adequate government supervision over agencies of industrial self-government" involved problems of such complexity and scope that a deliberative process, rather than the administrative facility characteristic of the code-making period, would have to be applied if any meaning was to be given to the term "adequate."

The new machinery, which represented a reasonable approach to the problems in hand, was for some reason abolished in June 1934. Staff functions relative to code authority organization and administration were transferred to a newly created Assistant Administrator for Field Administration. Thus "staff" functions, which had started to be closely integrated with executive "line" functions, were dissociated from them.

Compliance and enforcement. From the outset the NRA divided its participation in code administration into two more or less distinct activities: the supervision of code authority organization and administration, as mentioned above, and the supervision of code compliance and enforcement efforts. According to the paper plan, NRA was to exercise direct supervision over both trade practice and labor compliance work until code authorities established proper machinery and were authorized by NRA to take over these activities.[36]

Late in 1933 the NRA created compliance machinery as an integral part of the administrative structure. It consisted of a National Compliance Board, a Compliance Division, and a field organization consisting of regional offices in each state.[37] (See the chart on page 55.) The Compliance Division took over the functions of the Blue Eagle Division and of the voluntary local adjustment boards previously set up to secure compliance with the President's Re-employment Agreement.

From the beginning, official emphasis had been placed upon the self-enforcing aspects of code provisions. It was contended that compliance on the part of the majority of affected members of an industry would follow immediately upon the discovery of their rights and duties under a code. This theory flowed naturally from the contention that the provisions of each code had been sponsored and officially assented to by an applicant group legally designated as truly representative of the industry affected. It was further assumed that the recalcitrant minority could be led into the fold by persuasion of the majority. Only in a minor portion of cases was it contemplated that the coercive force of legal penalties would be required.

Based on this concept the compliance activity of NRA was largely limited to compliance as distinguished from enforcement efforts during the first few months of 1934 —that is, the stress was placed upon persuasion rather than upon application of the coercive force of the law.

---

[36] Method outlined in *NRA Bulletin No. 7*, January 1934.

[37] For a detailed description of the operation of early compliance machinery see *The ABC of the NRA*, pp. 96-110.

It was expected that code agencies, when organized, would be mainly responsible for the persuasion, leaving the NRA with only contingent and not very extensive compliance duties.

Not until March 1934 was there any evidence of an official shift in emphasis from compliance to enforcement efforts. As a part of the reorganization for code administration (referred to above) a Litigation Division, reporting to the General Counsel of NRA, was created. In general it was instructed to keep in close contact with the Compliance Division, the industry divisions, and the Special Assistant Administrator of NRA, and with the Department of Justice. Specifically it was directed to: (1) "co-ordinate all NRA litigation; (2) examine and review all cases which have been turned over to the courts; (3) in the name of the Department of Justice prepare and carry through litigated cases."

Each division administrator was instructed to designate an assistant for enforcement to co-ordinate the routine compliance and enforcement functions carried on by industry divisions with all other NRA compliance agencies.

Steps were also taken to decentralize enforcement efforts. State offices had been set up under the National Emergency Council and state compliance directors were authorized to refer non-compliance cases directly to United States district attorneys, after reasonable effort to secure voluntary adjustment, rather than (as previously instructed) referring them to the National Compliance Board at Washington. Official instructions to state directors read in part:

We must now proceed on the basis that one who is violating his code and who is not ready and anxious to comply and make restitution when informed of his non-compliance, must be brought swiftly and surely before the enforcement agencies of government.[38]

The plan for supervision of compliance and enforcement work was somewhat altered upon the appointment in June 1934 of the Assistant Administrator for Field Administration. In addition to his staff functions relative to code administration, this officer was given executive control of compliance functions, being charged with "supervision over the execution of policies governing compliance, enforcement, and code authority organization." His office absorbed the supervisory function previously exercised by the Special Assistant Administrator, and direction of the work of the Compliance Division. The compliance assistants to the heads of the industry divisions were abolished, thus retracing the steps taken to gear these divisions into the compliance mechanism.

Oddly enough the actual work of the field administration office was mainly directed toward refinement of internal administrative procedure. This sufficiently needed doing, but it hardly seemed the proper primary preoccupation of this office. In any case little progress was made toward a solution of the basic problems of code administration. One broad result was to disrupt the tendency started, under the previous reorganization, to increase the effectiveness of NRA supervision over the activities of code authorities.

The numerous changes in policy and method as sketched above did not remove the difficulties which were inherent in the compliance and enforcement problem. They continued to vex administration officials and code authorities. The shuttling character of NRA policy and method kept both code authorities and industry division

[38] *NRA Release No. 4293,* Apr. 6, 1934.

personnel in constant confusion. It contributed nothing to orderly administration. Throughout the second period of NRA development most deputies in charge of various codes used methods suggested by expediency to push the work of code authority organization administration, and devoted practically no time to compliance matters. One point that became increasingly clear during this period was that most code agencies were going to be ineffective, and that the NRA was saddled with monumental duties which had been no part of its original intention.

Finally in October of 1934 the entire enforcement machinery was overhauled by concentrating the supervisory function in a single director of enforcement and compliance and by decentralizing administrative work on a regional basis.[39] The office of field administration was dismantled and its functions dispersed.

Policy determination. Between June 1933 and September 1934, as already stated, there existed no real policy-making body. That is, there was no agency whose functions were limited to policy making and general supervision, as distinguished from administrative execution. The Special Industrial Recovery Board, created presumably to exercise general supervisory control over NRA, failed to function in that capacity. The exact relationship between the National Emergency Council and the NRA was never clearly defined, but there is no evidence that it functioned any more effectively as a general control agency for the NRA than did the Special Industrial Recovery Board.

From time to time, however, the Recovery Administrator established agencies within the NRA to advise on policy. Some operated effectively in formulating policy

[39] See p. 74 for description of structure.

and some not at all. None, however, had any power to effectuate policy—they were all advisory.

The first gesture toward the establishment of continuity of operating policy was made in September 1933 with the establishment of a Policy Board to—

> . . . work out a change in organization to accommodate the gradual merger of the Blue Eagle work into the work of code hearings and code administration and to free the time of the Administrator by a greater delegation of responsibility and authority. . . .[40]

Its membership was composed entirely of NRA staff officials. Later, in January 1934, the Policy Board was reorganized to include all division administrators, chiefs of divisions, and chairmen of advisory boards. It was instructed to:

> . . . Advise the Administrator on all matters of general policy arising in NRA and all other questions specifically referred to it.[41]

It occasionally met with the Administrator in an advisory capacity but promulgated no policy rulings.

These efforts to establish continuity of policy suffered from the weakness common to all policy-making bodies composed of administrative personnel. In the first place the members of such a policy body are ordinarily too absorbed in administrative detail to give considered opinions on general policy problems. And wholly aside from the time element, its recommendations on policy matters are inevitably colored by considerations of administrative expediency.

In the second place, complete discretion in the final disposal of policy recommendations is vested in the chief

[40] NRA Office Order No. 35, Sept. 16, 1933.
[41] NRA Office Order No. 55, Jan. 6, 1934.

administrative officer. At best such policy groups can function only in an advisory capacity. In any event, under the administrative conditions prevailing in the NRA during the first year, the policy group composed of administrative officials did not function effectively as a policy group, even in an advisory capacity.

From time to time various individuals and agencies within NRA made extra-official attempts to establish uniformity, at least in internal operating policy. Personnel of the Legal Division, for example, supplied the intellectual initiative in a number of moves to secure uniformity of procedure in the code-making process. One such effort resulted in the formulation of a so-called "model code."[42] This furnished the applicant group and NRA personnel with a handy pattern both as to physical form and minimum requirements for substantive content, to guide the drafting of proposals in the early stages of code negotiations. Model codes, however, played very little part in formulating the major content of codes.

Then, too, individual legal advisers throughout the entire code-making process tended to extend their rulings on particular questions beyond the issues of law, far into the realm of general policy. While other divisions operated to some extent as policy-creating groups, the Legal Division occupied a unique position in the extent of its extra-official activities. In general the legal staff was more adequate in numbers to carry its work load than that of other divisions, and was recruited on a selective basis designed to permit the necessary delegation of authority. Both by virtue of the caliber of its personnel and the

[42] The original "model" was issued in October 1933. It was quickly withdrawn because of objection to some of its provisions in certain quarters, and thereafter circulated as an aid in code making on an entirely unofficial basis. A revised edition was issued in April 1934.

absolute nature of its rulings on some basic points (truly representative, monopolistic tendencies, etc.) it occupied a dominant position in the formulation of some codes; and on the basis of legal rulings it deflated many an ambitious scheme embodied in other code proposals. Deputies looking in desperation for some source of advice detached from any one of the special interests represented in the code bargaining process, at times found the legal adviser to be the only one in a position to give such counsel. In the general absence of NRA policy it was not unusual for legal rulings to be adopted as standard procedure by the Legal Division, and eventually by the NRA. It was a process of policy growing out of administrative action. In spite of decided limitations, the general effect was salutary. Not a few of the constructive rearrangements in NRA operating policy and method are directly traceable to the intellectual leadership of the Legal Division.

A development of somewhat different nature is found in the history of the Review Division. It first came into informal existence through the code-checking activities of a group of individuals attached to the executive officer's staff. Their duty was to see that the proper documents were attached to final drafts of codes and that all mandatory provisions were included. In this process of mechanical checking, it was natural that at least the most extreme variations in code-making methods and code content would be brought to light. Such discoveries when called to the attention of NRA officials occasionally gave rise to policy statements designed to produce more even treatment of code formulation. In the large, however, the review function was negative in character, being designed to protect the Administrator from approving mechanically faulty documents.

A formally constituted Review Division was not established until February 1934. It was given substantial powers both of review and constructive recommendation. Specifically it was directed to review all codes, orders, rulings, etc. submitted for the Administrator's approval in order to "verify compliance with established policy" and to disclose "inconsistencies between such rulings." In addition to such negative activities it was empowered to study classification problems (see p. 149 for discussion) and to analyze approved codes as a basis for suggesting amendments designed to bring off-color provisions into conformity with "established policy."

In spite of its formally expanded functions, the Review Division's effective work was still largely limited, as it had been before, to spotting mechanical defects in documents presented for approval, with some expansion in the direction of checking for uniformity of procedural treatment. The more constructive portion of its function was absorbed by the policy boards mentioned below. It is interesting to note in passing that the Review Division was not formally constituted until the end of the active code-making period.

It was not until April 1934 that the NRA established any structure designed to remove consideration of policy matters from the necessarily superficial attention and partisan influences inherent in the acts of policy-making agencies composed of administrative personnel. At this time the Administrator established an Assistant Administrator for Policy and named three deputy assistant administrators to be in charge of policy matters dealing respectively with labor problems, trade practices, and code authority and classification problems. Each of the three advisory boards, the Research and Planning Division, and the Legal Division were instructed to assign full-time advisers to each of the three deputy assistant administrators for policy. Each of these deputy assistant administrators, partly because of the character of tasks with which he was confronted, partly because of differences of view as to desirable method, approached his work in somewhat different ways. Each, however, to a greater or less degree dealt with the day to day run of code problems; each to a greater or less extent made recommendations for more general policy.[43] It should be noted in passing, however, that their decisions were in all cases subject to the final approval of the Administrator. Some of their recommendations were adopted and some not; others were adopted and effectuated; and still others were adopted as policy but not actually translated into administrative action.

The work of another agency, the Advisory Council, has exerted increasing influence on policy matters. It was established in June 1934 to expedite the disposal of various matters on which the opinion of representatives of the three advisory boards was required. In many respects it expedited administrative work and certainly tended to counteract the separatist tendency which underlay the entire NRA structure, one which has acted as a drag upon effective administrative operation. The mould into which the code-making process had been cast, one of intense bargaining, and the absence of general administrative co-ordination, had developed highly individualistic attitudes among the various advisory boards, staff divisions, and technical divisions. In dealing with interpretations, exemptions, and so on, it was not at all unusual for the deputy responsible for making initial de-

---

[43] A more detailed description of the work with reference to trade practices will be found in Chap. XXIX; with reference to classification problems on p. 284.

cisions in such matters to find himself confronted with diametrically opposed recommendations from his advisers. Decisions were slowed to a point of stoppage, for it was necessary for the deputy to attempt to secure a reconciliation of these differences prior to making a decision on each of the innumerable cases of administrative business. The Advisory Council served as a channel through which authoritative opinions could be obtained from representatives of the various boards to cover all cases arising in the future out of similar circumstances. (For a discussion of the functioning of this Council under the general reorganization of NRA, see page 76.)

General Reorganization and Reorientation

At the end of the first year, in spite of numerous reorganizations and adjustments, both in structure and in method, the NRA was a sprawling, poorly co-ordinated, and relatively ineffective organization. Innumerable shifts in internal method had kept the administrative personnel in constant confusion, and the code authority representatives in a state of irritation. Morale both of NRA and industry agencies was anything but the best. Each NRA policy or procedural announcement, followed as it was by modifications, retractions, and explanations (for example, on price policy, budgets, and government contracts) gave rise to a series of "revolts" among the industry members of various codes. Contending factions had sprung up within the NRA itself. Public discussion and general opinion were both pointing toward a change of direction for NRA. The Recovery Administrator himself stated:

No one man can watch the operation of 450 codes—I hope we can reduce them to 250 by consolidation, but even that is too many for one man. It needs a commission. I think the War

Industries Board model was good—a commission of responsible executives sat to co-ordinate activity but it had no vote. Its chairman was responsible and had the final decision.[44]

In short the scene was set for substantial reorganization, or for collapse. Decided differences of opinion developed concerning both policy and the proper form of reorganization. These differences became entangled in an emotional clash of personalities. The subsequent reorganization, in its first stages, is not therefore to be regarded wholly as the result of a calm discussion of the problems in hand.

On September 27, 1934 the President radically altered the administrative structure of NRA by substituting a board for the single administrator form of control. (See the chart on page 69 for the NRA administrative organization as it exists at present, April 1935.) The National Industrial Recovery Board, composed of five members named by the President, and two ex-officio members (economic adviser and legal adviser), was established and authorized, subject to the general approval of the Industrial Emergency Committee,

. . . to promulgate administrative policies, to appoint, employ, discharge, fix the compensation, define the duties, and direct the conduct of the personnel necessary for its administration and to exercise all those powers heretofore conferred by executive orders upon the Administrator for Industrial Recovery.[45]

At the same time the Industrial Emergency Committee[46] was charged with general supervision of NRA activities. It was composed of the following:

[44] *NRA Release No. 7119*, Aug. 2, 1934; address of Recovery Administrator.

[45] Executive Order No. 6859, Sept. 27, 1934. By Executive Order No. 6993 of Mar. 21, 1935 the Board was increased to seven members; one new member to represent industry, and the other, labor interests.

[46] Created by Executive Order No. 6770, June 30, 1934; amended by Executive Order No. 6836, Aug. 31, 1934; and by Executive Order No.

PRESENT ADMINISTRATIVE ORGANIZATION OF THE NRA

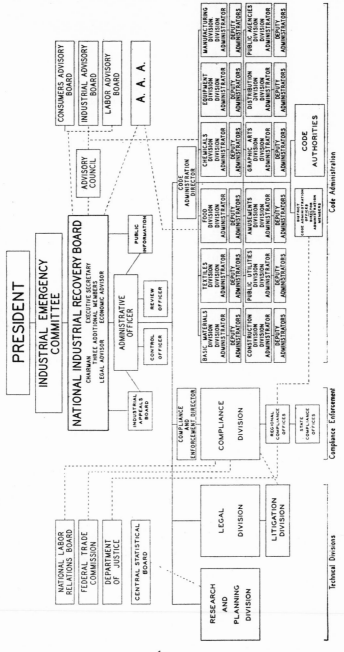

69

The Secretary of Interior
The Secretary of Labor
The Chairman of the National Industrial Recovery Board
The Administrator of Agricultural Adjustment
The Administrator of Federal Emergency Relief
The Director of the Committee

Among its other duties it was instructed "to determine, with the approval of the President the general policies of the administration of the National Industrial Recovery Act."[47]

First to be considered in connection with the re-organized Board are certain changes in internal administrative structure. More important and next discussed are matters dealing with the present composition of the Board and with the problems involved in securing continuity of policy under the existing division of authority and responsibility over NRA between various agencies.

Internal administrative reorganization.[48] The Recovery Board has been much concerned with internal administrative reorganization. Several definite adjustments have been made by the Board in administrative organization and procedure.

The Board has established a clear-cut distinction between the function of supervision and that of execution. Under the powers granted by the executive order the Board has chosen to devote itself primarily to formulating administrative policies and plans. It has placed wide authority and responsibility for executing its policies and orders in the administrative officer, who is the chief ex-

6860, Sept. 27, 1934. By Executive Order No. 6889-A, Oct. 29, 1934, the Industrial Emergency Committee was made a sub-committee of the re-organized National Emergency Council. Its functions remained the same.

[47] Executive Order No. 6860, Sept. 27, 1934.

[48] See the charts on pp. 49, 55, and 69 for the evolution of administrative structure.

ecutive official. All administrative operations have been functionalized and immediate supervision of each group has been placed under a unified control. In line with the plan, four co-ordinate divisions have been established, each headed by a director reporting to the administrative officer. The heads of these divisions have been titled respectively: Code Administration Director; Compliance and Enforcement Director; Review Officer; and Control Officer. Under the present administrative schemes the operating work of NRA centers in two divisions: Code Administration; and Compliance and Enforcement. The functions of all other divisions—Review, Executive, Research and Planning, and Legal—serve to facilitate these two basic operations.

Code administration. As in the past, routine administration of codes of fair competition is actively supervised by deputy administrators in charge of various groups of codes. The deputy's office furnishes the direct line of contact between the NRA and industry code authorities. All routine business connected with code administration is conducted by the deputy and his staff of assistants and advisers. As in the case of code formulation the deputy is required to secure opinions of advisers assigned by each of the three advisory boards and by the two technical divisions, before taking final action on matters of code modification, exemptions, interpretations, etc. which arise in connection with code administration. Under the reorganized NRA procedure, codes have been reallocated to divisions. For administrative purposes all codes are now grouped into twelve industry divisions; each division is headed by a division administrator.[49] The

[49] The 12 industry divisions are as follows: Basic Materials, Textiles, Food, Chemicals, Equipment, Manufacturing, Construction, Public Utilities, Amusements, Graphic Arts, Distribution, and Public Agencies. For comparison with earlier allocation of codes to divisions, see p. 51.

organizational features of one of the twelve industry divisions, together with the administrative assignment of codes to the various deputies and assistants, are shown in the chart on page 73. Other divisions are organized along similar lines.

In order to establish intimate points of supervision between the deputy's office and code authorities, particularly those located outside of Washington, full-time administration members on code authorities have been assigned to various regional offices. These administration members, each assigned to several codes, serve as the deputy's personal representative and report directly to him relative to the activities of code authorities.

One of the features of the structural reorganization of NRA was the establishment of a Director of Code Administration, charged with the overhead supervision of industry division activities, including field operations. His task is one of co-ordinating efforts of the various divisions with a view to securing uniformity of procedure on all codes, rather than the approval of detailed matters of business. The latter remains the function of division administrators. Formerly it was the duty of the Administrative Officer to see that the operations of all industry divisions were co-ordinated. Under this arrangement, proper supervision was impossible because of the multiplicity of routine matters requiring the attention of the Administrative Officer.

As the NRA is now organized the lines of authority and responsibility in code administration run uninterruptedly from the administration member in the field observing the activities of code authorities, to the deputy administrator in Washington in charge of a particular code, to the division administrator supervising a group

CONSUMERS ADVISOR
INDUSTRIAL ADVISOR
LABOR ADVISOR

DIVISION ADMINISTRATOR

ASSISTANT DIVISION ADMINISTRATOR

DIVISION COUNSEL | EXECUTIVE ASSISTANT | CODE ASSISTANT | TECHNICAL ASSISTANT

DEPUTY ADMINISTRATOR

DEPUTY ADMINISTRATOR
Fabricated Metal Products Basic Code
Electric and Neon Sign
Railway Break Beam Mfg.
Solder Mfg.

ASSISTANT DEPUTY ADMINISTRATOR
Bedding Manufacturing
Beverage Dispensing Equipment
Business Furniture, Storage Equip. and Filing Supply
Fire Resistive Safe Furniture Mfg.
Metal Hospital Furniture
Office Equipment Mfgrs.
Public Seating
Specialty Accounting Supply Mfg.

ASSISTANT DEPUTY ADMINISTRATOR
Aluminum Cooking Utensils Mfg.
Bank Instrument Mfg.
Floor Machinery
Musical Mdse. Mfg.
Photographic and Photo Finishing
Piano Mfg.
Pipe Organ
Portrait Painting
Vacuum Cleaner Mfg.

ASSISTANT DEPUTY ADMINISTRATOR
American Jeweled Watch Mfg.
Assembled Watch
Brush Mfg.
Clock Mfg.
Dry and Polishing Mop Mfg.
Medium and Low Priced Jewelry Producing
Silverware Mfg.
Watch Case Mfg.
Wet Mop Mfg.

ASSISTANT DEPUTY ADMINISTRATOR
Advertising Specialty
Athletic Goods Mfg.
Blackboard and Blackboard Eraser Mfg.
Corn Cob Pipe
Fishing Tackle
Fountain Pen and Mechanical Pencil Mfg.
Pencil Slat
Punch Board Mfg.
Small Arms and Ammunition Mfg.
Smoking Pipe Mfg.
Toy and Playthings Mfg.
Wood Cased Lead Pencil Mfg.

ASSISTANT DEPUTY ADMINISTRATOR
Beauty and Barber Shop Mechanical Equipment Mfg.
Dental Goods and Equipment
Blue Print and Photo Print
Dental Laboratory
Household Ice Refrigerator
Porcelain Breakfast Furniture Assembling
Prison Equipment Mfg.
Washing and Ironing Machine Mfg.

ASSISTANT DEPUTY ADMINISTRATOR
Artistic Lighting Equipment Mfg.
Artificial Limb Mfg.
Buff and Polishing Wheel
Chain Mfg.
Can Operated Machine
Collapsible Tube
File Mfg.
Fireplace and Furnishings Subdivision
Food and Meat Chopper Subdivision
Forged Tool Mfg.
Hair Clipper
Hand Bag Frame and Machine Knife and Allied Products
Metal Decorating Subdivision
Metal Safety Tread Subdivision
Optical Mfg.
Pipe Tool Mfg.
Rolling Steel Door Mfg.
Sterilizer
Surgical Mfg. and Wholesale
Vise Mfg.
Vitreous Enameled Ware Mfg.
Wheelbarrow Mfg.

ASSISTANT DEPUTY ADMINISTRATOR
Advertising Metal Sign and Display Mfg.
Can Manufacturing
Cap and Closure Mfg.
Cigar Container Mfg.
Cutlery, Manicure Implement and Painters and Paper Hangers Tool and Assembling
Fly Swatter Mfg.
Galvanized Ware Mfg.
Hog Ring and Ringer
Lock and Builders Hardware Mfg.
Metal Jacketed Jug Mfg.
Milk and Ice Cream Can Mfg.
Mine Tools Mfg.
Safety Razor and Blade Mfg.
Shoe Shank Mfg.
Steel Barrel and Drum Mfg.
Steel Package Mfg.
Plain Washer Mfg.
Saw and Steel Products Mfg.

ASSISTANT DEPUTY ADMINISTRATOR
Bolt, Nut and Rivet Mfg.
Bright Wire Goods Mfg.
Cut Tack, Wire Tack, etc. Mfg.
Cap Screw Mfg.
Drapery and Carpet Hardware Mfg.
Electro Plating etc. Mfg.
Hack Saw Blade Mfg.
Horseshoe and Allied Product Mfg.
Job Galvanizing Mfg.
Machine Applied Staple, etc. Mfg.
Machine Screw Mfg.
Machine Screw Nut Mfg.
Metal Etching Mfg.
Metal Treating Mfg.
Porcelain Enameling Mfg.
Screw Machine Products Mfg.
Slide Fastener Mfg.
Snap Fastener Mfg.
Socket Screw Products Mfg.
Tool and Implement Mfg.
Tubular and Split Rivet Mfg.
Wood Screw Mfg.

ASSISTANT DEPUTY ADMINISTRATOR
Complete Wire and Iron Fence
Corset Steel Mfg.
Flexible Metal Hose and Tubing Mfg.
Funeral Supply
Metal Spinning and Stamping Subdivision
Perforated Metal Mfg.
Pulp and Paper Mill Wire Cloth Mfg.
Spring Mfg.
Steel Wool Mfg.
Umbrella Frame and Umbrella Hdw. Mfg.
Upholstery Springs and Accessories Mfg.
Washing Machine Parts Mfg.
Wire Rope and Strand Mfg.
Wrench Mfg.

ASSISTANT DEPUTY ADMINISTRATOR
Architectural, Ornamental and Misc. Iron, Bronze Wire and Metal Spec.
Metallic Wall Structure
All Metal Insect Screen Mfg.
Greenhouse
Lighting Rod Mfg.
Metal Lath Mfg.
Metal Window Mfg.
Upward Acting Door
Open Steel Flooring Mfg.

of deputies, to the Director of Code Administration, and then to the Administrative Officer. Only matters involving policy determination reach the Recovery Board.

Compliance and enforcement. Under the administrative reorganization effectuated by the Recovery Board, compliance and enforcement activities have been centralized under the control of a Compliance and Enforcement Director. In authority this official is co-ordinate with the Code Administration Director. Both report directly to the Administrative Officer.

Two other distinct innovations have been instituted in compliance and enforcement procedure. A special assistant to the Attorney General has been named to direct NRA code litigation in all phases, including supervision over United States district attorneys in NRA matters and the preparation of court appeals cases. All compliance work has been decentralized on a regional basis. Nine regional offices have been authorized, each in charge of a regional director. Each regional office is set up as a complete operating unit staffed with advisers assigned from NRA divisions. The regional directors are directly responsible to the Compliance and Enforcement Director at Washington, but except in unusual cases, compliance cases are expected to be disposed of without being referred to Washington. (See discussion on page 261.)

Under the present organizational plan a clear-cut distinction has been made between the supervision of *code administration* and the supervision of *compliance and enforcement.* The distinction has been carried so far that the establishment of independent field organizations is contemplated with only a regional executive officer to coordinate their activities. While there may be some theoretical defense for the functional segregation of these two activities, it is highly doubtful that a duplication of field organization and personnel is either desirable or practicable.

Internal control. The service and advisory functions performed by the Review, Legal, and Research and Planning Divisions are dealt with in connection with other topics and require no further attention here, since their position in the NRA structure was not affected by reorganization.

One other highly important means of rationalizing procedure was provided by action of the Board. A control officer was named and given centralized authority over a number of vital functions which had hitherto been performed, if at all, by scattered divisions in NRA. This officer was given control over all matters relating to the planning of administrative methods and the provision of uniform methods of procuring and supervising personnel. His functions include (1) formulating internal operating methods designed to secure uniformity between divisions in the methods of conducting business (routing of communications, standard filing methods, form of reports, etc.); (2) preparation of operating budgets and supervision of finances; (3) establishment of personnel classifications and standards for determination of reassignment, promotion, dismissal, and so on.

Failure to supply such a centralized control over the service operations which are vital to the smooth functioning of any large organization furnishes the explanation for the existence of some of the worst spots of administrative confusion in NRA.

Composition of the National Industrial Recovery Board. The present composition of the Recovery Board represents a calculated attempt to project upward into the controlling agency, the general pattern of the NRA sub-structure. Just as the NRA machine was originally set up to include three separate divisions charged with actively furthering the respective interests of labor, consumer, and industrial groups, so the Recovery Board includes individuals who are presumed to be active champions of each of these three groups. There seems to be no good reason why the Board should be so constituted, particularly if the present sub-structure is to be retained. On the other hand, there are several important reasons why the Board should be constituted on an impartial basis.

In an operation such as the NRA, characterized throughout by the active controversy of special interests, it appears obvious both from the standpoint of administrative expedition, and equity, that final decisions should be made by a board constituted of individuals owing active allegiance to none of the special parties at interest in such decisions; in other words, by an impartial board. Viewed solely from the standpoint of administrative procedure, final decisions are naturally delayed if the process of bargaining and compromise characteristic of NRA administrative process must be repeated when matters come to the Board for final decision. Before reaching the Board, controversial questions are subjected not only to the scrutiny of deputies (in charge of the code or codes involved) and his advisers, but are also analyzed by the Advisory Council. In its present operations the Board draws heavily on the services of the reorganized Advisory Council. It will be recalled (see page 66) that the Council was originally composed of three members from each of the advisory boards. Under the reorganization the Council is still composed of nine members; two from each of the advisory boards, one each from the Division of Research and Planning and the Legal Division, with an executive director designated as a special assistant to the Board. All matters of non-routine business are cleared through the Council before being presented to the Board.

The Recovery Board as now constituted represents in pattern a complete duplication of this Advisory Council. In function it is different only in degree of authority. The Board still functions, as did the Administrator, without benefit of clear general policy. It has no stated function of determining general policy, and it serves as the final forum of compromise. Obviously, if an impartial board were to be appointed, its ability to function as such would have to be predicated upon the assumption that it had the power to promulgate policy. Immediate responsibility for such policies now rests with the Industrial Emergency Committee, to which attention may now be turned.

Determination of general policy. It has already been noted that in passing the Recovery Act, Congress failed to exercise what has ordinarily been considered the constitutional power and duty of the legislative branch of government, to declare unequivocally the basic objectives of legislative enactments, and to establish the administrative machinery and methods to be used in attaining these objectives. It delegated this duty to the President, who exercised it to some extent (1) by creating the skeleton of an administrative structure; (2) by establishing a policy body to exercise general approval over the acts of the administrative agency; (3) by selecting the instrumentality of voluntary codes of fair competition as the means of effectuating the purpose of the act; and (4) by retaining final power of approval (but not without exception) over the acts of the administrative agency. In net operating effect, however, the administrative agency actually performed in large measure, to whatever extent they were performed, both phases of the function of supervision and control: the promulgation of general policy, and the formulation and execution of administrative policy.

With the recent reorganization of the NRA a new alignment of authority and responsibility has been established. The Industrial Emergency Committee is empowered, subject to the approval of the President, to promulgate general policy relative to the administration of NIRA; the National Industrial Recovery Board is empowered to promulgate, subject to the approval of the Industrial Emergency Committee, administrative policy relative to the functioning of NRA. With one important exception, the supervisory relationship existing between the Industrial Emergency Committee and the Recovery Board is therefore similar, potentially at least, to that ordinarily prevailing between the legislative branch of government and administrative agencies. The important exception involves the time element and is particularly vital to the type of regulatory method adopted under the NIRA. (This exception will be dealt with in the next section.)

One of the first obstacles in the way of establishing continuity of policy for NRA is raised by the multiplicity of regulatory agencies created by the present Administration. The jurisdiction of many of these agencies overlaps that of others in many important respects. Even if there is no outright overlapping of jurisdiction, the total coverage is so broad that adoption by one agency of a given policy or method may vitally affect the success of another agency in carrying out previously adopted policies.[50] There can be little question that so long as a series

[50] One example serves to illustrate this point. The lumber and timber products code and the construction code may be administered by the NRA in such a way as vitally to affect the success of the Federal Housing Administration in its drive for home remodeling, etc., or may vitally affect the public works slum clearance projects.

of far-reaching programs are being carried on simultaneously by the Administration under a broad delegation of legislative power, supervisory control must be exercised on several levels if the entire program is to be co-ordinated either in terms of timing or ultimate objectives.

The obvious intent of the President in creating the Industrial Emergency Committee was to guard against the development of situations in which the efforts of one emergency agency cancels out those of another. It was, however, given special authorization to establish policies for the NRA. Whether in fact it will perform either of these functions effectively is problematical. Previous agencies with similar functions have not done so, and it resembles the earlier agencies in that its membership is composed of already overburdened administrative offivers of the government. The primary difference is that its executive officer is now a high official of the NRA, whose views on its operations are presumably approved by the President. Presumably named to serve as the chief co-ordinating official between numerous government agencies, he appears hardly to be in a position to give discriminating attention to both sets of duties. Constituted as it is, there is little to be said for the adequacy of the Industrial Emergency Committee as an agency to perform the policy-making duties delegated by the legislature. Nor has it shown any initiative in performing them. Whatever the degree of its adequacy, it suffers under the necessary defects of administrative bodies which are charged with performing policy-making and legislative functions.

LEGISLATIVE *VS.* ADMINISTRATIVE POLICY MAKING

If the legislature exercises its power to define policy and establishes administrative machinery to effectuate the legislative intent, the administrative agency is informed in advance as to the outside limits of its operating authority; and the interests affected by the legislation are advised as to the outside limits of their privileges and responsibilities. Both the administrative agency and the economic interests affected can estimate with reasonable assurance at least the minimum time period during which these maximum and minimum conditions will be applicable. Administrative procedure, on the one hand, and compliance with orders, rules, and regulations issued by the administrative agency, on the other, are planned and executed in terms of continuity of policy. These in general are the operating conditions characteristic of regulatory agencies such as the Interstate Commerce Commission, state public utility commissions, the Federal Communications Commission, and others.

If, on the other hand, the legislative body fails to establish an unambiguous definition of general policy and fails to make any specification as to administrative machinery or method; and if, by a process of delegation and redelegation, the real exercise of this function finally lodges at various levels in the executive branch, a wholly different set of conditions is created. Under such circumstances, the administrative agency, being wholly responsible to the executive, is subject to recomposition, and to redefinition of powers and duties at a moment's notice. Even in the exercise of its routine administrative function its acts are subject to veto by an executive agency. In like manner, the executive agency (such as the Industrial Emergency Committee), which by virtue of delegated authority is empowered to promulgate general policy for control of the administrative agency, is subject at any time to dissolution, reconstitution, or to a redefinition of powers. With such conditions prevailing there is no guarantee of any continuity in operating policy. In fact, there is no guarantee that general policy will be enunciated at all, except perhaps to meet particular operating situations as they arise. And there is nothing to deter the frequent adaptation of general policy to the shifting convictions of the controlling personalities, or to the waxing and waning influence of various individuals who pass in and out of the administrative scene.

Similar shifts may occur, and for similar reasons, when general policy is promulgated in the first instance by legislative action. The basic difference is that the phase of the cycle of adjustment, characteristic of executive control, is almost always shorter than that of the ordinary cycle of legislative adjustment. This naturally follows since control over administrative agencies is presumably delegated to the executive branch of government in order to secure flexibility in adapting policies and methods to changing conditions.

As already indicated, neither the devices of control and supervision originally established to govern the administration of the NIRA, nor those created under the reorganization of NRA, place any effective limitation upon the frequency with which both objectives and machinery may be altered.

In the NRA effort to organize industry and trade for "industrial self-government" perhaps the chief disturbing factors have been the absence of clearly defined policy and the consequent vacillation in method. There is no reason to believe that whatever efforts the NRA may make in the future to guide the idea of industrial self-government to maturity will escape the difficulties cast up by vacillating policy and method. And there is nothing in the present arrangement of direction and control to guarantee that general policy will be defined and executed according to relatively fixed standards and methods. There would seem to be little reason to believe that detailed regulatory control of the type essayed by the NRA can be effectively exercised in the absence of some guarantee that well-defined goals are to be sought by the application of reasonably stable administrative policies and methods. In one of its most crucial aspects the NRA problem sifts down to the discovery of ways and means of establishing some such guarantee.

Should the NRA be continued there are certain minima of legislative control in the absence of which it is impossible for such an administrative agency to function properly. One is the statement of objectives in unambiguous terms, together with the criteria of judgment and measurement to be used. Another is the provision of a form of administrative organization capable of maintaining continuity of policy and method. Another is the creation of an executive co-ordinating agency to adjust the activities of the multifarious new administrative agencies to one another. An impartial board is the only sort of superior administrative body which could rescue the NRA from its bargaining plane, and establish it on a basis of impartial administration. An organization such as the NRA can have no appropriate place in a system of representative government unless protected from the subjective whims of uninstructed officials.

In concluding this survey of certain aspects of NRA organization, various tests of performance could be stated more at length, relating in the early stages to its adequacy for creating codes, and in later stages to its adequacy for supervising the administration and enforcement of codes. But such tests are inconclusive apart from consideration of qualitative tests of the things to be administered and the problems and policies imbedded therein. The fundamental tests are only such as can be distilled from the evidence on all the diverse matters which make up the body of the present work.

CHAPTER V

THE CODE-MAKING PROCESS

In formulating rules and regulations to govern code making, the NRA was bound by few statutory requirements. As earlier examination has shown (page 9), the law required only that the representative character of applicant groups be determined and that "public notice and hearing" be afforded. All rules and regulations, administrative devices, and procedures designed to secure an orderly and legal process in formulating codes of fair competition were prescribed either by executive order of the President, or by direct action of the Recovery Administrator. Supplementing a basic organization including administrative officials and legal and research divisions, the NRA added to its structure the three advisory boards to represent the interests of business, labor, and consumer groups respectively at each step of the code-making process. In the interests of legality as well as to facilitate administrative action, it created the device of the public hearing. These elements of the plan are described as follows in a condensed official statement:

As to the machinery—the practical way of accomplishing what we are setting out to do, when a trade association has a code ready to submit and the association has qualified as truly representative, and after reasonable notice has been issued to all concerned, a public hearing will be held by the Administrator or a deputy. A Labor Advisory Board appointed by the Secretary of Labor will be responsible that every affected labor group, whether organized or unorganized, is fully and adequately represented in an advisory capacity and any interested labor group will be entitled to be heard through representatives of its own choosing. An Industrial Advisory Board appointed by the Secretary of Commerce will be responsible that every affected industrial group is fully and adequately represented in an advisory capacity and any interested industrial group will be entitled to be heard through representatives of its own choosing. A Consumers' Advisory Board will be responsible that the interests of the consuming public will be represented and every reasonable opportunity will be be given to any group or class who may be affected directly or indirectly to present their views.[2]

GENERAL CHARACTER OF THE PROCESS

In broad outline the plan laid down for code making was as follows: The applicant group submitted a proposed code which was assigned to a particular deputy administrator. When the group had been found to be properly representative within the meaning of the act, a series of preliminary conferences were held, over which the deputy presided. In addition to the code committee of the applicant group, these conferences were attended by a representative of each of the three advisory boards, of the Legal Division, and of the Research and Planning Division. When the proposals were in a form to be put on public display, a public hearing was called at which interested parties could appear. After the hearings the proposals proceeded to a further stage of negotiation. From this process a document finally emerged which was sent by the deputy to the Administrator. And finally it was the function of the NRA, or more specifically of the Administrator, to hold the finished product up to the light of public interest and advise the President whether it should be approved, modified, or rejected.

From the beginning to the end of the code-making process the functions of the NRA were somewhat ambiguously defined and are difficult to state accurately in official terms. As an agency charged with furthering the purposes of the act, it adopted a procedure which placed

[1] *NRA Bulletin No. 1,* June 16, 1933.

upon its deputy administrators (the active NRA agents in code making) types of duties of rather dissimilar character. In the early days of the NRA a somewhat idealized view of the proceedings was held. It was described as a "forum for co-operation."[2] The applicant groups were expected to bring in proposals directed toward the immediate NRA purpose of re-employment. Lest their proposals reflect too strongly their limited point of view, the proposals were, however, to be subjected to the scrutiny of the advisory boards, which were regarded as representing definable interest groups. Out of the ensuing discussion it was presumed that there would be substantial agreement among all parties concerned. In the degree that the parties at interest were unselfishly seeking to co-operate in promoting the immediate purpose, the function of the deputy could be defined as chairman of the forum, steering the proceedings toward a basis of agreement.

More or less from the beginning, however, the idealized version gave way to the realities of an out and out bargaining process, in which selfish interests were played against one another. No exact official recognition was given to the subtle difference between a "forum for co-operation" and an arena for bargaining, but the recognition of it crept into official language. Thus, the basis for arriving at decisions on the exact character of code provisions was described as emerging from the "controversy of conflicting interests."[3] In so far as this characterized

[2] "The machinery the President has set up is not a bureau and will not become one. It is rather a forum for co-operation." See p. 43.

[3] "The formula is designed, by controversy of conflicting interest, to arrive at truth and composition. This practice has been followed without exception. Without it there would be no formula or possibility of obtaining informed opinion on any of the three principal sides of the controlling questions pertaining to each code. The only alternative to

the proceedings, the position of the deputy might be described as that of a referee confining the contending parties within the rules.

In whatever degree they are appropriate, the "forum" and the "arena" concepts do not give a sufficient characterization. The NRA was the active proponent of certain ends, and it could not cast its agents merely in the role of chairmen or referees. The bargaining method adopted was only instrumental, in that the outcome was expected to promote the purposes in view. But the outcome could not be left entirely to bargaining. The deputy was therefore constrained to throw his weight in favor of provisions which he conceived to promote the purposes of the NRA. He might thus at times be lending support to one or the other of the bargaining parties, and at other times be initiating proposals and taking the offensive as one of the primary participants in the bargaining process.

In any case the bargaining concept must be retained at the center of the picture. This flows from the fact that the NRA provided its deputies with no substantive guides concerning the proper content of codes. No definite standards were established, stating the criteria to which code proposals must conform, either with respect to labor provisions, or trade practice provisions, or to forms of collective organization.[4]

The character of the general process described indi-

that sort of revelation through controversy is such long inquisitorial and academic proceedings as have contributed to the previous failure to control monopoly by the anti-trust acts." *NRA Release No. 2993,* Jan. 25, 1934.

[4] Lest this statement appear to misrepresent the facts, the seeming exceptions must be noted. With respect to hour provisions, it was required that a showing of favorable effect on employment must be made. With respect to wage provisions, a similar showing of addition to aggregate wage payments and of protection to ill-paid workers was called for. The general, mainly negative, requirements concerning trade practices will be

cates the importance initially placed upon the final function of the NRA, that of final review. Up to that point the proceedings were highly particularistic, based on an inward-looking view of the problems of a particular group, and the narrowly conceived contribution of that group to the program of the NRA. The full implications of code provisions so arrived at were presumed to be ascertainable only by looking at them in relation to the whole complex of inter-industrial relationships.

Viewed in its broad outlines the administrative method conceived by the NRA to guide the formulation of codes exhibits a direct intention to avoid playing into the hands of self-interested groups. Its preparations for bringing all points of view and all interests to bear on the process of code making might even be described as elaborate. Moreover, the plan was a direct administrative approach to the problem in hand, within the scope initially conceived. For it has to be remembered that the original procedure was devised to carry out a task of finite proportions. All the early planning for code making was on the plane of dealing with a few large associations, perhaps 10 at the start, and 30 to 50 eventually, covering the major fields of industrial employment. Re-employment and certain wage adjustments were to constitute the initial agenda, with perhaps some attention to trade practices of a conspicuously destructive character. Attention to the more basic problems of business practice and industrial organization was subject to postponement until a second and more leisurely phase of the NRA.

---

dealt with at a later point (See Chap. XXIX). The very general character of all these requirements emphasizes the absence of *definite* criteria and shows the extent of the open field for bargaining. In practice, certain rough criteria grew up by imitation and precedent, rather than by definite policy determination.

At the very outset of the NRA some trepidation was felt as to whether industrial groups would embrace the voluntary scheme offered by the government, involving, as was supposed, some initial sacrifice on the part of the co-operating groups. It was even felt necessary to practice some preliminary persuasion, to be sure that important groups would appear. No one seems to have envisaged the prospect of hundreds of small groups storming the gates with proposals of their own.

When within little more than a month some 400 codes had been filed for consideration, including large units such as textiles, oil, steel, coal, electrical manufacturing, retail dry goods, wearing apparel, lumber, wool, and shipbuilding, the officials were somewhat appalled by the proportions of the task undertaken.[5] The deluge of code proposals was, however, accepted as an opportunity to extend the benefits of the program.[6] This decision, accompanied by no consideration of the problems involved, entailed the discarding of the simple original plan, and opened up a troublesome chain of developments for the NRA.

CONSTITUENCY AND INCENTIVES OF APPLICANT GROUPS

In order to gain a clear view of what went on at the NRA, it is necessary to examine the character of the

[5] On this matter the General Counsel remarked that: "These prospects at the present time instead of discouraging us with any fear that industry may not respond to this call is rather appalling to those who must administer the law and who are determined to deal with this vast amount of controversial material without creating a huge governmental organization. In view of the staggering size of this undertaking it will doubtless surprise many to know that less than 400 persons have fixed employment up to date in the NRA." *NRA Release No. 93*, July 26, 1933.

[6] "Once launched there was no halting the code-making process. It had to be carried through so that every industry in the country and its workers might as quickly as possible have an even break of the recovery program's benefit." *NRA Release No. 5889*, June 21, 1934; statement of Recovery Administrator.

groups which initiated code proposals and the incentives which moved them to action.

The Trade Association Base

A dominant place in the NRA program was assured to trade associations when the administration chose the industrial self-government pattern of regulation, since such organizations formed the only available channel for immediate action.[7] Some sort of organized association existed in almost every sphere of industry and trade. Several hundred were national associations, the remainder regional and local. The principle of organization was usually that of common interest in given markets, and the pursuit of this principle led to the existence of separate associations for highly unimportant commodities. Because of the variety of products produced by typical enterprises, it was common to find that a single enterprise subscribed to the support of several different trade associations, each of which was concerned with some market in which it operated. Most associations led an independent existence, but there were striking examples of co-operative action between associations in closely related fields, as in the cases of lumber and electrical manufacturing. Not uncommonly, on the other hand, rival associations were to be found in the same field.

The scope of association activities differed from industry to industry, partly due to the uniqueness of the problems in each industry, partly to chance circumstances and

[7] The intended reliance of the NRA upon trade associations is seen in the following statement: "Nearly every principal employer belongs to what is called a trade association. These associations were mostly formed long ago for what mutual help the members could get by agreement within the law (the anti-trust laws). They were not very strong under the old law, but the new one makes them highly important. They are almost a part of the government and they can do and agree to many more things than they could ever do before." *NRA Release No. 11*, June 25, 1933.

personal factors. Some, as in copper and steel, covered practically the whole of important industries and were cartel-like in their activities. The same may be said of numerous associations in the fields of mining and manufacturing. A certain number of these were somewhat generally believed to be engaged in more or less effective avoidance of the Sherman Anti-trust Law. The activities most widely engaged in were the promotion of trade statistics, standardized accounting, and standards of competitive practice. Technical and market research, trade promotion, and legislative lobbying were also very common.[8]

In the distributive trades the strong units were commonly regional or local, though grouped under national associations with very limited functions. Trade promotion was the primary function and this commonly entailed an attempt to strengthen certain distributive channels as against others. Wholesalers' associations, for example, sought to bulwark the independent wholesaler against mass distribution by chain stores on the one hand, and against direct factory-to-retailer distribution on the other. There was also direct concern with trade practices, such as discounts, customer classification, and the like. From time to time special legislative questions agitated the distributors' associations, such as the battle over retail price maintenance. Though impracticable in most fields of retailing, price-control efforts were much to the fore in local associations in a few fields such as coal and ice. The officials of existing associations were the active agencies in initiating a major fraction of the codes. The system of codes is thus in large degree a direct off-shoot of the preceding trade association system.

[8] See United States Chamber of Commerce, *Trade Association Activities*, 1930.

With the code-making process under way, the NRA itself precipitated remarkable changes in the trade association situation. In the first place, the lure of a code brought many more or less moribund associations to life. In the second place, it induced the organization of many new associations, or led to the formation of informal groups, intent upon getting codes. Both the resurrection of moribund associations and the creation of new ones was often due to the initiative of particular individuals, frequently of the promoter type, to whose advantage in fees or salaries the existence of the group would accrue. In the third place, many of the older associations, to qualify as "truly representative" groups within the meaning of the Recovery Act, were compelled to solicit the co-operation of other associations or unorganized groups. The scope of a code-seeking group ordinarily had to be wider than the membership of a particular association. Since, however, the association was the nucleus of most groups, the voluntary classification of industry to which the pursuit of codes led was not unlike that which had previously existed in the structure of the trade association system.

Incentives

Casual observers of the NRA scene were nonplussed that committees of business men were crowding into Washington and staying for weeks and months for the privilege of increasing their costs by raising wages and reducing hours of work. For the most part they were there to secure a sufficient *quid pro quo*, hoping (as against official pronouncements) that the *quid* would sufficiently outweigh the *quo* to make the effort worth while in terms of profits. The imaginations of groups of business men were fired by the prospect of removing or mitigating the competitive handicaps to which they so largely attributed the unhappy absence of profits.

The positive incentives were: (1) relief from the anti-trust laws; (2) the authoritative enforcement of price-control devices; and (3) relief from competitive practices deemed to be ruining the market. These incentives, while closely related, operated with varying force on different groups. Relief from the anti-trust laws merely implies an opening of the way to certain types of voluntary agreement without the force of law. This is what some groups would have preferred, particularly in the industries where the conditions for monopolistic combination were propitious and where there was already a body of experience in co-operatively skirting or overlapping the boundaries of the law.

Such relief would, however, have been no relief at all to large areas of industry and trade. In many, if not most, areas of industrial production the ability to exercise any effective collective control over prices or business practices on a voluntary basis probably does not exist. The competitive forces are too active. To such groups codes gave promise of legal force to such agreements as were approved by NRA, permitting recalcitrant minorities to be forced into conformity. Given the prospect that such agreements would include price-control devices, such groups saw themselves approaching what they often regarded as the enviable position of industries in which more or less monopolistic powers were attainable.

There still remained highly competitive areas of business, in which even under codes it was hopeless to suppose that any effective fixing even of minimum prices could be achieved. Here, however, it was commonly thought possible to codify and enforce rules of business conduct which would diminish the severity of price competition and support a more stable level of higher prices. There were, for example, industries in which the major competitive trouble was conceived to be competitive wage cutting, and minimum wage rates were regarded as a blessing rather than the contrary by the more important elements in the industry. In other industries or trades rules limiting various types of current trade practice were thought to have some power to end the demoralization of the market price structure.

Of these various incentives, the second was no doubt the strongest and most accountable for the large number of code applications. The early flood was based on hope alone. Soon, however, favorable harbingers began to arrive. The first code provided for indirect control of production through limitation of machine hours, and the second prohibited selling below cost. On August 15 the electrical manufacturing code was approved. It contained a fully developed open-price reporting provision. And finally, on August 19 the approval of the iron and steel code and the lumber and timber products codes sent business hopes soaring. The former contained elaborate price reporting, merchandising, and minimum price protection provisions. The latter contained a forthright system of price fixing, and provisions for the control of production, including allocation. The promise of constructive relief from the anti-trust laws was proving no mirage.

One must guard against overstating the potency of these lures. Some groups applied for codes under what amounted to governmental coercion. Other groups, unable to see how a code would aid them directly, nevertheless joined the movement willingly in the hope that they would benefit from the widely advertised "increase in purchasing power." Some persons accepted onerous obligations in the hope that they were performing a public service. Conversely some proposed codes were tricky devices designed to benefit some groups of competitors at the expense of others. It must be recognized that every degree of public spirit and avarice, and of naïveté and sophistication of thought went into the coke-making process. No close observer of the process can, however, avoid the conclusion that the expectation of "improving" prices by collective action among competitors was the central motivating force.

This statement of fact must not be regarded as imputing to code proponents any more than the customary amount of human avarice. Years of propaganda against the anti-trust laws had weakened the popular fear of business agreements and combinations. The current popular theory that the depth of the depression was due to "unbridled competition" was axiomatic to a large part of the business community. The President's acceptance of the concept of "over-production" and his advocacy of higher prices, in unduly vague terms, invited the belief that almost any price-raising activities were laudable, especially when joined with the spreading of work and the payment of higher minimum wage rates. Among many code-seeking groups, especially at the beginning, there existed therefore a sense that they were acting in the public interest. It was not they, but the Administration, which had brought it about that activities once legally defined as "conspiracy in restraint of trade" had happily come to be regarded as a public service. As time went on, this atmosphere tended to fade and code proponents went about their tasks with a franker recognition of their pursuit of special self-interest.

It is not to be supposed from the foregoing that expert economic opinion concurred in the view that the setting up of price and production control devices was conducive to economic recovery. Nor is the idea to be conveyed that there was any official NRA policy which supported the drive for such devices. But to business men harassed by declining prices and critically uncertain markets, some promise of a way out of their particular difficulties was presented. In the actual code-making process they found it possible in substantial degree to get what they wanted. Apart from the power of the NRA to impose codes, applicant groups held the key to the situation. They could appear with proposals or not, as they pleased. Since most of them were little interested in negotiating with the NRA on the basis of the initial limited objectives, the NRA quickly adjusted its ideas to the situation, and thereby implicated itself in the immeasurably complicated task of dealing in short order with the whole realm of business practices for each of hundreds of groups. Speed was called for to achieve the initial objective of re-employment; while at the same time a comprehensive scope of negotiation was called for in order to secure the co-operation of groups. In due course this situation came to be regarded as normal by all parties concerned, except as in a quiet moment some tired NRA official might wistfully wonder whether it would not have been a better procedure to have stuck to the original plan.

THE STAGES OF CODE MAKING

The problems met in the actual code-making period, the methods used to dispose of them, the personalities involved—all combined to produce what might be termed the romantic adolescence of industrial self-government. A highly confused set of forces were at play, precipitate changes in methods were being made, new personalities were constantly moving in and out of the spotlight, producing a scene of seething action better

adapted to broad-brush painting than to analytical treatment. Projects were being conceived on bold scales and
executed with amazing speed and energy. What portions
of these projects were conceived as parts of an integrated
program, and what portions were created in the attempt
to control unforeseen situations after they had arisen is
probably known, if at all, only to those who created them.
The scene viewed as a whole gave the appearance of
being controlled more by the interplay of individual
personalities than by the actions of a single directing
agency.

In spite of the dynamic and confused nature of the
period, there are some lines of development which can
be traced throughout, and some vector forces resulting
from the action and counteraction of the code-making
era. Attention will be centered on these tangibles.

Before arriving at the NRA, most codes had a somewhat extended unofficial history. All the preliminary
drafting and the negotiation between interested elements
within an industry occupied trade association officials and
others for varying periods of time.

Treatment of codes, once in the NRA hopper, fell
into three broad phases.[9] (1) Preliminary checking, classification, and assignment to NRA deputies; (2) preliminary conferences and public hearing, and (3) final negotiations leading to approval. While every code at one
time or another passed through each of these phases,
there was decidedly no uniformity between codes, either
in the time consumed in the entire process from initial
preparation to final approval, or in the time consumed in
clearing through any given phase. Nor was there any

[9] For a detailed statement of the mechanical procedure followed in early
drafting of codes see *The ABC of the NRA*, The Brookings Institution,
1934.

uniformity between codes in the stubbornness of the problems encountered during any given stage of the code process. Some codes for example went directly to a deputy administrator, without preliminary examination. Some were in reality drafted during the period of pre-liminary conferences, either because of the wholly un-acceptable character of the applicant group's proposal, or because the original code proposal was split into two or more separate proposals. Public hearings on some pro-posals were held within two weeks of the date of filing, and final approval was secured in a few weeks. In other cases as long as four months was required to shape the code into acceptable form for public hearing; and a total of seven months of continuous negotiation was required for final approval. As the code-making process moved forward and administrative routine was perfected, some of the confusion so characteristic of the early code-making period abated.

Briefly stated, the NRA, during the era of greater code-making activity (from July 1933 to January 1934), was a tremendous mechanism operating at high speed, and in separate, loosely connected sections. It was per-forming activities ranging from routine administration to judicial determination, all with the same personnel and machinery. It was not an integrated organization but a collection of units.

Classification and Preliminary Analysis

With scores of code proposals pouring in daily and with hundreds of business representatives milling through the Commerce corridors, anxious to find one of the widely publicized government "referees" in order to start negotiations for a code of fair competition, the NRA encountered at the outset a largely unanticipated problem. A small, hurriedly assembled staff was assigned to the initial task of classifying codes into related groups, and allocating them to deputies in such a way as to assure uniformity of treatment. It was wholly baffled. Paradoxically enough the so-called "Control Division"[10] charged with this responsibility was the scene of some of the wildest confusion witnessed in NRA during its early months. Very little probing is necessary to discover the cause for bewilderment. As the plan was initially conceived the classification problem would not have arisen. No group of experts would have been required to assign a total of 20 or 30 proposed codes to 10 individual deputy administrators for negotiation, particularly when those proposals concerned such relatively well-defined industries as automobile manufacturing, iron and steel production, oil production and refining, and lumber and timber products. But with the deluge of codes, there began to appear, not only by tens but by hundreds, such strange titles as "ashes, cinders, garbage and scavenger," "gummed label and embossed seal," "long-distance furniture movers," "armored car operators," "wet mop," "dry mop," and "mop stick" industries. Those in charge were immediately faced with a problem for which no preparation had been made. The problem itself was clear, but the solution was elusive.

If any rationale were to be introduced into code negotiations and subsequent administration it was clear at the outset that uniformity would have to be obtained at least in the various provisions of all codes covering directly competing or closely related divisions of industries

---

[10] The Control Division served as a clearing house through which all contacts between any trade association or industrial or trade group were supposed to be made with the NRA. After the code passed preliminary analysis by the Code Analysis Division, the Control Division placed the industry representatives in contact with the deputy who was assigned to the code.

and trades. Obviously the manufacturers of rayon garments could not be allowed to secure privileges under code provisions which were not given to manufacturers of silk garments, without causing serious disparities in competitive conditions and consequent disruption of economic relationships. Less obviously, serious jurisdictional questions would ensue if an industry were permitted to define its membership in such a way that jurisdiction would be gained over similar operations carried on as minor phases of wholly unrelated industrial activity. In short the NRA problem was to secure in advance a classification of industry which was reasonable for the purpose of facilitating the negotiation of labor and trade practice provisions in the several areas of industry.

This was an entirely new problem within the purview of American government, and an excessively difficult one to attack, since the structure of American industry is highly unamenable to such classification. Business enterprises have not been developed with an eye to being classified for purposes of administrative control from above. Single enterprises engage in a most miscellaneous range of activities; some cut vertically through various levels of production and distribution; the types of marketing structure and strategy are myriad. To work out a scheme of classification under which to organize the joint administration of labor provisions and trade practice provisions for the whole of American industry is obviously a task of Herculean proportions. Without expecting to achieve more than a roughly helpful result, an effort to reduce the anomalies of classification and the conflicts of administrative authority to the minimum might naturally be thought of as the minimum preliminary requirement for any extensive collective interference with established economic relationships and business practices.

The facts in point here are that the serious import of

this problem was not at first realized, and that when realized effective measures were not taken to cope with it. The NRA proceeded without benefit of industrial classification and accepted codes of all degrees of importance, codes with overlapping definitions, codes which cut segments out of a larger industry, codes which cut vertically through the distributive trades. Initiative taken by deputy administrators during the later stage of code negotiations was largely responsible for securing some small degree of orderly classification.

During the first few months of the code-making period the NRA made an attempt to submit all code proposals to a centralized preliminary analysis before they were assigned to deputies for conference with the applicant group. This analysis was designed (1) to determine whether or not the applicant group was truly representative of the industry or trade covered by the proposed code, and (2) to evaluate the economic and social significance of specific provisions. Preliminary analysis was originally entrusted to the Division of Economic Research and Planning. But when the duties of the Division became too heavy, a Code Analysis Division was created to supervise the work of initial economic analysis.

The first function of the Division was to check statistical information furnished by applicant groups with respect to the number of firms engaged in industry, the character of the industry, aggregate capital investment, sales volume for recent years, number of employees, number of trade associations organized to serve the industry, etc. In this way the Division attempted to determine whether or not the applicant group could be declared "truly representative" of the interests it claimed to represent. At the same time, the by-laws and the constitution of the applicant organization were examined for the existence of inequitable restrictions on membership. Two obstacles were met here. Applicant groups commonly supplied inadequate data concerning the extent to which they were representative; and there was no quantitative definition of "truly representative." Tested by the three quantitative criteria of business units, output, and employment, an applicant association might show percentages of 20, 80, and 60 respectively. What might have constituted a fairly acceptable test of representative character in one industry might well have proved wholly inapplicable for another.[11] The Division was inevitably forced to adopt the rule-of-thumb method supported by means of estimation. In general it called specific attention to cases where it appeared that the applicant group could claim to represent less than 50 per cent of the industry, measured in terms of units, employment, capital investment, or output. In the case of associations of the highly localized trades, quantitative tests were, however, almost completely inapplicable, and findings could hardly be more than certain facts concerning the elements represented in the association and the regional distribution of membership. The findings of the Division did not determine whether or not the NRA should recognize a group as "truly representative." Discretion on this lay elsewhere, mainly between the deputy administrator and the Legal Division.

Different but equally troublesome problems were encountered in the attempt to evaluate specific code proposals. As previously indicated, no general economic principles had been officially adopted by NRA against which the desirability of various types of code provision

[11] In many instances the failure of applicant groups to be truly representative has given rise to serious administrative problems. See Chap. VIII.

might be checked. The Division was therefore forced to adopt its own standards. Codes were analyzed on this basis and the attention of the deputies in charge of various codes was called especially to certain price-fixing and production control devices which in the opinion of the Division were economically and socially undesirable. These analyses were furnished to the three advisory boards, the Research and Planning Division, and the Legal Division, as well as to the deputy. The recommendations of the Division were purely advisory in character.

The procedure outlined was short lived. With the creation of four industry divisions in October 1933 the Code Analysis Division was abolished and full responsibility for passing on the representative character of applicant groups was transferred to the deputies and their legal advisers. During its existence it analyzed and furnished comments on some 600 proposed codes. So far as is known, the activities of the Code Analysis Division constitutes the only attempt, during the active period of code making, to submit proposals to a central scrutiny based on uniform standards.

Lack of basic data, an inadequate and hurriedly assembled staff, and the general press for speed inevitably placed the preliminary analysis of codes on a more or less superficial plane. But many codes were never subjected even to this type of scrutiny, for a substantial number had been filed for consideration before the Division was organized; others because of pressure and administrative confusion went directly to deputies for conference, and still others grew out of codes already in the conference stage.

With the completion of the preliminary analysis, the code proposal was transmitted to the deputy administrator who had been assigned to carry on negotiations with the applicant group. One of the real problems created for the NRA organization by the code deluge was that of discovering deputies competent to carry on the exacting work of code negotiations. The NRA purpose was to command the services of men who had established reputations in their fields, who were temperamentally and intellectually capable of reviewing problems in terms of the broad public interest rather than from the standpoint of the narrower interests of an applicant group. Moreover, the specifications called for men with a practical turn of mind. And as a matter of policy no deputy was to be assigned to any code covering an industry in which he held substantial interests. Such specifications might have been partially met in staffing a small organization, such as was originally contemplated. No doubt during the formative period of NRA they were met, in some degree, by "drafting" leaders in various fields for tours of duty. But with progressive additions to the volume of work, the NRA was forced to adjust personnel ideals to the availability of material. Negotiations on the first major codes were supervised by deputies selected according to the original personnel plan. After that codes were in general distributed to the "least burdened" deputy and he in turn reassigned them to such assistants as were made available.

Fairly early the NRA had set up 17 general categories of industry classification under which codes were to be classified. In some degree the administrative divisions followed this classification, and there was even some intention of fitting code assignments of deputies into it. But in the dynamic growth of the organization, with new deputies and assistant deputies being added to the staff and new code negotiations being continuously opened, the administrative organization became very tenuously related to the industry classification.[12] Deputies came to have quite miscellaneous assignments, and closely related codes instead of being handled through a single office commonly were distributed among different deputies and even among different divisions.[13]

Preliminary Conferences

Preliminary conferences began as soon as proposed codes were assigned for negotiations, or, more accurately, as soon as the applicant group could secure the attention of the designated deputy. They were informal and private in character. The Recovery Administration was represented by a deputy administrator or an assistant deputy. The trade association or other group representing the code was represented by a steering committee, of manageable size, selected from its membership. Each of the three advisory boards assigned staff members to sit in on the discussions. The Legal Division and Research and

[12] That the classification of approved codes into 17 major industrial groups in many cases could serve no very useful administrative purpose is illustrated by merely listing from a random selection a few approved codes included under several of the 17 industry classifications. For example:

Miscellaneous Industrial:

    Cinders, ashes, and scavenger trade (largely trucking)
    Retail jewelry trade
    Retail trade
    Construction

Miscellaneous Commercial and Professional:

    Air transport
    Laundry trade

Motor bus
Restaurant
Transit

Transportation Equipment:

    Automobile manufacturing
    Domestic freight forwarding
    Funeral vehicles
    Inland water carriers
    Motor vehicle retailing trade
    Trucking
    Wholesale automotive trade

It should be noted here that the codes for air transport, motor bus, transit, domestic freight forwarding, and trucking were negotiated under the supervision of one deputy.

[13] For allocation of codes to divisions, see p. 51.

Planning Division each assigned advisers to aid the deputy in conducting negotiations. They might or might not be called upon to attend all conferences. During the early negotiations the function of each of these individuals consisted largely in keeping before the deputy administrator the point of view of the division or board which he represented.

At a very early stage of the negotiations the essentially bargaining character of the code-making process became apparent. Hostilities, however guarded, opened at this point. The code committee for the applicant group was able to observe the individual competence of the Labor Advisory Board representative; whether his individual efforts were going to be directed largely toward re-employment measures, or whether his official stand on labor provisions for the entire industry would be based on labor conditions previously secured by highly organized, but often relatively small, sectors of the industry. The code committee attempted to gauge the organized strength back of the Labor Advisory Board representative. Previous knowledge of this strength was not available in all cases to applicant groups, for, as in the case of trade associations, realignments, reorganizations, and revivals of moribund labor groups occurred rapidly under the incentives offered by the NRA code plan.

Personalities and motives were also disclosed for evaluation. The contending groups were able to acquaint themselves with the deputy's qualities, including the vulnerable spots in his make-up; and the deputy, in turn, was able to gauge the real motivating forces behind the proposals presented by the applicant group and behind the informal position taken by representatives of the advisory boards. Each "interest" in the coming controversy was taking measure of the others' strength.

As stated at an earlier point, there was no uniformity in the manner in which various codes were developed. Some passed rapidly through the pre-hearing conference stage and the real issues did not develop until after the public hearing, when the deputy attempted to secure definite agreement on contested provisions. Some brought long-standing and irreconcilable conflicts to the conference table. And at times the "forum for co-operation" turned out unscheduled products by giving birth to disruptive conflicts within applicant groups which had approached the code-making process inspired by the new co-operative spirit.

It was during this phase of code making that the NRA upon several occasions acted vigorously to keep the mounting number of codes from reaching wholly unmanageable proportions. In many cases several trade associations, competing for membership in a single industry or trade, had presented codes with widely varying provisions, each desiring to negotiate a separate code. When the overlapping claims were serious enough to command attention, the deputy attempted to induce the competing associations to combine under a single code. Efforts on this score were hampered by the illogical assignment of codes to deputies, which meant that conflicts often existed between groups dealing with different deputies. Glaring conflicts in jurisdiction usually came to light fairly early in the negotiations. But attempts to transfer codes from one deputy to another often met with telling resistance from applicant groups who wished to proceed separately or feared loss of ground by virtue of the attitude of the deputy or the necessary re-enactment of a whole series of negotiations. Complete lack of uniformity among deputies in the methods of negotiation strengthened this attitude on the part of applicant groups.

Where a deputy was in a position to do so, however, he often applied strong pressure to compel the composition of conflicts over jurisdiction. Failing in this, he sometimes refused to negotiate further with the individual associations. Unless the deputy was overruled by some higher official, the only avenue open to the industrial or trade groups then was to form a new or amalgamated association which could claim to be more nearly truly representative of the industry concerned. Negotiations were then reopened on the basis of a single code. Instead of completely breaking off negotiations temporarily, deputies perhaps more commonly fostered and exercised some guiding influence upon the attempt of groups to compose their differences.[14]

In the preliminary stages of negotiation, the effort was not to perfect code provisions, but merely to put them in a form acceptable for public hearings. This meant, among other things, that the deputy could inform applicant groups of certain essential things to include and to omit. The legal adviser pointed out clearly illegal elements in the proposals and suggested legal forms for others. Labor and consumer advisers could make known the points upon which they were in firm opposition and permit the proponents to decide whether they cared to take these points to public issue. Grosser forms of overlapping

[14] Two examples serve to illustrate the point. Some 30 codes of fair competition were presented to the Administration by various interests purporting to represent the coal-mining industry. The process of combining these various proposals into a single code, acceptable to all interests, presented an extremely difficult task for the Administration; one which required a long series of conferences, bargaining, and compromises, both on the part of the Administration and the industry. In the case of the trucking industry, two competing national associations and scores of regional groups filed codes. At the end of the first series of conferences between the deputy administrator and the associations, the Administration refused to negotiate further on the basis of separate codes and instructed the associations to pool their efforts and present a single code. When this was accomplished, negotiations were reopened.

and jurisdictional conflict could be uncovered and removed.

Public Hearings

In point of time the public hearing marked an interlude between the preliminary conferences and the real bargaining period leading up to approval. It gave the public a glimpse of the NRA machine in operation.

Early public hearings, particularly those on major codes, were occasions for considerable pomp and circumstance. Industrial and government dignitaries held the spotlight. There were numerous exchanges of formal well-wishes; expressions of confidence on the part of government representatives that industry had caught the vision of co-operative action between management and labor; and industry assurance to government that it had. This over, the procedure settled into the routine of provision by provision analysis and discussion of the code, punctuated by general arguments from all interests which demanded to be heard.

Public hearings were conducted on a formal basis and were presided over by the deputy or assistant deputy administrator in charge of the code. Ordinarily he was attended by technical advisers representing the three advisory boards, and by representatives from the Research and Planning Division and the Legal Division. Any person who could demonstrate a substantial interest in the provisions of the code under discussion was permitted to appear at the public hearing by complying with certain formal requirements.[15] Official procedure required that

[15] "Due notice" is defined and the methods to be used by NRA in giving notice of hearing or opportunity to be heard are set forth in Executive Order No. 6527, dated Dec. 21, 1933. Pursuant to this order an official bulletin board was set up in the NRA offices. Notices of all public hearings and opportunity to be heard were posted on this board. (Provided for in Administrative Order No. 2, dated Jan. 6, 1934.) It is interesting

requests to be heard be filed at least a day before the hearing date and include: (1) A statement of the person or groups represented by the individual desiring to testify; and (2) a simple statement without argument proposing either (a) to eliminate a specific provision of the code, (b) to modify a specific provision of the code, or (c) to add a new provision. In actual practice it was not uncommon for the deputy administrator to allow the presentation of testimony by individuals who had failed to comply with the prescribed procedure. The general idea behind the conduct of NRA public hearings was characterized by the Administrator as the "gold-fish bowl" method of administration.

Procedure governing the conduct of public hearings as well as the objectives to be attained have remained substantially the same throughout the entire code-making period. They were defined as follows by the General Counsel for the NRA at the time of the hearing on the cotton textile code, the first formal hearing conducted by NRA:

> ... these [public hearings] are not judicial investigations nor, strictly speaking, legislative investigations, but rather in the nature of administrative inquiries for the purpose of adequately advising the Administration of the National Recovery Act of the facts upon which the exercise of administrative authority must be predicated. ...
>
> No representative of a private interest favoring or opposing a code has any legal right to control or direct the presentation

---

to note that these precautionary measures occurred late in the code-making period. Previous to this time the Press and the trade associations were informally relied on in large measure to keep interested parties informed as to the time and subject of public hearings.

Under the present arrangement notices of important hearings are furnished to the Press, labor unions, federal government officials, governors of states, code authorities, compliance directors, first-class post offices, trade associations, and individuals on special mailing lists.

of evidence or the procedure in a public hearing, which will be subject to the sole control of the deputy administrator in charge, acting in conformity with any general regulations or with specific instructions of the Administrator. It will, however, be the purpose of the deputy administrator to give to all persons interested an adequate opportunity for the presentation of evidence in support of a code, or any objections to proposed code provisions, or any suggested modifications thereof, or additions thereto. . . .

These hearings will not be appropriate for the presentation of arguments upon issues of law. If any party in interest desires to raise any issue of law in connection with a proposed code of fair competition, he may file a written argument thereon with the deputy administrator. . . .[16]

At an early point in the hearing procedure all witnesses were officially advised that: "It is important to realize that the public hearing is merely a fact-finding device— not a device in which oratory or persuasion can win advantage." Not infrequently, however, the routine was interrupted by heated oratorical remarks from certain witnesses indicating some disagreement with the practical form of industry's proclaimed vision of the new era of co-operative action. There were charges of monopolistic motives in code provisions; there were charges that proposed hour and wage provisions were designed to crystallize into law existing exploitive hour and wage provisions, rather than to produce re-employment or otherwise to improve conditions of labor. As the making of codes moved further and further into local trades and small-scale manufacturing there were frequently recurring charges that the applicant group was not truly representative of the industrial or trade operations covered by its proposed code definition of "industry" and "members of industry."

The amount both of heat and light which was elicited

[16] *NRA Release*, June 27, 1933 (outline of procedure, unnumbered).

at public hearings varied in the widest degree from code to code. But to an observer of the scene two general impressions stood out sharply. One was the rarity of orderly and convincing presentation of factual evidence. In exceptional cases associations were able to present a relatively impressive array of data. And, in equally exceptional cases, the Division of Research and Planning was able to present extensive and well-digested data on the industry. But the slight statistical basis of knowledge which underlay code making came into the open at the hearings. Applicant groups were shown to have astonishingly little quantitative knowledge concerning their own industries, thus displaying the embryonic stage of the statistical work of all but a few trade associations. The reverse of this absence of explicit information was the large part played in public hearings by argument, contention, charge and counter-charge unsupported by evidence.

The other impression was the casual way in which intricate code provisions were passed over without analysis or clarification. Labor provisions ordinarily drew the major scrutiny and inspired the more eloquent oratory. Trade practice provisions became the focus of attention only when the business group was divided against itself and dissenting members brought the intra-industrial conflict into the hearings. But little calm dissection of the economic significance of the provisions took place. Nor was there much consideration of the administrative feasibility of provisions nor of the administrative means appropriate thereto.

Public hearings, in brief, presented the opportunity for interested parties to bring into the open their hopes and misgivings. They protected the NRA from such public criticism as would have developed had such an opportunity not been given, and permitted it the somewhat fictitious claim that its work was being done "in a goldfish bowl." Only in exceptional instances, when great opposition to provisions of the code was uncovered or unfavorable public reactions were generated, did it greatly affect the gradual forging out of the final form of code provisions, a process which started in the preliminary conferences and was continued and completed in the post-hearing conferences.

Post-Hearing Conferences and Final Approval

After the public hearing, negotiations settled down into an out and out bargaining procedure. Lines of difference between the various divisions of the industry and trade came clearly into the open; and the points of conflict between representatives of the applicant group and the various interests represented by advisory boards became sharply defined. All formal pretension was stripped away.

It was earlier pointed out that the NRA chose to construct codes through the process of controversy between conflicting interests rather than by use of any predetermined formula or by reference to uniform criteria. Each party at interest in the code controversy was expected to be fully partisan. Out of the clash of interests it was thought that "truth" would emerge and "composition" could be secured. Under such a system the code product was inevitably moulded by the interplay of four major sets of factors: (1) the constituency, motives, and strategy of applicant groups; (2) the manner in which the so-called advisory groups were organized and implemented; (3) the forces which conditioned the functioning of the deputy administrator; and finally (4) influences exerted by the technical divisions of the NRA. The

interplay of forces brought to bear by various combinations of these elements constitutes the real substance of
the code-making process.

Before turning to a discussion of this part of the
process, it appears desirable to digress somewhat from a
chronological treatment by indicating at this point some
of the implications of the NRA plan for final approval
of codes. The chronological treatment is resumed in the
next section of this chapter.

It will be recalled that in the official plan for codifying
industry on a voluntary basis, negotiation of codes and
final approval were regarded as separate functions. The
code-seeking groups and the advisory boards were to
engage in a controversy of conflicting interests supervised
by the deputy. Out of this welter of conflict, the basic
truth and validity of the proposals brought forth by
contending interests would be made clear to the deputy,
and presumably to the contending groups, for the composition of conflicts was to follow upon the emergence
of truth.

Such "truth" as emerged was, however, to be regarded
as conditional, being limited to points arising in the discussion of the problems of a particular industry. Once
the composition of contending interests had been secured,
the Recovery Administrator and the President were to
determine whether or not, in view of all considerations
affecting the public welfare, the agreement should be
given the force of law. Thus the plan recognized that in
an agency such as NRA, whose final rulings have the full
force and effect of law, and the jurisdiction of which
extends over the bulk of industry and trade, the segregation of the approving from the negotiating function is of
fundamental importance. From the beginning of the
NRA, official emphasis was placed upon the role played

by the Recovery Administrator and by the President as guardians of the public interest. The Administrator on numerous occasions stressed his personal responsibility for all acts of his assistants and defined his own position as that of an official umpire, rather than an active participant. During the early days of the NRA the President's responsibility was also stressed.[17]

In practice this segregation of negotiating from approving functions seldom obtained. Only a casual scrutiny of the process by which codes were formulated, their multiplicity, and the intricacy of their provisions is required to convince one that, in making its final decision, the approving agency would have to depend largely on the findings of the operating agency. Some independent analysis and evaluation of provisions by the approving agencies, as outlined in the formal statement of functions, might have been possible if codes had been highly restricted in number and simple in structure and implication. They were neither.

By the very nature of the case, therefore, detailed knowledge of the majority of codes, the real meaning of various provisions, the motives behind the inclusion of those provisions, and their probable operating results were known—if at all—only by those who had been in intimate and continuous contact with the code-making process. In the vast majority of cases, then, these things

[17] On this point the Administrator stated: "That [three principles: organization, co-operation, governmental participation] is the ground plan of NRA and the broad foundation of all that we had tried to do under the President's direct and personal guidance and I want to repeat and emphasize that not one single code has been approved without his personal and searching scrutiny and that at every critical point he has direct and intimate leadership." (*NRA Release No. 1137,* Oct. 10, 1933.) Later, by Executive Order No. 6543-A, Dec. 30, 1933, the President delegated to the Administrator his powers of approval, except for codes covering in general more than 50,000 employees.

were made known to those directly responsible for the protection of the public interest only through reports and recommendations of the deputy and his advisers. Under these circumstances the immediate responsibility for the evaluation of code proposals on the basis of general economic and social implications, rather than in the light of the immediate interests of any one applicant group, in actual operation fell upon the deputy administrator.[18]

The stage of approval can therefore be described in almost purely formal terms. As the outcome of the negotiations, the deputy transmitted a draft code to his superior officer concerning which he was supposed to certify "substantial agreement" among his advisers. Substantial agreement was a term of variable meaning. It did not mean that any of them entirely agreed. Nor did it preclude strong dissent on the part of one or two of them. In practice more often than not it probably meant that the legal adviser certified the legality of the content and the labor adviser was prepared to let the bargaining over labor provisions come to an end. In making his report, however, the deputy was required to take cognizance of all objections to code provisions, whether filed by advisory boards or technical divisions.[19]

The exact administrative procedure leading to final approval has varied from time to time. Originally the

[18] Because critical questions were being settled during the negotiations, parties who felt themselves being damaged by the proceedings were under the inducement to solicit the attention and aid of superior NRA officials. These might be the applicant group, labor interests, or other parties either involved in or external to the negotiations. No general description of these extra-official activities can be made, but, since in some instances they were of importance and modified the relation between deputies and higher officials, some mention of them must be made.

[19] The final report of the deputy was accompanied by (1) letter of transmittal containing findings of fact; (2) transcript of record on public hearing; (3) formal reports from three advisory boards, Legal Division, and Division of Economic Research and Planning.

line was direct from the deputy to the Administrator and then to the President, who retained power of approval for all codes. Later the power to approve codes for minor industries (usually those employing less than 50,000) was delegated to the Administrator. With the reorganization of administrative structure in October 1933, all codes were approved by division administrators before reaching the Administrator's office. A review section of the executive office (later expanded into the Review Division) was charged with final inspection before a code reached the Administrator's desk. During the active period of code making such checking served only to eliminate gross errors of form and the more obvious violations of administrative policy.

The deputy's function of making the initial report to the Administrator on the code has remained the same throughout the process. This report might recommend blanket approval of the code; might recommend stays upon the operation of certain provisions pending further investigation; or might recommend the modification of various provisions by administrative or executive order. The important point to observe here is that the qualifications and stays attached by executive order to final approval of codes were ordinarily those recommended by the deputy who supervised code negotiations.[20]

In exceptional instances codes were thrown back into the negotiating stage after reaching the desk of the President or the Administrator, due either to his personal objection to certain provisions or to convincing representations made to him that unfortunate consequences, economic or political, would flow from the provisions. Where a code as it left the deputy's hands was the object of strong

---

[20] They were of course transmitted to the President as recommendations of the Recovery Administrator, rather than of the deputy.

opposition in some quarter, it was not uncommon for the interested parties, whether business or labor groups or NRA or other governmental officials, to attempt to pursue it to the highest quarters in the effort to secure modification or reconsideration.

DRAMATIS PERSONAE

The full import of code negotiations, briefly described in the preceding section, can be grasped only through a clear understanding of the position of the various parties to the negotiations. These parties have been shown to be (1) the code committee representing the applicant group, (2) the representatives of the three advisory boards, (3) the representatives of the two technical divisions, and (4) the deputy administrator.

The Code Committee

The character of applicant groups and the incentives which brought them in have been sufficiently shown at an earlier point (page 88). Most code committees representing these groups approached the conflict with several distinct and inherent advantages over the other parties at interest. They had prepared the first draft of proposals and knew exactly what they contained, their subtleties and purposes. Theirs was the positive stand; it devolved upon the adversaries to demonstrate that what they proposed was undesirable, or to make a show of strength which would induce them to assent to alternate proposals. Moreover, in addition to their own intimate knowledge of their industry and its problems, they often commanded skilled legal and technical services. They were in possession of all of the statistical evidence which was available to their adversaries, plus masses of data selected from private sources to prove the chaotic conditions existing in their

industry when such conditions needed proving. And finally, within limits, they held the key to the entire procedure, for they had voluntarily initiated the negotiations
and could terminate them at will.

On the other hand they started off as strangers in a
land foreign to their experience. Many of them consisted
of somewhat fragile combinations of disparate intra-industrial factions. They differed greatly in the definiteness
of their goals and the articulateness of their thinking.
And all of them, as against the strategic advantage of their
voluntary appearance, faced the power which the Recovery Act provided to impose a code irrespective of the
wishes of the members of an industry. In the ensuing
negotiations they were therefore in a strong, but not im-
pregnable, position.

The Advisory Boards

In code negotiations the gamut which the applicant
groups had to run was mainly formed by the representatives of the advisory boards, though reinforced by the
representatives of the Legal Division and the Research
and Planning Division, and in certain special ways by the
deputy. Both official statements of the functions of Industrial, Labor, and Consumers' Advisory Boards, and
formalized descriptions of their powers and duties indicate that they were intended to play, not only a secondary but a uniform part, in the code-making process. That
their position was to be secondary follows naturally from
the fact that the applicant group controlled the initiation
of the process, and formal power of final approval or
disapproval lay outside the power of the boards. The assumption that each board was to be equally well implemented in giving advisory opinions and that such
opinions were to be given equal consideration in final

code decisions is implicit in the plan. In the actual code-making process, however, equality in the influence exerted by the various advisory groups was not maintained. This departure from the theory of the formal plan can be explained only by analysis of the constituency and functioning of the advisory groups.

Industrial Advisory Board. On the theory that the Recovery Administration, acting in its capacity of impartial umpire, should neither control the findings of its advisers nor be controlled by their recommendations, the membership of the Industrial Advisory Board was appointed by the Secretary of Commerce, and the recommendations of the Board were made purely advisory in character. As originally constituted the Board was composed of 21 members selected from among business leaders, not to secure regional representation, but with a view to securing representation from industry at large. In its advisory capacity the Board was to test the proposals of each applicant group in terms of the interrelationships and conflicts of interest among business groups. Needless to say, the character of industrial and trade organization in this country rendered extremely difficult the formulation of definite policies to guide the Board's advisory operations. General policies of the Board have therefore changed with changes in its personnel. In an effort to secure greater continuity of policy, the Board was later reconstituted to include three resident members serving on a rotating basis.

In code negotiations the Board was represented by a staff of advisers partly made up of resident personnel, partly of men loaned by business concerns for given periods or for the duration of particular code negotiations. In practice these advisers were not often very prominent parties in the bargaining process. Very commonly the industrial adviser gave approval and support to the proposals of the applicant group. It was not unusual for an industrial adviser to lend active support to the applicant group in the bargaining with labor representatives. Important issues could be carried by the adviser to the Board, which might then throw its weight through direct approach to the Administrator or other high officials.

Appreciable differences developed between industrial advisers and applicant groups only when the proposals of the latter were so designed as to work to the distinct competitive disadvantage of another business group. Then there was occasion for inter-industrial diplomacy and even informal coercion on code-seeking groups to keep their demands within bounds. Barring duties of this sort, industrial advisers were in effect a second line of support for applicant groups.

Labor Advisory Board. The Labor Advisory Board was named by the Secretary of Labor. Like the Industrial Advisory Board its actions were thus removed from the immediate control of the Recovery Administration. The Board was made up of leaders of organized labor and one or two individuals presumably qualified to represent the interests of unorganized workers. It was expected to establish policies for labor bargaining, and theoretically its chairman served as the channel of contact between the Board and the NRA on labor policy. But in actual operation the work of the executive director of the Board in supervising the activities of labor advisers came more and more to be the means of formulating whatever consistency in policy was attained. A permanent staff of labor specialists carried on the routine work and served as representatives in the code-making process (and continued to act for it in the subsequent phases of code administration). In some code negotiations, however, a labor representative was assigned by a labor organization to speak for the organized workers of the industry. In such cases a member of the advisory staff served as technical assistant to the union representative.

General Board policies—such as the consistent stand for adequate labor representation in code administration, restriction of homework, safety and health provisions—were formulated by the Board in consultation with staff members. So far as is known, however, no single set of instructions or statement of policy was available to labor advisers during the code-making period. But there was never any ambiguity in the general position of labor representatives in the bargaining process.

Throughout the entire code-making period, the Labor Advisory Board operating through its code advisers, functioned as a well-defined and relatively well-implemented element in code bargaining. Its initial position on the major hour and wage provisions was almost of necessity defensive, since initial proposals were made by industry.[21] But in such matters as health standards, hazardous occupations, protecting wages above minimum, labor representatives took the offensive. Whether in a defensive or offensive position, they operated consistently and definitely as the applicant group's chief antagonist, always pressing for concessions which would in their opinion favor the position of workers in the industry under consideration. They operated according to no specific formula, depending for their success upon three factors: the bargaining advantage furnished by the purposes and mandatory provisions of the act; the in-

---

[21] This of course does not apply where the NRA assumed the initiative in the code process by unofficially threatening to impose a code (the bituminous coal situation for example). In such cases labor was in a better position to take the offensive.

genuity and energy of the labor advisers; and the bargaining strength of organized labor.

In the actual code bargaining procedure, labor's defensive approach usually consisted in the attempt to demonstrate that the hour and wage provisions proposed in codes would not reabsorb all the workers who had been attached to the industry involved during the 1926-29 peak period. On this generalized proposition the *prima facie* evidence was usually in favor of labor, since applicant groups had naturally incorporated hour and wage provisions at bargaining levels in their original proposals.

But in shifting from the defensive attempt to demonstrate the inadequacy of industry proposals to a positive support of their own demands for more favorable labor provisions, the labor advocates met several major difficulties. First, there had been no official definition of the re-employment levels to be sought through codes. In the second place, only in rare cases could there be given any convincing statistical demonstration of the probable effect on re-employment and payrolls in specific industries. Basic data on any comparable basis were almost wholly lacking for all except a few large and concentrated industries. Besides, most labor provisions were so complex, and contained so many contingencies, that accurate calculations as to their probable effects would have been impossible, even had basic data been available. (See Part III.) In the absence of better criteria the hour and wage provisions and other conditions of labor, where labor contracts arrived at by collective bargaining existed, ordinarily served as the bench mark for labor representatives in their negotiations with the applicant group for minimum wage, maximum hour, and other code provisions. This stand was usually taken regardless of the extent of union coverage in the industry.

Individual labor representatives, in support of their contentions for code proposals favorable to labor interest, drew heavily upon facilities of the trade unions, the United States Department of Labor, the United States Employment Service, the United States Public Health Service, and various other agencies dealing with labor problems. Data derived from these sources, while not always wholly applicable to the conditions in question, were usually the only ones available, and therefore difficult to refute. Thus, in most cases, labor representatives were implemented not only by a native aptitude for out and out bargaining procedure, but as well by data from government sources. All of these factors combined to facilitate the functioning of labor interests as pressure groups.

The actual power of labor advisers, however, varied in the widest degree between one set of negotiations and another. Where they were backed up by strong labor organizations they were in a strategic position and the codes for such industries reflect the advantage. But in relation to those extensive fields in which labor organization is rudimentary or non-existent, employers were in a much more strategic position for resisting labor demands. Whether, therefore, in the final stages of negotiation, the labor adviser or the applicant group was on the defensive depended upon circumstances surrounding the particular case.

Consumers' Advisory Board. From the beginning the Consumers' Advisory Board occupied an anomolous position in the NRA set-up. There are two major points of difference between the Consumers' Advisory Board and the other advisory boards—first, its composition and responsibility; and second, the nature of its constituency.

In explaining the reasons behind the creation of this Board the Administrator stated that,

> While the Administration itself is directly responsible for safeguarding the public welfare and effectuating public policy, the actual consumers' interest is a matter of primary and acute concern. If that is not watched—at all times and from every angle —the whole plan may be imperilled. To provide against this the Administration itself has chosen a Consumers' Advisory Board which is responsible for watching every agreement and every hearing to see that nothing is done to impair the interest of those whose daily living may be affected by these agreements. The thought in choosing this Board was to get wide regional representation by devoted people who have interested themselves in this problem and are willing to give their time and effort to this vital work.[22]

Thus in contrast to the Industrial and the Labor Advisory Boards, the Consumers' Board derives its existence from the Administrator, rather than from the head of one of the old-line government departments. Moreover, it was not until September 11, 1933 (after the approval of several precedent forming codes) that NRA procedure required the deputy's report recommending approval of codes to the Administrator to be accompanied by a written report from the Consumers' Advisory Board, as well as by reports of the other advisory boards, transcript of hearing, and other documents.

So far as constituency is concerned, the Consumers' Advisory Board theoretically had a broader support than either of the other two advisory boards. According to the theory, it should have drawn support from every purchaser whose interests stood to be affected by price changes or standards of quality resulting from the operation of codes. But this theory was rendered fictitious by the very nature of the consumers' interest. Contrasted

[22] *NRA Release No. 11*, June 25, 1933.

with the situation of the applicant group, and with the industrial and labor advisory groups, the consumers' interest lacked support from any well-organized or articulate underlying constituency.

Trade associations and powerful industrial groups were vitally interested in the outcome of code making; and the recommendations of the Industrial Advisory Board were supported by this organized interest. All labor was vitally interested in the way in which code provisions defined conditions of labor. Only a portion was effectively organized, but that portion was actively interested in extending its jurisdiction, and consequently threw its full strength into the struggle for favorable labor provisions. Similarly all consumers were vitally interested in the code process, for every code contained provisions which in operation might radically affect the purchasing power of every individual.

But in the economic process the immediate and tangible interest of most consumers is to be found either on the side of management or of labor. This fact was decidedly inimical to the progress of consumer organization. No organized basis for acting as a pressure group existed, either in initiating measures to protect this broad intangible interest, or in backing up the recommendations of the Consumers' Advisory Board in the code bargaining process. Consequently the active interest of most persons in the NRA program was identified either with the proposals of an applicant group, or with the position taken by the industrial or labor representatives. Those individuals whose immediate interests were not so identified had the assurance that the NRA proper and the President were responsible for the protection of the broad general welfare. Initiative in defining the consumers' interests and in devising strategy to protect these interests therefore came from within the Consumers' Advisory Board and its staff rather than from any organized constituency.

In formulating policies designed to carry out the mandate ". . . to watch every agreement and every hearing to see that nothing is done to impair the interest of those whose daily living may be affected by these agreements . . ." the Consumers' Advisory Board came full face upon the anomolous character of its position. On questions of quality standards of commodities it could, and did, take an unambiguous stand. But on matters involving prices, a clear-cut line between the "consumers' interest" and the "public interest" could be drawn only by emphasizing the consumers' interest in the lowest possible price on each commodity purchased, in contradistinction with his interest in the efficient and humane functioning of the economic and social system in general. On this basis a partisan stand against the elimination of child labor, sweatshop conditions, waste of national resources— against any type of provisions tending to raise the purchase price of a given commodity—might have been adopted and defended by the consumer representative in the code process. And, under the bargaining plan espoused by the NRA, had his contentions been backed by organized pressure groups, there is no reason why such a narrow concept of the consumer interest might not have been reflected in provisions of finished codes. But immediately upon the introduction of the broader concepts of economic recovery, social justice, and economic stability, the consumer interest loses its identity in that of the general public interest.

Partly by force of circumstances perhaps,[23] but largely

[23] Some attempt was made to organize consumers into pressure groups through the establishment of county consumer councils, under the direc-

because of the training and economic views of its membership, the Consumers' Advisory Board conditioned its operating policies on definite concepts of what types of controls, limitations, and privileges tend to produce a desirable economic and social system. In brief it chose to determine by analytical method what the Administration officially chose to determine by the trial and error method. The Administration itself, according to the official plan, was ". . . directly responsible for safe-guarding the public welfare." But the Consumers' Advisory Board, by seeking to impose on the content of codes its own concept of how to ascertain "public interest," automatically assumed the role of protector of the public interest. It thus ran the risk of incurring official displeasure for a too-ambitious definition of its functions, and was more or less afoul of this reef throughout the code-making process.

The Board's method called first for the collection of basic economic data, then for calm and objective analysis, and finally for evaluation of specific proposals in terms of the general public interest. Such a method could be made effective only through a laborious and time-consuming procedure. That this method was ill adapted to the tempo of the code-making process is illustrated by the fact that during a single week, selected at random, the Consumers' Advisory Board was called upon to express opinions on the provisions of 73 separate codes cov-

---

tion of the National Emergency Council. These groups, organized on an informal basis, were supposed to serve as the channel of direct contact between ultimate consumers and their government representatives—particularly in the NRA and the AAA. The paper plan called for the organization of some 200 county councils. At present only a portion of this number is functioning in some fashion. They did not serve effectively to consolidate the consumer interest into pressure groups for code-making purposes.

ering the operations of the most widely varying industries.[24]

The effective application of its adopted method was precluded both by official NRA choice of the trial and error method and by the speed at which the code-making process was carried on. Handicapped also by the absence of an organized constituency, the consumer representative was in most cases effectively sidetracked in the bargaining process. He was forced to operate almost exclusively as an adviser to the deputy on matters of general policy. In effect the Board attempted to furnish the deputy with the broad interpretations of public policy which the general directing agencies of NRA had failed to supply. Whatever success it encountered during the pressure period of code making, therefore, was not due to the equality of its bargaining position. Rather, it was due in some cases to the occasional recognition on the part of deputies that the type of economic and social bench marks being offered by the Consumers' Board was essential to consistent decisions on code proposals. In other cases the effectiveness of the Board was due wholly to the ingenuity and energy with which individual members of the Board and staff directed public attention to provisions of codes which exhibited the grosser forms of pursuit of special self-interest.

The foregoing analysis will make it clear that the representatives of each of the advisory boards occupied

[24] For illustration the following code titles are selected from among the 73: Saving, building, and loan associations; the powder-puff industry; funeral service; chewing-gum manufacturing; wrecking and salvaging; exterminating, fumigating, and disinfecting industry; infants' and children's wear; sawmill machinery; garter, suspender, and belt manufacturing; the heavy forging industry; automotive maintenance; outdoor advertising; and the manufacturing of ladies' handbags. Dexter M. Keezer (executive director of the Consumers' Advisory Board), *The Consumer under the National Recovery Administration.*

very different positions in connection with code negotiations. They were neither co-ordinate in function nor equivalent in power. The labor representatives were in a direct bargaining relationship with the applicant groups. The consumers' representatives, apart from the force of their interpretation of the public interest, had really no bargaining power at all except as they could convince deputies of the correctness of their contentions. As a bargaining element the industrial representatives were relatively inconspicuous. Correlative to the concept of bargaining is that of power, either positive power to force a position or negative power to damage by withdrawal. Power was usually inherent in only three parties to code negotiations, the applicants, the labor representatives, and the deputy himself.

Representatives of the Technical Divisions

The position of the legal adviser in code negotiations was nominally purely technical. It was his function to see that they were carried on according to prescribed rules and regulations, and that the result was in duly legal form. This nominal function is far, however, from describing the actual influence of legal advisers. From day to day they were continuously engaged in redrafting provisions, a circumstance which engendered initiative and kept them more or less continuously embroiled in the active discussion not merely of forms but of issues. Consequently they customarily stood in a very close advisory capacity to the deputy, on a broader plane than merely that of legal counsel.

Back of the separate legal advisers, the Legal Division of the NRA combined technical with general advisory and policy-making activities. This division was in effect the only clearing house for code provisions. With the multiplication of codes, typical problems of form arose. In practice the discussion of form is inseparable from that of intent, and in view of the vague NRA policies on content of codes, quite direct discussion of policy questions was equally entailed. As a result of this activity within the Legal Division, its influence ran out through the several legal advisers to color the thinking of deputies on policy questions. The ingenuity of its members in devising provisions capable of standing up in court was also, in a sense, a strong buttress to applicant groups in connection with trade practice provisions. It would be impossible, without great elaboration of detail, to create a sense of the subtle, yet omnipresent, influence which the Legal Division and its advisory staff exercised upon the process of code negotiations.

The representative of the Research and Planning Division had the technical function of collecting and analyzing the factual data concerning the industry involved, and of making certain findings concerning the effects of code provisions, such as the contribution of the hour provisions to re-employment, confined mainly to fact finding and arithmetical computations. His duties did not include the function of expert economic analysis. Since he was hindered by gaps in the source of information, they included a good deal of more or less elaborate guessing.

As in the case of legal advisers, the research and planning representatives were not strictly confined to their technical functions. But they did not ordinarily exert any comparable influence. This in part arose from the predilections of the division they represented. The Division of Research and Planning was manned by persons with more or less training and competency in economic analysis. This led to a bent toward an analytical approach not greatly unlike that of the Consumers' Advisory Board. General ideas on procedure antipathetic to the official trial and error method, and on the proper content of codes inimical to the desires of applicant groups, somewhat permeated the higher staff, which quite actively exceeded its technical function and tried to influence policy. Its primary predilections were against price and production controls, and in whatever personal ways their influence could be made felt, its representatives commonly threw their weight on the side of those predilections in code negotiations.

Deputy and Assistant Deputy Administrator[25]

The deputy administrator was ultimately charged with responsibility for submitting to the Administration a completed code with recommendations. His functions were multiple: supervising a bargaining process, entering the bargaining process to promote what he understood to be NRA policies, distilling the substance of controversy into the composition of agreement, and judging the desirability of the product. It is therefore important to inquire closely into the character of the material furnished to him as a basis for his final selection of the plane on which composition was to be secured, and into the factors which dictated the methods used in finally securing composition of interests.

Had any deputy administrator been so unrealistic as to have attempted to function in a judicial capacity during the code-making process—that is, first impartially taking the testimony offered by all contending parties and advisers, and then, by an uninterrupted study of the

[25] Officials of the ranks both of deputy administrator and assistant deputy administrator were the active agents in negotiating codes. In the current text, deputy administrator, or deputy, refers to both ranks.

record, formulating a final decision—he would have found himself in an embarrassing position at the end of the code process. The probabilities are that he never could have reconciled the conflicts in his own mind, and, if he had reached a satisfactory decision, that assent could not have been secured from the parties at interest.

In actual practice the deputy never evaluated the entire code in the light of a comprehensive and digested record. A code took form, provision by provision, out of bargaining and haggling. Even in the attempt to secure agreement by this process, the deputy found himself in possession of a remarkably flimsy set of materials to assist him in determining and defending his own position on proposals of far-reaching economic and social consequences. These materials fall into four classes. (1) There were volumes of conflicting testimony adduced by the two most active contestants—the code committee and the labor adviser. In great part it consisted of iteration and reiteration of a desire for specific proposals (or the reverse) supported, if at all, by whatever statistical evidence was at hand. Neither the testimony nor statistical evidence was entered on the record under oath. (2) Factions or individuals within the industry who objected to the current content of various provisions placed at his disposal a wide array of written and oral comment calling attention to the dire consequences which approval of the applicant's proposal would bring down upon particular groups of the industry. All of these impressions, although impossible of evaluation and sometimes not entered according to stated procedure, definitely contributed to the confusion of forces playing upon the deputy's decision. (3) From the Consumers' Advisory group the deputy obtained findings and recommendations based on a calculated attempt to reason out by economic analysis the possible implications of proposed code provisions, both in relation to the parties at interest under a single code, and in relation to the economic and social structure as a whole. This advice was oriented on a wholly different plane from that furnished by other agencies. It disputed the merits of the bargaining approach and introduced external criteria of public welfare. (4) And finally, the Research and Planning Division ordinarily furnished the deputy with some data and some analysis of the anticipated general economic effect of the code's operation. Here again, and by the very nature of the problem, the analysis was hasty and was drawn in the broadest terms. It was mainly confined to estimates of the effect in terms of payrolls and employment. Given the customary paucity of authentic data, reasonably accurate measurement of the economic consequences was patently impossible.

The simple fact of the matter is that however desirous a deputy might have been to base his decision on fundamental economic and social facts, he found few of them in the welter of contentious material placed at his disposal by the code bargaining process. He found only a guide as to how much each party at interest could be induced to recede from positions taken on various code proposals. On this basis he proceeded to an attempt to compose the outstanding conflicts.

In this effort the deputy had constantly to keep in mind the official NRA methods and policies under which he was required to operate—namely, (1) that speed based on an emergency situation was the essence of the entire NRA program ; (2) that re-employment considerations were to be held more important than long-term rehabilitation; (3) that the degree of his responsibility for the public welfare was to be weighed, not in terms of predetermined criteria, but in terms of what emerged from the code-making process; (4) that in terms of these factors the deputy's function, and therefore the measure of his competence, lay in getting codes completed as rapidly as possible, with a minimum of obvious deficiencies, and with the least possible friction.

Since each deputy was left largely to work out his own methods for getting codes through the mill, there was of course no real uniformity among deputies in tactics used to pull contending parties into line for final approval of codes. Many devices ranging from coercion to postponement were used to break deadlocks which inevitably occurred during the final stages of bargaining. Some applicant groups supported their proposals for production control and price-fixing devices by insisting that chaotic conditions existed in the industry. By such testimony they of course made an excellent case for executive action under Section 3(d) of the act, which permitted the imposition of codes on industries in which conditions inimical to the public interest existed. Consequently, if such an applicant group unduly delayed agreement they rendered themselves vulnerable to coercive action by the NRA.

Many serious deadlocks were broken merely by postponing final settlement of the issue. When neither party would recede from a position, and when arbitrary action on the part of the deputy would have terminated code negotiations, this method proved serviceable. It consisted merely in providing by a clause in the code that the contested matter would be reconsidered at the end of a specified period. Specific provision was ordinarily made for interim study and report.[26] In the meantime the

[26] The cotton garment code is an example, making provision for report within 90 days to determine whether the 40-hour week was producing

remainder of the code was to be put into operation.

Between these two extremes of outright coercion and postponement, the methods used by deputies to secure agreement on code provisions were dictated almost wholly by the alignment and the relative strength of the pressure groups involved in negotiations, and by the personal qualities of the deputy.

Two combined factors exerted a telling influence on the entire process; the pressure for speed and the absence of specific definition of policy. Since no one knew exactly what constituted a code which would in general protect the public interest—the public interest not having been defined by the Administration in terms of code provisions —the major criterion of a deputy's efficiency was in the expedition with which codes were put through the mill. Personal reputations were at stake on this basis of measurement. Consequently, it was almost inevitable that those charged with putting codes through should lend support to interested groups in such ways or propose compositions of conflicts of such sorts as tended to facilitate the code process, and should combat those which tended to act as a drag. It was under these circumstances that many deputies, perhaps unconsciously, assumed alternately the mantle of impartial umpire and special advocate.

The specific methods adopted by a particular deputy in the final stages of code negotiations were conditioned not only by the formal and actual requirements of the NRA plan and by consideration of speed, but as well by his qualities and training. On this point it is of course not possible to give any accurate characterization of deputies as a class. Personnel of this rank was recruited for the

---

substantial re-employment or whether the maximum work week should be reduced to 36 hours.

most part on an individual basis, that is, the small nucleus originally selected by the Administrator chose their own assistants, and so on down the personnel line. The result was naturally an operating staff of widely varying competence, bias, and temperament. Although on the side of personal qualities they were mostly of a rather superior sort, they were usually persons with no particular breadth of economic knowledge and in the main were strangers to the industries for which they negotiated codes.[27]

One fact was of special importance. Most deputies were drawn from the ranks of business occupations. By virtue of training and inclination they were therefore sympathetic with the business point of view.[28] This fact undoubtedly colored their views of what the proper content of a code was and affected the direction in which their influence was exerted during code negotiations. The weighting of such bias as deputies had is, however, less to be charged against them than against the responsible higher officials of the NRA. The amount of definitive guidance given them was slight. They were to exact as

[27] A problem in public personnel administration more difficult than that of securing industrial specialists for code drafting and code enforcement can scarcely be imagined. To secure at once persons well versed in the intricacies of the industry and yet free from bias and questionable interests was a difficulty of the first magnitude. Many persons would have had more confidence in the selections if eligibility for appointment had been determined more in the open by an independent personnel agency using a system in which the facts of education, experience, and interests were passed upon by a special committee of competent examiners of high standing, and one which left a reasonably complete record.

[28] It has been alleged that some of them were "planted" to protect the interests of groups or large enterprises. This of course is hardly subject to verification. It is true that some of them, as well as higher officials, were on temporary loan from business employments, and that most of them expected to return to private employment after a temporary tenure at the NRA. These facts, however, are merely a part of the general personnel problem and can be given no invidious interpretation other than the general effect of bias described in the text.

much as possible in the direction of re-employment; were vaguely instructed against price fixing; were left to assume that an applicant group knew more about the remedies for its problems than any one else; and were instructed in any case to get codes completed.

The one real guide which deputies had was what was already in approved codes. The same guide was open to applicant groups. Since in the earliest codes the NRA had gone far in granting collectives powers over prices and production, precedent granted wide scope for concessions of power. Wage and hour provisions of early codes and of the President's Re-employment Agreement also established what were in effect norms about which the range of proposals commonly fluctuated. Precedent was officially stated to be no guide. But this was a meaningless form of words which overlooked the actualities of the situation. In view of these various considerations the effect of bias on the part of deputies is to be discounted. In particular situations it was no doubt at times important. But if codes were to be completed at all under the plan adopted and with the expedition desired, it is doubtful if any other set of deputies derived from non-business fields could have made them much different. Almost every deputy probably felt a sense of inadequacy based on the degree of responsibility blindly assumed, and only lost it in the frenzied movement of the code-making process.

SUMMARY

Viewed in its entirety the code-making process as it was actually conducted presents a series of striking contrasts with the formalized statement of the conflict of forces out of which "truth and composition" were expected to emerge.

The early formal picture was one of a small number of

highly competent and impartial officials, conducting a series of orderly conferences and hearings, during which a group seeking to co-operate in the drive for re-employment presented basic proposals for the consideration of the NRA. In order to guarantee unbiased treatment of the proposals and to protect the interests of other affected parties, proposals of the applicant group were to be exposed to the test of public hearing and to the partisan attack of the accredited representatives of three equally well implemented groups. Since the constituency of each of these groups covered the entire range of industrial, labor, and consumer interests, the applicant's proposals were in effect to be subjected to the ultimate test of conformity with the public interest. By such alchemy the deputy was to forge a document which would operate equitably upon all interests concerned. That it constituted an equitable arrangement for the groups immediately subject to its provisions would be attested by the fact that a group "truly representative" of the trade or industrial operations concerned had assented to its provisions. That it was a document which would not be detrimental to the public welfare would be adequately attested by the approval of the President, or his agent, the Recovery Administrator, acting as guardians of the public interest.

The real picture was one of numerous officials, ranging the entire scale in individual competence and motives, struggling under pressure of time to secure, by whatever method available, some common ground for agreement among a number of contending groups. In this confused struggle the deputy sometimes lost his identity as an impartial referee and appeared as an active participant in the controversy, lending support first to one group and then to another according to his own conception of desirable economic and social controls, or his notions of how to facilitate progress on the code. The nice alignment between advisory groups and their stated functions suffered strange distortions. By reason of circumstances their advisory functions were forced into bargaining patterns. As a result, the theoretical parity of their advisory opinion was destroyed, for one of the groups was strongly organized to operate as a pressure group, the second mildly so, and the third not at all. In order to function at all, the latter, the consumers' group, was compelled to adopt a method which was alien to the entire NRA scheme.

Commonly, the code scene disclosed two active and distinguishable contenders in the drafting of labor provisions: the code committee and the labor group. The bulk of the former was somewhat enhanced by the shadowy embodiment of the industrial advisory group, though this board at times was an influence in restraining rather than promoting the attitude of code committees.

In the making of trade practice provisions the lines of conflict were less clearly drawn. Frequently the controversies within the code committee itself were the hardest to resolve. But there were continuing seeds of conflict in those price-control and other restrictive provisions which the consumers' advisory group opposed in principle. While the "consumers' interest" was a somewhat formless shadow, the deputy administrator was subject to some inhibitions imposed by the vague NRA policy against granting direct powers of administrative direction in matters of price and production control. Other inhibitions arose from questions of legality. A good deal of the time spent upon the negotiations of such provisions therefore was taken up with bargaining upon the details of formulas, rather than with the more direct form of bargaining which was possible on wages and hours.

Throughout the whole process the deputy's actions were notably dictated by the desire to bring the negotiations to an early end. For many codes, especially smaller ones, the negotiations could be much foreshortened by the application of formulas established by precedent. But for many others, extended and at times bitterly controversial negotiations were required.

As code making extended to include hundreds of separate groups, it became impossible for the Administrator to exercise his separable function as "protector of the public interest." He was forced to depend more and more upon the judgment of his agents and sub-agents that specific code provisions would not operate contrary to the public welfare. The structure of each code had become so intricate and the codes had become so numerous, that only these agents and the participant groups had any comprehension of the potential effects of given codes upon the public welfare. But each agent was operating largely independently of the others, and without any specific standards by which to gauge the public interest.

CHAPTER VI

THE CODE STRUCTURE

Basic codes to the number of 550 are spread over almost the whole of American trade and industry. The most important exceptions are certain public utility industries—railways, telephone and telegraph, gas, and electric light and power. Anthracite coal also has no code. Even these exceptions, barring railways, are due to no lack of effort, but merely to failure to reach agreement. The coverage runs to such extremes of difference as retail trade, mining, investment banking, and trucking. By number of employees, the major coverage is over local trades and services. The large majority of codes, on the other hand, relate to various fields of manufacturing. No general picture of the composite code structure can be given in any brief space, but the more striking characteristics can be portrayed. (See Appendix D for a complete list of codes.)

GENERAL CHARACTERISTICS OF THE CODE STRUCTURE

Certain fields of industry have a unitary character which, if there is to be formal organization, dictates a single body for the whole group. This is particularly the case with the various mineral producing industries. The basic factors are the specialization of plants and the standardization of products. An industry like iron and steel is less homogeneous by reason of the greater diversity of products. On the other hand the high degree of financial concentration and a history of past association with respect to a well delimited field of operations defines a unitary area of group interest for purposes of code organization. It would be possible to go through the classi-fication of the large recognized fields of industry and define large groups therein which, if organized, are pretty well bound to be in a single organization.

Further examination, however, exhibits the fact that throughout the various fields of manufacture, the several large classifications include subordinate groups which, in terms of market interest, have their own unitary char-acter and are collectively bound together by no intimate ties of common interest. The degree of this internal hete-rogeneity varies widely from one general area to another, but its existence is the key to an understanding of the whole code structure. It is the basis of the separatist influ-ences which led to the large number of codes. What has to be grasped is, on the one hand, the character of the forces which worked against separatism and therefore led to large code groupings, and, on the other, the character of those which worked for separatism and promoted small groupings.

The code groupings for lumber products are illuminat-ing in this connection. The lumber industry has widely scattered producing areas, a large number of firms run-ning from very large to very small, integrated and un-integrated firms, numerous distinct types of lumber and finished product, and severe competition within each branch of the industry, between the several branches, and between the industry and other industries. There were therefore no clear lines of mutual interest dictating how it should be organized for code-making purposes. Po-tentially there was a field for separate codes dealing with the preparation of lumber in its various stages and for diverse groups of products, running into a considerable number at the stage of fabrication of final lumber products. No clear pattern for administrative convenience stood out.

Two types of influence appear to have been definite. One was the very intricacy of the competitive pattern. There appeared to be little possibility of market control without the existence of a co-ordinating agency with supervision over many fields of specialized production. The other influence derived from the history of past association. The various branches of the industry had strong associations above which stood a super-association. The separatist tendencies of the various regional and product groups were thus held in check, and a large number of related groups co-operated in the formation of a single basic code, with numerous administrative subdivisions. The result was a code of quite astonishing scope and complexity, covering everything from the felling of trees in Oregon to the making of baskets in Jersey City.

The separatist influences were not, however, entirely inoperative. Furniture manufacturing, a major industry in its own right, was the largest group to maintain its independence. Some of the groups acting independently were of the utmost insignificance, such as the wood plug "industry." Thus in the outcome one finds a group of codes covering wood products ranging in importance, by number of employees, from over half a million at one extreme to less than 200 at the other. Somewhat similar experience is reflected in the codes for the various branches of paper and paper products manufacturing. As in the case of lumber, 22 well-organized branches of the paper industry co-operated in securing a basic code with administrative subdivisions. Two or three important branches, such as newsprint and paperboard, secured separate codes. There then appeared a whole series of separate codes for specialized paper products, some of them ridiculously small and unimportant. Some other chance might have brought waxed paper and water-proof paper together under the basic code. Or some other train of events might have prevented separate codes for tags and gummed labels, or for paper drinking cups, food dishes and paper plates, cylindrical liquid-tight paper containers, and fluted cups, pan liner and lace paper. But again in the light of actual primary interest in price control and modified competitive practices, even the most unimportant of these groups may have seen no approach to the universal goal except through separate codes.

The preceding illustrations may be generalized into the statement that every industry concerned with early processing of important basic materials contains a large code group. Every such group in turn covers some part of the later fabrication of the materials. But surrounding such codes are satellite codes. The extent to which the large code covers later processes of fabrication derives from two relationships: (1) the extent to which enterprises engaged in the earlier processing of materials extend their operations into further fabrication; and (2) the extent to which in the past associations of specialized manufacturers have maintained close co-operative relationships with associations of the processors of materials. The relevancy of these observations would be substantiated by further inquiry into the fields of rubber, leather, and textiles.

The heterogeneity of large industrial classifications becomes much more marked in those fields where manufacturing is relatively or completely divorced from the early processing of materials. There are a few large manufacturing industries of a highly unitary character, such as automobile manufacturing and shoe manufacturing.

But they are exceptional. One has, for example, only to look at the classification of industrial machinery. This covers scores, if not hundreds, of specialized products, such as printing machinery, most of which are produced in specialized plants. No basis of common market interest unites them. They had their separate associations which severally initiated code negotiations. Nor did the separatist interest end there. Printing roller maufacturers stood away from the printing machinery group, and ring traveler manufacturers from the textile machinery group. On the other hand, a common interest in labor aspects of the NRA operated as a unifying influence which induced between 40 and 50 groups to co-operate in securing a single basic machinery manufacturing code. A similar development took place in the field of light metal manufacturing. In each of these two large fields, therefore, there exists a large code representing a federation of groups, surrounded by a considerable number of smaller independent codes dwindling away in size to those of the utmost insignificance.

The situation in the garment industries is somewhat different. Fairly well-defined areas exist with appropriate associations. The outcome is therefore a relatively small number of fairly large codes, covering most garment-making operations. Even here, however, petty groups arose, leading to such codes as the shoulder pad code. A good deal of difficulty was experienced in suppressing factional elements due more than anything else to the existence of unionized and non-unionized shops.

In the food manufacturing industries the separatist tendency ran wild, leading to a whole army of petty codes.

One could go on indefinitely presenting additional illustrations. No further accumulation of details is necessary, however, to make perfectly explicit the fact that, if product groups primarily interested in market control are recognized, the pattern of industries presented is bound to include elements of every degree of size and importance.

Were the practice of entering codes for petty product groups followed extensively, the number of codes could run into many thousands. The fact that only 550 basic codes have been approved is evidence that most products found a home with others under more capacious definitions, rather than independently. It remains true, however, that most of the codes are for small industrial groups.

A rather different picture arises when one looks at certain localized industries and trades. In localized industries like baking and printing, or in local trades like grocery retailing or cleaning and dyeing, or in trucking services, a very large aggregate number of people are employed, so that national codes for these callings are necessarily very large.[1]

In the retail field, representatives of the various types of retail outlet in some degree co-operated in code applications, as for example in securing the general code for

---

[1] Calculations made from unofficial figures prepared in the U. S. Bureau of Foreign and Domestic Commerce yield rather striking results. The figures are very rough approximations of current facts since they are taken from 1929 and 1930 census data and therefore exaggerate the number of employees under codes at the present time.

Over 7 million employees are to be found under 17 codes covering retailing and local services, each applying to 100,000 or more employees and averaging nearly 450,000. Nearly 5 million more employees are to be found under five other codes with highly localized operations and markets—construction, trucking, baking, graphic arts, and daily newspaper. These 22 codes, covering mainly small-scale localized operations, thus account for more than one-half the persons under all code groups. There are in addition a considerable number of similar codes of smaller size. Of the 21 codes covering more than 250,000 employees, 11 are in this group, including the 4 largest codes.

retail trade with its nine large divisions. On the other hand, the separatist influences were very strong, and the NRA commonly bowed to such forces, as in approving separate codes for such retail groups as coal, monument, tire and battery, meat, and jewelry. These forces are not hard to understand when examined in particular cases, granted the purpose of codes as understood by the interested parties.

The diversity in the size of code groups and the predominance of small codes are shown in the accompanying table. An analysis of the data in this table, supplemented

DISTRIBUTION OF EMPLOYEES AMONG NRA CODES, AUG. 8, 1934[a]

Employees per Code	Number		Per Cent		Cumulative Percentages	
	Codes	Employ-ees (In thou-sands)	Codes	Em-ployees	Codes	Em-ployees
1– 4,999	283	473	54.7	2.1	54.7	2.1
5,000– 9,999	68	456	13.2	2.1	67.9	4.2
10,000– 19,999	51	701	9.9	3.2	77.8	7.4
20,000– 29,999	24	576	4.6	2.6	82.4	10.0
30,000– 39,999	14	480	2.7	2.2	85.1	12.2
40,000– 49,999	12	519	2.3	2.4	87.4	14.6
50,000– 99,999	23	1,560	4.4	7.1	91.9	21.6
100,000–249,999	21	2,971	4.1	13.5	95.9	35.1
250,000–499,999	15	5,492	2.9	24.9	98.8	60.1
500,000–999,999	3	1,739	0.6	7.9	99.4	68.0
1,000,000 and over	3	7,054	0.6	32.0	100.0	100.0
Total	517	22,022	100.0	100.0	100.0	100.0

[a] From Leon C. Marshall, *Hours and Wages Provisions in NRA Codes*, 1935, p. 4.

by certain additional data, shows the following striking facts:

1. The 50 per cent of the codes which is made up of the smaller codes covers a total of only 369,463 employees; the 50 per cent of the codes which is made up of the "larger" codes covers 21,652,614 employees. Or, stated entirely in percentage

terms, the 50 per cent smaller codes has 1.7 per cent of the employees; the 50 per cent "larger" codes has 98.3 per cent of the employees.

2. The range in number of employees is from 45 in the animal soft hair industry to 3,453,771 in the retail trade code. The median number of employees is 4,000; the average number is 42,596.

3. The three codes which have 1,000,000 or more employees each are 0.6 per cent of the codes, but they embrace 32.0 per cent of the employees. The six codes which have 500,000 or more employees each (this includes the 1,000,000 and over group) are 1.2 per cent of the codes, but they embrace 39.9 per cent of the employees. The 21 codes which have 250,000 or more employees are 4.1 per cent of the codes, but they embrace two-thirds (64.8 per cent) of the employees.

4. The 283 codes which have less than 5,000 employees each make up 54.7 per cent of the codes but only 2.1 per cent of the employees. It develops that 62 codes have less than 500 employees each; 108 codes have less than 1,000 employees each; 181 codes have less than 2,000 employees each; 232 codes have less than 3,000 employees each; and 256 codes have less than 4,000 employees each.[2]

The NRA shut out a mass of potential codes by refusing to negotiate with regional groups. By this process of exclusion, it rid itself of a large majority of proposed codes, about 4,000 in number, so that it finally had to deal with only something over 1,000 through code negotiations. This number was further reduced by combinations of applicant groups, either voluntarily or under pressure from NRA officials.

The general picture of the code structure cannot be completed without recalling that many codes include subordinate groups with more or less autonomous administrative powers. Some such multiple codes are bound closely together under the extensive supervisory powers

[2] Leon C. Marshall, *Hours and Wages Provisions in NRA Codes*, pp. 4-5.

of the topmost administrative agency. At the other extreme are loose federations under the so-called "umbrella" codes. How far the minute subdivision can go is illustrated by the fact that under the fabricated metal products code there are four supplementary codes for screws, and separate supplementary codes for machine screws and machine screw nuts.

The number of identifiable groups in the code structure is thus seen to be much larger than is indicated by the number of basic codes. No authentic count of the actual number is available, but it may be estimated at something over 1,000.

The essential reasons for the variety of size and constituency of code groups may be summarized as (1) the nature of the inducements to groups to secure codes, centering on control of the market, (2) the scope of existing trade association organizations, (3) the peculiar characteristics of industries and the relations of groups to their particular markets, (4) chance circumstances and personal factors, and (5) the absence of any reasonable tests as to size or classification within the NRA itself. While not exactly of the first importance, this matter of size has been accountable for vast expenditures of time and money, both within NRA and outside, in the effort to establish and administer insignificant codes. And, more particularly, it ties up with other circumstances, to be mentioned later, in making the administration of codes unduly cumbersome.

SPECIAL ASPECTS OF THE CODE STRUCTURE

In the absence of any central pattern of industrial classification, almost every recognized general area of industry was covered by numerous codes, large and small. Certain consequences of this fact are indicated by a study of the code definitions of industries, and are confirmed by an investigation of the problem of code administration. In the first place, many definitions in codes overlap one another, explicitly or implicitly, creating jurisdictional conflicts between code authorities. In the second place, principles of classification create anomalous areas of code coverage. In the third place, by reason of the characteristic diversity of operations within particular firms, it is the exceptional firm which finds its activities comprehended within the limits of a single code. Many enterprises, not always large ones, are compelled to operate under numerous codes.

Overlapping Definitions

The responsibility for the existence of overlapping definitions is various. On the side of applicant groups there was an almost universal effort to secure broad definitions. The primary reason for this was to cover as fully as possible a given competitive area. A secondary reason was the desire to secure as broad a base as possible for purposes of assessing the cost of code administration. In part the overlapping of definitions was due merely to insufficient care by the NRA in scrutinizing and editing definitions.[3] On the other hand, there were instances in which the existence of conflict of definitions was clearly pointed out during code negotiations without causing it to be eliminated. Rather than delay the completion of a code, or perhaps in some instances for political reasons, the NRA knowingly permitted these conflicts to be crystallized into law.

Very commonly the difficulty has been a generality

[3] In this connection it is illuminating that a careful comparative study of definitions of industries did not begin in the NRA until the spring of 1934, as code making was drawing to a close.

or vagueness of definition which opened the way for later controversy between code authorities. For example, the code definition of the electrical manufacturing industry is "the manufacture for sale of electrical apparatus, appliances, material or supplies, and *such other electrical or allied products as are natural affiliates.*[4] This opened the way to very wide claims of jurisdiction by the electrical code authority or its subdivisions. A similar vagueness led to controversy between the road machinery and farm equipment code authorities with respect to authority over tractors.

Somewhat different instances of overlapping definitions are those occasioned by overlapping areas of activity between different general levels of productive operations. Of this sort is what is perhaps the most serious jurisdictional conflict that has arisen, that between the machinery manufacturing codes and the contracting supplements of the construction code. The primary conflict is with respect to installations. In some cases the effect of these supplements is a conflict between their explicit terms and what had been supposed to be the implied scope of the machinery codes. In other cases, the conflict is explicit. The contractors fear that manufacturers, working under less onerous labor provisions, will by reason of lower costs encroach upon the contracting field. Having set up rigid bidding rules, they fear also that these may be undermined. The manufacturers perhaps are most perturbed by the labor implications, since they have commonly worked on an open-shop basis and do not wish to become implicated in the labor relationships characteristic of the construction industries. The issues reach deeply into the industrial relations and trade practices of disparate groups, present disturbing prospects of

[4] Italics supplied.

future complications, and make contact with all sorts of settled habits and prejudices.

Important conflicts of definition occur in the garment codes. The mere names of a few codes, (women's) coat and suit, men's clothing, underwear and allied products, dress, cotton garment, knitted outerwear, blouse and skirt, infants and children's wear, and undergarment and negligee are indicative of the problem of classifying particular items under the several codes. Starting with brief and general terms under the earlier codes, the definitions grew more and more complicated, until under the infants' and children's wear code, coming as it did subsequent to all the other important garment codes and overlapping all of them, the definition is marked by appalling elaborateness. Jurisdictional conflicts were sharpened by the specific terms of the cotton garment code. Until modified by executive order this code had labor provisions less onerous to employers than those of the other garment codes. In consequence manufacturers attempted to conduct as many of their operations under it as they could at all plausibly claim the right to do. The encroachment of garment making upon the retail trade area also complicated the situation.

The confusing parade of definitions of industries brought in its train a minor but troublesome problem, that of finding a home for "lost" articles, not clearly covered by any definition. A few thousand specific articles or services are mentioned in code definitions, and innumerable others are included by clear implication. But no one has the slightest idea how many or what articles out of the hundreds of thousands of products of industry are outside or on the borderline of definition.

Experience under codes excellently illustrates the difficulties of defining an industry for purposes of establishing collective instruments of control. The NRA problem is only partly that of technical definition and classification, being equally one of stilling the seas of jurisdictional conflicts, many of which are the result of its own hasty procedure.

Conflicting Principles of Classification

Since applicant groups were not required to conform to any outlines of industrial classification laid down by the NRA, the groupings cut across one another. The actual outcome is highly variegated, but a somewhat oversimplified conception of it can be secured by examining two sets of contrasting types.

"Horizontal" and "vertical" codes. An aspect of definitions which results in administrative complications is the fact that some codes are "horizontal" (that is, apply to a single stage of manufacturing, processing, or distributing), while others are "vertical" (that is, apply to two or more successive stages). The great majority of codes are horizontal in character. Most manufacturing codes limit the scope to the "manufacture" or "manufacture for sale" or "manufacture and first sale" of the defined range of products. Similarly there are numerous codes for distributing trades which confine the provisions to a particular field of wholesale or retail trade. At the other extreme are a few codes, such as that for oilburners, which cover the whole trade life of a commodity from manufacturing to retail sale. In between lie a considerable number of codes with varying degrees of vertical scope.

Out of the first 450 codes, about 25 manufacturing codes include general wholesaling. A few more apply to wholesaling carried on by manufacturers, and a considerable number apply to affiliated selling agencies.

Very few manufacturing codes, not over ten but including the important cases of ice and petroleum, are defined to apply to selling at retail. One thoroughgoing vertical code, the baby chick code, early cropped up at all sorts of unexpected points to annoy hardware stores, grocery stores, mail-order houses, and others who found themselves subject to it.

The garment industries furnish illustrations of both vertical and horizontal codes. The men's clothing, underwear, and dress codes cover only "manufacture" or "manufacture and sale by the manufacturer," while the coat and suit code covers "manufacture and/or wholesale distribution." The hosiery industry goes further and includes "manufacturing, finishing, repairing, selling, and/or distributing by manufacturers at wholesale or retail, or distributing by wholesalers and selling agents." The corset and brassiere code similarly covers wholesale and direct-to-consumer and custom-made retail selling. The degree of vertical effect of the garment codes cannot, however, be clearly visualized merely by reading definitions. For example, a serious controversy arose almost immediately after the approval of the coat and suit code, as to whether its terms applied to garments made in the workshops of retail dress shops, either custom made or for stock. Nothing in the definitions permits one to know whether half a dozen codes, with non-uniform wage and hour provisions, are to be made operative in such workshops. Only administrative interpretation or code amendment can determine such issues, after a period of uncertainty and controversy.

The term "vertical" is not merely applicable to codes which overlap both fabrication and distributive agencies. Very striking instances are those which cover the passage of basic materials through to the point of ultimate fabrication into specific end products. Thus the steel code is a vertical code with respect to certain end products like steel rails and wire. The lumber code reaches from trees to crates. The cotton textile code is in a sense vertical in that it covers a group of products and processes which may be utilized in a connected series of productive operations, and which may be carried on in different plants or by different firms. By amendment, moreover, it has been made to cover the activities of brokers and other wholesalers of the products of the industry.

With hardly an exception, vertical codes are codes which cover preparation of raw materials, or fabrication, or other form of original production, extending from there into later stages or forms of production or distribution. There is, in other words, no clear case of a code which combines wholesaling and retailing without covering the earlier production of the products distributed.[5] This fact is illuminating, and points to the central logic of almost every vertical code, that the enterprises in the industry are unequally integrated with respect to a series of productive and distributive operations. Under the lumber code, for example, no logical cutting-off level can be found between the sawmill and the local sash and door factory.

The varying degree of vertical integration of certain productive processes may work in the direction of larger and more comprehensive codes, in view of the difficulty of finding any convenient boundaries for separate code constituencies. On the other hand, vertical organization

---

[5] The food and grocery trade may perhaps be regarded as a *de facto* exception to this statement. There are separate codes for wholesaling and retailing, but there is a central administrative agency composed of representatives of both branches of the trade. The builders' supplies code and the retail lumber code also contain features which make it possible to regard them as exceptions.

creates its own anomalies and disturbances. In particular it contributes its quota to the sum of multiple application of codes to particular enterprises. Distributive agencies find themselves in some degree subjected to rules concocted mainly by and for manufacturers.

Just as some horizontal codes reach into queer, out-of-the-way spots, so do vertical codes penetrate precincts far removed from those of the persons whose representatives are responsible for their existence. Though the number of manufacturing codes which reach down to the retail level is quite small, some of them not clearly vertical on the surface have the effect of placing restraints upon the freedom of distributors. Thus one might never suspect that the business furniture code is in part a vertical code if he failed to read one sentence in the supplemental code for steel office furniture, which imposes a system of resale price maintenance. Instances of this sort have raised a serious question within NRA whether the manufacturing groups which sponsored such codes are "truly representative" of distributors and whether therefore the terms of such codes are binding upon the latter.

The common criticism of many vertical codes is that they are designed to make price-control devices effective through a series of stages, and to "freeze" certain channels and practices of distribution. Granting the existence of this element, one must go more deeply into the structure of industry for a comprehensive explanation. American industry and trade is not neatly divided into horizontal strata, within one of which each group of competitors is neatly confined. The simultaneous organization of groups, some on the horizontal principle and some on the vertical principle, does, however, create jurisdictional overlappings somewhat analogous to those created by the organization of labor on the conflicting principles of craft unions and industrial unions.

"Straight-line" and "circular" codes. Most manufacturing codes cover the fabrication of single or closely related products usually deriving from particular basic materials and selling competitively in particular markets. These may be called "straight-line" codes without pressing the physical analogy too hard. On the other hand, there are codes which cover a miscellaneous range of complementary products of diverse origins which are associated on the basis of their ultimate convergence on a common destination. Of such sort are the codes for automotive parts and equipment, farm equipment, road machinery, toys and playthings, funeral supplies, office equipment,and athletic goods. These may be called "circular" codes.

In important instances the distinction is somewhat hard to apply. In practice, also, the distinction between the two types is less clear than would at first appear, since in the latter type there are commonly a number of separately administered product subdivisions. It may appear to make little difference whether brake linings are in a division of the asbestos code or of the automotive parts code. Nevertheless these cross-cutting principles do add complications, particularly in the way of adding to the cases of multiple coverage. Rubber manufacturers who make rubber balls find themselves under the toy code and the athletic goods code. A manufacturer of automobile tool kits finds himself under the wrench code.

Had the constituent product groups not associated themselves in seeking a single code, many of them would have been applicants for separate codes rather than members of some other large code-seeking group. The circular type of grouping has thus probably reduced the number of basic codes and made the degree of multiple coverage less than it would have been had the straight-line principle been followed throughout. It does, however, create particular cases and kinds of overlapping which would not otherwise exist.

A few codes acutely display all the weaknesses of overlapping definition and conflicting principles of classification, thus adding greatly to the confusion of multiple coverage and to the scope of jurisdictional disputes. The industrial safety equipment code is a rather extreme example. It is a circular code, covering a miscellaneous list of complementary articles. It is also a vertical code, covering both the "industry" and the "trade." The "industry" is defined as "the manufacturing and/or assembling and marketing" of a miscellaneous list of safety devices. The "trade" is defined as "the importing and/or distributing and/or selling" of the same range of articles. In the second place, there is a "shot-gun" definition: After citing 28 specific items, the definition adds "first-aid kits and materials for same used in industry, transportation, and service." This appears to make the code applicable to every company that produces drugs, adhesive tape, and absorbent cotton, and to every wholesale and retail druggist. Not content with this the code is made applicable, both as to manufacturing and merchandising at all stages, to all "like instruments and/or equipment worn or used in industry, transportation, trade, commerce and service to protect workers from injury." It is quite impossible under such a definition to prognosticate over what range of items the code authority will claim jurisdiction or to what number and type of establishments its authority will ultimately reach.

Multiple Coverage

In terms of administrative consequences, a less temporary and more stubborn difficulty than any of those mentioned is created by the diversity of operations of individual enterprises. Any scheme of industrial classification, except the vaguest, is bound to cut through the activities of most such enterprises. The actual definitions of industries and trades to be found in codes accentuate the difficulty. It is quite clear, for example, that if there are separate codes for the retailing of food, tobacco, and drugs, or for ice, coal, lumber, and building supplies, most enterprises engaged primarily in any one of these activities will be subject to the terms of more than one code. The possibilities in this direction are especially extensive in the field of manufacturing when the principle of association is that of specific types of product.

The fact of multiple application of codes to single enterprises has two rather different aspects. One aspect is that an enterprise is subjected to several codes covering the several lines of products which it produces or distributes. The difficulty connected therewith is that of isolating the operations relating to each in such a way as to apply the non-uniform labor and trade practice provisions of the several codes to the appropriate operations. The intricate way in which the operations of single enterprises are overlaid by the terms of a multiplicity of codes derives directly from the large number of small codes.

An example of this difficulty is that of a certain New England factory which produces washing machines, vacuum cleaners, electric motors, and other lines, the number of applicable codes being ten. Certain work rooms are specialized by products and the workers therein are clearly under a single code. On the other hand, there are metal, wood-working, and other shops where parts are made or materials processed for all departments. A single workman may in a single day work under two or three codes. Or at a single moment different workers in the same shop may be working under five or six codes.

The other aspect of multiple coverage is related to the

sweeping terms of some definitions which cause them to penetrate into odd and remote places. Thus, the contracting codes reach into a manufacturing enterprise making repairs upon its plant. The graphic arts code includes "all persons who are engaged in publishing or printing, or who use any of the processes or partial processes used in printing, or *who produce any printed matter of whatsoever description,*[6] or who sell any printed matter of whatsoever description in competition with persons who produce such printed matter," except daily newspaper publishing, book publishing, and the products of photoengraving, electrotyping, stereotyping, and similar products. The consequence of this definition is that the provisions of the code reach into innumerable business, educational, and eleemosynary establishments, wherever indeed any press work is done. The set-up paper box code is another ubiquitous visitor, reaching into every plant which makes cardboard boxes for its own use. Similarly penetrating are the seven subdivisions of the wooden package division of the lumber code. The definition of the "light sewing except garments" code is an invitation to an active code authority or executive officer to run around hunting for jurisdictional territory wherever anything is stitched.

The number of codes which, like those just mentioned, may insinuate their way into the operations of numberless firms is of course rather limited. On the other hand, there are a sufficient number of codes relatively sweeping in their terms to make it certain that almost every enterprise of any size will find itself subject to the terms of some code or codes thoroughly irrelevant to its main lines of activity. The principle and purpose are clear enough: to guard the interests of the principal parties at interest in every competitive situation. Looking outward

[6] Italics supplied.

from the vantage-point of those interested in particular products, this appears to them not only reasonable but essential. When generalized, however, into a structure of hundreds of codes, the resultant multiplicity of other codes coming back upon them creates difficulties and annoyances in the conduct of their affairs.

A somewhat contrasting aspect of definitions lies in the fact that areas of direct competition have not in some cases been fully included within the definition of a single industry. This is the direct opposite to the cases of broad and vague definition designed to reach every competitive element. The result is that identical functions are divided among various codes. Where there is any considerable difference between the wage and hour provisions of the codes, a competitive advantage is given to one group as against another. This is aptly illustrated by the provisions of the trucking code and the retail trade code. Wholly similar trucking operations are being carried on by delivery fleets owned by retail stores and by for-hire truck operators performing delivery operations for retail stores under contract. Trucking operations performed by store-owned trucks are excepted from the jurisdiction of the trucking code. Since wage and hour provisions of the retail trade code are much less onerous than those of the trucking code, the situation tends to induce stores to purchase and operate their own delivery equipment at the expense of the independent trucker. Few instances are so direct and obvious as that of trucking, and the matter broadens out to cover the whole field of competitive relationships between substitute commodities and services under different codes.

A knowledge of the structural complexities of codes is essential to an understanding of the problems of code administration. The codes to be administered are for the interlacing and overlapping industries described.

CHAPTER VII

AGENCIES FOR CODE ADMINISTRATION

To administer the provisions of the several codes it was necessary to create a new set of administrative bodies. The almost invariable practice was to provide for a "code authority" (other designations are used in some codes) for each basic code. This is the only agency mentioned in the majority of codes. In a considerable minority of codes, however, provision is made for subordinate administrative bodies and for committees of various sorts. A large number of other agencies not mentioned in the codes have actually been created, and other existing agencies have been made parts of the administrative structure.

The pattern of administrative agencies thus created has a more than superficial importance. Among its longer run objectives the Recovery Act was intended to furnish the basis for continuing forms of collective action by business groups. If the code system is to be continued, its administrative structure must be regarded as an extension, of a very novel sort, of the machinery of the federal government.

Very little thought was given to the creation of the structure. In each code negotiation it was recognized that some agency must be responsible for active supervision of the code. Such an agency was designated, presumably representative of the various elements of the industry or trade. It is possible to regard these agencies merely as the several individual bodies responsible for code administration, and to test them merely by the adequacy of their individual performances. A more general and deeper purpose is served, however, by attempting to get a clear understanding of the whole complex pattern. In this way a better view is obtained of what is implied in the idea of "industrial self-government," and the foundation is laid for a sounder judgment on the merits of the code system as an addition to the system of American government.

GENERAL CHARACTER OF ADMINISTRATIVE PROVISIONS

The statement of the powers and duties of the code authority is usually in the most general terms. Thus, Section V of the electrical manufacturing code defines them as "administering, supervising, and promoting the performance of the provisions of this code by the members of the electrical manufacturing industry." Very commonly there is added some such empowering clause as the following, taken from Article III of the code for the business furniture, storage equipment, and filing supply industry: "Subject to the approval of the Administrator, this committee shall issue and enforce such rules, regulations, and interpretations, offer such amendments hereto, and designate such agents and delegate such authority to them as may be necessary to effectuate the purposes and to enforce the provisions of this code." Review of certain administrative acts by the NRA is provided for, either specifically or in such general terms as the following, also taken from the business furniture code: "Any action taken by the National Emergency Committee, or by any divisional code committee or by any divisional planning and classification board may be reviewed by the Administrator, at his option, and modified or disapproved." This may be generalized into the statement that the NRA accepts a contingent responsibility for the proper administration of every code. The actual responsibilities of a code authority are to be found only by reading the whole code. They are simple or elaborate in the degree that code provisions are simple or elaborate.

The attempt to visualize the machinery of code administration from a study of administrative provisions of codes confronts several serious obstacles. In the first place, the method of selecting the primary administrative agency, or code authority, is not stated in numerous codes. The actual method can only be found by inquiring into the later history of each code. In the second place, where the method of selection is stated in general terms, the procedure is sometimes indefinite. Thus, it may be stated in the code that the members of the code authority are to be "elected by members of the industry," without providing for any electoral procedure. In the third place, the constituent membership is not always precisely stated. In one case, where there were to be "not less than twelve" members, the actual initial number of members was 35.

In the fourth place, the structure of the code authority, as shown in the code, often gives no idea of who will actually exercise the administrative functions in practice. Many codes authorize the delegation of functions of the code authority to other agencies. Apart from this, administrative practices may be adopted voluntarily, or may be imposed by the Administrator. Some code authorities are large in size, or the membership is widely scattered geographically, leading to the setting up of an administrative committee, and in some instances, of a further administrative sub-committee. Or again, actual administrative functions may be mainly carried on by specialized committees, such as those on trade practice compliance, industrial relations, cost accounting, and statistics. Or there may be set up regional committees with administrative powers for particular geographical areas. Moreover, the day to day administrative activity is likely to be centered in a single official. Thus a code authority, which is usually the only administrative agency mentioned in a code, may come to be in practice a body which meets only rarely as a policy-making and review board.

In the fifth place, the stated functions of code authorities vary so greatly from code to code, or the activities to which their energies are directed vary so greatly, that the picture of administrative agencies which can be secured from a study of the codes only slightly forecasts the form which they will take. Thus, a code authority charged with price fixing develops an organization for that purpose. In another case the primary activity may be the maintenance of compliance with the labor provisions.

In the sixth place, a good many code authorities, though formally set up in conformity with the terms of codes, have found it impossible to function effectively by reason of inadequate financial support, or inability of the members to agree on lines of action, or recalcitrancy on the part of members of the underlying industry. And finally, in some industries it has been impossible even to effect an initial organization of the code authority, or one which the Administrator would approve as conforming to the terms of the code and the meaning of the act.

The foregoing considerations make clear that a study of codes alone will give no accurate idea of how codes are administered. This can only come through the accumulation of detailed knowledge concerning administrative organization and activities under specific codes. Nevertheless, an examination of the provisions of codes furnishes the necessary starting point for a treatment of the administration of codes, and throws much light upon the character of the administrative problems from industry to industry.

METHODS OF SELECTING CODE AUTHORITIES

The methods by which code authorities are chosen vary widely from code to code. Roughly, however, they may be divided into those in which established trade associations are given a dominant part and those in which they are not. A survey covering 400 approved codes shows that 218 of the 400 place trade associations in a dominant position, with minority representation for non-member associations in 101 of the 218 instances. There is labor representation on 21 of the 400 code authorities, and consumer representation on 2.

A more detailed examination of 110 codes, including the first 100 codes and 10 later codes, shows that trade associations are given a dominant position in 63 instances. In these instances, the methods of selection of the code authorities vary greatly. In the largest number of cases, 28 out of 63, the code simply names a single association, or its board of directors or executive committee, as the national code authority. Eight others are chosen by the association or its directors, which comes to practically the same thing. In 16 cases the majority of the code authority is made up of representatives of a single association, with a minority chosen by members of the industry who are not members of the association. In one case there is added a minority representing labor. In 5 cases, the code authority is made up of representatives of two or more associations. In 5 other cases, two or more associations choose a majority of the code authority. In 3 of these cases there is a minority chosen by non-members of associations, and in 2 cases a labor minority.

Among the 47 codes which do not formally delegate dominant power to associations, 21 do not specify the method of selection at all, merely calling for a "fair method of selection," or some similar phrase. Eleven other codes call for selection by "members of the code" or "members of the industry," in some cases specifying the basis of the franchise and in other cases not. In 7 codes the code authority is made up of members selected by members of the several trade divisions of the industry, and in one case the members are elected by geographical areas. There are several variants on the principle of sellection by trade divisions. Thus, taking 4 cases where some members are selected by trade divisions, in one case there is a minority selected by an association; in a second case there is a minority elected at large; in a third case, in addition to a minority elected at large there are certain special members; and in a fourth case there are members elected by geographical areas, plus the original code organization committee. There are other special methods of selection: for example, one code authority is to be appointed in its entirety by the Administrator. Another is made up of members chosen by regional code authorities.[1]

[1] The 110 codes examined may be distributed as follows according to the method provided for choosing the code authority (or its membership where designated), and according to whether single or multiple administrative agencies have been created:

		Single Agency	Multiple Agencies
1.	"Fair method"	17	4
2.	(a) Chosen by "members of code"	2	—
	(b) Chosen by "members of code," with majority from association	—	1
3.	(a) Chosen by "members of industry" (in some cases at meeting called by association)	8	1
	(b) Chosen from industry, by trade divisions	—	7
	(c) Chosen from industry, by geographic divisions	—	1
	(d) 3(b) + 3(c) + code committee	—	1
	(e) 3(b) + minority at large	—	1
	(f) 3(b) + minority at large + special members	—	1
	(g) 3(b) + minority by association	—	1

The fact that numerous codes do not in words establish the dominance of trade associations in the selection of code authorities need not mean that associations will not achieve dominance in practice. For example, a "fair method of selection" approved by the Administrator may turn out to be one by which an association selects a majority of the members. Again, where elections are held, an association may promote a group of candidates successfully. It is therefore to be expected that trade associations will dominate more code authorities than would appear from a mere analysis of the codes.

Pending the determination of a "fair method" of selecting a code authority and pending the holding of elections, under many codes it was necessary to set up a temporary code authority. Frequently the code committee served as the temporary agency or dominated its appointment. In some instances a trade association selected the temporary body, while the permanent body was

4.	(a)	Association or its directors named as code authority	18	10
	(b)	Association or its directors named as code authority with non-association minority	5	4
	(c)	Association or its directors, with additional members appointed by association	1	—
5.	(a)	Chosen by association or directors	7	1
	(b)	Majority chosen by association or directors, with non-association minority	2	4
	(c)	Majority chosen by association or directors, with non-association minority and labor minority	1	—
6.	(a)	Chosen by two or more associations	1	4
	(b)	Chosen by two or more associations, with non-member minority	2	1
	(c)	Chosen by two or more associations, with labor minority	2	—
7.		All appointed by Recovery Administrator	1	—
8.		Chosen by regional code authorities	—	1
		Total	67	43

elected by the members of the industry. The holding of elections was sometimes a rather difficult process, and the facilities and personnel of established associations were of assistance. Some importance attached to the temporary bodies, since their early acts set the tone of admininstrative action, their election procedure speeded or delayed the implementation of codes, and their behavior focused the forces of code politics.

The place of trade associations in controlling the administration of codes is far from fully displayed by examining basic code authorities. In those numerous codes which have subordinate code authorities the subordinate agency is very commonly an association of persons selected by it. Thus, the numerous divisions under the lumber code, the fabricated metal products code, the machinery and allied products code, the paper and pulp code, and the graphic arts code are administered by or in close relationship to established trade associations. This close relationship between code authorities and trade associations is entirely in harmony with the purposes of the NRA. It is, however, necessary to understand that code authority functions are separate and distinct and of a quasi-public character.

TYPES OF ADMINISTRATIVE ORGANIZATION

For preliminary analysis codes may be divided into two groups: First, those which provide for a single code authority, and, second, those with administrative agencies for groups subordinate to the primary code authority. The latter group may be subdivided into two main sections—those with regional agencies and those with agencies for product groups, partly overlapping each other. In addition, there are other miscellaneous types of administrative subdivisions, most of which may be classified either as processing groups or as trade groups. The term "product group" is confined to groups engaged in primary production of materials or fabrication of products. Trade groups are those engaged primarily in some form of merchandising or contracting. Processing groups are less easy to define, but the term refers to groups primarily engaged in certain intermediate processing of materials in preparation for fabrication. There are not many of the latter, since most processing is covered by the grouping according to products. It is necessary to give warning that the actual administrative organizations to be found under codes are extremely varied, so that any such general classification is merely indicative and provisional, to be modified and supplemented by more detailed analysis.

The great majority of codes provide for a single administrative agency or code authority. Included in this group are some of the most important industries. For example, the boot and shoe, iron and steel, and automobile[2] codes specify single agencies. Industries having a relatively high degree of financial or geographical concentration or consisting of a relatively small number of units are more likely to fall into this group. In conjunction with one or more of these factors, relative narrowness of the line of products covered also plays some part. A very large majority of the codes in this group are for quite small industries. It is also true that many codes with multiple agencies are also small, so that it is not possible to secure any clear correlation between the importance of an industry and the elaborateness of its administrative structure. Though in a small minority as to number, the codes with subordinate administrative bodies

---

[2] This is not strictly accurate since there is a special committee to administer trade practices for the funeral vehicle and ambulance branch of the industry.

do, however, average much larger by the test of employees, so that such codes represent a distinct majority of the employee coverage of NRA codes.

The extent to which administrative subdivisions are incorporated in codes may be summarized by an analysis of the first 425 approved codes. There were in all 148 codes which provided for such subdivisions. Seventy-nine codes provided specifically for regional subdivisions. Of these nearly half related to retail trade or local services or production for highly localized markets, as in the case of ice and baking. Eighty-two manufacturing codes provided for product subdivisions. A few of these also had special processing subdivisions. From 15 to 20 codes provided for trade subdivisions. This is a somewhat miscellaneous group, the most important code thus classified being the construction code with its contracting supplements. The indefiniteness of the number is due to the difficulty of clearly differentiating some trade divisions from other types.

Any such count is necessarily inaccurate, due to the vague wording of some codes, and is merely indicative in a rough way of the extent of the phenomenon. It overstates the current facts in the sense that a number of codes simply authorize code authorities to establish subdivisions, and this has not in all cases been done. It understates them in so far as code authorities are exercising their discretion in setting up agencies not mentioned in codes, or are delegating their authority. The figures do not indicate the magnitude of the areas of trade and industry covered by the codes with subordinate administrative agencies. It was noted at an earlier point that more than one-half of the employees potentially under NRA codes are to be found under 22 codes with elaborate regional administration. Nearly 2.5 million employees are to be found under 8 large natural resource and manufacturing codes out of the 82 with product subdivisions.

Without closely estimating the magnitude of the remainder of the codes with subordinate administrative agencies, it is clear that a large major fraction of all employees under the NRA system are under codes of this sort. This fact is of importance for understanding the character of code administration. Under such codes the direct administrative oversight of the members of an industry or trade is not exercised by the national code authority, but by a subordinate agency. The supervisory functions of the former are therefore mainly those of guiding the activities of the latter, rather than themselves directly policing the industry and administering the provisions of the code. This in turn bears upon the supervisory relationship of the NRA to code administrative agencies. The NRA is represented on all basic code authorities by one or more representatives called administration members. In some instances it is also represented on subordinate agencies. But in so far as this is not true, which is commonly the case, the direct administration of the code provisions is in the hands of bodies which have no direct contact with the NRA. There is thereby created for the NRA the problem of how it can keep itself informed and perform its supervisory functions with respect to the thousands of agencies with which it has no direct intercourse (See Chapter IX).

There is no direct and simple explanation for the exact form and degree of complexity in code authority organizations. The endless vagaries of form in this, as in other aspects of codes, derive from the code-making process, which furnished no basis for uniformity or for consistency of principle. Back of these vagaries, however, to some extent stand thoroughly explicable reasons for many of the forms.

Since most of the codes give no real indication of what the administrative structure will be like in practice, the following discussion is mainly based upon knowledge of post-code developments. The examination will be facilitated by separate treatment of regional agencies, product group agencies, and special and mixed types.

REGIONAL AGENCIES

Regional administration is provided for in numerous codes and is actually developing under others in which it is not mentioned. The forms which it takes are diverse by reason of the differing situations to which it is applied.

Distributing and Service Codes

From an administrative viewpoint, the dominant physical fact about codes covering selling of goods or services to the final consumer is that the members are numerous and widely scattered. No national code authority could exercise any effective supervisory function over such units. The situation requires the existence of regional or local agencies, and they are almost universally found in such codes as retail trade, retail food, retail coal, retail lumber, laundry, cleaning and dyeing, barber, beauty parlor, restaurant, hotel, and retail tire. Certain other localized, but not retail, services, such as warehousing and trucking, follow the same principle. Again, a number of types of manufacture for local use, such as baking and ice manufacturing, are of the same order. Some violence is done to careful analysis by lumping all such codes. Their problems are in many respects quite different. The common elements which alone permit them to be described together are their geographical diffusion, large number, and small size.

In this field of local trades and services the number of subordinate administrative agencies reaches a large figure. The retail trade code authority has set up over 700 local agencies. Some of those in metropolitan areas have subordinate or associated agencies for outlying communities. The food and groceries code authority has set up 110 district agencies and over 600 local agencies. The usual pattern is on three levels, the national code authority, regional code authorities (in some codes, one for each state), and local code authorities. But some codes, particularly the retail trade code, have no intermediate agency, the local agencies being set up by and directly responsible to the national code authority.

It is impossible to learn from most codes how many agencies will be set up. Thus under the retail fuel code, the national code authority is merely authorized to divide the country into regional divisions for each of which there is a divisional code authority. The actual number established is 49, but not by states. The divisional code authorities in turn are authorized to delegate power to agencies for "marketing areas." The subdivisions may be counties, legislative districts, cities, trade areas, or any arbitrary carving up of territory, and the probable number is estimated at about 700. The establishment of such agencies is optional, so that one may find some divisions completely organized, and others with little or no local organization. These agencies may be local retailers' associations, though they may cover a wider area than a mere locality. In the latter case a single agency may utilize the services of several local associations or may have to organize its own staff for detailed local supervision. The indefiniteness of the codes is further illustrated by the retail rubber tire code, which merely authorizes the national code authority to "define regional, district, and other trade areas" and to establish "a control board or boards for any region, district, or other trade area, and to discharge through such board or boards such of the powers and duties reposed in the code authority as may be necessary for the effective administration of this code."

Even where the code seems rather more definite, the actual organization does not always follow the code pattern. Thus, the trucking code originally provided for regional administration at four levels, national, regional, state,[3] and district, in a descending hierarchy of powers. In addition, state authorities were authorized to create divisional agencies for different branches of trucking. In practice, the state code authorities are the only subordinate agencies which have been established on a functioning basis. The regional authorities have been abolished by amendment of the code, with provision, however, for temporary inter-state code authority committees on special problems transcending state jurisdictional lines. No action has been taken by state authorities to set up district and divisional code authorities, and it appears probable that local committees or associations will serve the state authority in lieu of formal local code authorities. In some degree this attenuation of administrative organization is in the interests of economy, and in part it reflects the experience and judgment of those charged with administrative duties. The food and grocery distributors set-up similarly deviates from the pattern provided in the code.

A few wholesaling codes provide for regional agencies, not of course on the minute scale of retailing. This is especially the case with the commodity divisions of the wholesale or distributing code, mentioned at a later point.

The potential aggregate number of regional and local agencies runs to many thousands. The geographic areas to which they apply are defined in each code or under

---

[3] The jurisdiction of state code authorities is not always strictly defined by state boundaries.

the powers granted in each code, severally. Some attempt is being made by the NRA to get code groups to re-define the boundaries of their subdivisions in conformity with a commercial map which has been drawn up, but with little success. Very serious problems of financing arise in the attempt to make the regional systems opera-tive. Of another sort are the problems of exercising adequate government supervision.

Natural Resource Codes

Regional organization is characteristic of most of the codes covering the mining and quarrying operations for such products as coal, gypsum, and limestone. Closely related thereto are other industries engaged in the first processing of minerals such as cement and lime. The boundaries of such regions roughly delimit what are thought of in the industry as natural marketing areas. The purpose is commonly to facilitate the operation of price-reporting and price-control systems, amounting in some instances to highly developed marketing plans. The number of marketing zones set up in codes is not large, running usually from 10 to 15. This fact is not, however, indicative of the ultimate set-up, since the ap-propriate number of zones may be expected to derive from the peculiar facts of each industry, including the geographical location of mineral resources, transportation costs, and so forth. At one extreme are the highly local-ized operations under the code for crushed stone, sand and gravel, and slag. This is reflected by the provision for 16 regional committees which in turn can set up any number of district committees for local marketing areas. No such extensive local subdivision, however, could be expected for marble quarrying or cement manufacturing.

In the field of minerals, by far the most important

codes are those for petroleum and bituminous coal. The extraordinary complexity of the former derives from the fact that it is a vertical code, covering all operations from original production to final retailing, and its peculiar features are aside from the immediate topic of discussion. The bituminous coal code exhibits exceptional administrative features which are worthy of mention in the present connection. The usual pattern of codes for mineral producing and processing is a strong code authority with subordinate regional committees. By way of striking contrast, the coal code parcels out almost all effective administrative power to the code authorities of the five regional divisions and the subdivisions thereunder. In view of the past history of the industry, which made agreement upon a code almost miraculous, this deference to the separatist tendencies within the industry is understandable. Nevertheless, the allocation of power in this fashion ignores the overlapping market boundaries of the several areas. Since the most important function of the divisional code authorities is that of price fixing, problems of market adjustment arise that can only be effectively handled by an agency of national scope. The *de facto* solution was first to constitute the administration members of the several code authorities into an informal coordinating agency. Thereafter by administrative order the adjustment routine was expanded and formalized by creating a committee representative of the several regional divisions. By amendment to the code an arbitration board was established in January 1935. The original extraordinary decentralization of power was obviously unstable and additions to its super-structure were predictable necessities.

The type of regional administration characteristic of mineral industries, based on market areas, is to be found in a number of industries engaged in fabricating earthen and rock products. Thus, there are a number of such codes for clay products alone, including five for various types of tile. Other types of products fall into the same class. The rationale is exactly the same, that of exercising some control over regional markets of highly standardized products which by reason of transportation costs can move only limited distances from the area of production.

Manufacturing Codes

There are a few manufacturing codes for which the requirements of regional administration are not greatly dissimilar to those already noted for retail trade and service codes. This is particularly true of the important ice and baking codes, and for the commercial relief-printing branch of the graphic arts code. In these instances the operations are highly localized, and in part consist of final distributing as well as manufacturing operations. This situation is reflected in the administrative organization. Under the ice code there are 10 regional advisers who supervise the activities of 44 committees of arbitration and appeal, which serve the territories of the several regional trade associations. These committees in turn have local representatives in the various market areas within their respective regions. The baking code provides for state and local agencies in much the same terms as various retail codes. The graphic arts code has a highly complex structure of interlinking regional and product agencies which will be noted at a later point in this chapter. Industries of this type are exceptional, and the regional organization of other industries is much less highly developed.

The number of miscellaneous manufacturing codes which provide for regional administration is small, and in most instances the number of agencies and the character of their duties are not specified. Where defined, the regions are usually few in number—for example, five for novelty curtains, five for boat building, and three for coffee. The bedding code stands out as an exceptional instance with 29 regional divisions. A number of industries, like photo-engraving and boat building, exhibit characteristic traits of localism in their markets. Others, however, exhibit no such traits, and the explanation has to be attributed to other considerations.

The primary reason for regional organization for other purposes than the control of regional markets or regional price reporting is to facilitate general compliance activities. A secondary reason lies simply in the utilization of pre-existing trade associations for carrying on administrative duties under codes even when the markets are in no sense regional. Both these points are illustrated by the furniture code. This code was sponsored by two large associations, one covering the South and the other the rest of the country. The code authority maintains only a skeleton organization and delegates almost all its administrative functions to the two associations. Directly supervised by the associations are 15 zones, set up by the code authority, each with a zone director and compliance committee. In some instances these zones and officials derive from sub-regional associations; in others it has been necessary for the code authority, through the two large associations, to set up the agencies. The purpose of these regional offices and committees is almost strictly confined to adjusting trade practice complaints, since under the furniture code "control of the market" activities are very limited.

From a study of codes it is impossible to secure any impression of the potential extent of regional organization in manufacturing industries. This is in part because the codes providing for regional administration commonly leave actual organization for later action by code authorities. But particularly it is because regional offices may spring up under any code, and there is no means of foreseeing the extent of this development. It is, however, to be expected that they will exist in almost all industries with numerous and widely scattered membership. This is evidenced by the setting up of regional compliance offices under the cotton garment, coat and suit, and men's clothing codes, though no intent to organize on regional lines is to be found in any of these codes.

With respect to the mere physical difficulty of establishing an effective administrative organization, it may be repeated that the existence of numerous widely scattered units militates against ease of administration. Thus, to take industries of comparable importance, the highly concentrated steel and automobile industries present incomparably lesser administrative problems than the scattered lumber, ice, and graphic arts industries. Within a narrower range, the scattered units of the cotton garment industry are more difficult to supervise than the more concentrated men's clothing industry. Industries like lime, salt, and cement are of a lesser order of administrative difficulty than crushed rock, sand and gravel, and slag. Where units are not only small and scattered but also mobile, as in the motor transportation codes, the difficulties are even more striking.

The duties of regional officers may be expected to vary according to the character of the market and the terms of the code. Where markets are national in extent, regional agencies are likely to be engaged mainly in compliance activities. Thus the regional offices of the cotton garment code authority are mere outposts of the national code authority, to implement its primary interest in maintaining adherence to the wage and hour provisions of the code. Where markets are more localized, the same may be true in some instances. On the other hand, codes which contemplate any important degree of market control in localized markets will almost necessarily give the regional agencies other administrative duties. It may perhaps be taken as axiomatic that almost every industry which has regional trade associations will have some form of regional code administration, utilizing the associations for that purpose.

AGENCIES FOR PRODUCT GROUPS

Of the more than 80 codes providing for product subdivisions almost all are for the fabricating industries, though in the case of lumber such organization reaches back to the raw material stage. A good reason is usually to be found for the existence of subdivisions where they exist. There is, however, no general rationale for the existence of product subdivisions in some codes, as against their absence in others. To obtain a true understanding of the reasons for subdivisions, and for their exact nature and scope, would in fact require a knowledge of the history of each code in its formative stages.

Origin of Divisional Organization

A number of important codes, it has already been pointed out, grew out of a history of past co-operation between trade associations in closely related fields. Such are the lumber, electrical, and rubber codes. In other instances the history was quite the reverse. Separate code-seeking groups found a basis for common action during the course of code negotiations. Sometimes this move was self-initiated, sometimes the result of pressure brought by NRA officials. Other groups associated themselves in advance of code applications.

After some early experience of making codes under which constituent product groups maintained their separate identity and administrative powers, the idea came to be regarded as having great merit and a good deal of effort was expended, both inside the NRA and outside, in inducing related groups to get together. One of the elements of merit, from the NRA point of view, was a purely procedural one—it cleared the docket of scores of separate code hearings. There was, too, a growing feeling that numerous small codes were undesirable for a variety of reasons. Another element lay in the fact that powder-puff codes and hog-ring codes sounded ridiculous and furnished a basis for public ridicule. A more objective and weighty merit of the scheme centered largely in the securing of identical labor provisions for closely related areas of production, where entirely separate codes would increase the annoyances of multiple coverage.

It was not, however, until the spring of 1934, in the face of hundreds of petty pending codes, that concerted efforts were made by certain officials to head off further proliferation by amalgamation of proposed with existing codes. The policy was not easy to put into practice on a wide scale. This arose in part because negotiations on pending codes were commonly in an advanced state, and the path of least resistance for deputy administrators was to carry them on toward completion, rather than open new negotiations of a long-drawn-out character. In part it was because of the unwillingness of applying groups to be merged with other groups. In part it was because there were many proposed codes which did not reasonably fall under any of the codes already approved.

In those instances in which smaller groups found a basis of co-operation in securing a single basic code, each was ordinarily unwilling to lose its identity. With respect to trade practice aspects of codes, most constituent groups felt strongly the need for administering their own affairs. There often existed also obvious elements of expediency, as for example in connection with utilizing well-established trade associations in a variety of administrative tasks for which they were fitted by experience. Strong traditional lines of cleavage also militated against closer union, often supported by the vested interests of trade association officials.

Types of Subdivision

In spite of their diverse origins and special circumstances, it is possible to class most of the complex manufacturing codes into two groups on the basis of, first, the existence of recognized subdivisions within a given industry; and, second, the combination of dissimilar industry groups under a common code. The first of these is characteristic of industries in which there is a considerable degree of technical integration between the first processing and further fabrication of some basic material. This is a partial explanation of the subdivisions under the glassware, rubber, paper and pulp, asbestos, cork, leather, lumber, and textile codes. The textile codes are especially good examples.

Any acquaintance with the textile industries displays the existence of a number of relatively clearly defined divisions within each industry. For purposes of devising special trade practice rules or for administering the general rules of a code, each of these divisions has a natural coherence and common interest. This is especially true of industries like textiles where plant size is not typically very large, so that there are numerous plants specializing in the products or processes of the several divisions. It is natural under the circumstances to find in such codes the recognition of the divisions, each with its own subordinate administrative agency. Thus in the wool textile code, typical divisions out of the total of 15 are worsted men's wear, blankets, worsted spinners, combers, scourers and carbonizers, and piece-goods selling, which show the industry to be subdivided along both product, processing, and trade lines.

On the other hand, the so-called "umbrella" type of code like the machinery and allied products code brings together a number of potentially separate codes, usually because of the desire to give greater uniformity to the labor provision throughout fields of industry which, though closely related and overlapping particular firms, produce quite dissimilar products independently of the processing of the basic materials. This description covers all those codes which have at an earlier point been called "circular." The refractories code, the farm equipment code, the scientific apparatus code, the automotive parts code, and several others are of this type.

The distinction between these types is not clear cut. In the making of some of the codes mentioned like lumber and paper, as well as in others like electrical manufacturing, graphic arts, paperboard, and chemicals, both sets of influences were present. The distinction needs to be made, however, by way of making clear that some of the codes with multiple administrative machinery have a much higher degree of organic unity than others.

Codes with product subdivisions run from very small, for example the mica code, to very large, for example the paper and pulp code. The number of divisions runs from one to more than 50. Every degree of intricacy in the relationships of the constituent groups exists. In a few instances there is a double process of subdividing. Thus under the automotive parts and equipment code, the primary divisions such as the accessories division and the replacement parts division are being broken down into subordinate product groups such as hot-water heaters and axle shafts. The intricacy of the relationships between product groups usually cannot be deduced from the terms of codes nor from the number of groups. Under some codes, particularly the "umbrella" codes, the several groups lead a quasi-independent existence. On the other hand, under the lumber code a highly intricate set of relationships exists among the numerous subdivisions, due in large part to the exigencies of administering price and production control provisions for groups of products that are somewhat competitive with one another.[4]

Administrative Divisions and Supplementary Codes

Were the function of a subordinate administrative agency merely to administer the uniform terms of a basic code, the picture of code administration could be much more simply drawn. Actually, however, the agencies of product groups, while administering some common provisions, are usually intended to administer provisions special to the particular divisions. One cannot grasp the significance of the rubber code or the business furniture code from reading the basic code. It is in the rules of the subordinate divisions that the kernel of "self-government" is usually imbedded.

The codes in their original approved form often give scant indication of their future content. For example, the leather and electrical codes merely indicate the intention to have divisions of the industry without naming the

[4] The price control features of the code have in part been superseded.

divisions or describing the type of administrative agency or stating its functions. In other cases, as in the cotton garment code, subdivisions of the industry are named and are utilized in choosing the code authority, but no prospective functions as administrative agencies are mentioned. A somewhat different example is that of the furniture code, which indicates an intention to use certain trade associations as administrative agencies, without indicating whether there is any expectation that they will submit for approval special trade practice provisions. Inquiry within various industries indicates that in many such instances it is the intention that such divisions should later present and be made autonomously responsible for special trade practice provisions. In a number of codes this is made more explicit, as for example in the electrical code, by stating the intention to study trade practices in the various branches of the industry and to submit for approval provisions applicable thereto. What this means one can discover only by following later developments.

Autonomous divisions, though highly diverse in character, may be reduced to two formal categories, according to whether they do or do not have supplementary codes. Where there is no supplementary code, there may be added to the basic code a list of special provisions applying to the several divisions. This is true, for example, of the graphic arts code, the lumber code, the rubber code, the paper and pulp code, and many others. The content of these special sections varies in the widest degree from a single supplementary provision at one extreme to full-fledged documents on trade practices, cost protection, price reporting, and statistical reporting at the other. Some of these supplements are to be found in the original editions of codes. Others have been added from time to time. Administrative divisions may, on the other hand, have no provisions except the basic code. Differences on this score may exist under the same basic code.

A supplementary code is a formal document which is arrived at by going through the whole routine of code making as though it were a separate code. Commonly, the supplementary code authority is less fully subordinate to the national code authority than the ordinary divisional agency, and has certain direct relationships with and responsibilities to NRA which do not exist in the case of other subordinate agencies. The existence of supplementary codes is commonly related to the structure and history of the industry. They occur particularly in codes which represent new realms of association, where the placing together of groups under a common code is not built upon any past history of close association. The basic codes represent certain minimum provisions upon which the separate groups have been able to agree, especially with respect to labor provisions, but their purpose to maintain their separate and autonomous administration shows the influence of those same separatist tendencies which have been discussed at an earlier point.

In spite of these facts the formal distinction between supplementary codes and the divisional organization of other codes lacks real significance. On the side of procedure, while the Recovery Administration might approve provisions for product subdivisions without extensive conferences and hearings, in practice any important proposed rules go through a procedure approximately as elaborate as that for securing a supplementary code. Again on the side of actual power, divisional code authorities often have autonomous powers quite as great as those of supplementary code authorities. The significant fact is that hundreds of product groups, whether they have supplementary codes or merely divisional rules and organization, are the active agencies in administering the codes.

Certain facts concerning the multiplicity of administrative agencies may be given a clearer outline by taking the most extreme example from among the codes which provide for supplementary codes. There are not many such basic codes, fewer than 25 in the first 400 codes. Some of these are small and unimportant, with few subdivisions. Several of them are, however, of particular importance and interest in a study of the administrative aspects of the NRA.

The leadership for a single basic code arose spontaneously within the light metal industries, and eventuated in the Fabricated Metal Products Federation, with over 100 constituent associations and hundreds of individual members. While a large number of groups thus co-operated, many others equally eligible for membership went their independent paths to the attainment of separate codes. At one time it looked as though the number of supplementary codes under fabricated metal products would run as high as 150 or 200. So petty were many of the product groups that there was no reason, on the same principle of classification, why the number might not just as well have been 1,000 or 5,000. Under this one basic code there began to be reincarnated in miniature the history of the NRA, repeating and exaggerating the folly of setting up minute product groups which endlessly overlapped the activities of particular enterprises. The reason was identical—the interest of each product group in price-control devices. The procedural weakness was also identical. There was at NRA the same receptive welcome to each applying group. Then each supplementary code had to go through the whole prolonged code-making process, the pressure of interested groups, the haggling with advisory boards.

In consequence the supplementary codes which were approved followed no uniform pattern of provisions or terminology, and they started to overhang the metal trades with the prospect of scores of applicable accounting, reporting, and cost protection systems. By October 1934 there were more than 50 supplementary codes. But before then the imbecility of the process was recognized on all sides and a presumably simpler procedure for procuring more uniform provisions and less elaborate agencies had been devised. In practice this procedure turned out to be little less complicated than the earlier one. Meantime the process of grinding out petty supplementary codes ceased and has not been resumed. In so far as the remaining groups have any part in code administration, it is informally through their trade associations, and not as duly constituted agencies.

The machinery and allied products code has a somewhat similar history with differentiating features. Under this code are nearly 50 supplementary codes, a few of which provide for further product or regional subdivisions. These groups are highly autonomous.

The groups under the electrical code are bound by closer ties of past association, and the basic code, by reason of its fuller content, leaves less in the way of non-identical provisions to be put into supplementary codes. The code authority too has a more direct responsibility to supervise the making of supplementary codes and to co-ordinate the administration of them. The original intention appears to have been to negotiate numerous supplementary codes. After a few had been approved, however, a change of plan occurred. At present, certain *de facto* administrative functions are performed under some 22 product groups. Beyond that trade associations are presumably engaged in certain aspects of administration without official status.

From code to code, by small degrees of difference, the administration of complex codes moves from extreme decentralization over toward a situation where the administrative pattern is more uniform and the co-ordinative mechanism more fully developed. It is not to be supposed that these varieties of administrative situation derive merely from differences of effort or wisdom on the part of those responsible for code negotiations. They derive, also, as stated earlier, from different histories of industrial co-operation. Even more fundamentally they derive from the varying structure of different large areas of industry.

When supplementary codes and autonomous product divisions are taken into consideration, it will be seen that, with respect to trade practice provisions, the number of codes is really much greater than the official number of basic codes would indicate. The separatist tendency in industrial grouping was shown at an earlier point to be fully evident from the list of primary codes, but the scope of this tendency is only to be discovered by a census of the groups which maintain their separate subordinate identities.

Whether small groups are independent or are subordinate divisions under a basic code, the number of administrative agencies is unchanged and the executive acts to be performed are substantially the same. There does, however, exist a better prospect for the ultimate elimination of overlapping functions and agencies if groups are from the start associated even in a loose federation.

MIXED AND SPECIAL TYPES

Subordinate administrative agencies cannot be fully displayed under the separate headings of regional agencies and product groups. There are codes which combine these forms; codes which are subdivided on other lines, mainly trade and processing; and codes which combine trade and regional forms.

Mixed Types

The combinations of forms are too diverse to be displayed accurately in any brief space. They may, however, be advantageously illustrated.

The most numerous instances are the various combinations of regional and product groups. One of the most intricately organized industries is printing under the graphic arts code. This code is in effect a federation, covering 15 "industries" such as commercial relief printing, gravure printing, and trade type-setting. Each constituent industry has its own national code authority. These several divisions have subordinate organizations on a regional basis. The commercial relief-printing code authority, for example, has set up 17 zone agencies which in turn supervise about 120 regional code authorities, below which are local associations of printers. The constituent industries are divided into four groups, each of which has a national appeal board, and above these stands the topmost administrative authority, the national graphic arts co-ordinating committee. The national appeal boards may set up regional appeal boards. Under the dual organization of national and regional code authorities and national and regional appeal boards, direct administrative responsibility inheres in the former, while the latter are primarily judicial in function, adjudicating disputes which overlap the jurisdictions of the various constituent industries. Provision is further made for the amalgamation of two or more regional code authorities or regional appeal boards operating in the same area when considerations of convenience or economy dictate.

The administrative structure is further complicated by the existence of 17 so-called "national product groups," separate from the 15 national "industries," and covering the distribution of such products as greeting cards, tickets, commercial stationery, posters, and maps. Each of these has an "administrative agency," but is not subdivided regionally. Overlapping jurisdiction among these "product groups" or between any of them and any of the "industries" is provided for through the appeal boards upon which the product groups have special representation.

All members of the printing trades, whether under the "industry" or "product group" classification, are subject to the wage, hour, and trade practice provisions of the basic code, but each "industry" and "product group" is privileged to draw up supplementary trade practice rules for itself alone. Depending upon the scope of activities of a particular enterprise, with respect to the various aspects of its business, that enterprise may be subject to the authority of any number of "national code authorities" or "administrative agencies," or both, all under the basic graphic arts code. In effect, the graphic arts code is a federation of 15 national printing codes with regional subdivisions and 17 national product wholesaling codes without subdivisions, each largely autonomous, all possessing certain common provisions, and the whole complex welded together by an elaborate set of co-ordinating and judicial agencies.

No other code provides a similarly intricate interrelationship of product and regional administration and of administrative and judicial machinery. Others, however, are built on highly complex lines, in particular the lumber code. In external form its more than 40 divisions and subdivisions are product groups. In actual practice, however, a number of the associations which act as administrative agencies are in effect regional associations and serve as regional agencies for lumbering operations. On the other hand some of the fabricated product groups have set up regional subdivisions, as in the case of the railroad cross-tie division with its seven regional agencies.

As noted earlier, the furniture code has a regional set-up. But it also includes two autonomous product groups which operate entirely outside that set-up. Under the fabricated metal products code the electroplating supplementary code provides for the setting up of twelve district committees.

The wholesale or distributing code gives examples of mixed trade and regional groupings. One of the 24 commodity divisions, wholesale dry goods, further divides itself into seven commodity subdivisions and at the same time provides for regional agents. In several instances of which this is typical it is quite impossible to prognosticate the character of the relationships between the commodity subdivisions which are national in scope and the regional offices which are the creatures of the parent division. All that the code does is to adapt itself to the existence of separate groups and recognize the necessity of regional agencies. But the whole operative system of administering interrelated agencies can only be discovered by detailed examination of subsequent developments.

The important construction code is in some respects like the graphic arts code, in that it is a federation of groups of contractors, which severally maintain a high degree of autonomy and which must by the nature of their operations organize on a regional basis. The construction code is similar to the graphic arts code also in providing a special appeal mechanism for settlement of conflicts between its several groups.

The intention to organize regionally is to be found neither in the construction code nor in the various supplementary codes. In fact, however, such organization is going forward. For example, in the preliminary plans of the general contractors' division there is provision for 49 state agencies and 250 local agencies. Each of the contracting groups under the construction code is proceeding with regional organization and by February 1935 the number of agencies functioning was approaching 1,500. Should each group go forward with local organization, the number of official administrative agencies under this one code might reach 5,000 or more. This development lends weight to an observation made at an earlier point that it is impossible to tell from most codes what the administrative organization will eventually be.

Special Types

Scattered at large in one code or another are to be found provisions for special types of administrative subdivisions incapable of accurate classification. A few may be called "processing" subdivisions, such as the combers division under the wool textile code. A number may more or less accurately be called "trade" subdivisions. The outstanding case is the wholesale or distributing code, which provides for supplementary codes for each of some 24 commodity divisions. The retail trade code has supplementary codes for booksellers and retail custom fur manufacturing. The cotton textile code, like several other manufacturing codes, has a supplementary code to cover jobbing activities.

The classification of other cases is less clear. Thus

under the canvas goods code one division of the industry includes manufacture for resale by jobbers or for sale to industrial or governmental purchasers, the other includes made-to-measure canopies and awnings, and all "taking-down, storing, repairing . . . and renting" of various canvas products. In part the distinction is by products, in part by type of purchaser, in part by character of service. Under the loose-leaf notebook code, the two divisions are made up respectively of manufacturers who sell for resale by distributors and those who sell direct to industrial, commercial, and institutional users. The sewing machine code has a special division for rebuilders. The various subdivisions of the fur-dressing code and of the two miscellaneous junk and scavenging codes are mainly defined by product groups, but they relate to trade rather than industrial operations. The construction code, mentioned above, provides supplementary codes for each of several branches of contracting.

Most such miscellaneous instances of subordinate organization have no particular importance in themselves, with the exception of wholesaling and construction; but taken together they do add to one's understanding of what the problems of organizing for industrial self-government are. They add to the roll of organized groups, and expose the odd corners of group interest.

INTER-CODE CO-ORDINATING AGENCIES

An aspect of code administration which should be mentioned in the present connection is the provision, actual or prospective, of "co-ordinating committees," mainly to negotiate settlements of jurisdictional differences between code authorities. A few codes provide for specific committees for particular purposes. Thus the cotton garment and men's clothing codes by a joint amendment set up an inter-code committee to recommend and administer adjustment between the two industries with respect to boys' pants and men's cotton wash suits. The retail lumber and builders' supplies codes provide for joint interpretation committees to adjust the operations under the two codes to each other. In some other codes a general co-ordinating committee to act jointly with similar committees of other code authorities is mentioned. Again provision is made for temporary co-ordinating committees to act *ad hoc* with respect to particular questions arising between code authorities.

A number of the later codes provide for so-called "trade practice committees." These are narrower in function than general co-ordinating committees, being particularly designed to consider trade practices mutually affecting manufacturers and distributors. Their origin lay in the complaints of distributors that provisions of manufacturing codes improperly control their actions. The function of such committees, acting jointly, is to establish trade relationships mutually satisfactory to the interested groups.

Most codes do not provide for committees of these several kinds. In its general instructions to code authorities, however, the NRA indicates its intention that such committees, either permanent or special, be appointed and that they take the initiative in adjusting jurisdictional or other conflicts between codes. The expressed desire of NRA is that it be appealed to only as a court of last resort in such disputes. The analysis of code groups which has been made makes it unnecessary to emphasize how many questions there are to fill the agenda of such committees.

It is not possible to say how widely the method is being used. But up to the present there is extensive evidence with respect to the widespread failure to follow the method. Only much more experience than is now available can permit any informed judgment as to whether the method itself is appropriate.

CONCLUSION

Taken singly, the administrative structure of any one code is not difficult to impress upon the mind, nor is the reason for its form usually difficult to comprehend. The fundamental administrative problem in each case is that of adjustment to the peculiar characteristics of the particular industry or trade. The more elaborate structures follow the elaborate pattern of the producing and marketing system to which the codes apply. Quite clearly if codes are to be fully administered, the agencies appropriate thereto must be adjusted to the varying characteristics of the business situations covered. In given instances the system of administration for a code more often seems essentially too simple to cope with the problems involved, rather than the contrary.

When, however, an over-all view of the system of agencies created under the NRA is taken, considerations of a different character arise. The attempt to comprehend the whole system is somewhat bewildering. For any ordinary observer the effort is not worth making. But it has to be remembered that this aggregate of agencies constitutes a vast extension of the framework of government. As such it has to be kept under administrative supervision by officials of the government. It therefore becomes an appropriate subject of inquiry whether the system as such lends itself to satisfactory inclusion within the administrative scheme of government.

The present chapter has the importance merely of a map of the country of code administration. Whether or not the code system can be properly administered is not something that can be judged from such a map. It is in the operating processes that the crucial evidence is to be found. The next two chapters will be devoted to an analysis of the evidence, the first dealing with the code agencies themselves, the second with the relationship of the NRA to the administration of code provisions.

CHAPTER VIII

CODE ADMINISTRATION

The meaning of "code administration" is summarized by the NRA as follows:

There are two aspects to code administration; one, planning and progress, and two, compliance.

The term "normal code administration" is intended to include such functions as:

(a) Economic planning and research for the Industry.
(b) Reports and recommendations of conditions in the industry.
(c) Collection of statistical data, preparation of cost accounting methods, etc.

The term "administration for compliance" is intended to include:

(a) The instruction and education of those subject to the code as to their responsibilities thereunder so as to anticipate and avoid complaints of non-compliance.
(b) The adjustment of complaints of non-compliance by education, fair findings of facts, and the pressure of opinion within the industry.
(c) The adjustment of complaints by arbitration, conciliation and mediation.
(d) The rendition of reports to the enforcement agencies of government in those cases where all other means have failed.[1]

With respect to "normal code administration" the responsibility of the NRA is to see that a code authority faithfully fulfills the administrative duties imposed upon it by the code and does not abuse its powers. With respect to "administration for compliance" the same statement may be made. But to it must be added the fact that the

---

[1] *NRA Release No. 1847*, Nov. 22, 1933.

NRA takes a special responsibility for effecting compliance, being organized to carry on trade practice compliance activities before code authorities are prepared to engage in compliance activities or at whatever point the code authorities' efforts are ineffective or abortive, and to exercise special supervision over compliance with labor provisions. The whole organization of the NRA is built on the supposition that it *will not* have to perform any of the functions of "normal administration" and *will* have to perform extensive compliance functions.

GENERAL FEATURES OF CODE ADMINISTRATION

The subdivision of duties within a code authority customarily takes two forms: first, the various committees of the code authority itself, and second, the departmentalization of the employed staff. The second of these is much affected by the extent to which a code authority organizes its separate staff or alternately delegates its functions to trade associations or professional management firms. Where code authorities act wholly for themselves, an examination of their organization will give a fairly accurate picture of the scope of their activities. Where they delegate power, however, such information can only be secured by inquiring into the activities pursued in behalf of code authorities by the agencies utilized.

The twofold definition of code authority functions, compliance and normal administration, is the general guide to the internal committee and office organization. In the early history of most code authorities, however, the principal activities were neither, but rather those of organizing for the performance of functions. Very commonly this stage lasted for months and in a sense it constitutes a continuing sphere of action since few code authorities are fully implemented to perform the functions which their codes impose upon them.

Compliance

Compliance activities fall into the two general categories of trade practice compliance and labor compliance, for each of which appropriate machinery is supposed to be set up. The formal NRA requirement with respect to trade practice complaints is the setting up by the code authority of a trade practice complaints committee and of a procedure for the adjustment of charges of violation of trade practice provisions. In practice this formal requirement leads to the most diverse forms of office and field organization. The organization must be such as is appropriate to the character of the tasks. The varying difficulty of effecting compliance with trade practice provisions may be envisaged from the varying characteristics of different trades and industries. In the larger and widely diffused industries the necessity for a large corps of agents is apparent. The lumber code authority has about 200 field agents. An exaggerated instance was the provision in the proposed budget of a single division of the retail solid fuel industry for 52 inspectors. Under some codes the formal requirement of a trade practice complaints plan covers an elaborate hierarchy of investigatory and adjustment agencies and personnel, while under other codes the code authority itself performs such simple routine functions as are called for. Where regional organizations exist, they are the outposts. Where supplementary codes or autonomous divisions exist, each requires its appropriate agencies.

The obligation of organization for labor compliance is somewhat less mandatory. Complaints of violation of labor provisions may arise either from other members of the industry or from workers. In the former case it is permitted to handle them through the same procedures as those for trade practice complaints. In all cases of complaints from workers, however, the required agency is a joint committee composed equally of code authority and labor representatives. Since joint action is required, the obligation to organize cannot be placed solely or directly on code authorities, and the efforts to create joint agencies face a variety of obstacles arising out of employer-employee relationships in the several industries. In some industries code authorities are averse to the idea and have attempted no organization, one reason among others being that they do not wish to create friction with their members by disciplining them on labor matters. They prefer to let the government do this. In the absence of voluntary agencies in most industries the labor compliance function rests largely on the regional agents of the NRA. There are industries in which labor compliance is considered the most important feature of code administration which still do not utilize the joint committee plan. Complaints from workers are left to NRA agencies, but the code authority itself actively seeks and disciplines violators. The cotton garment code authority is of this sort, employing a considerable field and office force in its compliance division.

With respect to either trade practice or labor violations, it is not to be supposed that the formal organizations and procedures prescribed by NRA give a realistic view of the way in which compliance activities are actually carried on. In industries where code authorities pursue such activities at all assiduously, they devise such means as they think appropriate to the problem, both for uncovering violations and for disciplining violators. The disciplinary means are perhaps as often as not informal persuasion and coercion of a sort not to be discovered on any organization chart or in any manual of procedures.

Other Administrative Duties

The miscellaneous functions of code authorities may be classified as preliminary, special, and continuing. The preliminary functions are those of organizing for the performance of other functions. In part this consists of satisfying certain requirements of NRA. Thus it has been necessary, with a few exceptions, for code authorities to submit by-laws, budgets, and trade practice compliance plans to NRA for approval. Where accounting and cost-finding systems are authorized or required by the code, these have to be devised and submitted for NRA approval. Where administrative subdivisions are to be set up, elections frequently have to be held, and the procedure and result approved by NRA. Where inter-code jurisdictional conflicts occur, negotiations between code authorities and between them and NRA are required. All sorts of problems of implementation arise, such as setting up of office and field staffs, taking a census of the industry, setting up reporting systems, and arranging the delegation of powers to trade associations or other agencies. Preliminary interpretations of code provisions must be sought from NRA, and an intensive campaign of education carried on within the industry. Except for the three items of by-laws, budgets, and compliance plans, there is no uniformity in the character of these initial obligations, because of the varying provisions of the codes and the varying structure of the several industries. Some code authorities in well-organized and concentrated industries have rapidly prepared themselves for the continuing duties, but the much more widespread experience has been that the phase of organization has been extended into many months of harassing preliminaries.

The special duties of code authorities arise in part from

certain demands of the NRA for information not available during code negotiations. Thus the cotton garment code authority was required to make a series of special studies, such as the relation of North-South wage differentials to costs of living and the effect of the 40-hour week on employment. Special studies in various industries cover such topics as productive capacity, hazardous occupations, wage differentials, imports, and other topics designed to throw light on the operation of the code or to exhibit the problems of the industry more clearly. Other special investigations are provided for in codes at the instance of the industries involved. For example, in many industries there is the desire for more or less elaborate marketing plans which were not permitted to get into codes, but which code authorities are authorized to prepare and submit for later consideration.

These special duties merge into the continuing functions in the sense that every code authority is charged in a general way with the duty of studying the operation of the code and proposing modifications. The general function is whatever may be implied by the phrase "industry planning." There is, however, a wide range of specific continuing duties.

What code authorities are obligated to administer are the specific terms of particular codes. It is therefore difficult to speak in a general way about code administration. The problems presented to each code authority are in greater or lesser degree unique. The same provisions in different codes may be accompanied by entirely unlike administrative problems. Thus to devise and secure adherence to a system of uniform accounting may be relatively simple in one industry and entirely impossible in another. The range of administrative agenda differs from code to code. A few of the simplest codes require little more than the maintenance of certain wage and hour provisions and the reporting of statistics, while others require administration of systems of accounting, price reporting, price fixing, production control, and so on, and necessitate the most intensive fact-finding studies.

The same general functions call for varying elaborateness of organization. For example, in some industries statistical reporting requires a large and highly trained staff, and in others very little work or skill. In some cases the code authority has organized its own technical staff, in others delegated such work to a trade association, and in others employed the services of an outside agency. Similarly, no general statements are possible with respect to the character of the internal organization for purposes of supervising the operation of accounting systems, operating price-reporting systems, inventing cost formulas, educating the members of the industries in their interests and duties, and so on. It can, however, be seen that if a code authority in an important industry is organized for the full performance of its functions, the administrative staff must contain a number of expertly trained executives and staffs of considerable size. In declining scale of importance the organizations trail off at the other end to petty codes in the small office of some professional trade association manager.

THE MEMBERSHIP OF CODE AUTHORITIES

The NRA has followed the principle that a code authority shall consist of members properly representative of the underlying business interests in the industry, except in a small minority of cases where labor is also represented. To secure this result the NRA has in a majority of instances allocated controlling power to trade associations, usually, however, providing for an elected non-association minority. In a smaller number of instances the code authority is constituted mainly by elections. To the voting members thus selected is added one or more administration members appointed by the NRA.

Code Authorities and Trade Associations

It was at the start considered axiomatic at the NRA that agencies for code administration should be closely related to, if not identical with, voluntary trade association organizations. Any careful thought upon the relationship between trade associations and code authorities was, however, very belated. Initially it would appear that the various strong associations which applied for early codes were thought of as being in themselves the appropriate administrative agencies. As the code-making process continued, it became increasingly clear that in a large majority of instances no sufficiently representative and reputable association existed to which could be exclusively delegated the function of administering a body of law. It therefore became necessary to define the functions of code authorities and to set them up as something other than the creatures or *alter egos* of trade associations. Associations were, it is true, in a majority of instances given an important representation on such bodies. But in only about one code out of four is the membership of a code authority exclusively dictated by a trade association.

The failure of associations and code authorities to have quite the same underlying constituency has created some difficulties in defining the appropriate range of activities of each. For example, many associations promoted statistical reporting services and had expert accounting staffs for the education of their membership in uniform accounting procedure. They also engaged in trade promotion activities, political lobbying, and technical research.

Statistical service is a necessary adjunct of code administration, while trade promotion is distinctly outside the appropriate sphere of code authority action. In many instances code authorities have merely utilized and paid for the technical services of trade associations. There has, however been a distinct tendency for them to set up their own agencies, in some cases taking over and developing an existing trade association department. This tendency of course narrows the scope of trade association action, and by making the code authority the primary representative agency of the industry is thought to threaten the existence of many trade associations. It is feared that the functions still performed by the associations will not be sufficiently important to the industry to attract a large voluntary dues-paying membership.

In some instances there is the opposite fear that the code authority, by being largely the creature of an association, will not be adequately representative of the industry. This situation has disruptive possibilities, particularly in industries where there has existed a strong non-association or anti-association element.

From the start the practice developed among some code authorities and trade associations of using the code as a means of "forcing" the growth of membership in associations. In some instances this amounted to nothing more than attempting to persuade members of the industry that full benefits under the code were only attainable if they were members of the correlative trade association. Various degrees of misrepresentation developed. This sometimes arose out of the misapprehensions of association officials or code authority members. But the latter sometimes took advantage of the ignorance and mental confusion of members of the industry. Misrepresentation reached the point of suggesting, if not stating, that members of the industry were required to join the association if they wished to participate in benefits under the code. The abuses in a considerable degree were associated with regional associations and subordinate code agencies rather than with national associations or code authorities. From scanty information one cannot estimate the extent of such practices, nor generalize much about the occasion for them. They appear, however, to have developed particularly in industries where the members were of a type to be ill informed, and in connection with associations relatively weak numerically and in need of funds, or those of chronic ill repute. The sporadic appearance of such manifestations is partly to be explained only in terms of the varying standards of ethical practice followed by trade association officials.

Quite apart from any abuse of power, the working out of a satisfactory *modus vivendi* between associations and code authorities is commonly attended by difficulties, involving allocation of functions and personnel, methods of financing, distribution of expenses, and so on. During the early months of a large number of codes problems of this sort were very confusing to all persons involved, including officials of the NRA who had not themselves clearly foreseen their character. The trade association division which was set up within NRA primarily to deal with such questions was largely abortive, since the problems were at the start of a detailed sort which were difficult to generalize. The perplexing problems of organizing and defining the functions of code authorities continued to be on the hands of deputy administrators. The question of trade association functions sank into the background, and only gradually as code authorities found their feet were they able to give careful scrutiny to the problems of mutual adjustment. The process of clarification was hastened by the code authority budget rules which were promulgated in the spring of 1934. Since each code authority had to submit a budget for approval by NRA it had in the first instance to define the intended scope of its activities. This in turh compelled NRA to attempt some clarification of its thinking upon what code authorities could and could not do.

There still exists, however, no uniformity concerning the manner of adjustment of functions. Some associations have curtailed their activities to the scope of code authority functions and the two have become in effect identical bodies. Some code authorities on the other hand maintain only skeleton organizations and farm out their functions to associations for a fee. Many code authorities hire the services of the same professional management concerns which have previously acted for the associations. Such a concern is then acting for an association in certain capacities and for the correlative code authority in other capacities. The various types of adjustment have been too numerous to describe in any general way. The problem is in many instances a continuing one, with the ultimate outcome undiscernible. As in so many other matters concerning NRA, the uncertainties about the permanence of NRA prevent a solution. Associations which otherwise might willingly change their scope in adjustment to the code authority face the possibility that by doing so they may in another year find the code authority gone, their own organizations disrupted, and the industry left in a highly disorganized state. It is therefore not to be expected that definitive adjustments will be made in many industries until the future of the NRA is made definitive.

The Basis of Representation

The only problem of code authority personnel with which the NRA has concerned itself is that of securing a membership properly representative of the *business* elements in the industry. The problems in connection therewith are on the whole analogous to those which were discussed earlier in connection with the representative character of the committees applying for codes. Very few industries, as defined in codes, are so homogeneous that factional interests are not present. On code authorities the non-association minority is likely to represent such an interest. Under the more comprehensive codes, the factional interests are commonly more numerous. In a sense the principle of code authority membership is that representation should be given to each element of the industry or trade which merits recognition. The actual membership under most codes is, however, a very rough approximation to this ideal. Associations are taken as units, and no recognition given to the existence of factions within associations. When, therefore, the officials of an association are the dominant element, as they are under a large majority of codes, the principle of control deviates somewhat from the political principle of majority rule, being rather that of a majority of a majority, and in some instances a majority of a minority. Non-association minorities also are commonly accepted as units, without regard to the disparate elements therein. And where code authorities are elected, it is commonly by the industry at large, establishing majority rule regardless of factions and possibly without representation of minorities.

Under the more intricate codes, well-defined interest groups are usually recognized. Thus chain stores and mail-order houses have representation on the retail trade code authority. The several associations representing product groups under the cotton garment code are each represented. But in such instances representation commonly goes no further than recognition of a number of associations.

The basis of representation is made more difficult to define by reason of having to consider both the number of members of an industry and their respective contributions to its output. Thus, quite typically, an association will include a minority of the members of an industry, but will account for a majority of the value product. There are such extreme instances as an association with 10 per cent of the membership and 90 per cent of the output of an industry. In the example just mentioned, the association was made the sole authority for one division of the lumber code. Where the size of a minority of a code authority was to be determined, the tendency has been to give primary weight to dollar volume. On the other hand, some electoral plans have been devised which deviate strongly toward greater recognition of the democratic principle. Concerning problems of devising and supervising electoral procedures no mention need be made. The plans appear to have worked out with less friction and dissatisfaction than might have been anticipated. All such problems occur within the existing framework, based on the principle of sole representation of business interests.

This principle has not gone unchallenged, and the basic challenge has derived from certain concepts fostered by the NRA itself. In the making of codes the three advisory boards were conceived to represent "pressure groups." The deputy administrators served in a dual role, as protectors of basic NRA policies and as umpires in a conflict of interests, and on the whole more the latter than the former. A code is thought of as a compromise product, adjusting the interest of the various parties at interest. Out of the same line of thought derives the proposal to place labor members and consumer members on code authorities. The idea of pressure groups is carried from the field of code making to that of code administration. Given even minority representation it is conceived that the interests of these groups could be kept continuously in sight and the danger that codes become merely collusive agencies of profit seeking minimized.

The official view of the functions of pressure groups has not, however, gone so far, and with a few exceptions no provision has been made for any group representation on code authorities other than that of the business interests involved. The administration member, backed by the NRA organization, has been clothed with all the responsibilities of protecting the public interest against abuses of power by the code authority. The few instances of labor representation derive from labor's bargaining power, and not from any policy of the NRA.

The theory of pressure groups has impregnated the administrative structure to the degree that the administration members of each code authority *are supposed* to have a labor adviser and a consumers' adviser, with access to all code authority records and the right to be heard at code authority meetings. This set-up, first promulgated in January 1934 and repeated in official pronouncements from time to time, has never been made effective. Such proposals as the Consumers' Advisory Board has made to put it into effect have been largely ignored or vetoed. The Labor Advisory Board has never pressed for the appointment of labor advisers. It takes the view that labor interests should be directly represented on code authorities and refuses to compromise that principle by accepting what it regards as an evasive half-recognition of labor's interest in the administration of codes. There is evidence that the responsible officials of NRA, during the tenure of General Johnson at least, were actively opposed to the appointment of such advisers, and no evidence that any one outside the Consumers' Advisory Board had the slightest interest in pressing the matter to effective completion. This aspect of code administration may therefore be set down as a matter of administrative dead wood or window dressing.

The issue is really much more fundamental than its casual treatment by the NRA might indicate. Its character is sharply seen in the more extreme proposal that code authorities be composed equally of representatives of business interests, labor, and consumers, with a public chairman. This proposal sharply challenges the conception of "industrial self-government" which the present form of code authority supports. It presents the view that if industry is to be organized collectively, it must be defined as including all the groups at interest, and not merely the single group concerned with making a pecuniary gain from industrial operations. There is great force in this contention. It recognizes what is true, that under the aggregate terms of codes as they now exist there resides a considerable power to restrict the productivity of the economic system to the detriment of the population dependent thereon in their roles both as workers and consumers, so long as such powers exist. It is very difficult to defend the present basis of representation in the hands of the only persons to whose interest it may be to restrict productive activity. This is even more true if public officials, as has tended to be the case, condone or favor such action.

The issue is thus seen to be twofold in character. One

question is whether powers which could be used to produce "contrived scarcity," detrimentally to the public interest, should be permitted to exist. The other is, given the existence of such powers, under what form of administration the potentially detrimental consequences can be prevented. The particular proposal under discussion— a tripartate agency composed equally of labor, industry, and consumer representatives—is directed to the second of these questions. What is implied is that, in collective control of industries, other principles than those of business enterprise must be controlling. The threat to the powers of the business community thus implied is so great that it might easily prefer to scuttle the ship of formal self-government rather than divide authority on the bridge.

In the form proposed this threat is not serious nor imminent. It arises in another form, however, in connection with the character of the supervision to be exercised by the NRA over code authorities, discussed in Chapter IX. If powers such as the codes create are continued, there is every reason to suppose that the character of the governing bodies will remain the subject of continuing agitation.

THE ORGANIZATION AND IMPLEMENTATION OF CODE AUTHORITIES

Late in the autumn of 1933, after a considerable number of codes had been approved, it became apparent within the NRA that the setting up of a fully qualified code authority would in many cases not be easily accomplished. The process of organizing code authorities went forward at a slow rate, and the many perplexities and conflicts of the industries involved were thrown back into the laps of the deputy administrators responsible for the codes at the NRA. The NRA was not well organized for such problems, since the administrative organization was still built mainly on the principle of expediting proposed codes rather than perfecting the administration of approved codes. The early procedure for facilitating effective organization was haphazard, differing from deputy to deputy, and division to division.

Effecting an Organization

Belatedly recognizing the magnitude of the problem of code authority organization, the NRA took halting steps toward doing something about it.[2] During early 1934 counsels within the NRA were so divided upon the proper relationships of the NRA to code authority activities that very slow progress was made even in drawing up instructions for code authorities. At one extreme were those who felt that code authorities should be agencies of a real "industrial self-government" almost independent of governmental oversight; at the other extreme were those favoring extensive governmental oversight and regulation. Special controversies existed with respect to the administration of labor relationships, the extent of required statistical reporting, and a variety of other topics. All this was to the detriment of a clear-cut statement of policy and procedure. The consequence was the omission from early instructions of all reference to certain vital aspects of code administration.

It was not until after the code authority conference in March 1934, which dramatized the necessity, that any serious attention was given to problems of code administration. Divisional administrators were then given staff assistants for code authority organization. Also, a separate personnel of administration members of code au-

---

[2] The history of the changes in NRA organization for facilitating code administration is outlined in Chap. IV.

thorities, appointed more or less *en masse,* were expected
to assist in perfecting organization under the several
codes, but turned out to be of relatively minor aid.[3]
Though these steps somewhat facilitated the progress of
organization, detailed assistance to code authorities in
effecting an organization remained a function of the
deputy administrators. While some of them were in a
position to turn their attention primarily to such problems, many of these officials were so immersed in code
making until summer that their attention to code authority problems was relatively secondary and cursory.

The situation with respect to code authority organization may be stated in general terms as one in which the
NRA progressively brought more pressure on code
groups to hasten their organization, and progressively
fitted itself to give more aid and guidance to the process;
but also one in which the progress of code authority organization was primarily dependent upon the initiative
of the code groups. The NRA seems to have intended
to rely on private initiative, and only started to concern
itself actively in the matter as experience disclosed the
difficulties of many in getting organized. On this account
it was always much in arrears in the aid and counsel it
was prepared to give. The delinquency of the NRA
should not be overstressed, since the major difficulties
were those inherent in the codes and in the industries to
which they applied. More effective NRA aid could have
reduced the initial confusion, but perhaps not have done
much more. This view is confirmed by the fact that organizational difficulties persisted under many codes even
after the NRA had fitted itself to give more active guidance. Of a somewhat contrary sort, however, is the fact

[3] For full discussion of administration members of code authorities see
Chap. IX.

that, as the NRA gave increasing attention to the matter, it began to prescribe stricter requirements and more elaborate procedures for authenticating code authorities which, however salutary, slowed down the process of organization.

The difficulties were not serious in the case of code authorities consisting of well-established trade associations. In such instances the executive committee of the association could start to function promptly as the code authority, with a well-trained trade association official as the principal executive officer. These simple cases were relatively few. Nevertheless, a number of others presented no great difficulty. In industries having responsible associations the election of non-association minorities could proceed with promptness and little friction where the method of election was clearly set forth in the code.

Other types of situations, however, presented difficulties or delays of different degrees of magnitude. In some cases, the code did not provide in detail for the method of electing minority members but required that the code committee devise a satisfactory plan and have it approved by the Administrator. In other cases friction existed between association and non-association members over points not clearly defined in the code. In some cases where the electoral procedure depended upon the temporary functioning of the original code committee, factional quarrels impeded progress. Some associations were jerry-built, hastily devised organizations thrown together for the purpose of getting a code and ill prepared for responsible administrative functions. A few were little more than the personal vehicles of promoters who had assembled the membership for the purpose of getting a code under which the promoter anticipated fees or a well-paid executive position. A number of codes pro-

vided no procedure whatever for selecting a code authority. This situation arose particularly under codes of
hitherto unorganized or ill-organized industries, or of
industries with rival organizations, or in a variety of
situations in which industries were ill prepared for undertaking the responsibilities of "self-government."

These difficulties were overcome with varying facility,
except in a troublesome residue of cases where they have
never been resolved. Typically, a period of months
elapsed after the approval of a code before it had a properly authenticated administrative body. Experience is
gradually exposing to view a number of codes under
which it seems improbable that effective organization can
ever be accomplished.

Implementation of Code Authorities

Effecting an organization of a code authority which
will be recognized as official by the NRA is merely the
first phase of the problem. Before such bodies can operate they have to provide implementation of their functions, and it is in this second phase that the more serious
difficulties arise.

Preliminary requirements. At an earlier point (page
203) certain formal preliminary steps required by NRA
were set forth. Within the NRA there exists a formal
routine procedure covering each of these matters. NRA
approval or disapproval is commonly a mere ratification
of actions taken by some subordinate official in the course
of routine procedure. With respect to such matters each
code authority approaches the NRA through the avenue
of the assistant deputy or deputy administrator assigned
to the particular code. The latter initiates the routine
which again ends with him, as he transmits the official
NRA action back to the code authority. In more informal

ways the various deputies may be in relatively close contact with code authorities, the deputy for an industry being the person at NRA to whom the members of a code authority naturally turn for consultation on questions of organization and procedure.

The other informal ways in which code authorities, or individual members, officials, or counsel, contact the NRA are not capable of generalized description. On matters of importance they may go past the deputy straight to a divisional administrator for preliminary consultation. They may consult members of the Legal Division or discuss labor questions with officials of the Labor Advisory Board. They may adopt backstairs methods to reach the higher administrative officials. In large part this informal procedure has been used for expeditiously settling special problems of organization, inter-code frictions, and the like, often upon the advice or with the intervention of the deputies. Naturally it is subject to some abuse based upon personal friendship and "pull," but not to any degree that can be regarded as "abnormal" or notably scandalous. It does, however, occasion departures from strict rules of administrative priority and impartiality.

From the side of code authorities comes continuous pressure for greater freedom of action. Having undertaken the responsibilities of code administration they tend almost universally to take the view that the NRA should adopt a procedure of relatively passive supervision. Its principal function is commonly thought of as a supplementary policing agency to assist them in driving recalcitrants into line. Perhaps the most annoying thing to them about codes and administrative orders is the number of things that can only be done "with the approval of the Administrator." This situation imposes upon them the necessity of creeping to Washington hat in hand, and subjects them to long-continued administrative delays within NRA. In practice it places great powers within the hands of junior officials of the NRA. It is the primary source of the complaints against "bureaucracy." For purposes of freeing their hands and permitting dispatch there appears to be some consensus among code authorities that codes and administrative orders should largely be freed of the phrase "subject to the approval of the Administrator," substituting therefore some such phrase as "unless disapproved by the Administrator within ____ days."

The implied remedies which accompany charges of administrative delay are of a highly questionable sort. It is implied that NRA should waive supervision in the interests of speedy code authority organization and action. It is further implied that the NRA should accept the codes as written and waive further questions of principle in the matter of implementation. This pressure for a free hand is very heavy, but not easily defensible. One reason is that, with exceptions, code authorities are not at the outset agencies to be relied upon as proper public agencies for administering a body of law. The other reason is that the codes are such defective documents, so precipitately drawn, that extremely important matters of principle and policy are at stake in the early stages of implementation. Given this situation, supervision is essential, though by more definite policy decisions and improved internal organization at NRA delays might be made less serious.

Budgets. For many code authorities, the delay in approval of budgets was initially the most serious of all. Not being financed, they were unable to proceed to action. The interim period in which no effective code administration existed was lengthened. In its first phase the budget problem arose out of the multiple coverage of codes. Code authorities set about billing assessments to all known firms subject to the code. Business men received demands or requests for payment from unexpected sources and in undue multiplicity, much to their surprise and displeasure. The NRA order[4] that a firm was tentatively to be assessed only by the code authority representing its principal line of business.cared for the problem in part. On the other hand it created new ones. Some code authorities, particularly for small industries, were thereby made unable to finance their activities. The routine of applications for exemptions from the order then kept many code authorities long in doubt concerning the scope of their collecting power.

The second phase of the problem was the requirement that no assessments could be levied until a budget had been approved by NRA. The reason for this was partly legal, arising out of the very uncertain legal status of compulsory assessments. The Legal Division of NRA only with difficulty found a procedure which it was prepared to defend in court. The other reason was the unwillingness of NRA to leave the basis of assessment and the amount and direction of expenditures to the complete discretion of code authorities whose competency, and in some cases honesty, it had reason to distrust.

The sudden promulgation of the assessment policy created a convergence of budgets upon NRA, and it spent the spring and summer of 1934 digging itself out from under the heap. After the preliminary rush it has still remained impossible to work out satisfactory budget plans for a large number of code authorities. As late as March 2, 1935 only 298 budgets had been approved

[4] Administrative Order No. X-36, May 26, 1934.

under the 550 basic codes then existing, and only 89 under the 223 supplementary and joint codes. Some of the remainder were operating on a voluntary assessment plan, but a good many were very slightly operative for lack of funds.

These administrative features make up only part of the budget problem. The other is relative to the ability of a code authority to collect funds from its underlying constituency. For a good many groups, especially those previously having well-organized trade associations, this has been a very minor problem. They financed themselves voluntarily over the period of administrative delay, and they have a constituency able and willing to stand the expense. Their problem is confined to making collections from a recalcitrant minority, without prejudice to their ability to engage in administrative action. Some avoid even this necessity by retaining a system of voluntary payment.

Under a great number of codes, however, there exist all degrees of unwillingness or inability of the constituency to pay, arriving finally at that residue of code authorities which are unable to collect enough money even to effect an operating organization. Several groups of starving code authorities may be roughly distinguished. There are the very small industrial codes for which adequate organization would require a prohibitive rate of assessment. There are the smaller codes which require regional and local organization, as in the case of the more petty retail codes. There are the codes under which members have lost hope of attaining their objectives. And, somewhat overlapping the others, there are the codes with constituencies essentially unamenable to organization and collective action.

One of the critical problems facing NRA is that of

adjusting code administration to the financial realities. There are a considerable number of codes concerning which nothing can be done except to liquidate them. Concerning many of the remainder it is questionable whether the money they can raise is sufficient to support even a moderately effective administration of the provisions of the code. Above these there may be said to exist a general state of relative poverty. Contrary to common opinion even the largest budgets are commonly inadequate. The large budgets are mainly for codes requiring numerous local agencies, most of which are still financed on a basis of slow starvation.

The budget problem runs head-on into questions both of political expediency and of economic policy. On the side of expediency the question is how severely the NRA will dismantle whole codes or parts of codes to bring nominal administrative duties into line with bill-paying capacity. The problem merges at points into the general compliance problem. To make the nominal NRA structure close to the real appears to be not only a proper immediate objective, but a higher form of expediency than temporary but ultimately disastrous face-saving. Economic policy is involved since ability to collect assessments is partly associated with the existence in codes of provisions favored by industries, especially price-control devices, which are out of line with present NRA policies. It remains to be seen how far code administration can be financed if a serious effort is made to put such policies into effect through compulsory code revision.

Special code provisions. The several codes require implementation appropriate to their particular context. Without attempting to display the scope of the problem, one may note a few ubiquitous types of provision which require special implementation.

About 70 per cent of the codes make some provision, mandatory or permissive, for *uniform systems of cost finding,* usually linked with a rule against selling below cost. For a variety of reasons little progress has been made toward installing such systems.[5] The present situation is that only about 6 per cent of the codes providing for cost protection have formally authorized systems, that almost none of these have operative systems, that a large portion of the code authorities have little hope of devising administrable systems, and that the higher officials of NRA entertain doubts both on the score of feasibility and of public policy. Since these provisions were the cornerstone of the hopes of a large number of applicant groups, a revised scope for NRA is clearly ordained by the breakdown in this field. The alternatives are a more actively competitive situation or a higher degree of discretionary administrative control over prices.

More than half the codes provide for some system of *open-price reporting.* No statistics are available to indicate the extent to which they are operative. In the field of relatively standardized commodities, many such systems have been established. In the fields of lesser standardization, however, not only are the technical difficulties greater but the resistance to reporting is frequently severe. This is especially the case where code provisions do not adequately safeguard confidential information. During code making there was a stampede to include price reporting with little reference to feasibility. Current experience is now sorting out both the spheres to which it is inherently inapplicable and the administrative methods which cannot be successfully used.

Statistical reporting along lines laid down by the NRA is an obligation under every code. The NRA has, how-

[5] For discussion of this subject see Chap. XXIII.

ever, never promulgated a general scheme of statistical reporting for public purposes. Most code authorities are also authorized to call for statistical data as a necessary adjunct to their function of "industry planning." Under a few codes highly competent statistical departments are operating and the members of the industry are reporting rather fully on payrolls, production, and so forth. But on the whole statistical reporting under codes is in a highly rudimentary stage.

A serious weakness with much of the statistical work to date is that it has been directed toward proving something to the NRA. Thus the cotton garment code authority wished to prove that the 40-hour week had increased employment. The cotton textile code authority wished to prove that limitation of machine hours did not threaten a scarcity of textile products. So long as code authority statistical departments are charged with supporting arguments to be made to the NRA, they cannot fulfill their proper function, which is to present an unbiased account of the state and trends of the business situation. Since adequate trade statistics are the basis and *sine qua non* of intelligent collective action in industry, the larger functions of code authorities cannot be developed without extensive implementation in this field. Whether, given a good statistical service, code administration will operate to the public interest must be judged on other grounds. Without it the prospects of any useful form of industry planning are very dim.

Experience with the three types of provisions mentioned will sufficiently illustrate the fact that even fully authenticated code authorities are only partially, and in some cases slightly, prepared to perform the administrative duties with which they are charged by the codes.

Organization of subordinate agencies. Given the existing codes, it is quite clear that the administrative organization has to be adapted to the structure of the industries as defined therein. For effective administration the code authority must be organized for contact with the activities of the individual enterprises subject to the code. There are many codes for which this is impossible except through subordinate agencies for regions or groups. The proliferation of such agencies by the thousand is therefore not an aberration, but a necessity of code administration. The essential correctness of proceeding to the extensive delegation of authority to minor agencies cannot be called into question. Under those codes which call for regional or divisional agencies, the first primary responsibility of the national code authority is that of seeing that the subordinate agencies are properly organized. Where subordinate bodies are necessarily the active administrative agencies, code administration can be said to have actively begun only where they are on an operative basis.

All codes requiring *local administration* were relatively slow in achieving a full administrative structure. Experience, however, was very mixed. A few such as retail trade, retail solid fuel, retail and wholesale food and groceries, and commercial relief printing (a division of the graphic arts code) energetically pushed their local organization and were rather fully organized by the summer of 1934, though even they have a good deal of mere paper organization. Others have lagged, and some have made approximately no progress. One reason for relative failure is the budget problem, already mentioned. The other is the peculiar difficulties of local organization in some trades and industries, the trucking industry being a peculiarly striking example. To what extent local organization is lacking or inoperative in such miscellaneous industries as the various contracting divisions of the construction code, the retail monument code, the baking code, and so on, there is no way of knowing, except by detailed examination of developments under each type. In a few instances, the attempt to organize locally has been given up. And in the service trades, especially those deprived of their trade practice provisions, local organization is pretty much at a standstill.

The immediate prospects of a number of codes are linked with their inability to effect or finance regional organization. On strictly administrative grounds, this ranks as one of the most troublesome problems now facing the NRA.

Detailed data concerning the progress of organizing *divisional agencies* is nowhere available. Relatively complete organization can be reported under a number of important codes such as lumber, paper, and others where strong underlying trade associations were prepared to promote organization. Elsewhere, no estimate can be given of the extent of organization, nor any opinion expressed concerning the prospects of effective organization. Some evidence, however, exists that many subordinate groups are in the same situation as some of the independent code groups, hampered by problems of financing and internal division, or otherwise deterred from effecting an organization.

One difficulty in ascertaining the state of organization arises from the diverse ways in which subordinate administration can be carried on. Under a single basic code it is possible that at a given time some divisions may have supplementary code authorities; some may have divisional committees; some may have unofficial administration by trade associations; and some may have no administrative agency. Moreover, some of the agencies may act for themselves and others may delegate their functions to outside agencies.

Any general picture of subordinate organization could only be drawn up within NRA and this has not yet been done. Oddly enough, there was little official interest at NRA in assembling such administrative information until late in 1934. There has been a steady stream of it into the Control Section of NRA, due to the requirement that certain agencies be approved by the Administrator as to methods of selection and personnel. Most subordinate agencies do not, however, require such approval. These are also supposed to be reported, but the reporting has always been in arrears and no serious effort has been made to digest what is reported. Much undigested information has been lying in the files, casual in character and conforming to no system of administrative reporting. By reason of this deficiency the law of the land has in some degree been administered by persons and agencies, and at places, entirely unknown to any public official. Higher officials of the NRA have had no means of surveying the complicated structure of administrative agencies which is arising. They have not known the extent to which the contemplated structure is or is not in existence. These are of course reparable deficiencies. A good deal of progress has been made in digesting information on regional organization, and the Recovery Board has evinced an interest in the assembling of other information. Until recently, however, this has been perhaps the worst example of the defective informational service within the NRA.

Special problems of jurisdiction. The process of preparing code authorities for effective action has been impeded by the existence of the various overlappings which were displayed in Chapter VI. These were shown to be

(a) the multiple coverage of codes over single enterprises, and (b) the indistinct jurisdictional boundaries of many of the codes.

The relation of *multiple coverage* to code authority budgets has already been noted (page 221). The budgetary aspects of the matter are really of minor importance. They would have been capable of relatively simple administrative adjustment had it not been for the ineptitude of the NRA in failing to foresee and provide for the problem before it arose. Other aspects are essentially more important.

One of the most serious issues to arise was how to adjust the varying wage and hour provisions to the operations of a single enterprise. The somewhat indefinite NRA policy has been to require classification of workers under the several applicable codes, and where this is impossible to apply the provisions most favorable to labor. How difficult the technical problems of doing this are can only be determined from acquaintance with specific plants. The situation has created unfortunate psychological repercussions, in that it has been a matter of universal annoyance for every business firm to have to attempt to make its own adjustments—studying codes, studying its operations, uncertain what its obligations are, and vainly seeking light and guidance from the code authority and from NRA.

A simpler way out would be to permit a particular firm to follow the provisions of the code governing its principal line of business with respect to unclassified workers. This would greatly simplify the problem for most enterprises. But, however reasonable, it appears to violate the codes. It gives rise to strong resistances, especially from the labor side, which supports the "most favorable to labor" principle. It favors some competitors as against others. Many officials, too, think that when it is to a business man's interest to do so he would fail to carry out his classification of labor as far as he reasonably ought.

There is no real solution of a strictly administrative sort, since the basic defect is in the composite code structure. The plain fact is that the delimitation of code boundaries does not create proper boundaries within which to apply standard labor conditions. Much less confusion might, however, have prevailed had the NRA met the problem at the start with a definite but somewhat elastic policy decision, capable of some adjustment to the various large fields of industry and trade. But on such points the NRA was, and is, a split personality. While officials charged with retail codes insisted that such codes could not be operated except on the basis of a single set of labor provisions, the legal officers doubted the legality of such a solution, and other responsible officials thought it to be unnecessary. On such questions, also, the NRA is surrounded by the spears of opposed interests on none of which it wishes to impale itself. In detail therefore particular situations are dealt with by the several administrative officials in non-identical ways for similar cases, while in the more troublesome cases which reach the higher officials "half-policies" or *ad hoc* decisions are applied where the resistances are not too great. Preparations for code administration stumbled along under the burden of such handicaps, leaving both code authorities and individual enterprises much in doubt concerning the character of their several responsibilities.

Other problems of an analogous sort are those relating to the other general provisions of codes. The most common provisions are those dealing with cost accounting, "cost protection," price reporting, statistical reporting, and general trade practices, including merchandising

plans. Other important code provisions, but less ubiquitous, are those relating to price fixing and production
control. From the point of view of individual enterprises
subject to numerous codes, some of the problems are
technically almost as difficult as that of labor classification,
or would be if they were fully implemented. By reason of
the slowness of many code authorities in attempting to
put them into effect, they have not been widely recognized as creating serious problems for individual enterprises. Moreover, since these are the things for which
code proponents were almost universally working, they
arouse less resentment even when troublesome. If and
when codes are fully implemented, however, some queer
situations will arise.

The matter of cost accounting is a striking instance. If
a company produced products covered by 20 codes, each
of which required members of the industry to follow a
costing system set up by the code authority, it would be
legally obligated to set up 20 such systems. This idea
has no substance except humor. The problem is not one
that any one can solve. It is simply an absurd situation
which the NRA will have to remove.

Some idea of what might happen under fully implemented administration of codes may be illustrated by a
hypothetical company primarily engaged in the manufacture of chemicals and subject to 25 codes, which found
itself expected to contribute to the support of 15 code
authorities; to apply with respect to different parts of its
operations 10 sets of maximum hour and 20 sets of
minimum wage rates; to report statistics to 25 code authorities; to introduce 14 systems of cost accounting; to
report prices to 12 code authorities; and to market its
products under 25 different sets of trade practice rules
including 5 highly developed merchandising plans. It is

not likely that anything of this sort will ever really happen. Non-administrable or unduly onerous obligations are more likely to be, if not eliminated by NRA, disposed of by mere sabotage.

Another type of perplexity was introduced by the executive order[6] which required that every bidder for a government contract certify that he "is complying and will continue to comply with each approved code of fair competition to which he is subject." The fact is that very few large contractors or manufacturers were able to make any very assured declaration to that effect for two reasons. First, they did not know to what codes they were subject. Having found attempts being made to establish jurisdiction by a printing code authority because they printed their own publicity, by a paper box code authority because they made paper containers, or by a lumber code authority because they made their own crates, they were unable to say what blow would strike next. Second, they were not certain that they were living up to all the codes which they recognized as applying to them. Or perhaps it would be more accurate to say that they were usually certain they were not, since they had not discovered how to adjust their operations to the diverse labor and trade practice provisions of the several applicable codes. The problem was further complicated wherever sub-contracting took place, since original contractors had in effect to swear to complete compliance on the part of sub-contractors. It was necessary even for the most conscientious bidders to sign affidavits with fingers crossed and in serious trepidation lest they incur future penalties. Though described above in the past tense, the problem is not ended. It is another one of those which may be expected to be rectified in some degree in the course of time, but it

[6] Executive Order No. 6646, Mar. 14, 1934.

will be in a highly unsatisfactory state so long as the present multiple coverage by numerous diverse codes continues. In the outcome it seems likely that the problem will not be how particular enterprises can be made to live up to all their existing and potential obligations, but rather how they can be relieved of many of them.

No further description of *jurisdictional conflicts* need be made beyond what is already to be found in Chapter VI. They need merely to be recalled, as presenting a serious obstacle to getting code authorities into the stride of their regular duties.

The early bent of code authorities was to stake out broad jurisdictional claims and to appeal to NRA to support their claims. NRA officials were hounded by code officials asking for official and definitive solution of inter-industry questions. Individual enterprises likewise demanded immediate knowledge of their responsibilities under the several codes to which they were nominally subject. Most of the questions were of minor importance and without important economic implications. A few attained a major importance, where the interests or habits of substantial groups were endangered.

The petty questions, however insignificant from an external view, were not in the aggregate so petty in their effect upon the progress of code administration. They subjected effective code administration to a delayed start and to serious psychological handicaps. They threatened to swamp some codes in a morass of ill feeling and administrative delay.[7]

In this atmosphere the mechanism of inter-code co-

[7] In this connection, it is not a little enlightening to observe that industrialists, long contemptuous of the jurisdictional struggles of labor unions, are themselves capable of equally bitter conflicts among themselves, sometimes on the strength of clear group interest, sometimes by reason only of custom or prejudice.

ordinating committees did not flourish, failing the presence of reasonable forebearance and patience on the part of code officials. Consequently the time of NRA officials was much occupied with the attempt to placate the feelings and settle the disputes of code authorities or to determine the status of individual enterprises confused by the uncertainty and annoyed by the multiplicity of their obligations.

The jurisdictional questions have been of a very harassing sort. Officials have often been ill informed as to the specific facts, and often indeed there has been no reasonable answer, only an arbitrary one, since the problems arise out of an irrational code structure. There have been many "by guess and by God" quick decisions which create new confusions and new fights, and many prolonged delays in making any decision at all. The vast mass of "exceptions and exemptions" which has flowed out of the NRA is mainly attributable to an attempted adjustment to the circumstances of multiple coverage and jurisdictional conflict.

With the passage of time the initial pressure of such problems has tended to diminish. Much progress can be reported for some codes. On the other hand, the will to settle inter-code disputes through co-ordinating machinery external to the NRA appears to exist in very slight degree. This form of implementation is therefore little developed and shows no sign of developing extensively.

The foundation of definite information is far too insubstantial to support any confident quantitative statements of fact concerning the progress of code authority organization and implementation. But a few facts, mainly qualitative, are entirely clear. (1) There are codes for which code authorities cannot be organized. These are very few. (2) There are others which, though organized, lack the money or the will or power to perform their functions at all adequately. These are relatively numerous. (3) Full implementation exists under very few codes. (4) Most codes contain provisions incapable of implementation or administrative supervision. (5) The phase of preliminary organization and implementation occupied so long a period for most code authorities that experience in the actual performance of administrative duties is still very limited. (6) The delays in organization have made subsequent administration much more difficult.

ROUTINE ADMINISTRATION

The basic data for a study of code administration consist of the particular activities of particular administrative agencies engaged in attempting to perform particular functions prescribed by particular codes. No one is in a position to generalize from a comprehensive knowledge of that range of data. Such general comments as follow must therefore be understood to derive from highly fragmentary knowledge. This is a lesser handicap than might be supposed, since such information as accrues shows that the problems of code administration fall into fairly clear-cut categories. The typical problems can therefore be stated quite confidently.

The Code Authority Outlook

The code authority outlook is dominated by the primary purpose of mitigating the severity of competition. Since this is the purpose of codes, as seen by the proponents thereof, the first and most obvious duty is that of effecting general compliance with the terms of the code. The assiduousness of code authorities in pursuing this duty is the first test of their competency.

In the second place, an examination of the activities of any code authority almost always discloses that primary emphasis is placed upon one or two lines of collective action which are deemed by the industry to be of special importance. What these lines are can usually be discovered by access to code authority minutes where available, by analysis of the activity of code authority staffs, by reading of trade journals, and by personal contacts with responsible officials. Thus, under the fertilizer code, primary emphasis is put upon the operation of the open-price reporting system. The active interest of the commercial relief-printing code authority is the introduction and maintenance of rules for minimum price determination. The lumber code authority and its subordinate bodies devote themselves to price fixing and production allocation (or did, until their price-fixing powers were stayed). The cotton textile code authority is primarily interested in limitation of machine hours.

This may be generalized into the statement that each code authority has one or two pet devices for supporting the price structure, and that its activities focus thereon. Complaints of non-compliance which come in from members are of course subject to routine investigation and adjustment. But the active search for non-compliance is usually reserved for the critically important provisions. Though perhaps on insufficient evidence, it seems possible to place code authorities in three groups, according as their primary interest is in price reporting, "cost protection," or wage and hour maintenance, the last being a relatively small group.

Once the initial problems of organization are past, many code authorities are able almost to retire from active duty. They can turn over policing and technical duties to an employed staff, or delegate them to an outside agency. There are probably scores of code authorities whose members have little more than nominal duties. This is especially the case under small codes where, with a limited membership in the industry, administration is almost confined to routine reports, bulletins, and long-distance telephone calls. A high degree of attention to continuing administrative functions is a characteristic only of those code authorities which possess considerable scope for discretionary action, or which are required continuously to adjust serious conflicts of interest. The actual degree to which code authorities turn over routine administration to an employed staff depends perhaps as much upon personal factors as upon the objective character of the duties. A very typical outcome is that responsibility is drawn into the hands of one man who may be the chairman of the code authority, or one of its members, or its legal counsel, or its executive secretary or other employed agent.

Local Administration

For reasons of many different sorts, local code administration is in a highly precarious situation. The NRA is thoroughly alive to the problem, and is promoting negotiations toward attaining a simplified structure of local agencies. This attempt is directed not merely to a solution of the budgetary difficulty, but also to achieving greater uniformity in code provisions. Under present conditions of multiple coverage there can be little doubt that local establishments are disregarding the terms of codes covering their minor operations, whatever the degree of compliance with major codes. Whether the separatist tendencies which account for all the separate codes can be overcome is highly doubtful. But if they cannot, local adherence to the terms of codes will never be effectively enforced through code machinery.

Another general aspect of local administration turns upon labor provisions of codes. For the most part local trades have no basis of labor relationships upon which to build a system of voluntary agencies for the adjustment of labor complaints. It therefore appears that almost the whole responsibility for labor compliance activities will remain, where it now is, with the local compliance agencies of the NRA or of the regional labor boards, unless some sort of local trades councils with labor representation can be developed—an outcome which there is no present reason to anticipate. In consequence, though local agencies may be expected to have some grist of labor complaints laid by employers against competitors, their activities may be expected to center on the observance of the trade practice provisions of codes. On this plane, the prospects of local administration vary from code to code depending upon the character of the provisions, the interest of the several constituencies therein, and the quality of the local agents.

It is impossible to display here the unique array of provisions of the several types of codes. A few special problems may, however, be distinguished. Most retailing codes, beyond labor and store-hour provisions, are mainly devoted to general merchandising practices with little attempt at price control. A critical rule in most such codes is, however, one against settling below invoice cost plus some stated per cent for overhead. Such a provision is clearly non-administrable. What it does do is to permit examination of invoices in cases of strikingly low prices, and therefore make possible elimination of "loss-leader" tactics. The probability of local compliance rests very much upon whether the local constituency is sufficiently interested in the provisions to give real support to local agencies. Different types of retail outlet have different interests in the rules, and the problem is that of keeping recalcitrant minorities from becoming majorities.

Codes for more specialized types of retailing contain provisions of more critical importance. This is particularly true of those like retail solid fuel which provide for minimum price determination. This is the focus of the entire interest in the code. Given this provision, the trade is prepared to finance itself amply to provide extensive inspection of operations. Situations of this sort are, however, precarious in two ways. In the first place, if, as seems possible, NRA policy against price fixing materializes into actually taking such provisions out of codes, the prospect is that no serious effort will be made to administer the code. In the second place, fixed prices may be a standing invitation to new competition, to the detriment of existing enterprises. Another aspect of such provisions is that they invite administrative abuse. Some local agencies are so intent upon maintaining adherence to prices that they are rather less than squeamish in the methods of enforcement which they apply.

What has just been said applies with equal force to most of the codes for the local service trades. The cleaning and dyeing code illustrates the precarious situation of local price fixing, as well as the lapse of interest in code administration when it is withdrawn. A whole group of service codes from which the trade practice provisions have been removed are marked by almost complete lack of voluntary effort at enforcement.

Early experience under most retail and service codes has not been conducive to later effectiveness. Codes went into effect and for months the code authority was fully occupied in merely organizing the mechanics of a nation-

wide local organization. Meantime complaints of violation merely accrued, clogging the compliance machinery
of NRA. The failure of complaints to be promptly disposed of undercut local supporting sentiment and played
into the hands of dissenting merchants. Many merchants
also became confused and impatient over the demands for
assessment or claims of authority from various code authorities. The whole scheme tended to fall into disrepute.
The code authority thereupon was faced with the peculiarly difficult task of resuscitating a dying sentiment of
support as its organizational activities reached from community to community. No one can presume to estimate
the extent to which this sort of development has taken
place throughout the numberless localities of the United
States. It is, however, known to be sufficiently widespread
to have started many local agencies upon the performance of their duties under a heavy handicap.

Quite apart from the intrinsic difficulties of organizing for local code administration, this result in part derived from a failure of imagination at the NRA. Pending the readiness of local code agencies to function, no
local NRA agency held the fort. The NRA local compliance boards, or alternative agencies, might have been
maintained in a position of real prestige and power.
"Policy" announcements, ambiguous in terms and mis-
interpreted by the press, were confusing. The inherent
difficulties of doing retail business under a multiplicity of
codes, if realized, were not remedied. The multiple
assessment tangle was unnecessarily permitted to spread
resentment and confusion. Merchants were left completely in the dark on how to adjust themselves to
multiple labor provisions. Certain special doubts about
the legality of local regulations also militated against
conformity. These considerations of course have an ap-

plication wider than the local trades. But it was the latter which were furthest removed from knowledge of what went on at Washington, and least accessible either to NRA or to their own code authorities.

In view of such considerations it would be foolish to be optimistic about the effective enforcement of most of the retail and service codes. In the field of NRA politics the matter is of great importance, since it is in its retail manifestations that the public at large comes most directly into contact with the NRA and any decided weakness at that point forebodes a weakening of the popular support upon which the effectiveness of the NRA program rests.

In more fundamental terms the problem of enforcement is secondary to a more important one. Among high officials of the NRA there has always existed a strong doubt whether the code system ought to have been extended to local trade at all. Experience with such codes has strengthened rather than mitigated the doubt. There is a clear tendency to beat a retreat in this field by way of attempting to simplify the terms of such codes and in some degree to combine them. In some instances the primary question is whether the code shall be retained at all.

The internal NRA situation on this point during the spring and summer of 1934 was very interesting, illustrating the astonishing capacity of the NRA to be traveling in one direction while its official thinking was moving in another. The code-making machine went relentlessly ahead grinding out more of the same, simultaneously with the development of an almost universal private belief among the responsible officials that the resulting codes were undesirable and non-administrable. (This is analogous to the way in which it continued to

grind out petty product codes long after they were considered to be undesirable.) One difficulty with NRA
treatment of the problems of local trade arises out of the
fact that, though half of the coverage of NRA codes lies
in this field, hardly any of the staff has had any intimate
acquaintance with the problems of the distributive and
service trades. The administrative difficulties that have
arisen have tended to give rise to mass disillusionment
and defeatism among NRA officials.

Altogether, the future of retail and service codes is
left in a highly problematical position. Will NRA aban-
don them, or some of them? Will they be amalgamated?
Is local enforcement feasible on any terms? Will NRA
policy, averse to price control, cause the content of some
of them to be radically altered? If so, will the groups
involved try to enforce the remaining provisions? Will
the courts uphold the right of the government to regulate
local trade? Such are some of the many uncertainties. In
any event effective local administration is in prospect for
no more than a few of the many retail and service codes.

Other Fields of Administration

It will not be possible to present detailed evidence
concerning the state of code administration in the many
fields where it is proceeding. The character of the problems and some idea of the prospects may, however, be
gained from a few briefly stated illustrations, grouped
under two headings: natural resource codes and manufacturing codes.

Natural resource codes. No codes present more difficult
administrative problems than those of the petroleum,
coal, and lumber industries. All are widely scattered,
cover thousands of operators, and contain special price-
fixing features, and in the case of petroleum and lumber

provide for production control. The character of these codes differentiates them from most others by indicating an intent to pursue collective control further than elsewhere, for what are possibly very sound reasons of public policy.

The only one of the three in which the administrative means have been constructed on a scale realistically adjusted to the magnitude of the task attempted is the petroleum code. In this case responsibility has been removed from the NRA to a separate bureau.[8]

From the industry's point of view, great improvements were achieved under the bituminous coal code, and both wage compliance and price control have been more successful than might have been anticipated. The Planning Committee for Mineral Policy of the National Resources Board makes the following review:

> Despite numerous criticisms, the code has achieved a great measure of success. Criticisms of delay on the one hand and of over-hasty action on the other are natural in so new and so large an undertaking. Complaints of discrimination are heard from individual producers. Correlating price differentials between competing districts has proved difficult. Evasions threaten to reach grave proportions unless the power to force compliance is upheld by the courts. Yet in comparison with the competitive chaos which preceded it, the code is a great achievement.[9]

Less sympathetic opinions, often deriving from direct experience, emphasize the weaknesses which the committee mentions.

The evidence appears conclusive, however, that the powers and means now available are inadequate to keep

---

[8] A special study of the petroleum industry under its code is being made at The Brookings Institution, which makes it desirable to reserve comment.

[9] National Resources Board, *A Report on National Planning and Public Works in Relation to Natural Resources*, 1935, Pt. IV, pp. 402-03.

the forces of competition under restraint on a continuing basis. The code, therefore, is a half-way house from which it is possible to go on or to return. Since it is improbable that the coal industry will be thrown back into dependence upon an open market, the present stage of code administration may well be merely an interim stage in a process of developing organization in which the exercise of collective power will go far beyond that provided in the code.

Under these circumstances a subtle struggle for power is going on. Code authorities are seeking to gain more definitive powers to discipline members of the industry. They are also attempting to minimize the degree of government supervision. A very disturbing philosophy is abroad that the exercise of even greater monopolistic powers than those now possessed should be permitted, backed up by even greater exercise of coercion. The NRA philosophy and procedure are being shown to be inherently inapplicable to the problems of "regimenting" the coal industry with due regard for the public interest. What actual changes in the forms of control are likely to emerge, it is useless to prognosticate. But it can be said without question that no foundation of agreement has been laid for proper relationship between the government and the industry.

The prospects for the lumber industry are even more problematical. There is no crystallized opinion in favor of further government intervention, and the characteristics of the industry are highly unpropitious for successful market control, except in certain specific products, due to the great variety of products, the large number and scattered location of business units, and the intricate pattern of competitive relationships. The price-control provisions have already broken down and been abandoned in some divisions. Production control, relatively much more successful, is still in a precarious situation, and the habit of wage compliance is far from being well established, especially in the South. No public policy exists and no well-laid plan is current for the effective maintenance of collective action on an extensive scale. On the scale introduced by the code itself, the prospect is for reversion to a relatively complete competitive situation, except as certain branches of the industry are more amenable to control.

Copper and other lesser minerals marked by a high degree of business concentration have unique characteristics which nothing in the philosophy of the NRA quite touches. They represent fields well adapted to cartellization, and have in the past exhibited a strong tendency toward monopoly. Their codes touch only their immediate difficulties in relation to their markets, and cannot be said to touch the major problems of public policy with respect to industries of this type.

When one looks at such industries, and particularly coal, it becomes apparent how ill conceived it is to have the administrative mechanism relating to them a mere part of the whole overwhelming complex of the NRA. The duties involved are not to be stated in those simple NRA concepts of re-employment and fair trade practices. What is involved is the reconstruction of the forms of control in large areas of American industry. This is not a function that can properly be delegated with primary authority to "self-governing" groups, since a whole series of issues of public policy are raised by any proposed lines of development. Higher NRA officials cannot consider these issues in odd moments of respite from a thousand other duties. Nor can such extensive responsibilities be properly placed on subordinate officials. Every consideration, therefore, dictates that whatever administrative responsibility the federal government takes for supervising the reconstruction of the natural resource industries be removed from the NRA.

Manufacturing codes. Concerning the large manufacturing groups a good deal of information on administration is available. Because of the greater importance of their activities the NRA has kept itself relatively well informed, and their problems have received some degree of publicity. For the most part, well-established associations are the responsible agencies and financing is relatively adequate. Concentrated mass production industries like steel[10] and automobiles are those least marked by compliance difficulties and best equipped for carrying on routine administrative duties. What several of these codes do is not to settle, but to sharpen, the issues of public policy with respect to their operations. Steel and cement, for example, are industries wherein the monopolistic tendencies are very strong, and their codes make concessions to these tendencies. However effective the administration under the code, in terms of public policy the administrative organization must be regarded as unstable, since it appears highly improbable that quasi-monopolistic organization can be facilitated by the government without developing correlative public means of control. The real policy decision has therefore yet to be made between depriving these industries of powers which they now have, or extending them subject to public supervision.

Other large manufacturing industries of a more highly competitive character have been affected in important

[10] A special study of the steel industry under its code is being made by the Bureau of Business Research of the University of Pittsburgh in conjunction with The Brookings Institution.

ways which, while they are properly discussed under the heading of economic consequences, directly affect administrative action. Of this sort is the disturbing character of the wage differentials under the boot and shoe code, which has grave consequences for the compliance situation and for the interest of members of the industry in the effective continuance of the code.

The cotton textile code is one of those entailing most active administrative attention, and is a particularly good illustration of the interest of code authorities in particular objectives, in this instance limitation of machine hours. This code also illustrates very well the strong and weak points of code organization. The weakness here is intense absorption in the current market situation and action with respect to it of a very questionable sort, with a correlative neglect of the more fundamental study of the industry's problems and the issues of public interest connected therewith. The strength is in some degree derivative from the weakness. A foundation of greater knowledge of the industry is being laid upon which to formulate a more permanent policy with respect to the forms and powers of collective action. Evidence on enforcement under this code is not extensive, except to the extent of conclusive evidence on the maintenance of much higher minimum wage rates than existed before the code and on the effectiveness of the machine-hour limitation. The concurrent economic consequences in relation to higher wage brackets, stretch-out methods, production, and prices are the subject of economic studies which cannot be reviewed here. As code No. 1, the cotton textile code has been rather a pet at the NRA, and probably more is known about its operation than about that of any other important code. For this reason it furnishes a rather interesting laboratory for the study of code administration, economic consequences, and questions of public policy with respect to the "taming" of highly competitive industries.

Some of the most active and well-financed code authorities are in the larger garment industries. Compliance with labor provisions is the primary desideratum in these industries, and one can see by comparing them how closely the relative concentration of an industry is correlated with ease of administrative supervision. The relative ease of effecting compliance also appears in these industries to be closely correlated to the degree of labor organization, which has some relationship to geographical concentration. The way in which evidence is interpreted permits widely varying judgments concerning the degree of administrative efficacy. There is on the one hand conclusive evidence of the riddance of the more harrowing sweatshop conditions and on the other evidence of widespread deviations from strict compliance with labor provisions. Similarly at variance are evidence of clique control and hounding of certain elements and evidence of serious attempts at intelligent industry planning.

Compliance activities in the garment industries are much facilitated by the use of NRA labels without which no article can be legally sold. The administration of labels is through the code authorities, under regulations laid down by the NRA. As first administered, the regulations were very loose and notable abuses of power by some code authorities occurred; nor can the situation yet be said to be satisfactory. Some code authorities have been disposed to regard it as proper to withhold labels, and therefore the power to do business, from persons they thought were violating the code, without too careful a regard for all the legal niceties. The NRA under its regulations frankly admits the principle that using labels may combine the function of a method of assessment with that of a compliance weapon. On both scores it is a relatively effective measure though a private trade in labels has sprung up which tends to diminish control. Officials close to the situation consider it essential both for financing and enforcing these codes. Certainly it places them in a very advantageous position as compared with other codes. Nevertheless, the use of labels as an instrument of compliance raises very grave questions both of legality and of public policy. The power to deprive an enterprise of the right to do business is not a power to be bandied about, especially under the direct administration of a body made up of competitive rivals. How this power can be exercised under any of the powers granted in the Recovery Act is one of those mysteries of legal interpretation of which an understanding is not vouchsafed the lay mind.

More than half of all codes apply to small product manufacturing groups with less than 5,000 employees and averaging little more than 1,500. Concerning the administration of these codes detailed information is very meager. Indirectly, through personal channels, some word does, however, come out of this dark hinterland of code administration. The reports are extremely varied. One knows that there are codes of this sort that are unfinanced and inoperative. Many of them one knows also to be administered from the office of some professional trade association executive or lawyer, who may have a whole group of them under his charge. For the most part, aside from their pre-existing trade association functions, they have little *raison d'être* except price control and may be presumed to be operating in that field so far as they are able. Some reports indicate relative satisfaction within the industry concerning the state of business under the code. But in any quantitative way it is impossible to generalize concerning the extent to which such groups are finding it is impossible to achieve their objectives, or how seriously they attempt to enforce the codes, or how successful they are.

Some facts are of public record. Of these the most important are that practically none of them are provided with official NRA machinery for dealing with labor complaints; and that very few have approved cost-finding systems wherewith to follow out official forms of price control. The NRA appears to be committed to the idea that these small codes ought not to exist. The prospects of their continuance are therefore problematical, though to date the efforts of NRA have been entirely of a persuasive sort and have made no serious impression upon the the separatism which called them into existence.

The activities of the numerous autonomous divisions under the "umbrella" codes are similarly difficult to report upon for the same reasons. The state of organization is, however, not quite so hidden, since some information can be secured through the agencies of the basic code. No serious penetration into knowledge of this field of small groups is possible to any other agency than the NRA, and its researches have so far been highly fragmentary.

Code Authorities and Their Constituencies

A code authority seldom has the whole-hearted support of the underlying constituency. The disaffection is not confined to that unwilling minority which every code was intended to coerce. The more important trouble is that which derives from experience under the codes.

Much of it flows from months of disorganization in which non-compliance went unchecked and spread in widening circles of competitive pressure. Partly it is attributable merely to impatience under restraint, partly to ignorance of what the code authority is doing and confusion of mind concerning obligations and objectives. Other elements, however, deserve careful notice.

In the first place, code authorities themselves commonly represent somewhat discordant elements. On the highest level this is overcome by sincere co-operative attempts to operate the code without favor. On the lowest level it leads to clique control in the interests of a dominant element. In between, some degree of internecine conflict is a common attribute of code administration. In the second place, some code authorities have been guilty of misrepresentation, as in using their influence to force persons into trade associations. In the third place, code authorities tend to be distrusted by reason of their access to confidential information. The distrust may arise from known breach of trust or from mere suspicion. But it is inherent under many codes, quite apart from the personal probity of officials.

Nothing can alter the fact that code authority members are also competitors. The fact that they have access to intimate business information is sufficient to strike terror, resentment, and suspicion. Price reporting which necessitates identification of customers is a case in point. Access to books is another. There are many others. Even reporting of sales for the determination of assessments is a disturbing element. In some instances, such information goes directly to the code authority. More commonly it goes to a "confidential agency" so-called, but since this is commonly the creature of the code authority, code authority members can have access to it if they wish. The reluctance or refusal of the constituency to report is therefore based on very solid reasons. Interestingly enough, experience shows two opposite administrative effects of this situation. One is the abuse of confidential information by code officials. The other is a tendency of officials to lean backward in the attempt to be above suspicion of abuse, even to the point of some laxity in pursuing cases of non-compliance.

With due regard for instances where abuse is made impossible, it appears that much underlying sentiment will not support the existing rules for handling confidential information. The suggestion comes with astonishing frequency from members of industry that a government agency be made the "confidential agency." Any serious limitation of their access to information will seriously disturb the administrative methods of some code authorities, since they use this power as a means of scenting or establishing violations of crucial code provisions. The problem is, however, sufficiently critical to threaten the continuance of the code system in some industries.

Of a different character is the inadequate power of code agencies to secure the information which would furnish evidence of non-compliance. The limitation upon the power to subpoena information is the heart of the matter, and operates to the special disadvantage of subordinate agencies with powers more limited than those of the code authority. It is not suggested here that a wide power of subpoena should be granted, the intention being merely to disclose the difficulty.

One tendency of code authorities in the exercise of their powers is a not too accurate application of the code rules, a tendency to adjust the rules to specific situations by condoning deviations from the strict rule. In view of the character of the rules they are sometimes expected to administer, this is understandable. But it is not exactly a desirable development that a vast body of business law be administered by agencies which feel free to engage in administrative modifications of the law.

Another tendency is to exercise more power than the code authorities legally possess by way of coercing or persuading members of the industry. This may be illustrated from experience under needle trade codes which require manufacturers to mark their products with labels secured from the code authority.

Another type of extra-legal coercion exists in connection with the administration of cost-finding systems. Where systems have been approved, it is doubtful whether much serious effort is being made by code authorities to require them to be followed. Where they are not approved, the rule against no selling below cost is sometimes invoked as though they were effective. In either case, they actually give rise to discretionary price control. Firms whose prices are deemed to be "out of line" can be warned that their books are to be examined to see whether their prices are above costs as computed under the mythical system of accounts. This scheme can be further extended, as at least one code authority has done, by issuing a list of prices for quotations below which it will subject a firm to examination.

In the field of persuasion, the lines between a group of men acting as association officials, as unofficial leaders of an industry, and as a code authority majority are very blurred. A common situation is that the powers conferred by the code are not adequate to the objectives of the industry leaders. This is especially true of price control. To official code administration is added some extra-legal persuasion and co-operation. No extensive or adequate data exist on the point, but it would be extremely interesting to know the extent to which the administration of codes and the making of inroads upon the Sherman Act are the twofold activities of controlling groups. A certain ironical humor exists in the fact that there are groups of men who accomplish "self-government in industry" partly by administering one body of law and partly by breaking another.

In pursuing their compliance functions, code officials at times find that initiative on their part complicates their relationships with the underlying constituency. So long as complaints come from members of the industry, these officials are in an unambiguous position. Their duty is to investigate the complaint, attempt to secure voluntary compliance where violation is established, and pass on to NRA agencies those complaints which cannot be adjusted on a voluntary basis. In practice, valid complaints do not flow in very freely. One reason for this is no doubt an aversion to tale-telling. More important is the inability of members of the industry to make valid complaints because of lack of precise knowledge. Also there is some ignorance of correct procedure and some unwillingness to commit complaints to writing. And finally lax enforcement has made sending of complaints seem somewhat futile. It therefore happens that much of the responsibility for uncovering non-compliance devolves upon code officials. But when they take on what amount to detective and prosecuting functions, their position in relation to their constituencies is subtly changed. They modify their status as impartial representative administrative officials. The ambiguity of function involved in policing, representing, and engaging in competition with the underlying membership of the industry is a source of considerable embarrassment.

In some degree the attitude of NRA toward code authorities is accentuating this tendency. It is adding emphasis to the public character of their responsibilities. This was illustrated by the removal of members from the cotton garment code authority, because they were parties to a legal action against the government to prevent the executive imposition of an amendment to the code. However appropriate such action,[11] a body of persons thus limited cannot at the same time be in any real sense representative of the members of an industry. There arise tests of loyalty as between obligations as a quasi-public official and as a representative of an industrial group.

This situation accentuates the anomalous situation which is developing in industries where the code authority and the directorate of a trade association are coincidental bodies. It raises the question whether a single body of men can, at the same time, be the policing agency for a body of trade rules with the force of law and the representative and spokesman of an industry on points on which the industry and the government are not in agreement. Additional embarrassment is added when such a body is also charged with long-range industry planning.

Except for a limited number of codes as to which the inherent difficulties support a fairly confident opinion, it is not to be supposed that any one can prognosticate the relative success of different code authorities merely from the character and severity of the difficulties presented by the formal structure of the industry. The qualities of the agents and the underlying sentiments of the constituent membership of the industries will often no doubt be the deciding factors.

[11] No opinions on the merits of the particular action are expressed here in the absence of sufficient knowledge to support an informed judgment.

GENERAL CONCLUSIONS

If the purposes of code groups be not challenged, the only grounds upon which to criticize the code system are those of administrative inefficacy. Such criticism reduces to a few points: (1) whether the groups are sufficiently coherent to permit a continuing, self-supporting existence; (2) whether the provisions of codes are of an administrable character; (3) whether the pursuit of a particular group interest on the one hand and the adjustment of conflicting group interests on the other hand are simultaneously attainable; (4) whether an appropriate administrative personnel is available; and (5) whether the scheme of human relationships established can be maintained.

Serious difficulties have been shown to exist on each of these points. Much of the administrative structure is therefore unstable and insecure. Examined in detail, some of the weaknesses are seen to be capable of removal. This, for example, is perhaps true of the present handling of confidential information. Others are less easily remediable. This is true of all troublesome elements inherent in the large number of codes deriving from separatist influences and corresponding to no reasoned scheme of industry classification. Others are characteristic of particular industries in which no solid foundation of collective action has been laid, or the characteristics of which are inimical to the control of competition. Others are related to the qualities of the administrative personnel, and still others to anomalous types of human relationship which the codes create.

Detailed knowledge of the present status of code administration, fragmentary as such knowledge is, permits therefore a whole series of adverse judgments concerning the particular scheme of "industrial self-government" which has developed under the NRA. By reducing the administratively feasible list of methods, it reduces the area of sensible discussion. At this level of observation one can confidently say that much of the code structure cannot stand because of practical unworkability. There are other parts which stand up only with the assistance of extra-legal support. With respect to the non-administrable parts the only question is that of the means of liquidating the experiment.

Conversely, there are parts of the code structure which can stand as now constituted. And, as will be further shown in the following chapter, there are other parts which, while unable to stand on the basis of the contemplated means of "self-government," can be made effective if the government will add sufficient supporting aid. Concerning the latter areas, the continuing problems are not those of technical administration, but those of public policy. Without going into them at this point, two of them especially relevant to the present text can be stated briefly in the following terms: Whether the collective pursuit of special self-interest by separate self-constituted groups furnishes a sound foundation upon which to build a permanent reconstruction of economic relationships; and whether the government wishes to become deeply implicated in enforcing code provisions with which code agencies were expected to, but cannot, effect compliance.

All paths of examination of code administration converge upon one fundamental conclusion, that the primary problems arise out of the desire to control the market, and that no real simplification of the problems is in prospect so long as the separatist interests intent upon market control furnish the foundation upon which NRA is built. This observation is equally true of the detailed duties of each code authority, the relationships between code authorities, and the relationships between code authorities and the government. Meantime, code administration proceeds in the absence of any determination, based on careful analysis, concerning the areas within which, and the extent to which, the principle of market control may be properly made effective as an instrument of public policy.

The function of code administration which is described as "long-range industry planning" is almost wholly absent from the current scene. Subordinated to immediate exigencies and interests, it has occupied the attention of code authorities but little. The NRA experience is not entirely unenlightening, however. The character of the preoccupation of code groups makes it highly questionable whether their administrative agencies are in a position to make much socially useful contribution to thought and action in this field.

CHAPTER IX

THE NRA AND CODE ADMINISTRATION

The NRA carries responsibility for seeing that codes are properly administered and that compliance is effected. The situation which has been shown to exist with respect to code administration roughly defines the character of NRA's responsibility. The extent of that responsibility cannot, however, be visualized without recalling the following basic facts: (1) that there are 550 basic codes and a roughly equivalent number of identifiable autonomous groups officially charged with code administration; (2) that administrative duties are delegated to hundreds of trade associations and other agencies which do not formally occupy an official status; (3) that administrative duties are delegated to many thousands of official regional and local agencies, and to other unofficial regional agencies. The discussion of activities of the NRA in this field may conveniently be broken into three parts, compliance, supervision of code agencies, and attempts to simplify the code structure.

COMPLIANCE

For both code authorities and governmental agencies, compliance work starts off from the favorable situation that the great bulk of reputable business men desire to discharge their obligations under the codes. The moral foundation for this sentiment is the common preference for obeying the law rather than the contrary. This is supported by the self-interested expectation of benefits to be gained from the operation of codes. Among the well-intentioned and sufficiently prosperous firms many techni-

259

cal violations derive simply from making what seem to them reasonable *de facto* adjustments to their obligations under a multiplicity of codes. Others arise from ignorance or misunderstanding.

General Aspects of the Compliance Problem

The experience of the NRA compliance agencies demonstrates that the compliance problem is almost wholly a problem of the behavior of small business units, complicated by regional or local circumstances. In general, compliance is likely to be poorest under those codes where the size of units is smallest, and among the smaller units under any particular code. There is almost no compliance problem among large manufacturing enterprises, except for minor technical violations. Compliance is also worst in economically backward regions where customary standards of business operation are difficult to adjust to the requirements of codes. Thus, in the large, compliance is a more difficult problem in the South than in the North. Or, to illustrate more specifically, compliance under the canning code is much poorer in the Ozarks than in New York State.

Instances of widespread violations under particular codes usually represent widening circles of competitive interaction, starting from certain persons who engage in willful violation for a variety of reasons: out of native avarice, or because they feel unfairly dealt with, or because the terms of codes are peculiarly onerous. Such violation is in many instances the device of desperation. Whatever the reasons, the activities of violators impinge immediately upon their competitors. The failure of the compliance machinery to move promptly in the suppression of violations induces not merely the spread of competitive non-compliance, but a state of business sentiment inimical to compliance. Thus a good many codes have been marked by progressive decay of supporting sentiment.

The Responsibility of the NRA

The NRA responsibility for compliance, since late 1933, has been carried out through a system of special compliance agencies which has gone through a series of reorganizations (see Chapter IV). The present structure of compliance agencies is headed by a compliance and enforcement director. Under him the primary units are the Compliance Division of the NRA, 9 regional compliance directors, and a compliance officer for each state, with a number of sub-offices. The administration is now largely decentralized. Complaints of violation go first to state offices. They are investigated and if possible adjusted there through a staff of investigators and adjusters. Those incapable of adjustment by state offices, or for which the state office does not wish to take responsibility are referred to a regional office. Only a small residue of complaints reaches the Compliance Division.

Throughout this whole machinery the NRA has no direct powers of enforcement. Certain indirect powers exist, however, in so far as removal of the Blue Eagle or threat of prosecution are effective. Under some codes also the label provisions amount to direct coercive power.

For purposes of preparing cases for legal prosecution there exists a staff of lawyers under a Litigation Division attached to the Legal Division. Lawyers from the Litigation Division are attached to state and regional offices. Since these lawyers are not directly subordinate to compliance officers the latter cannot finally choose to have a case prepared for litigation. This is a point of conflict between the legal and compliance officials of the NRA.

Even a litigation officer cannot go directly into court with a case. He prepares it and submits it to the United States district attorney in the district. In practice he actually goes into court and advises the district attorney upon the conducting of the case. A plan is being worked out whereby litigation officers may be appointed special assistants to district attorneys, thus permitting them to take responsibility for conducting cases. Final determination to prosecute, however, lies entirely outside NRA agencies, and in the hands of United States attorneys. The whole scheme of relationship between compliance officials, litigation officials, and Department of Justice officials has been rather cumbersome technically, and rather delicate in terms of human relationships. Some improvement in these respects, however, may be noted, and in particular a better working basis between the NRA and the Department of Justice.

Another pathway from the phase of adjustment to that of enforcement is the passing of cases from the Compliance Division to the Federal Trade Commission. This has been utilized to some extent. The procedure of the Commission is not, however, well adapted to speedy handling of a large number of cases. There exists also a considerable lack of sympathy and wide diversity of outlook between officials of the Commission and of the NRA. The liaison is therefore not very intimate. And it is made less so by placing the compliance work on a basis of geographical decentralization with more reliance upon direct court action.

The compliance agencies of the NRA have been continuously loaded with a larger range and volume of duties than were ever planned for. During the period of code authority organization these agencies were the sole compliance machinery for each code. They still retain a large measure of direct responsibility, since most codes are not properly implemented for compliance work. They also have contingent responsibilities for adjusting unsettled cases passed on to them by code authorities.

The extent of these responsibilities is rather astonishing. This is especially true of labor compliance. As of March 2, 1935, plans for joint employer-employee agencies to adjust labor complaints had been approved under only 17 out of 550 basic codes, and not all these were operative.[1] The prospects of extending such machinery widely are very slight, though many code authorities will no doubt continue active, if informal, pursuit of violators of labor provisions. Officially, however, the NRA compliance agences are wholly responsible for the labor provisions of almost all the codes. The magnitude of the task is dimly reflected in the 118,000 labor compliance cases which had been handled by NRA state offices up to February 1935, all coming to them in the form of complaints, mainly from individual workers. Since code provisions are law, this method of passively waiting for violations to be voluntarily reported hardly seems to discharge the government's obligation. Even on the present basis, the staff is highly inadequate for the task imposed. But if any adequate inspection service were to be set up, the staff of federal agents would have to be tremendously augmented.

Code labor provisions arose as part of the contemplated system of "industrial self-government." But they have ceased except in a minor degree to have any administrative relationship to the system. Without forethought or intent there has sprung up a tremendous new field of federal administration. This situation dictates a complete reconsideration of the subject of federal labor leg-

[1] See also Chap. XVII.

islation. Does the federal government wish to have laws prescribing conditions of employment with enforcement through its own direct agents? If so, does it wish merely to inherit the outcome of the code-making process, or does it wish to modify or replace code law through other procedures? And what type of administrative machinery does it wish to employ?

With respect to trade practice provisions, the NRA agencies have of course a less sweeping responsibility, since code agencies are more active in this field. There are some codes representing large areas of industry with which NRA agencies hardly have to concern themselves at all. On the other hand, the obligations of the NRA are much more extensive than is generally imagined. As of March 2, 1935, no trade practice complaint plan had been approved for 40 per cent of the 550 basic codes. The 332 approved plans represented every degree of operative effectiveness. The codes which have ineffective machinery for trade practice compliance work add up to a large fraction of American industry and trade. The existence of this area in which "self-government" is not really operative raises questions of the same sort as those in the preceding paragraph.[2]

[2] The following is the official record of the Compliance Division of the NRA on complaints handled by NRA state offices.

Complaints	Labor	Trade Practice
Received	118,441	31,687
Closed	97,281	24,249
Adjusted 64,577	17,945.	
Investigated, no violation found 32,704	6,304	
Referred to other agencies without action by NRA state office	3,041	2,161
Referred to Compliance Division and district attorneys	3,533	1,892
Pending, February 16, 1935	14,586	3,385

No record exists of the number of complaints handled by code authority agencies. Extensive samples indicate that such agencies handle several

Special Elements of Weakness

The complaint is almost universal from code officials that observance of codes is undermined by the defective compliance work of the NRA. This is a poor reward for the Herculean efforts of compliance officials. At the same time it is true in a limited sense. Compliance situations run from a high level under some codes and in some communities, down to a very low one elsewhere. One judges that compliance averages out at a fairly low level, and the means do not now exist in the NRA to make it much better. The responsibility is rather difficult to assess.

It must be remembered that the load of duties which the NRA compliance agencies bear derives from the inability of code agencies to perform the self-governing functions which were originally expected of them. This outcome was fairly certain from the start in the field of labor compliance. The obvious was neglected until the Administrator precipitated it in the spring of 1934 by requesting code authorities to submit plans for the handling of labor complaints. On the trade practice side, the degree of weakness was less easily foreseeable except as to certain groups which appeared to have no foundation for collective action. Where conditions were more

---

times as many trade practice complaints as go to the NRA, but that the number of labor complaints handled is a minor fraction of those handled by the NRA.

The figures on complaints are no guide to the state of compliance. Complaints sometimes accrue in the largest numbers under codes or in regions where enforcement is most actively promoted, and reflect a relatively good compliance situation rather than the contrary. Conversely there are codes or regions where compliance is .bad which give rise to few complaints. An accurate idea of the state of compliance can only be discovered by special investigation. Sample studies have been made by the Compliance Division, but over much of the field of NRA action opinions on the general compliance situation have to be based on rather rough indicators.

propitious, much of the weakness developed in the pro-longed periods of preliminary code authority organization. The length of these periods and the subsequent barriers to prompt code authority action, due to NRA requirements, are the basis for the common charge that NRA procedural delays are primarily responsible for administrative weakness. No point would be served here by re-examining the mutual recriminations, noted earlier, that code authorities are weak because they are kept in leading strings and that they are kept in leading strings because they are incompetent or unrepresentative.

Given the situation in which the NRA does bear its present responsibilities, the question is why it is so ineffectual. The answer naturally is manifold. One answer is in the matter of personnel. The greatest diversity exists, for example, in the management of state compliance offices. Others relate to the characteristics of some of the trades and industries, regional economic situations, and the fundamental habits and preconceptions of a people.

Granting these difficulties, the question still stands whether the NRA could have been much more successful. There appears no doubt that the answer is in the affirmative. Two general contributing causes are of importance: first, the lack of imagination which kept the organization always in arrears of current needs, and second, the unwillingness to build up a vast army of federal compliance officials.

The weakness started with the intense preoccupation of both the NRA and industrial groups with law making and with organization for routine administration during the first year of the NRA. During this period compliance under most codes was of a purely voluntary character. Where circumstances were especially contributory to non-compliance, it developed well in advance of any appropriate machinery for dealing with it. As compliance agencies developed, many officials in close contact with developments were able in some degree to visualize the character of their organizational and personnel requirements. But to impress these needs upon the higher officials was another matter. During the active period of code making the Compliance Division was a stepchild, neglected and undernourished.

This neglect did not spring merely from deferring attention to compliance problems. It arose also from a general concept of what the NRA was, which covered a somewhat romantic idea of the proclivities of business men and of the capacities of code agencies. The higher officials of the NRA under the régime of General Johnson looked at the NRA as a means of aiding groups in attaining real self-government. Most of them probably still look at it in much the same way. In this view the government's police work was secondary and mainly temporary. This outlook worked in two ways: either it blinded them to the administrative consequences of what they were doing, or made them hesitant to support that part of their creation necessitating an army of federal officials, which had been no part of their intent.

An especially critical aspect of inadequate staff concerns litigation. An organization for preparing cases for litigation was slow in being developed. Since its establishment it has been continuously understaffed, making it impossible to dispose even of flagrant cases of non-compliance with dispatch. Some improvement in this respect is being made under the latest organization of compliance agencies.

In connection with this inadequacy of legal staff there has grown up a very odd, or at least antiquated, theory of the function of litigation, to the general effect that the conviction of a few outstanding violators is to create a psychological state of fear conducive to compliance. Whatever the services of prompt justice in discouraging crime, the customary theory of justice does not permit legal officers to overlook the offences of known willful violators of law. This is exactly what has been done under NRA compliance machinery. The outcome is a system of "selective justice,"[3] under which a few violators are selected to be made examples of, with no pretense of prosecuting other cases of similar nature. But even this system has not been sufficiently manned to establish "the fear of God."

A related weakness has been the hesitation to litigate certain kinds of cases. This is especially true of cases under the local trade and service codes, many of which represent a very low degree of compliance. In approving such codes the NRA failed to keep code jurisdiction within reasonably well-established concepts of interstate commerce (or at least within a reasonable estimate of juristic flexibility). The fact that the bulk of operations covered by many codes can only by the most strained interpretation be claimed either to be in or affecting interstate commerce has led to a marked timidity on the part of NRA enforcement officials in pressing court cases dealing with these operations. This timidity is even more marked in the case of the Department of Justice attorneys who are legally responsible for the conducting of court cases. Chronic violators have operated with impunity to the disadvantage of complying competitors. Prestige both of NRA and of code authorities has of course suffered in consequence.

---

[3] This happy phrase is used with the consent of the lawyer who invented it, who claims no proprietary rights.

There is another aspect of local trade litigation. Public opinion appears unsympathetic to prosecution of small violators, and the publicity is almost uniformly unfavorable. Whether political considerations based on this fact sway the legal officers of the government one is unable to report.

When all these special aspects of the compliance problem have been given due weight, it remains to be said that the fundamental difficulties arose from the initial failure of the NRA to follow a general policy of keeping codes within reasonable limits of administrative feasibility. It permitted codes to contain patently non-administrable provisions. It approved codes which outlawed the confirmed and competitively essential practices of large sections of the group subject thereto. It approved codes for groups which had little underlying sentiment of support or no history of co-operation or means of effective collective administration. A considerable mass of the NRA accomplishment consists therefore of provisions, or even in some instances whole codes, which are little more than writing on the sand.

The non-administrable character of many code provisions is now openly admitted by the highest NRA compliance officials. This was brought out in relation to price-control provisions by the compliance director at public hearings on January 9, 1935.[4] He also noted the contagious character of non-compliance in the following words: "From a compliance standpoint experience seems to indicate that ineffective or inoperative price provisions seriously affect code compliance. . . . Not only do unworkable code provisions hamper the effective administration of other provisions in the same code, but they encourage violations of other codes. . . ."

[4] See Chap. XXIII.

"Unenforceable" is of course not an absolute concept, but is in some degree relative to the means available. This is sensibly brought out in a report to the Recovery Board by William H. Davis, a former chief of the Compliance Division.[5] At one extreme of trade practice provisions he places (1) those "which aim to build up higher business standards, . . . which apply equally to all members of the industry; and provisions the legality of which has been well established. . . ." At the other extreme he places "(3) provisions which experience has shown to be economically unwise or unenforceable." In between he places "(2) provisions which do not affect all members of the industry in the same way and consequently give rise to charges of discrimination against individuals or groups; and provisions prohibiting practices which are not clearly recognized to be unfair in themselves, and as to the propriety or wisdom of which there is no common agreement, and no firmly established precedent." Given the present state of enforcement machinery, much of the area of unenforceability lies in this middle area.

The more careful analysis of the compliance problem has to run in terms of the applicability of particular types of provision to the circumstances of particular areas of trade and industry. The problem centers in those areas least amenable to the suppression of competitive forces, whether by reason of geographical dispersion, large numbers of units, absence of supporting sentiment, or other reasons.

There is no longer any serious discussion of attempting to enforce *all* provisions of *all* codes; the question is *what* provisions of *what* codes. The correlative problem is that of the means and degree of the dismantling of

[5] *NRA Press Release No. 8940.*

codes. On this point the NRA has been up to the present struck with paralysis. The bases of this immobility are numerous. Perhaps the most telling consideration is the thought that even the non-administrable provisions of codes create a situation preferable to that which would exist if they were rescinded. Thus it may be impossible to enforce the wage and hour provisions of the fisheries code or the canning code, and equally impossible to withdraw the provisions without creating still more severe wage competition. A second consideration is the desire not to sacrifice the principle of certain types of provisions, particularly labor provisions, until an alternative means of attaining the objective has been devised.

A third consideration is the existence of group pressures which it is thought impolitic to over-ride. The price hearings in January 1935 were perhaps mainly designed to assemble evidence that price-control provisions were ineffective, to get code groups to admit the point, and then to get them to forego them voluntarily. But on this point the proceedings missed fire, since the groups were unwilling to give up the principle of price protection, and insisted upon an effective means as the price of giving up the ineffective means. This drives the question directly back to the arena of economic policy, where it belongs. But the NRA is not willing at present to act decisively on the policy question, since if it did it would precipitate a widespread collapse of the structure of its creation.

This introduces the fourth consideration, that it is thought impolitic for the Administration (the present federal administration as distinguished from the NRA) to admit the magnitude of the errors of the NRA by starting an active process of imposed alteration or cancellation of codes. This point is not to be too heavily emphasized, since official thinking is probably most concerned over the first two considerations mentioned above.

From this analysis it is evident that the present situation is an impasse. The revision of codes is not being pressed. The army of officials necessary to create a moderately effective compliance mechanism is not being recruited. It is a highly undignified position for the federal government to be in. In due course it will have to be dealt with. Since this is so, there are very weighty grounds for thinking it a more intelligent form of expediency for the government to initiate a program of revision, rather than to be forced into it later under less auspicious circumstances.

SUPERVISION OF CODE AUTHORITIES

It may be taken for granted that the activities of code authorities have to be supervised. Contention to the contrary blinks all the relevant facts. What they administer is a body of law. Being interested parties to the body of the law which they administer, their impartiality is obviously not wholly to be relied on. Their powers are built upon the disciplinary and coercive powers of the government. It is therefore inconceivable as a matter of public policy that they should be given full authority either to administer the definitive terms of codes or to exercise the discretionary legislative and judicial powers contained therein. The problems are those of how much and in what respects.

Conflicting Principles of Policy

No consensus has ever existed within the NRA over the character of its supervisory functions. The argument is not over any formal matter of definition, but over questions of basic policy. The central question is the content of the phrase "industrial self-goverment" which has been ever present in NRA discussions. Given the provisions of codes, what is to be the degree of autonomy of code authorities on the one hand and the degree of governmental participation on the other, in the collective regulation of business enterprise and in planning for industrial development?

The opposite poles of the argument center around flat affirmative and negative answers to the question whether the code authorities as constituted can be expected to administer the terms of codes in a manner compatible with the public interest. The affirmative answer in general follows the line of thought that the terms of the codes are to be regarded as recognizing a public interest in the enforcement of those terms; that the code authorities represent the interests that will be competitively damaged by lax enforcement of the terms; and that they may therefore be expected to be faithful and assiduous in the performance of their duties. This position is re-enforced by a very pervasive business philosophy that what a representative group of persons in each industry thinks best for the industry should be accepted as *prima facie* in the public interest.

The negative answer in general suggests that most code authorities are not fully representative of all the business interests in the industry; that other groups than the profit-seeking group have a vital interest in the operation of the industry; that most codes, far from being definitive and final, are highly experimental and contain provisions detrimental to the public; that most codes permit the exercise of so much discretionary power that a code authority's functions are not purely administrative, but contain important legislative and judicial elements; and that, while exercising quasi-public functions,

the members of code authorities almost universally entertain a business man's viewpoint, which is at variance with
the habit of mind necessary to a faithful public servant.

So far as its pronouncements and formal requirements
are concerned, the official NRA position appears to be
about midway between the poles. Initially inclined rather
toward the affirmative arguments, its officials through
experience made continuous concessions to the negative.
Much of the hesitant intervention in code authority affairs rose in connection with problems of organization
and implementation already noted. With the passage
of time and changing personnel, the NRA bent toward
closer supervision has tended to develop into a definite
policy. But concerning the degree and precise objectives
of such supervision counsel has remained divided and
policy obscure. The issue splits on whether the concept
of "self-government" or that of "regulation" shall be in
the ascendant.

Administration Members of Code Authorities

The administration member of a code authority is the
visible evidence of the NRA's supervisory responsibility.
Given the debarment of labor and consumer groups from
any active part in code administration, the administration
members are in a highly crucial position. They are the
only direct avenue through which the NRA can follow
the performance of code authorities and the principal
avenue through which the purposes and policies of NRA
can be interpreted to code authorities. They are the outposts of NRA in American industry, its eyes and ears.
They are potentially the sole well-informed advisers
upon those matters which require the approval of the
Administration. They are the primary guardians against
administrative slackness or abuse. On its face the position

is of paramount importance to the successful supervision of code administration. This is made the more true by the large number of codes, a situation which prevents the NRA officials at Washington from being in close touch with the code authorities of any but a few of the largest industries.

The obvious generic importance of this class of functionaries makes all the more remarkable the handling by the NRA of matters concerning administration members. Within the NRA, high officials have always declared the importance of administration members. But until recently no series of overt acts gave weight to the words. The early history was one of carelessness all along the line—in considering the potential character of their services, in conceiving the requirements of the position, in the selection of personnel, in educating them to their duties, in scrutinizing their performance, and in utilizing their services.

In the early phases of NRA the position of administration member was commonly occupied by the deputy administrator who had supervised the making of a code. In view of the other responsibilities of deputies, membership was largely perfunctory, and some of them never attended a meeting of the code authorities to which they were assigned. About January 1934 an active movement began to replace deputies with persons outside the NRA.

Internal controversy developed over whether they should be a body of public officials attached to the NRA staff or outside persons who would serve on an unpaid or *per diem* part-time basis. The latter plan was adopted and constituted a victory for those who wished a minimum of government supervision. As may well be imagined, the building up of a panel of suitable persons from which to make selection was not simple. Nor was the problem solved. The divisional administrators, instead of having fore-armed by slow degrees, suddenly sent their code authority organization assistants into a spasm of finding persons to serve. A special effort was made to secure appointments before the meeting of the code authority conference on March 6, 1934, to permit a favorable "progress report." By this process *someone* was found for most of the then existing codes by the time of the conference. They were mainly business men from other lines of business than those covered by the codes to which they were assigned, but there was a heavy sprinkling of military and professional men and professors. Most of them were strangers to the appointing officers, and little was known about their personal qualifications. In the first instance this important category of public officials was filled with unknown quantities.

These officials started their labors under serious handicaps. They were not usually well versed in the problems of the industry to which they were assigned, and the fact that the minor part of their time was spent on code matters retarded their rapid progress in knowledge. They were only vaguely familiar with the policies and procedures of the NRA, which gave the most perfunctory attention to educating them in their duties. They lacked power to initiate action. And as time went on there appeared little evidence of intention at the NRA to utilize their services in any important way. Obviously no general comment can be made upon the adequacy of personal performances. There have been conscientious and intelligent administration members, and the contrary. One also knows deputies to have been assisted by, or to have paid attention to, the reports of administration members, and the contrary. On the whole, however, deputies appear to have proceeded through the summer of 1934 with but minor reliance upon administration members.

As a system of supervision, the plan had little opportunity to demonstrate its qualities. During most of 1934 the NRA was not internally organized to review the activities of administrative members. And by autumn the argument for the abandonment of the system was in the ascendant. Under the Board which succeeded to the Administrator's powers in October 1934, the alternative plan of creating a class of permanent officials to act as administration members with a rank about equivalent to that of assistant deputy administrators, has been accepted and is being put into effect. This is the plan rejected earlier in the year and its adoption may be supposed to indicate some revision of policy in the direction of closer administrative supervision. Some pains are being taken with the choice and training of these officials. Most of them will be located in regional offices and each will be assigned to several codes which have their headquarters in or near the same city. The system is a reasonable one, in the sense that it establishes the minimum direct oversight which can be justified over code authorities as now constituted. The casualness of the earlier system is removed, and there is every likelihood that the new type of official will conduct himself with a sense of the obligations of a public servant far more than was generally true of the earlier type. The system as such of course gives no assurance of proper administration of codes. As was seen at earlier points, the problems of code administration lie deeper than mere problems of supervision. And as will appear in the next section, the problem of supervision is not itself solved.

In the code structure, as it now stands, there exist the most striking anomalies with respect to the existence of administration members. Every basic code, large or small, has one or more such members. The same is true of most, if not all, the more than 200 supplementary codes. Some of the regionally organized codes have one for each major regional division. There are thus administration members assigned to each of the 49 divisions of the retail solid fuel code. In striking contrast, the only agency under the graphic arts code having one is the topmost agency. None of the 15 national code authorities thereunder are supplied, though the largest of them is in size perhaps more than equal to the 100 smallest independent codes. Product divisions of vastly greater importance than many supplementary codes and with equally great autonomous powers do not have an administrative member. The actual assignment of these officials therefore fails to provide a reasonably effective system of supervision.

Internal Organization for Supervision

At an earlier point (page 218) the relation of deputy administrators to code authorities was described. This has remained a relatively direct relationship and the administration members have been relatively a secondary or supplemental link. Above the deputy administrators a closely articulated hierarchy of officials is built up on paper. In practice the striking fact about the organization is the extensive decentralization of power. This derives mainly from the tremendous volume of detailed work at the rim of the administrative wheel and the impossibility that much knowledge of it should move in to the hub. This creates a peculiar necessity for analytical staff work which will permit the higher officials to secure an accurate apprehension of the problems and activities of the lower officials.

During 1934 the NRA was continuously experimenting with its internal organization for supervising code administration (described in Chapter IV). The skeleton organization attached to each administrative division for the performance of staff functions was abolished in June 1934. The official who at that time was made executive head of compliance activities was at the same time given co-ordinating staff functions for code authority supervision, direct executive responsibility for which remained with the divisional administrators. Oddly enough, he was assigned no staff to review the activities of code authorities or code authority members and devised no routine by which he could be reasonably well informed concerning such activities. In particular, no scheme of centralized scrutiny and analysis of administration member reports was devised. The deputy administrators therefore remained the only persons in a position to know the work of any code authority or administration member intimately. How carefully they followed it, it is impossible to say. Certainly there was no higher official within the NRA in a position to express an informed general opinion concerning the character of the performance of administration members or of code authorities. This is about where matters stood when the new Board took over the Administrator's duties in October.

It is not possible to say from external evidence that the responsible officials before that time attached any importance to careful oversight of the activities of code authorities. In words they did, without supporting deeds. The question arises whether the failure to develop staff analysis of code administration represented mere ineptitude in organizing the NRA to perform its functions, or an unannounced policy of minimum supervision, or the somewhat unconscious consequence of certain personal predilections. No one is in a good position to supply the answer, but so far as may be judged, the answer is a qualified affirmative to all three suggestions. In practice the NRA policy is commonly to be found less in reasoned official documents than in the implications of official acts. The drift of policy has flowed from certain basic patterns of thought of particular officials. The arrangement of relationships between the NRA and code authorities was placed in the hands of persons who leaned strongly to the "self-government" school of thought; who in other words conceived that code authorities should have a maximum of administrative discretion. The outcome can hardly be said to represent a deliberate attempt to "capture" the NRA by "industry-minded" officials. It appears to reflect rather the absence from the minds of certain persons with a business background, even when placed in official position, of any set of concepts wherewith to consider the relations of government to business enterprise other than the hackneyed thought that the less government supervision there is the better. It must be added, lest the state of the facts be too much attributed to personal convictions, that the mere tenacity of administrative officials in the NRA in protecting their spheres of action against invasion has militated strongly against the introduction of reasonable changes in internal organization.

The preceding observations exhibit the fact that the NRA did not until recently begin to effect an organization through which the higher officials could know what was going on in the field of code administration. They have therefore lacked the foundation of knowledge upon which to consider intelligently the duties and responsibilities of the NRA with respect to code administration. Whether, with such information at hand, they could have improved the performance of code authorities very much, is another matter entirely.

More recently there is evidence of a new movement in respect of administrative supervision. This may be granted a sincere intention to throw more light on the situation and to move more vigorously both in the direction of compliance activities and of supervision of code administration. But the organizational superstructure has very odd features. The system of field administration devised in the summer of 1934, apart from its defects of form and performance, at least imbedded the sound principle of keeping the closely related functions of compliance and code supervision in intimate administrative connection with each other. The new system divorces them, placing each under a separate official of co-ordinate rank with no effective liaison between them. Each has set up an independent regional organization, a step so absurd that its continuance can scarcely be imagined. Compliance work has been drastically decentralized on a geographical basis, which was inevitable under the mounting responsibilities. But, going their independent ways, compliance officers proceed without benefit of counsel or review by the deputy administrators who are the officers in immediate charge of code administration. If this system is carried out to its logical end, the compliance director will have in effect to create a body of officials similar to deputies to deal with code authorities on compliance matters, thereby taking away a large fraction of the function of the present deputies and depriving them of those contacts whereby they know the character of the performance of code authorities. The present deputies' functions would thereby be confined to supervision of the "routine" as distinguished from "compliance" functions of code administration.

There is no reason to suppose that the present structure of relationships between compliance officials and officials of the administrative divisions will stand very long as now defined. The cycle of complete reorganization has run at about three-month intervals. Since the present structure is so ill designed to compose the intricate intra-NRA relationships, it may be regarded as highly unstable and destined to continue the cycle. The current development appears to derive from the influence of certain personal factors mitigating against close co-ordination of functions, and to feed on a panicky apprehension concerning the compliance situation.

Meantime staff work of an analytical and informational sort, though in process, makes little progress. There is nowhere in the NRA a directory of agencies engaged in code administration. Nobody knows how many there are. Nobody knows how many provided for in codes are nonexistent or inoperative. Nobody knows how many not provided for in codes have been created. Nobody knows to what extent administrative duties are delegated to extra-official agencies. It is almost impossible to overstate the neglect within the NRA to reduce the picture of the structure of code administration to a form wherefrom a higher official could grasp the character of the empire over which he rules. And it is a very intricate empire.

In concluding the discussion of supervision of code administration, it is desirable to look squarely at what the task is. The NRA confines its efforts to supervision of basic code authorities and of some major subdivisional agencies. It trusts to these agencies to exercise appropriate supervision of other subordinate agencies. This is supervision of code administration only in the most limited sense. To a very large degree, and for a large major fraction of the coverage of codes, the actual performance of administrative duties under codes is performed by subordinate agencies with which the NRA has no contact. The construction code is very slightly administered by its code authority or by any of the national divisional agencies. Even the state agencies of the latter are a minor element. The real job is done by the local agencies. The cross-tie division of the lumber code is out of the range of vision of any NRA administrative officer, and the administrative agency of its Northeastern subdivision is still further out of range. The same is true in all the different industries with intricate administrative organizations, which far outweigh in coverage those like automobiles and steel, where the opposite is the case.

The plain fact is that the NRA cannot possibly supervise code administration without an army of officials. Its whole reliance, in the case of the intricate codes, is upon (1) the probity, energy, and public spirit of those upper code authorities with which it maintains contact, and (2) complaints of misconduct on the part of subordinate agencies which are transmitted either to the administrative or compliance divisions of the NRA. It is not impossible that over a fairly long period of time a quality of personnel in the upper reaches of code administration might be attained in some instances which if adequately staffed might perform the supervisory functions with relative adequacy. But the situation does not now exist nor is it in early prospect.

With respect to those code agencies which are, or are in process of becoming, subject to supervision, the problems are of another sort. The primary point is whether the code authorities can operate effectively under the degree of supervision now imposed. In particular, the control of budgets, the administration of minimum price provisions, and the variety of things that can only be done with the approval of the NRA officials are at issue. There are no general statements to be made on this point, because the requirements are of diverse character and effect for different codes. There are, however, unquestionably a good many codes, the code authorities of which have been greatly hampered by administrative delay within the NRA. Some claim (with what justice no opinion is offered) that their efforts are made almost of no effect. Without estimating the administrative ills attending, one must note the existence of a degree of mutual defeat between the supervisory rules which the NRA feels obligated to impose and the allotted duties of code authorities. Nor is the situation likely to improve. Indeed, in its essential features the system of code administration appears destined to be encumbered by increasing elements of bureaucratic delay.

SIMPLIFYING THE CODE STRUCTURE

By January 1934, it was apparent to any observer that the pressure system of code making had produced a code structure which was marked by serious structural defect. Various officials began to regard the code structure as a Frankenstein to be tamed. The large number of codes and sub-code groups was commonly and properly thought to involve serious difficulties, to private businesses in adjusting their operations to the code system, to code officials in performing their functions, and to the NRA in promoting compliance and supervising code administration. An active movement was therefore started to simplify the whole structure for purposes of administrative efficacy.

In the spring of 1934 an official was charged with responsibility for promoting simplification. The movement started with a classification of industry. Actual codes were classified under the categories set up. Codes were then reassigned to divisional and deputy administrators on the basis of this classification, in the effort to facilitate inter-code adjustments. Quite apart from the merits of the particular classification, this move was the beginning of wisdom in the internal administrative reorganization of the NRA.

The second move was to reduce the number of codes radically and to eliminate overlapping. During the ensuing year something was done by way of adjusting a great many specific cases of overlapping jurisdiction and multiple coverage. Approximately nothing, however, was done by way of removing any of the basic defects of the structure. In some ways, indeed, the means of adjustment added to the over-all complexity since it overlaid the whole structure with a tangled mass of exceptions and exemptions.

Very little has been done by way of reducing the number of codes, and very little can be expected through the conventional NRA process of negotiation. Some code groups, it is true, are prepared to succumb because of the costs of separate code administration. Others are disillusioned concerning the benefits to be gained and may consent to be absorbed into larger groups. Quite conceivably there are other groups which through negotiation will find merits in closer association. Very special attention has been given to simplifying administration of retail codes by amalgamation or federation. Significant developments are more easily imaginable in this field than elsewhere, but the prospects cannot be classed as hopeful. Elsewhere the prospects are poor for any considerable degree of amalgamation or federation in the early future. There seems to be little spontaneous drift in that direction, and the separatist interests which created the situation in the first place are in full force. Some negotiations are in progress and some minor combinations will no doubt come from them.

Assuming that some considerable degree of combination were to take place, the administrative consequences would not be striking. The usual form of combination is that of making one group into an autonomous division under a basic code. Some economy might be achieved and a somewhat less troublesome situation of overlapping and multiple coverage. But the number of administrative agencies would not be reduced nor the difficulties of governmental supervision diminished. The ways in which administrative supervision can be simplified are either by not attempting it on an extensive scale, by substantive changes in the content of codes, or by eliminating code organization in some fields where it now exists. The only way in which turning separate code groups into divisions of other basic codes could be expected to diminish the NRA's supervisory functions would be for it to cease supervising subordinate groups. It is possible that this outcome is in the minds of some officials, as part of a more general movement to increase the degree of "self-government."

Related to the development just mentioned is another, still more in the background: that of the possible federation of related basic codes under a sort of super-code authority, charged mainly with co-ordinating functions. To the extent that such organizations developed they would in some degree supersede functions now inherent in the NRA. This type of development may be thought of as an imaginative extension of the now almost inoperative inter-code co-ordinating machinery. It may also be thought of as a gradual approach to the elimination of small codes. The objectives have not been made very clear by those who support the idea. In some degree it epitomizes the thinking both of those who want more and more fully organized "self-government" and of those who want more "economic planning." The matter is, however, of interest only as one of the long-range potentialities and is not related to the solution of administrative difficulties in the early future.

CONCLUSION

The situation which now faces the NRA as an enforcement and supervisory body may be concisely stated. The range and volume of its duties go far beyond what was anticipated. It cannot with even moderate adequacy discharge its responsibilities for compliance. Nor can it discharge its responsibility for supervising the administration of codes by their own administrative agencies. Its present administrative machinery is already jammed by the mass of detailed problems which converge upon the higher officials from the rim of the administrative wheel. Yet to discharge its duties, additions to the machinery of startling magnitude would be required. A decision to retain the NRA with approximately its present coverage and range of duties entails one of two alternatives: either the flagrantly ineffective administration of a body of law, or the creation of an army of federal inspectors and officials under a decentralized system of executive organization. These are unpleasant alternatives, and imply the judgment that on strictly administrative grounds, divorced from the policy considerations to be considered at length in later portions of this book, the NRA ought not to continue to be what it now is.

The dark picture of the prospects of code administration is believed not to misinterpret the state of the facts.

It does not perhaps give sufficient credit for sincere and able efforts at code administration, wherefrom more encouragement might have been lent to those who think the principle of collective action to be the proper foundation of a new national economic policy. Nevertheless the existing situation represents an outcome of code operation other than was ever intended by anyone. Quite regardless, therefore, of anyone's interest in code operations or his bias on matters of economic organization, the administrative difficulties are necessarily high on the current agenda of discussion concerning the future of the NRA. Their character is not in the least changed by anyone's interest in the outcome.

In the following chapter attention is given to the question whether the NRA has inherent in it the ability to reform its own administrative weaknesses. Clearly one's judgments concerning such weaknesses must be softened if it can be shown that they are merely the defects of haste which over a period of time can be eliminated. The next chapter should be read as a body of summary conclusions applicable to the whole preceding group of chapters which make up Part II of this book. In writing this body of conclusions, it has been impossible to escape overstepping the boundary of strictly administrative considerations, since the latter are so organically related to the body of code rules which make up the subject matter of administrative action.

CHAPTER X
SUMMARY AND CONCLUSION

There have been presented in the preceding chapters an outline of the administrative system which has developed under the NRA and an analysis of the administrative procedures and problems. In the present chapter the more striking elements of the whole confusing complex are stated in summary form. In addition the forms and procedures are subjected to the test of certain criteria properly applicable to any extensive experiment in the field of administrative law making.

SUMMARY

Under a very broad and indefinite grant of power, the NRA has been operated as an administrative, law-making, and adjudicating agency without effective legislative or executive control.

The attempt was made to achieve within a short period three radically different objectives: relief of unemployment through spreading work, promotion of recovery, and reforms and modifications of the competitive system. In order to facilitate the first two objectives, the NRA administrative organization and method were geared for speed in the production of codes. It was thought that, substantial recovery accomplished, machinery and method could be adapted to the requirements of efforts directed toward basic reform; and that the product could be adjusted wherever necessary to policy formulated on the basis of operating experience. Under pressure the range of subject matter covered by codes went far beyond the limited early objectives.

The code-making process was marked by haste and by an overwhelming burden of duties upon responsible administrative officials. No clear instructions were given to NRA officials responsible for negotiations with industry groups except that codes were expected to effect reemployment and to establish minimum wages. The constituencies of applicant groups, being self-determined, fitted into no scheme of industrial classification, and the number of such groups took the NRA entirely unawares. The code structure, therefore, "just grew" rather than being a part of any contemplated plan. Code making proceeded on a bargaining basis. It proceeded without benefit of carefully analyzed factual data concerning the industries involved. Implications of trade practice provisions and forms of collective action were not closely examined nor thoroughly understood. The primary purpose of most applicant groups was control of the market, and the presumption was permitted to prevail that, short of overtly monopolistic powers, their views of their own needs conformed to the purposes of the Recovery Act.

No objective economic analysis of the terms of codes was made independently of the code-making process, so that final approval was ordinarily mere rubber-stamping of the recommendations of a deputy administrator whose efficiency was rated in large degree according to his facility in expediting the completion of codes. Codes were thus given the force of law in almost complete absence of knowledge concerning the probable economic consequences.

For the administration of codes there has been built up a vast network of code authorities and subordinate agencies which constitute in effect a unique extension of the machinery of the federal government. The exact legal status of these bodies is much in doubt. The propriety of attempting to administer a new body of law through agencies made up of representatives of the private interests to which the law applies is very questionable. Experience indicates that in practice impartial administration is difficult to secure through such agencies.

A great variety of factors have conspired to make code administration unsatisfactory. The characteristics of many trades and industries are antipathetic to the types of control attempted. Policing is ill financed. Factional disputes are common. Many code provisions are non-administrable. The multiplicity, vagueness, and multiformity of the rules make it impossible to apply them reasonably to the situations to which they are made legally applicable. Individuals learn with difficulty what their rights and obligations under the codes are. Doubts concerning the legality of provisions exist. Competitive pressures lead to widening circles of non-compliance. The system of code rules thus is only in partial effect, and where in effect is subject to weaknesses and abuses of power.

The NRA itself is helpless to remedy the situation materially. While charged with responsibility for the proper administration of all codes, it has been overtaken with a range of duties which it never anticipated. Its responsibility for compliance, originally regarded as contingent, has become primary, and it is unable to meet the situation effectively. The system of code administration which has been created is such that the NRA cannot guarantee the proper administration of codes.

It is impossible at this point to delineate lines of constructive action in purely administrative terms. The administrative forms in their origins are very closely related to the positive content of codes. The forms of code administration were, in other words, devised to cope with the types of provisions which were written into codes.

Many judgments must therefore be postponed until those provisions have been canvassed. There are, however, certain general considerations relating to the delegation of legislative powers that can be brought to bear upon the situation.

THE NEMESIS OF TRIAL AND ERROR

In undertaking its task the NRA went beyond all past experience in the use of delegated powers, and in fact rejected such experience as there was. It was able to do so because of the extent and vagueness of the powers which were allocated to it by Congress.

Starting then with a vast amount of delegated power, vague statements of policy, and no defined form of organization, the President fell heir to those responsibilities which Congress neglected. The President was therefore charged with definition of policy and creation of organization and procedure—duties promptly passed on to the Administrator for Industrial Recovery. Thereupon, lines of administrative action were adopted the propriety of which is to be seriously questioned.

The choice was made to retain full authority in the hands of a single administrative official. The initial limited objective was to negotiate with private business groups to secure their co-operation in spreading work and increasing payrolls. The scope of the negotiations was not, however, defined, either as to the groups to be recognized or the permissible content of agreements with them. The latter was left to be determined by what was called the trial and error method. The principle of action prevailed as against the stated alternative of academic conjecture. The statement of alternatives is obviously a false one, since it leaves out of account the dictates of experience and common sense, unless they be regarded as subordinate categories under the heading of conjecture.

To support the application of the trial and error method to the processes of social change, it is necessary to assume, either that experience furnishes no basis for the application of rational principles of policy and procedure, or alternately, that the attainment of some immediate and tangible goal in a given program is inconsistent with, or of prior importance to, rational analysis of the varied social consequences of the line of action pursued. The latter may be said to comprehend the principle of emergency.

The method of scientific experimentation, which is a highly refined version of trial and error, has of course been a necessary concomitant of scientific progress. But in practical application it has been hedged about by considerations of social responsibility. Thus new materials and techniques of medical science are subject to rigid tests of efficacy before being made available to the medical practitioner. The laying of a rational basis of inference concerning the probable effects has to precede practical utilization of the results of the method.

Novel procedures of government of course do not permit a comparable process of preliminary experimental isolation. Political experiments can be carried out nowhere except on the body politic. The results of such experimentation are at once imbedded in the body of human relationships, and the mistakes are never fully cancelled. This is no argument against experimentation when there are sound reasons to believe that the aggregate gain will outweigh the incidental mistakes. When, therefore, specific situations exist which are deemed to require novel methods of public regulation, one of three initial requirements must be regarded as definitive in governing the action of the responsible governmental agencies: either the range of experimentation must be initially limited to proportions which will not be widely damaging if the trial results mainly in "error"; or it must be possible to determine in advance with reasonable assurance that the methods adopted are well adapted to the removal of the abuses or weaknesses attacked, without collateral consequences of a more damaging character; or that the means exist to eliminate the unforeseen detrimental consequences of the policies and procedures followed.

The NRA proceeded to ignore these tests. The trial and error method, combined with the doctrine of action, was applied with amazing and indiscriminate vigor. The area within which action took place was extended, in the midst of action, far beyond the limits which had been set in the more sober preliminary deliberations. Experimentation proceeded beyond the boundaries of caution with thoughtless disregard of consequences. The trial and error method worked far beyond schedule both on the trial and on the error side, in ways that made almost impossible the introduction of corrective elements. Administrative experience was ignored and administrative consequences were unforeseen.

Up to the present the NRA has moved to remedy its minor defects in detail, but has failed to cope with any of its major errors of structure or content. How far it has an inherent power to do so is problematical. The very foundation on which it is built, bargain-made agreements with private groups, is a powerful deterrent to reform. Serious effort at constructive reform invites collapse of the structure by impairing the foundation. This inadaptability to basic changes is the final commentary upon the particular form of the trial and error method which was adopted. This comment is without prejudice to the initial objectives of the NRA and without reflection on any parts of its accomplishment in detail. It is relative entirely to the total character of the organic structure that has been reared.

ELEMENTS OF ADMINISTRATIVE REFORM

The administrative defects were in no sense a necessary corollary of the powers delegated, but followed from lack of foresight and wisdom in the use of those powers. There existed far more experience and a sounder basis for rational foreknowledge of consequences than was ever taken advantage of by the NRA. Nevertheless the possibility of such highly defective action as that of the NRA owes its existence to elements of unwisdom in the law.

Under circumstances requiring extensive delegation of legislative power to administrative agencies, and even where such agencies are temporary, there is a minimum of control which the legislative branch needs to exercise. With this point in mind, constructive suggestions can be made.

1. It is much to be desired in connection with Congressional delegation of power that the specific objectives of the law be stated in unambiguous terms, and that the standards of judgment and measurement to be used by the administrative agency in pursuing the objectives be stated in as definite terms as possible. Undoubtedly, difficulties are involved in the definition of objectives and the establishment of standards which will serve as real administrative governors and guides. On the other hand, if a reasonably restricted definition of legislative intent cannot be written into a law, it is doubtful whether the public interest will be secured by chancing the varying interpretations which are likely to be placed upon it under executive direction.

2. In the degree that, under the regulatory scheme undertaken, the standards of measurement are largely subjective and considerable discretion must be placed with the designated agency, it becomes important that the legislature, if it is not completely to abdicate its function, establish an administrative organization capable of maintaining continuity of policy and method. (This logically follows since the basic rights of individuals subject to the provisions of a law are determined in large measure by the specific rulings of the designated agency rather than by the original action of the legislature. The activities of this agency therefore become, in effect, legislative rather than administrative.) With respect to both the points mentioned, Congress failed in the proper performance of its legislative duty when passing the NIRA.

3. The superior authority for such an organization as the NRA needs to be a board rather than an individual, and impartial rather than representative. Members need to be appointed for a stated period and to be removable only for cause. Its primary responsibility should be that of promulgating and supervising the execution of *administrative* (as distinguished from *general*) policy. Given functions of the sort stated, it would appear to be axiomatic that they cannot be performed properly by a representative board engaged in continuous bargaining and playing for group advantage. Whatever its character, such a board can only be expected to function in a reasonably effective manner when, in terms of objectives and standards, it is properly instructed concerning the character of its functions, something that has never been done for the responsible officers of the NRA..

4. Since Congress has chosen to create, or to delegate the power to create, a multiplicity of agencies which by virtue of indeterminate definition of powers and duties

can be operated at cross purposes, there is no alternative
to the establishment of an executive co-ordinating agency.
Granting this necessity, the functions of such an agency
need to be defined and limited. It should for example
have no power, such as the Industrial Emergency Committee now has, to promulgate policy affecting any single
agency, nor the power to veto the administrative policies
and acts of any given commission or board except upon
definite showing that they are at cross purposes with acts
and policies of other agencies regarded as having prior
importance in the circumstances.

The fundamental purpose of co-ordination is the elimination of inconsistencies and the promotion of united action toward definite objectives. Given proper legislative
determination of general policies, the necessities are reduced to co-ordinating the lower orders of administrative
discretion. In the absence of such determination with
respect to the NRA, either by Congress or by the President, the task of co-ordinating the work of the NRA with
that of other governmental agencies is quite hopeless.
The primary necessity is therefore not co-ordination, but
clarification of purpose.

It is not to be supposed that a mere meeting of the
formal administrative criteria just mentioned guarantees
appropriate action in the public interest. Objectives, however clearly stated, may be unwise. Forms of organization
and procedure, however technically sound, may miscarry
through defects in the human element. But to ignore the
dictates of experience in such matters is merely to com-
pound the probabilities of unwise action.

Should Congress continue the powers delegated under
NIRA without essential clarification of objectives and
standards or prescription of organization and procedure,
it is problematical whether any improvement in the qual-

ity of administrative action may be expected to occur. Certainly experience has demonstrated to the NRA that the delegation of general policy-making functions to the executive arm in no way diminishes the necessity for performing them. But this is merely posterior enlightenment coming from past errors. Whether this new wisdom can be used effectively is another matter.

The difficulty is that the NRA is almost wholly occupied with the attempt to administer the province of action which it has created. The primary present requirement on the side of policy is, however, to determine whether it should continue, and if so, to what end and in what form. The inertia of forward motion on the track of administrative action is antipathetic to the appropriate action on matters of policy determination. The NRA in its present form is distinctly unfitted for the performance of this function.

Whatever body falls heir to the present empire of the NRA will find itself in continuous difficulties for all the various reasons that have been displayed in the preceding chapters. If it were not assumed that the NRA was to be reformed, it would be rather foolish to discuss matters of administrative organization. Assuming the intention to reform, importance attaches to such matters. No more delicate task could be assigned to any group of men than the processes of disentanglement, partial dismantling, salvaging, adjustment, and constructive effort through which it might be attempted to put the NRA. Should the present delegated legislative and judicial functions continue to be commingled in the persons of administrative officers who have not time even for the proper discharge of their executive duties, the continuance of the principle of muddle is as predictable for the future as evidence of it is observable in the past. As the

NRA "acted" itself into an indiscriminate reconstruction of the control of American industry without ever making any rational and deliberate choice to do so, it may equally "act" itself into a further series of unpremeditated consequences.

As a case study in administrative law the NRA appears destined to become a classic. As a phenomenon, it offers strong confirmation of the traditional prejudice against extensive delegation of legislative power to the executive arm of government. The necessity for some degree of such delegation being, however, admitted, the peculiar warning is against following a principle of "action" unlimited by rational ("academic") analysis of processes, clear definition of objectives, careful selection of procedures, and in general the appeal to experience.

Were it necessary to judge the NRA purely on the basis of its merits as an administrative system, it would be marked for the most radical metamorphosis of form. The future of the NRA is not, however, to be blocked out entirely on the basis of an administrative study. The future of the body of substantive law which it has erected is at issue in any such discussion. Form, content, and processes become intertwined, and final judgments must represent a distillation of conviction from the whole complex.

PART III

THE WAGES AND HOURS PROVISIONS OF CODES

CHAPTER XI

THE APPROACH TO LABOR PROVISIONS

In the words of the President the National Industrial Recovery Act was passed to "put people back to work —to let them buy more of the products of farms and factories and start our business at a living rate again." While industrial recovery was to be the first task, another task moved with it, that of planning a "better future for the longer pull." The labor provisions of the codes of fair competition reflect an attempt to carry out these two objectives. These provisions may be classified in terms of the following sub-objectives:

1. Limiting the hours of work to the end that available work may be shared among a greater number of workers.

2. Setting the minimum wage rates in an attempt to provide "living wages" for all and to enlarge the purchasing power of the lowest paid classes.

3. Making some arrangements for wage rates above the minimum—still with increased purchasing power as an objective.

4. Guaranteeing the right of collective bargaining as stated in Section 7(a).

5. Abolishing child labor by setting a minimum age of 16 years, which was seldom qualified or decreased and was increased to 18 years in some industries or in hazardous occupations. Though not required by the act, this clause appears in every code.

6. Making provision for various other situations by "special clauses." Some of these pertaining to stretch-out, consecutive work hours, etc., are peculiar to certain industries; others, such as provision that state laws apply where more stringent, have more general application.

7. Providing for statistical reporting not only of labor conditions but also of other factors in business operations. The specific

situations on which reports are most often requested are wages above the minimum, hazardous occupations, handicapped employees, and standards of safety and health. Commonly, there is a general provision that reports shall be made or information given as may be required, and this may be interpreted to include labor conditions.

Practically all the codes follow the frame-work of this classification. A few have no clause on wages above the minimum; two codes, presumably because of the technological situation, set no minimum wages for unskilled workers; one has no hours limitations; but in the main these seven headings represent the structure into which the labor provisions are fitted. In the later stages of code making these seven divisions are commonly brought under three sections or articles of the codes: (1) hours, (2) wages, and (3) general labor provisions.

The three chapters which follow are primarily concerned with an analysis of the wages and hours provisions of the codes. There is no discussion of child labor or statistical reporting provisions, and the "special clauses" which are discussed are those which bear more or less directly upon wages and hours. The collective bargaining aspects of the codes are considered at length in another portion of this volume.[1]

THE PATTERNS FOR CODE LABOR PROVISIONS

Although the general structure of the codes of fair competition was determined by the National Industrial Recovery Act and by the Administration's plans in connection with it, the cotton textile code—the first code approved—and the President's Re-employment Agreement established patterns which exerted a powerful influence upon subsequent codes. Other early codes also set significant precedents. Since, however, it would com-

[1] See Pt. IV.

plicate the story too much to examine all of the precedents in close detail, attention is here confined to the earliest precedents, the cotton textile code and the President's Re-employment Agreement.

When the cotton textile code went to the President for approval, its labor provisions were short and simple. There was to be a minimum wage of $13 a week with a differential of $1.00 for the South—learners, cleaners, and outside employees were excepted. Weekly hours were limited to 40 (with two shifts permitted)—repair shop crews, engineers, electricians, firemen, office and supervisory staffs, shipping, watching and outside crews, and cleaners were excepted. Children under 16 years were not permitted to work in the industry; and the collective bargaining provisions required by the act appeared. Reports were to be made every four weeks on hours worked and minimum weekly rates paid.

However, when the President approved the code on July 9, 1933, he issued an executive order modifying it; and within a week further modifications were made on the basis of representations by the industry. The outcome was a code which fell somewhat as follows into the National Recovery Act structure:

1. Hours of work. Office employees were limited to 40 hours per week averaged over six months—the first averaging provisions of the codes. Other employees were limited to 40 hours per week. A tolerance of 10 per cent was permitted in the hours of repair shop crews, engineers, electricians, and watching crews —the executive order had attached to the unlimited hours previously given these classes the condition that time and one-half be paid for overtime.

2. Minimum wages. The minimum of $13 a week with a differential of $1.00 for the South was retained—learners, outside employees, and cleaners were excepted.

3. Wages above the minimum. This provision in essence maintained the former weekly wage and the existing differentials among the wage rates in the higher brackets, but existing differentials between the higher paid classes and the minimum were not maintained.

4. *Collective bargaining.* The mandatory provisions of the act were included.

5. *Child labor.* Children under 16 years were not permitted to work in the industry.

6. *Special clauses.* In addition to a provision dealing with the stretch-out, there were others which included: plans for employee ownership of homes in mill villages; a stipulation that maximum hours governed every employee even if he worked for more than one employer in the industry; arrangements for further study and report upon the situation of cleaners and outside workers; and a guarantee of the minimum wage regardless of whether the employee's compensation was based on a time rate or upon a piece-work performance.

7. *Statistical reporting.* Reports were to be made every four weeks showing actual hours worked by the various occupational groups of employees and minimum weekly rates of wages. A report was also to be made on emergency time worked.

Such is the initial pattern for the wages and hours provisions of the codes—a pattern that in its brevity and simplicity was followed by the other two codes approved in July 1933. Although brief and simple, the cotton textile code contained the basic elements which achieved elaboration in later codes.

In the closing days of July, another pattern became available, that of the President's Re-employment Agreement. This "blanket code" profoundly affected later codes in the matters covered and the phraseology used.[2] A brief résumé of its provisions follows:

1. Hours of work. A 40-hour week was set for the "white-collar" workers; a 35-hour week was set for factory or mechanical workers or artisans. (This was in effect changed to a 40-hour week in manufacturing industry by the many substitutions that were later made.) There was provision for certain exemptions from the maximum hours requirements.

---

[2] For the labor provisions of the "blanket code" see Appendix B.

2. *Minimum wages.* The wages for the "white-collar" workers was formulated in terms of population differentials and ranged from $12 to $15 per week. The wage for the artisan group was 40 cents an hour with a time period differential which permitted the rate paid in July 1929 but in no event less than 30 cents an hour. This arrangement, in effect, gave both a geographic and population differential.

3. *Wages above the minimum.* Wages in excess of the minimum were cared for by a provision which purported not to reduce compensation notwithstanding the reduction in hours and to increase pay by an equitable readjustment of pay schedules. (The meaning was far from clear, but it greatly influenced later code making. The provision is discussed at some length in Chapter XIII.)

4. *Collective bargaining.* Section 7(a) was incorporated by reference.

5. *Child labor.* Certain exceptions from the 16-year limit were permitted.

6. *Special clauses.* The minimum wage of the factory group was to be a guaranteed minimum regardless of whether the employee was compensated on a time rate or a piece-work performance. There was to be no resort to subterfuge to frustrate the spirit and intent of the agreement. (Both of these provisions soon became "standard.")

7. *Statistical reporting.* There was no provision in this field. Later, it is true, an attempt was made to secure by mail a census of results. The returns were upon the whole too inadequate to justify careful analysis.[3]

While the cotton textile code and the President's Reemployment Agreement established precedents which

[3] It became necessary immediately to issue a series of interpretations—21 were issued by Aug. 21, 1933. In so far as these interpretations dealt with labor considerations, they: (1) specified groups of employment not intended to be covered by the agreement, (2) provided time and a third for hours worked in excess of the maximum by employees on emergency maintenance and repair work, (3) authorized certain seasonal reductions and certain other modifications of hours of operation in store or service industries, (4) regulated the minimum wage for apprentices and part-time workers, (5) added to the employees covered in paragraph two, (6) excused managerial or executive workers receiving more than $35 per week from the maximum hours provisions, and (7) added to the list of workers included in paragraph four. (See Appendix B, p. 901.)

code makers definitely tended to follow, other important factors impinged upon the situation. A full account of these factors would deal with the influence of the various advisory boards, especially the Labor Advisory Board and the Industrial Advisory Board; with the representations made by skilled-trade association executives and attorneys who appeared before the Administration; with the constructive and destructive manipulations of representatives of powerful industry groups; with the backgrounds of changing attitudes of deputies and division administrators; with gradual formulations of policy, usually in terms of what had already happened; for a small number of codes, especially in the apparel industries, with union collective bargaining patterns; and with all the other forces brought to bear upon this novel method of law making.

Thus, while patterns of a sort were early set for the NRA codes, many forces were beating against them; and though many of the elements of these patterns survived the attacks and appeared in the latest codes, others were battered down and disappeared after but slight use. New patterns (the "model" codes formulated as unofficial guides by various NRA branches are an example) appeared from time to time, but it is doubtful whether any of them were as influential as the cotton textile code and the President's Re-employment Agreement.

THE STATISTICAL APPROACH

In December 1934, the NRA codes had covered about nine-tenths of the total employees eligible for coverage under the law. The accompanying chart gives a picture of the entire field of employment, breaking that field into three parts: (1) the unemployed; (2) the gainfully occupied in industries not subject to NRA; and (3) the gainfully occupied in industries subject to NRA. The latter (and lower) part of the chart is of present interest. That part shows how the NRA codes crept in during July 1933 and by December of 1934 had extended into 90 per cent of the area. A portion of the area, however, is still uncovered. The estimate of the Research and Plan-

NRA COVERAGE OF THE FIELD OF EMPLOYMENT
DECEMBER 1934[a]

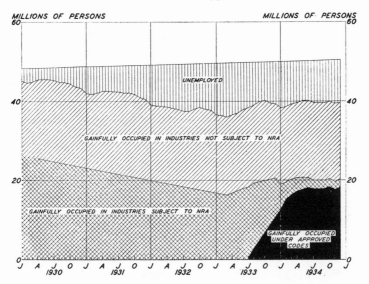

[a] Adapted from a chart in *Report on the Operation of the National Industrial Recovery Act*, NRA Research and Planning Division, February 1935, p. 30.

ning Division of NRA is that, as of the end of 1934, there were approximately 2 million employees not under codes, although the bulk of these were under the President's Re-employment Agreement.

In the chart on page 310, we extend our treatment to February 20, 1935 (when 550 NRA codes—exclusive of the 19 AAA "labor provision" codes—had been approved and some 22,190,000 employees covered),[4] to make a time comparison between codes approved and employees covered. In terms of approving codes, the NRA work has stretched out; in terms of covering employees, the bulk of the work was done in the first nine months. This first nine months accounts for the approving of only 68.4 per cent of the NRA codes of February 20, 1935, but it accounts for the covering of 90.8 per cent of the code employees of that date. The codes approved from April 1, 1934 to February 20, 1935

CODES AND EMPLOYEES COVERED, BY TIME OF APPROVAL
(550 codes approved by February 20, 1935)

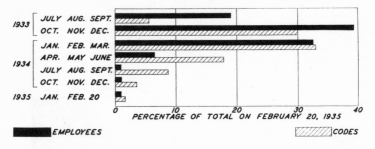

covered relatively few employees. This concentration of employee coverage in the hurly-burly of the first nine months of code making, during which conscious policy formation was at a minimum, explains in part certain contradictory and chaotic situations in the employment provisions of the codes.

[4] The figures for employees used in this connection are those taken from NRA Research and Planning Division, *Report No. 60* (and supplements). This report gave the information as of the latest available date, and about 70 per cent of the employees are in terms of 1929 figures. Necessarily, these figures are in continual process of revision and, while the chart on page 309 reflects the latest revisions, no other tables and charts in these chapters do so. Accordingly, there is a discrepancy between the data for this chart and the other set of figures used in the discussion.

It is evident that very wide differences exist among the various codes with respect to the numbers of employees covered.[5]

CODES AND EMPLOYEES COVERED, BY INDUSTRY GROUPS
(517 codes approved by August 8, 1934)

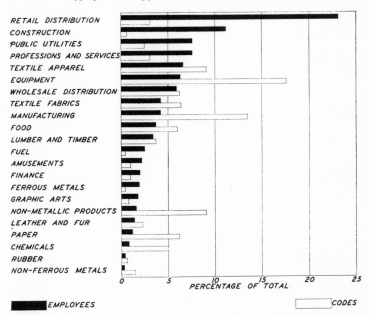

Among the NRA industry classifications in the chart above, the following stand out as having many employees in proportion to the number of codes: retail distribution, construction, public utilities, and professions and services. The following have many codes in proportion to the number of employees covered: equipment, manufacturing, non-metallic products, paper, and chem-

[5] The contrasts in number of employees covered by single codes are striking. The range is from less than 50 employees in one code to more than 3 million in another. An examination of the 517 codes with their 22,022,000 employees reveals that 3 codes cover 32.0 per cent of the employees, while 283 codes cover only 2.1 per cent. See p. 147.

icals. Codes, in fact, are not limited to an "industry" of any specified size. The range is wide and the smaller codes are surprisingly abundant.[6]

In the statistical handling of the codes, the variation in the size of the industries covered is not the only complicating factor. Another such factor is the splitting of some of the codes into divisions (with differing labor provisions) or, for other codes, the addition of supplements (sometimes with labor provisions differing from the basic code, sometimes not). The difference between a supplement (or division) and a code is often slight. Supplements do not necessarily cover a small number of employees; the use of them is quite likely to point to an industry well enough organized to bring rather varying parts together under a single code (with supplements) rather than to permit each part to go under a separate basic code.[7]

To ignore in the tabulations the supplements and divisions of the codes and to consider only the basic codes is to ignore the labor provisions of certain important supplements and divisions—especially unfortunate is the omission of the supplements to the construction code. On the other hand, to include each supplement and division in the tables on the same basis as a code is to give undue importance to the labor provisions of certain codes which have large numbers of supplements, all of which follow the basic code in those provisions.[8]

[6] The first code with less than 1,000 employees was approved Sept. 18, 1933. The next·one did not get in until Oct. 23; then came one on Oct. 31 and three more on Nov. 4; whereupon the gates were open wide to small industry codes.

[7] The construction code is an example of an industry brought under one basic code (with supplements) ; the paper codes provide an example of an industry under many basic codes.

[8] The outstanding instances of this padding are the fabricated metal products code (with 45 supplements) and the machinery and allied products code (with 41 supplements). The fabricated metal products code specifically states that "all employment provisions of such supple-

And whether the count is made in terms of basic codes only or in terms of codes, supplements, and divisions, there remain such incongruities as that of the retail code with more than 3 million employees carrying no more statistical weight than the animal soft hair code with less than 50 employees.

In order to satisfy all these objections, three methods of handling the codes are utilized in the chapters which follow.[9] (1) The first is according to basic codes (a total of 517); (2) the second method adds to the 517 basic codes the 143 supplements approved by August 8, 1934 and the 35 additional divisions which had different labor provisions (a total of 695); (3) the third method weights each of the 517 basic codes by the number of employees covered (a total of 22,022,000).[10] In some

---

mentary codes shall conform with the basic code," and the machinery and allied products code provides that the supplemental codes shall include by reference all the provisions of the basic code. Nevertheless, when the tabulation includes supplements and divisions on the same basis as codes, the labor provisions of the fabricated metal products code are counted as 46 and those of the machinery and allied products code are counted as 42. (See, in the table on page 315, the figures for equipment and manufacturing where the increase of codes, supplements, and divisions over basic codes is largely due to the two codes under discussion.) This weighting seems disproportionate since the labor provisions were actually passed upon only in the basic code.

[9] The discussion of hours and wages provisions has been confined to the 500 NRA codes and the 17 labor provision codes which were in effect on August 8, 1934. This sample covers 22,022,000 employees and includes practically all the important codes. In fact, between August 8, 1934 and February 20, 1935 only 50 NRA codes and two labor provision (AAA) codes, with combined coverage of 505,000 employees, were approved.

[10] In weighting the codes, the full force of all the employees covered by the code is thrown behind the provisions of the basic code or behind that division of the basic code which seemed most representative. In the following codes, some choice of a representative division had to be made and the division named (in italics) is the one whose labor provisions are taken not only for the weighted codes but also for the 517 count. Wheat flour milling, *"B" mills;* feldspar, *mining;* petroleum, *drilling, etc.;* salt, *processing;* pyrotechnic, *commercial fireworks;* shipbuilding and ship repairing, *shipbuilding;* graphic arts, *lithographic printing;* motion

connections the term "weighted codes" is used in referring to this last basis of computation.

In connection with the weighting of the codes, a warning note should be sounded. It should be remembered that there are no figures on employees for specific provisions of codes—only for a code in its entirety—so that when a code with 350,000 employees is spoken of as having a 40-hour week, it does not necessarily follow that all the 350,000 employees are under a 40-hour week. Indeed, practically all the codes except certain employees from the basic hours. Another difficulty is in the figures for employees. Prepared by the Research and Planning Division of NRA,[11] many of them had to be estimated and the figures are for varying years, mainly 1929 and 1930. Some idea of the dangers lurking in the use of not completely reliable figures having so wide a range may be seen from the following illustration. One-half of the codes covered only 369,000 employees. If an error of 10 per cent were made in the figures of one code —the retail trade code with 3,454,000 employees—that error would have as large statistical consequences as the data of nearly half the codes. A related difficulty lies in the fact that, because derived from earlier years, the

---

picture, *production;* coal dock, *Northwest;* rubber manufacturing, *rubber.* The retail codes presented a special problem. Their labor provisions vary according to the length of time the store is kept open. In consequence, no one "group" is taken as representative of the code, but different provisions are taken for different purposes. For example, though one group has a 4b-hour week, the code itself is classed as a more-than-40-hour code (according to the other two—sometimes three—groups) ; but when it comes to deciding what is the highest and what the lowest wage under the code, all the groups are considered.

[11] *Report 60* (and supplements). The first 517 codes covered 22,022,000 employees—21,688,000 under NRA codes and 334,000 under labor provision (AAA) codes. Revisions have changed some of the figures in this report, two of the most significant changes being those for the automobile and petroleum codes.

figures give an exaggerated weight in terms of present employment to those industries in which unemployment is greatest, for example, construction.

The accompanying table brings out some of the differences resulting from the use of the three methods of counting. A comparison of the three percentages given for any one industry is particularly telling. Note, for instance, the equipment industry which, according to the

DISTRIBUTION OF CODES AND EMPLOYEES AMONG INDUSTRY GROUPS

	Number			Percentage Distribution		
Industry[a]	Basic Codes	Codes, Supplements and Divisions	Employees (In thousands)	Basic Codes	Codes, Supplements and Divisions	Employees
Total	517	695	22,022	100.0	100.0	100.0
Food	31	40	811	6.0	5.8	3.7
Textile fabrics	33	34	935	6.4	4.9	4.2
Textile apparel	47	47	1,460	9.1	6.8	6.6
Leather and fur	12	12	314	2.3	1.7	1.4
Ferrous metals	2	2	420	0.4	0.3	1.9
Non-ferrous metals	8	8	55	1.5	1.2	0.3
Non-metallic products	47	48	355	9.1	6.9	1.6
Fuel	2	4	560	0.4	0.6	2.5
Lumber and timber	19	19	731	3.7	2.7	3.4
Chemicals	26	32	184	5.0	4.6	0.8
Paper	32	32	263	6.2	4.6	1.2
Rubber	3	4	97	0.6	0.6	0.4
Equipment	91	154	1,386	17.6	22.2	6.3
Manufacturing	70	104	931	13.5	15.0	4.2
Construction	3	19	2,465	0.6	2.7	11.2
Public utilities	13	13	1,680	2.5	1.9	7.6
Finance	5	5	449	1.0	0.7	2.0
Graphic arts	4	9	394	0.8	1.3	1.8
Amusements	5	7	490	1.0	1.0	2.2
Professions and services	16	17	1,664	3.1	2.4	7.6
Retail distribution	16	32	5,092	3.1	4.6	23.1
Wholesale distribution	32	53	1,288	6.2	7.6	5.9

[a] The classification of the codes according to industry groups follows the NRA classification as it stood in August 1934. Since that time the NRA has made minor modifications in the grouping. For the list of the approved codes according to this classification, see Appendix D.

method of counting used, includes 22.2, 17.6, or 6.3 per cent of the total count; retail distribution, which includes either 3.1, 4.6 or 23.1 per cent of the total; and construction, which includes one-tenth of all codes in one count and less than one-hundredth in another.

CHAPTER XII

MINIMUM WAGE PROVISIONS IN THE CODES

As indicated in the preceding chapter, approximately nine-tenths of the employees over whom the National Industrial Recovery Act assumed jurisdiction are under codes. The bulk of the remaining one-tenth are covered by the President's Re-employment Agreement, originally planned to serve as a stop-gap until January 1, 1934, but later extended. Clearly the code structure of hours, wages, and working conditions is in a position to exert a powerful influence upon business operations, and indeed upon the whole economic pattern. The present chapter will examine that part of the code structure connected with minimum wage provisions and at the outset two points may well be made.

In the first place, the minimum wage of the codes is not a single, definite thing. It varies according to industries. At one extreme is the code for needle work in Puerto Rico, which sets a minimum of 12.5 cents an hour; and at the other the wrecking and salvage code, which provides a minimum of 70 cents for New York City. It varies also according to geographic areas, according to the population of the city where a plant is located, according to sex, and occasionally according to wages paid in 1929. It varies according to class of work, unskilled production workers and clerical workers frequently being differentiated, and additional classes occasionally being given minima. Then, there are exceptions which constitute sub-minimal arrangements for certain occupations, for learners and apprentices, for the old and handicapped, for office boys, juniors, and others. In fact the minimum wage pattern of the NRA codes may well be likened to a mosaic.

In the second place, the effect of a minimum wage provision is far reaching; it is not confined to the actual recipients of the specified minimum. In a considerable number of industries the minimum rate of pay has traditionally served as a base for the entire wage structure. This tendency has persisted in the codes, for, as will be seen in the subsequent chapter on wages above the minimum, the clauses frequently relate the wages in the higher brackets to the minimum rates. Even where the formal code clauses do not maintain this relationship, there are many instances in which custom has tended to do so. The minimum wage pattern in the codes accordingly has a significance far beyond its immediate and obvious application.

THE MINIMUM WAGE FOR UNSKILLED PRODUCTION WORKERS

The minimum "wage floor" so frequently referred to is really a complex of staircases. There has been much talk of the "wage floor" that is set by the codes—much talk of the 40-cent and the 35-cent wage floor. There is of course considerable justification for this form of expression, for to a great extent the minimum wage rates do fall into such patterns. In a general way, one can say of the male unskilled production wage rates[1] that in

[1] In order to bring the present discussion within compassable dimensions, it is confined to those recipients of the minimum wage who may be termed unskilled production workers, or to that class of workers which best corresponds to this designation in such industry groups as finance, professions and services, wholesale distribution, retail distribution, and the like. Two of the 517 basic codes (coat and suit with 455,000 employees and print roller and print block manufacturing with 150 employees) do not set minimum wages for unskilled production workers. They are, accordingly, excluded from this discussion.

To promote comparability, all rates have been put on an hourly basis.

almost one-half of the codes the highest minimum wage is set at 40 cents while in most of the other half it falls between 30 and 40 cents.[2] Only a few codes (less than a tenth of them) set rates higher than 40 cents and but a handful (10 codes) have top minima less than 30.

At first hearing this general statement does sound like a description of a wage floor of relatively few levels. If, however, the situation is presented in detail, as is done in the chart on page 320, it at once appears that "staircase" is a more appropriate word. The upper staircase represents the highest minimum wage of the codes; and the lower staircase represents the lowest minimum wage to which the worker may be dropped by a geographic, population, or time period differential.[3]

When the codes are weighted by the number of employees covered, the wage staircases still remain—with, however, quite different spacings. This will be observed

---

This method, of course, conceals the cases where rates are in weekly terms. The detail of minimum wage rates as they are given in each code may be found in Leon C. Marshall, *Hours and Wages Provisions in NRA Codes.*

[2] In this 30 to 40 per cent group the most popular rate is 35 cents (appearing 78 times). The 32.5 cent rate appears 53 times, and the 37.5, 43 times. The 30 cent rate is provided in only 12 codes.

[3] A time period differential takes the form of a reference back to an earlier date, usually 1929. The method of reference is that of providing that the 1929 rate shall apply, but in no event less than a specified rate shall be paid. An example of this type of variant is found in the following paragraph from the fabricated metal products code.

"On and after the effective date the minimum wage which shall be paid by any employer to any employee engaged in the processing of products of the industry or any labor incident thereto shall be 35 cents per hour for males and 30 cents per hour for females in the Southern wage district, unless the hourly rates for the same class of work on July 15, 1929 were less than the above-specified minimums in the Southern wage district, in which latter case the minimum hourly rates shall not be less than the rates in effect on that date; but in no case shall the minimum rates be less than 80 per cent of the minimum rates of 35 cents for male employees and 30 cents for female employees in the Southern wage district."

MINIMUM WAGE FLOOR FOR 515 CODES
1. Percentage Distribution of Codes Unweighted by Employees

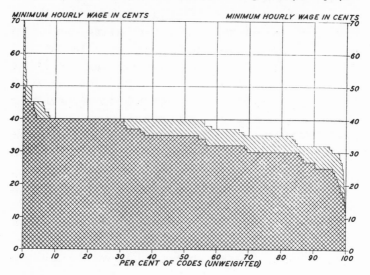

2. Percentage Distribution of Codes Weighted by Employees

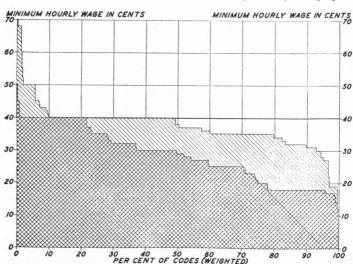

from a comparison of the upper and lower sections of the chart on page 320.

In both charts, if the subtle effects of the time period differential are for the moment disregarded, the higher and lower staircases may be described in simple terms as respectively (a) the Northern, large-city minimum and (b) the Southern, small-town minimum. It is quite likely that the bulk of the workers on the minimum wage are *between* these two staircases.

The spread results from differentials the sizes of which range from 2.5 to 40 cents an hour. In almost one-half of the codes with differentials the extreme range in the rates is 5 cents or less per hour; but in more than half the cases the differential climbs over 5 cents—in a few cases to more than 15 cents an hour. Generally speaking, the textile codes have the smallest differential—usually 2.5 cents per hour—while the equipment, manufacturing, non-metallic products, and retail distribution codes have larger differentials.

The range of the minima having differentials (as well as the range of the undifferentiated minima) in the various industry groups is shown in the chart on page 323. In the left-hand section of the chart are bars showing for each industry group the number of employees under codes with minimum wage rates. In the right-hand section of the chart, for each given industry group, the areas resembling tubes indicate, for the codes with differentials, the weighted average of the highest and also of the lowest minima (wage rates being weighted by number of employees under the codes); while stretching to the right and to the left of the tube-like areas are lines running to the highest and the lowest minima. In the codes with no differentials, there is of course only one rate for the unskilled production workers. For each industry group, the weighted average of these is designated by a thick vertical line, while to right and left are lines extending to the highest and the lowest minima in the group.

When this chart is set over against the chart on page 320, it at once becomes apparent what industries are primarily responsible for the position of the staircases, and especially what ones are primarily responsible for the spread between the lower and the higher staircase. For example, retail distribution (which has an enormous number of workers) immediately stands out as having a low bottom to its differentials; so also two other industry groups with large numbers of employees (public utilities and professions and services) have relatively low bottom minima. These three industries are a large part of the reason why the lower section of the chart on page 320, which presents the staircases in weighted form, has its bulk thrust well to the left as compared with the situation depicted in the upper section of the chart.

The mass of detail reflected in the chart on page 323 is too great to justify full textual analysis, but attention may properly be called to a few outstanding features. It is noticeable, for example, that the low minimum of 12.5 cents per hour for the 100,000 employees under the needle work code for Puerto Rico causes the entries for the textile apparel industries to assume somewhat spectacular form, as do also the differentials ranging from 30 to 70 cents in the comparatively small wrecking and salvage code[4] in the construction group, and the high

[4] The wrecking and salvage code with its somewhat bizarre bar is included for the sake of completeness of the statistical presentation. Only one code is included in the "average."

In the left-hand section of the chart, it will be observed that the textile apparel group has only one million employees. It will be remembered (see note 1, p. 318) that the coat and suit code with 455,000 workers did not have a minimum rate for unskilled production workers.

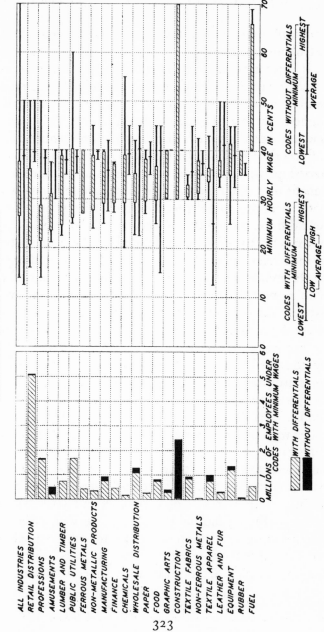

(and differentiated) minima for the bituminous coal and petroleum codes.

It is interesting, too, that the weighted average wage where there are no differentials is typically higher and seldom much lower than the weighted average of the highest minima of codes with differentials. It has frequently been asserted that a minimum which has no differentials tends to be put at a low figure so that no hardships will be worked in the areas accustomed to the benefit of a differential. On *a priori* grounds one would not expect this to be true. The industries which did not seek differentials in the process of code formation might be expected to be industries located in high wage districts, or industries relatively little affected in their labor costs by the minimum wage, and hence somewhat indifferent with respect to the level set. Furthermore, one would expect that industries which felt the need of low rates would have greater success in negotiating these low rates by proposing differentials rather than low undifferentiated rates.[5] As the chart shows, these *a priori* considerations are substantiated by the statistical facts.

The section of the chart summarizing the data for all industries is deserving of at least a glance. It shows for codes with differentials a weighted average high of 37.6 cents per hour and an average low of 26.5 cents per hour, but the extremes are 70 cents and 14 cents. For codes with no differentials, the weighted average is 38.7 cents an hour with extremes of 12.5 cents and 50 cents. Such ranges as these (and these data cover only unskilled production workers with no allowance for office and clerical workers or for other occupational groups which have minimum rates) demonstrate the danger attendant upon

[5] There were instances where high differential wages were set which will not be really operative, because few if any of the plants in the industry are located in such a way that the high rate is applicable.

too simplified a statement of the pattern that is set by the minimum wage provisions of the codes. The truth is that it is a very complex pattern. It was developed largely on the theory that every industry is "different"—a theory that tends to be concealed by statistical treatment.

The foregoing is an understatement of the influence of differentials in that sex differentials are disregarded. In one-fourth of the codes (129 out of 515) such a differential appears. This also is an understatement since it includes only the cases in which the sex differential is definitely so labeled. In addition, there are a few instances of rates for "light and repetitive work," and it is reasonable to suppose that low minimum wage rates for particular types of occupation, and indeed for whole industries in some cases, were inserted with awareness that the rates were mainly for women.

The use of the sex differential is somewhat concentrated in certain industrial groups. It is very frequent in the paper codes; somewhat less frequent in the manufacturing, equipment, non-metallic products, food, and chemical industries; and in many groups it does not appear at all. Usually the differential is small—in three-fourths (74.2 per cent) of the cases the highest female minimum wage is 5 cents per hour or less below the corresponding male rate. True, in nearly one-half of these cases another type of differential—usually geographic— is applied to the female rate. Confining attention to the highest rate, we find that the almost invariable situation is that these workers receive a minimum hourly rate of more than 29 cents and less than 40 cents per hour. There are only eight exceptions to this rule; and 30 cents, 32.5 cents, and 37.5 cents are the rates most frequently used.

The sex differential, clearly enough, serves definitely

to increase the complexity of the minimum wage structure for unskilled production workers. Its introduction into the charts would increase the spread between the wage staircases, and would place lower minima for several industry groups in the chart on page 323.

So much for a general view of the minimum wage structure of the codes. It may be worth repeating that this view does not extend to the final boundaries of the subject. The treatment has been confined to unskilled production workers and the class nearest thereto in industries in which the term "production worker" seems a misnomer. There has not been and in this treatment will not be consideration of office and clerical workers or of other classes of employees who are allotted minimum wage rates. Then too the treatment of exceptions from the minimum, including the sub-minimal rates, is postponed to a later point.

SOME SIGNIFICANT FEATURES OF THE GEOGRAPHIC WAGE STRUCTURE

Thus far, it has appeared that approximately one-half of the codes (261 out of 515 here under examination) make provision for differentials in their minimum wage structure. If, however, the matter is stated in terms of employees, four-fifths are under codes with differentials; and the figure rises to nine-tenths if the construction code with its 2.4 million workers is included in the list.[6] If allowance is made for the fact that many industries are so located that a geographic differential had no application and hence was not inserted in the code, it appears that very seldom in terms of employee coverage was

[6] This inclusion could easily be defended. The code permits regional agreements which may cover not only wages in the higher brackets but the minimum wage as well. The data here given, however, treat the construction code as having no differential.

there failure to grasp an opportunity to apply differentials. A summary percentage statement of the extent to which differentials are applicable to the minimum wages of unskilled production workers is given in the table below—it will be obvious from the figures that the construction code is included in the no-differential group. Basic codes are given in the first column and codes weighted by employees in the second.[7]

DIFFERENTIAL	**50.7**	**81.0**
Population only	5.6	8.7
Geographic only	33.4	21.8
Population and geographic	7.8	42.3
Time period	3.9	8.2
NO DIFFERENTIAL	**49.3**	**19.0**

About two-thirds (64.1 per cent) of all workers concerned are under codes which contain either a geographic differential or a combination of geographic and population differentials. In addition, almost a fifth of the workers are under codes which have either a population differential (8.7 per cent) or a time period differential (8.2 per cent). Since large cities are more characteristic of the North than of the South, a population differential serves to some extent as a geographic differential. A time period differential, which ties back to the traditional wage structure, has some of the consequences of a population, a racial, a sex, and a geographic differential. In fine, directly or indirectly a geographic wage structure is a characteristic feature of the codes and this structure deserves examination.

Technically, a geographic differential is applied to the minimum wage, but confining attention to this technical

[7] The left side of the chart on p. 323 gives a picture of the number of employees in codes with differentials and in codes with no differentials —this according to industry groups. The blackened area leaves no doubt of the weight of the construction code in the no-differential group.

situation may serve to conceal very important issues. What proportion of the total employees in the industry work at the minimum wage? Is the industry one in which, either through custom or code provisions, the minimum wage has powerful repercussions upon the wages in the higher brackets? Upon the answers to such questions as these depends the significance of geographic differentials in their effect on business costs.

It was not feasible, in advance of code making, to formulate a detailed policy on geographic wage structures. From the very first, NRA policy provided for sectional or geographic differentials in the minimum wage.[8] From the very first, too, it was recognized that many factors entered in: the historical development of the industry concerned, differences in cost of living, differences in productive efficiency, differences in market competition and marketing costs, differences in climate, and other pertinent elements. But while the existence of such factors as these was recognized, it never proved possible really to measure them or even to allocate to them relative significance in a particular situation.[9] In consequence, related industries and even competitive industries were given differentials of varying size (or no differential what-

[8] This is especially true as between the North and the South, and the South is sometimes subdivided into the South and Deep South. In certain instances, the geographic differential was worked out in terms of other sections of the country, as for example between the Eastern and Western clothing markets.

[9] The general attitude of the Administration was reflected in the President's statement on Apr. 22, 1934 in connection with the bituminous coal agreement, when he said: "On the question of Southern wage differentials the Recovery Act recognizes differentials according to locality. It is not the purpose of the Administration, by sudden or explosive change, to impair Southern industry by refusing to recognize traditional differentials. On the other hand, no region has any right, by depressing its labor, wages, and hours, to invade with its cheaper produce an area of higher wages and hours and thus to impose its lower standards on an area of higher standards."

ever), and the differentials were applied to varying districts. It should be added that the instances are rare in which the geographic differential was worked out in terms of the entire wage structure of the industry concerned; and the instances are almost non-existent in which the entire wage structures of competitive or otherwise related industries were worked out co-operatively.

The complexity which resulted from this rather haphazard handling of the problem can be illustrated by an examination of the codes under the NRA industry classification called "manufacturing." A survey of the 46 codes classified as "manufactured products" discloses great diversity in the treatment of the minimum for unskilled production labor; in the treatment of office or clerical labor; and in the use of female differentials and the relationship of such differentials to the basic production wage. Nine different ways (out of the possible twelve sketched in the following chapter) of handling wages in the higher brackets are utilized. The range is from detailed wage schedules or basing points in the higher brackets to no provision whatever.[10] Eleven codes set a lower minimum wage for the South but the definition of the South is identical in only two industries—in *eleven* codes there are *ten* different boundary lines for the somewhat vague "South."

While the presumption is strong that absolute uniformity should not exist as among the industries of a particular group, it is incredible that all the divergences found here, whether in wage rates or in wage districts, are economically justifiable.[11] It appears from this sam-

[10] See pp. 102-05 of Leon C. Marshall, *Hours and Wages Provisions in NRA Codes.*

[11] For a full account, covering the wage rates and the wage districts of all industry groups, see *Geographic and Population Differentials in Minimum Wages,* a pamphlet prepared under the supervision of Leon C. Marshall by the Division of Research and Planning of the NRA.

ple, which could be paralleled in almost every industry group, that the present code structure of geographic differentials has been neither carefully planned nor consistently applied. Must this, in the nature of the case, continue to be true? Can a consistent policy be worked out? Several schools of thought exist with respect to the policy that should guide in this matter.

Some persons advocate a uniform national minimum wage sufficient to furnish a minimum standard of living. They insist that if there are factors which properly cause variations in wage rates, these variations should appear only in the wage rates above the minimum. Other advocates of a uniform national minimum wage contend that wages for each class of labor, the skilled classes as well as the unskilled, should be uniform throughout the country in order to maintain "fair competition" in an industry. They argue that no manufacturer should have an advantage over his competitor by reason of lower wage rates. Competition, they say, should be restricted to factors such as style, quality, nearness to markets, efficiency in production, and the like. Even though this policy might necessitate the relocation of plants which have gone into certain areas because of cheap labor supply or might throw men out of work by the introduction of labor-saving machinery, these persons contend that the final result would be the most efficient organization for production.

Others believe that the pre-code differentials should be maintained. These persons contend that it is not the purpose of the National Industrial Recovery Act to relocate industry in accordance with some notion of efficiency, but rather to promote recovery. This can best be done, they insist, by making the type of contribution to purchasing power that would attend the raising of the existing wage level in every district by some definite amount. In this view, the procedure in setting minimum wages should include that of determining differentials existing prior to NRA, and then maintaining those differentials. Some of the proponents of the pre-code *status quo* view contend that these existing geographic differentials have a logical basis in fact, representing differences in cost of living, in the nature of the labor supply, in the lower productivity of labor in one area as compared with another, and other such factors. Others think that these existing differentials have no logical basis; but that their disruption would force many plants into bankruptcy with resulting hardships to labor and the community—thus tending to retard recovery rather than to hasten it.

Others advocate a gradual elimination of differentials. This third approach would compromise the two points of view given above. It sets as its *goal* a uniform national minimum wage below which no workers should be paid; but it holds that much hardship would result from the *immediate* introduction of such a policy.[12] It suggests the procedure (1) of ascertaining the extent of pre-NRA differentials, and (2) of agreement on a program of gradual elimination.

Others would make "fair" competition the touchstone of the differential wage structure. In setting minimum wage rates, they hold, NRA should take into consideration a large number of factors which influence the cost of doing business and should make an effort to equalize those costs. There is no agreement with respect to the factors which should be considered, but commonly mentioned are the following: cost of living, nearness to raw

[12] One advocate has put the matter thus: "The NRA may on occasion and with caution place a temporary crutch under the inefficiencies of the past, but it will not subsidize the inefficiencies of the future."

materials, nearness to markets, relative productivity of labor, nature of the labor supply, ability of industry to pay, stage of mechanization or development, and competitive nature of the products. It is argued, for example, that if certain Southern manufacturers are distant from the market for their goods, NRA should equalize this burden by permitting lower wage rates. Or it is argued that if certain Western areas suffer from lack of an adequate labor force, their competitive position should be equalized by a lower wage scale.

Other principles have been urged, but these four will serve to indicate the issues involved and the conflicting points of view. At the one extreme are many Southern industrialists who contend they were not properly represented in the code-making process with the result that insufficient differentials were approved. They further assert that they are not now properly represented in code administration and are therefore handicapped in securing amendments or exemptions. They would move, and promptly, to the restoration of the earlier differentials. At the other extreme are those who are thoroughly convinced that the differential structure is fundamentally an unfortunate historical development for which there is no defense in economics or in social welfare. They would move, and promptly, to the elimination of all differentials—geographic, population, sex, time period, or racial.

There is no easy solution of the problem. The Administration is here faced with an extremely difficult and complicated issue which raises the fundmental question of the *purpose* of control of wage rates in industry. To such a question there is no single answer that will be satisfactory to all. Even if there were, it would at once appear that the geographic wage structure is not a single problem but a whole series of problems in which the conflicts of interest are many, and agreement among the conflicting interests difficult to achieve. Everything considered, it is clear that the Administration has not hit upon any real solution of the difficulties inherent in the territorial wage structure; and it is equally clear that no promising solution is in the making.

WORKERS EXCEPTED FROM MINIMUM WAGE PROVISIONS

Even yet the full complexity of the minimum wage structure of the codes has not been stated. In addition to the varying rates set for unskilled production workers, in addition to the smaller number of variants of the minimum wage of office and clerical workers, in addition to the many cases in which minimum rates were allocated to other occupational groups, in addition to the diversities and contradictions in geographic wage structures—over and above all these is the fact that certain classes of workers are excepted from the minimum wage provision. Of the total codes, supplements, and divisions here under consideration (695), the number given below excepted the specified classes from this provision.[13] In certain cases the number providing safeguards is also given.

Old and handicapped .440
    Safeguarded by a number limitation . . 163
    Wages set 166
Office boys and girls .326
    Safeguarded by a number limitation . . 259
    Safeguarded by an age limitation 94
    Wages set 326
Learners 310
    Safeguarded by a number limitation . . 290

---

[13] The supporting detail may be found in the *Tabulation of Labor Provisions in Codes Approved by August 8, 1934*, a pamphlet prepared by Leon C. Marshall and distributed by NRA at the hearings on employment provisions, January 1935.

Some of these classes (such as outside salesmen, collectors, etc.) were excepted on the ground that the employer should not be expected to guarantee a minimum wage to persons working under circumstances which make it impossible for him to supervise their expenditure of time and effort. Others were excepted with the definite intention of applying to them a sub-minimal rate.[14] Four of the latter groups—learners, apprentices, office boys and girls, and the old and handicapped—are so important that it is appropriate to discuss their status.

Consider first the exception of learners and apprentices. As the codes are formulated, it is not always possible to draw a sharp dividing line between learners and apprentices; accordingly, the classification in the table is somewhat arbitrary. In the main if the learning period extends one year or more, or if there is definite provision for indenture, apprentice contract, training course, or the like, the term "apprenticeship" is applied. All others are regarded as learners, regardless of code terminology.

[14] In the case of watchmen, the exceptions from the minimum wage are not as many as would at first be expected. It is to be remembered, however, that the long hours typically worked by watchmen ordinarily operate to bring about a sub-minimal hourly wage for this group, whether or not formal mention is made of that fact.

It will be noticed that with respect to the 310 instances of learners, there are typically safeguards covering the permitted number of such persons, the length of the learning period, and the wages that must be paid. The number limitation is ordinarily in terms of a stated percentage of the number of employees, usually 5 per cent.[15] As for the wage base, the typical arrangement is to set it at 80 per cent of the minimum wage. The limitation of the period during which a worker may be classified as a learner is usually placed at 13 weeks or less, with a considerable number at 6 weeks or less.

In addition to the 310 learner cases, there are 121 provisions for apprentices, three-fourths of which fall in the equipment industry group.[16] These apprenticeship provisions, as the table shows, usually have safeguards with respect to the numbers who may be utilized and the conditions surrounding the apprenticeship training. The limitation on numbers is typically placed on a percentage basis, and there is typically provision for formal indenture, indenture contract, or course of training. The code provisions on apprenticeship, however, quite fail to tell the whole story. They must be considered in connection with an executive order issued on June 27, 1934,[17] which

[15] This statement is not as informing as it appears. In some codes the provision is for a percentage of the *total* employees; in others it is a percentage of a *particular class* of employees; in others the learners are grouped with some other occupational class (such as junior employees, messengers, office boys and girls, and the like) in calculating the percentage. These remarks with respect to the percentage method of limiting the number of learners have application also to the old and handicapped, the office boys and girls, and the apprentices.

[16] Forty-two of the 90 cases in the equipment group are due to the machinery and allied products code, with its 41 supplements. But even if these 41 were deducted, the apprentice cases would still fall heavily in the equipment group.

[17] The following paragraphs, taken from this executive order (No. 6750-C) state its essential features:

"(1) A person may be employed as an apprentice by any member of an industry subject to a code of fair competition at a wage lower than

permits any member of an industry subject to a code to establish an apprenticeship system under the general direction of the United States Department of Labor, with state agencies provided for supervision of the training. By the end of January 1935, state committees had been set up in all the states; state plans had been officially approved for 15 states; and plans were pending for 8 additional states.

As for the old and handicapped, the table shows a total of 440 instances in which codes or supplements contain a provision applicable to this class of workers. Here also, an examination of merely the code provisions leads to erroneous conclusions. The many instances in which there are no limitations set to the number of such workers and no lower limits set to the wage that may be paid them are mainly to be explained by the provisions of an executive order of February 17, 1934,[18] supplemented by

the minimum wage, or for any time in excess of the maximum hours of labor, established in such code, if such member shall have first obtained from an agency to be designated or established by the Secretary of Labor, a certificate permitting such person to be employed in conformity with a training program approved by such agency, until and unless such certificate is revoked.

"(2) The term 'apprentice,' as used herein shall mean a person of at least 16 years of age who has entered into a written contract with an employer or an association of employers which provides for at least 2,000 hours of reasonably continuous employment for such person and his participation in an approved program of training as hereinabove provided."

[18] The essential provision of this executive order (No. 6606-F) runs thus: "A person whose earning capacity is limited because of age, physical or mental handicap, or other infirmity, may be employed on light work at a wage below the minimum established by this code, if the employer obtains from the state authority, designated by the United States Department of Labor, a certificate authorizing such person's employment at such wages and for such hours as shall be stated in the certificate. Such authority shall be guided by the instructions of the United States Department of Labor in issuing certificates to such persons. Each employer shall file monthly with the code authority a list of all persons employed by him, showing the wages paid to, and the maximum hours of work for such employee."

an office memorandum of March 21, 1934. These documents authorize the employment of such persons under safeguards to be administered by a state agency which is to be guided by instructions issued by the United States Department of Labor.

The classification "office boys and girls," as used in the table, includes "messengers." If there were included the 55 cases of excepted "junior employees," the total of these exceptions would mount to 381 of the 695 codes and supplements. Here also the device commonly used to limit the numbers of such excepted employees is that of a certain percentage—usually 5—of total employees or of the employees in a specified class, the method varying from code to code. A definite age limitation is set in only 94 instances. As for safeguards on wages, 80 per cent of the minimum wage is again popular, although not so popular as is true of learners or the old and handicapped. The reason for this lower degree of popularity is at once apparent; office workers are commonly paid at a weekly rate, and accordingly the minds of the code makers would easily turn to expressing this particular sub-minimal wage in terms of a smaller number of dollars per week.

In summary of the occupational classes excepted from the minimum wage provisions of the codes, it is to be said:

1. The stated exceptions appear, *prima facie,* reasonably and properly safeguarded. Presumably, the operative situation varies from case to case, the variations depending upon some combination of the technique of the industry, the vigor of code administration by the code authority, the degree of compliance, the effectiveness of the Department of Labor in the matters in which it has been given a commission, and the like.

2. It is too early to have many dependable records of actual performance, but foreshadowings of such records seem to indicate that the exceptions for learners, for the old and handicapped, and for office boys and girls will be the ones most open to criticism. There are instances— with as yet inconclusive evidence concerning whether they are many or few—where these exceptions seem to operate to cause few workers to receive minimum wages while many are paid sub-minimum rates.

3. Particularly worthy of attention is the fact that the code system and the Recovery Act have been used as the occasion for establishing national supervision, through the Department of Labor, of apprenticeship and the working opportunities of the old and handicapped at sub-minimum wages. This is certainly novel.

SPECIAL CLAUSES

In addition to the wage provisions which almost invariably are in the codes, there are frequently, in the section on general labor provisions, clauses (here called "special clauses") which bear more or less directly on wages. They are not abundant in the early codes; but they increase in number fairly steadily as the code-making process continues. The special clauses that deserve at least summary treatment at this point, and the number of codes that contain them, are as follows:[19]

Minimum rate holds irrespective of method of wage payment	655
More stringent laws hold	630
No reclassification of jobs or employees to avoid code provisions	595
No sex differential on the same type of work	456
Method or time of wage payment specified	188
Wage deductions to be voluntary	159
Home-work provisions	97

[19] This count is in terms of the 695 codes, supplements, and divisions here under examination.

It will be observed that the pattern set in the cotton textile code to the effect that a code establishes a minimum rate of pay which shall apply irrespective of whether an employee is compensated on a time-rate, piece-work, or other basis, has been almost invariably followed. A "standard" clause to cover the situation quickly emerged and was all but universally adopted.

Another special clause that soon became standard and was widely utilized (630 times out of 695) is the one that laws more stringent than code provisions shall prevail. A common form reads thus: "No provision hereof shall supersede any state or federal law which imposes on employers more stringent requirements as to age of employees, wages, hours of work, safety, health and sanitary conditions, insurance, fire protection, or general working conditions than are imposed in this code." This of course covers much more than wages.

Next in frequency (595 instances) stands the clause designed to prevent subterfuge and especially to prevent improper reclassifications. The form that finally became more or less standard ran: "No employer shall reclassify employees or duties of occupations performed or engage in any other subterfuge so as to defeat the purposes or provisions of the act or of this code."[20] With a similar general objective, Executive Order No. 6711 of May 15, 1934 forbade the employer to dismiss or demote any employee for making a complaint or giving evidence with respect to an alleged violation of any code of fair competition.

Because of a persistent fight waged against sex differentials by the Women's Bureau of the Department of Labor and by the Labor Advisory Board, there are 456

---

[20] A grotesque illustration of subterfuge is indicated by the report that some of the Southern negroes found themselves advanced to the rank of "executives" and thereby excepted from certain code provisions.

provisions that female employees performing substantially the same work as male employees shall receive the same rate of pay as male employees, and that where they displace men they shall receive the rate of pay received by the men they displace. There are cases where this clause appears in codes which make definite provision for sex differentials.

In 188 instances there is regulation of the method or time of wage payment, and in 159 instances deductions from wages except at the will of the employee are forbidden.[21] A "model" clause is the following: "An employer shall make payment of all wages in lawful currency or by negotiable check therefor payable on demand. These payments shall be exempt from any deductions for pensions, insurance, sick benefits, shortages, fines, property damage, or any other purpose except as specifically authorized in writing by each employee. Wages shall be paid at least semi-monthly, and salaries at least monthly."

An interesting effort is made in the codes to grapple with the problem of home work, which is treated in 97 of the codes and supplements here under consideration. The treatment ranges from absolute prohibition to regulation by a state agency according to instructions issued by the United States Department of Labor—the latter being authorized by an executive order of May 15, 1934.[22] A standing committee in NRA deals continually

---

[21] Special studies have been made of this subject, the most notable one being that on "The Economic and Social Implications of the Company Store and Scrip System," completed by the NRA in October 1934.

[22] The following, taken from this order (No. 6711-A), is expressive of the typical situation with respect to homework regulations:

"A person may be permitted to engage in home work at the same rate of wages as is paid for the same type of work performed in the factory or other regular place of business if a certificate is obtained from the state authority or other officer designated by the United States Department

with the problem and a special investigation of it by the Women's Bureau of the Department of Labor came to fruition in late January 1935. Even so, the surface of the problem has barely been scratched.

Although not mentioned in the table on page 338, the activity in connection with safeguarding the safety and health of employees deserves notice. When such a provision appears in a code, it is usually drawn so as to give any standards that are accepted the force of the code itself. A committee of the Labor Advisory Board works intensively with the United States Department of Labor in formulating these standards—another interesting development in industrial relations.

The foregoing pages show the complex, relatively unco-ordinated, even internally conflicting character of the code minimum wage structure. There is complexity, lack of co-ordination, and conflict growing out of plural minima for individual industries, differentials of various types on these plural minima, some so-called minimum rates that are in no accepted sense of the term minimum wages, several types of divergently stated sub-minimal rates, astonishing spreads of the minimal rates within groups of related industries, varying structures in competing industries—and all these in a multiplicity of detail and endless variety of combinations. It is to be said, too, that the type of quantitative analysis used in these pages has tended quite definitely to minimize rather than mag-

---

of Labor, such certificate to be granted in accordance with instructions issued by the United States Department of Labor, Provided—

"(a) Such person is physically incapacitated for work in a factory or other regular place of business and is free from any contagious disease; or

"(b) Such person is unable to leave home because his or her services are absolutely essential for attendance on a person who is bedridden or an invalid and both such persons are free from any contagious disease."

nify the complexity. To understand the wage-rate provisions of any code, that code must be subjected to close scrutiny and exact analysis. Each code is a case by itself. Collective treatment blurs the diversities.

There is no blinking the fact that the present structure is too much an outcome of lack of dependable data, haste in code formation, and impatience with attempts to formulate guiding policies (or should one say the strong conviction that time was so essential that reasoned policies had to be sacrificed?). The existing structure is too much the result of "bargains" struck in a period of emotional stress and snap judgments. Certainly if the country intends to continue a minimum wage structure it should find some more rational scheme than the one now in effect.

CHAPTER XIII

WAGES ABOVE THE MINIMUM

In many industries—in most manufacturing industries—the wages paid to semi-skilled and to skilled workers are a much more significant element of labor costs than are the wages paid to unskilled workers. Because of this fact, the provisions in the codes dealing with wages in the higher brackets, as they are frequently called, have an importance far greater than would be inferred from the few lines they occupy in the various codes.

THE BACKGROUNDS OF THE CODE PROVISIONS

These provisions had to be shaped in the process of code negotiation without any pattern available in the Recovery Act itself and without any precise formulation of policy by the Administration. There was, of course, an underlying assumption with respect to the role of purchasing power in recovery. "The idea," said the President when signing the act, "is simply for employers to hire more men to do the existing work by reducing the work hours of each man's week and at the same time paying a living wage for the shorter work week." This, perhaps, was of some guidance in setting the minimum wage rate, but it helped not at all in the higher brackets.

A more precise prescription was initially stated in the cotton textile code, but very promptly events took a turn which blurred considerably this precision. When the President approved this code, he inserted in the executive

343

order of approval the following statement: "The existing amounts by which wages in the higher paid classes, up to workers receiving $30 per week, exceed wages in the lowest paid class, shall be maintained." This was definite: the approved technique for maintaining purchasing power was to increase the wages in the higher brackets by an amount equivalent to the increase that was made in the minimum wage. As is well known, the increase that was made in the minimum wage in this particular case was quite substantial. It is accordingly not surprising that, within a week after his order of approval, the industry persuaded the President to substitute a provision[1] which shifted the emphasis to maintaining the former weekly wage, with secondary emphasis upon the maintenance of differentials as they existed *above* the minimum wage, *and without relationship to changes made in that minimum.*

In the closing days of July 1933 (or two weeks later than the above-mentioned revision of the cotton textile code), the President's Re-employment Agreement was formulated. In this agreement, paragraph 7 provided that the employer was to agree with the President "not to reduce the compensation for employment now in excess of the minimum wages hereby agreed to (notwithstanding that the hours worked in such employment may be hereby reduced) and to increase the pay for such employment by an equitable readjustment of all pay schedules."

[1] The provision read thus: "The amount of differences existing prior to July 17, 1933, between wage rates paid various classes of employees (receiving more than the established minimum wage) shall not be decreased—in no event, however, shall any employer pay any employee a wage rate which will yield a less wage for a work week of 40 hours than such employee was receiving for the same class of work for the longer week of 48 hours or more prevailing prior to July 17, 1933."

This statement profoundly influenced later phraseology but its influence did not make for definiteness of meaning. Almost before the ink was dry on the promulgation of the agreement, it was deemed necessary to issue a series of interpretations, and quite lengthy interpretation was the lot of this particular paragraph. The net of it all was confusion. In general, the maintenance of the former weekly wage was urged, provided the hours were not too greatly reduced; but anything that was done was to be "equitable." Regarded as a formulation of law that was to be complied with, it is doubtful whether the interpretation had any really operative meaning.[2]

To sum up, such ideas as "purchasing power to aid recovery," "maintenance of weekly wages," "maintenance of long-standing differentials," and "equitable

[2] From the interpretation, the following paragraphs may be cited as the ones of most influence in later formulations:

"The policy governing the readjustment of wages of all employees in what may be termed the higher wage groups requires, not a fixed rule, but equitable readjustment in view of long-standing differentials in pay schedules; with due regard for the fact that payrolls are being heavily increased, and that employees will receive benefits from shorter hours, from the re-employment of other workers, and from stabilized employment which may increase their yearly earnings.

". . . an employee previously paid by the day, week or month will receive as much for the shorter day, week or month.

"An employee previously paid by the hour will receive as much per hour, but as shortening his hours will reduce his actual earnings per day or week, his compensation per hour is to be increased by an equitable readjustment.

"There is no fixed rule which can be applied to determine what is an equitable readjustment. In general, it will be equitable to figure what the employee would have earned at his previous rate per hour in a normal week in the industry, and then to increase the hourly rate so as to give him substantially the same compensation as he would have gotten for that normal week. But consideration must be given to other factors, including: Is the existing rate high or low compared with the average rate paid in the industry? Will the resulting adjustment result in an unfair competitive advantage to other employers or other trades or industries? Will a long-standing wage differential be lost if there is no increase in the existing rate?"

adjustment" were the main elements of the intellectual climate in which the provisions governing wages above the minimum were formulated. Perhaps it gives a wrong impression to speak of an intellectual climate. Perhaps it were better to speak of a series of intellectual climates, since many and rapidly changing forces beat upon the Administration in the process of code formulation. Naturally enough, industrialists, especially after the first flush of enthusiasm had faded, displayed a preference for clauses which would give them considerable elasticity in their operations—for clauses which vaguely called for "equitable" handling and left the employer or the code authority the judge of what constituted equity. The workers, on the other hand, especially as their attitude was voiced by the Labor Advisory Board, had a strong preference for introducing detailed wage schedules, or at the very least several basing points;[3] or for clauses which definitely demanded the maintenance of former full-time weekly earnings; or for clauses which required the maintenance of wage differentials. As regards this last position, the Labor Advisory Board of course wished this maintenance to be in relationship to the changes that occurred in the minimum wage; equally, of course, many industrialists wished to follow the pattern of the cotton textile code which, disregarding changes made in the minimum, spoke only in terms of maintaining the differentials *above* the minimum. Curiously enough, in view of the great expectations that existed in the early days with respect to the role of collective bargaining, the idea that the readjustment of wages in the higher brackets should be solely a function of collective bargaining had few advocates, and their voices were drowned in the roar and confusion of the arguments of other opposing camps.

[3] In contrast to "wage schedules," "basing points" set minima for few (usually one or two) classes of semi-skilled or skilled workers.

THE TYPES OR CLASSES OF PROVISIONS

In view of the dearth of expressed policy and the lack of precision and definiteness in the patterns available, it is not surprising that the persistent struggle between code sponsors and labor representatives over this, the most significant problem in the wage field, resulted in a wide variety of provisions governing wages in the higher brackets. The variety is so great, and the minor shadings so subtle and at times so cryptic, as almost to defy classification and generalized description. To meet as well as may be the difficulties of the situation, a classification approximately expressive of truth will at once be presented, and specific content will be read into it as the discussion proceeds. This classification is in terms of five stated main classes which can, when desired, be broken down into the twelve classes numbered in the table on page 348. This amount of detail is an irreducible minimum if a realistic examination is to be made of the interacting wage provisions of particular codes.[4] Even 12 classes fail to do justice to the complexity of the situation that exists in this vitally important aspect of wage structure. The distribution of the five principal types of provision by industrial groups is shown in the chart on page 349.

Detailed wage schedules and basing points cover a surprising proportion of the workers. At first thought, it seems astonishing to find 6,112,000 employees (27.8 per cent of the total) under the codes having this type of provision. Upon examination, however, it is found that 60 per cent of these are covered by two codes—the construction code, which provides for *later* regional collective bargaining on wage schedules, and the trucking code, which has a basing point in the sense that a differential

---

[4] For a statement of the type of clause in each code, see Leon C. Marshall, *Hours and Wages Provisions in NRA Codes.*

COVERAGE OF VARIOUS CODE PROVISIONS GOVERNING WAGES ABOVE
THE MINIMUM

Provision	Codes		Employees	
	Number	*Percentage Distribution*	Number (In thousands)	*Percentage Distribution*
A. (1) Wage schedules or basing points...	46	*8.9*	6,112	*27.8*
B. Emphasis on maintaining weekly wages	131	*25.3*	10,296	*46.8*
(2) Maintain, plus other provisions...	29	*5.6*	811	*3.7*
(3) Maintain, no other provision.....	64	*12.4*	6,738	*30.6*
(4) Partly maintain...............	38	*7.4*	2,748	*12.5*
C. (5) Maintain differentials..........	55	*10.6*	1,620	*7.4*
D. Equitable adjustments.............	197	*38.1*	2,539	*11.5*
(6) Equitable differentials..........	25	*4.8*	407	*1.8*
(7) Equitable adjustment—PRA.....	11	*2.1*	41	*0.2*
(8) Equitable adjustment, no reduction hourly rates..............	120	*23.2*	938	*4.3*
(9) Equitable adjustment alone......	41	*7.9*	1,153	*5.2*
E. No positive requirement for change...	88	*17.0*	1,455	*6.6*
(10) Policy statement or equivalent...	63	*12.2*	542	*2.5*
(11) Report only..................	11	*2.1*	418	*1.9*
(12) No clause...................	14	*2.7*	494	*2.2*
Total......................	517	*100.0*	22,022	*100.0*

wage ranging from 55 cents to 30 cents is provided for "drivers and skilled labor." Four other large codes with only basing points (bituminous coal, petroleum, men's clothing, and motor vehicle parking and storage) bring the count up to four-fifths of the total. In other words, detailed wage schedules in the codes exert only a modest influence. Their role is largest in the textile apparel, amusement, and graphic arts industries—industries where strong unions succeeded in having the essential features of collective bargaining wage agreements formalized into the law of the land. It remains to be seen whether this will prove a blessing or a curse to all parties concerned, including the public.

Blessing or curse, the Labor Advisory Board, with in-

creasing insistence, has sought the inclusion of detailed
schedules in codes where an approved strong union so
desired. At the present time, the Board believes that
codes should characteristically have, at the very least,
one or more basing points for wages in the higher brackets
—this as a device to "prevent the minimum wage from

DISTRIBUTION OF EMPLOYEES IN EACH INDUSTRY IN
ACCORDANCE WITH TYPE OF "HIGHER BRACKETS"
CLAUSE IN THE CODE COVERING THEM

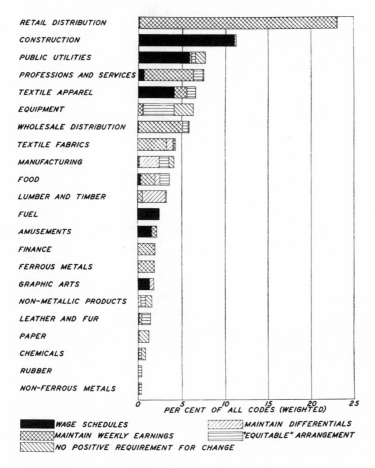

becoming the maximum." The Board seems not desirous of a *general* program of collective bargaining to determine wage schedules, lest this bargaining proceed under a type of unionization unsatisfactory to it.

The maintenance, wholly or in part, of former weekly wages applies to almost one-half the workers under the codes. Classes 2, 3, and 4 of the table on page 348 cover provisions governing such maintenance; the codes in those classes take in a total of 10,296,000 employees.

Clauses are placed in Class 2 when they provide for the maintenance of former weekly earnings *plus some other significant type of safeguard,* typically the maintenance of differentials. This is, of course, a fairly high standard in wage requirements. A typical clause runs thus:[5]

The weekly compensation for employment now in excess of the minimum wages herein provided shall not be reduced (notwithstanding that the hours worked in such employment may be hereby reduced). Wage differentials existing prior to June 16, 1933 shall be maintained for all employees receiving $35 per week or less.

The upper limit of $35, by the way, occurs frequently, not only in Class 2 clauses but also in others.

Less stringent are the clauses of Class 3 which require the maintenance of former weekly earnings *without significant supplementary safeguard,* although there is frequently a provision for "equitable adjustment." The clause in the retail code, although hardly typical, is reproduced since it applies to so many workers:

The weekly wages of all classes of employees receiving more than the minimum wages prescribed in this article shall not be reduced from the rates existing July 15, 1933, notwithstanding any reduction in the number of working hours of such employees.

[5] See also note 1, p. 344, where the corresponding clause from the cotton textile code is given.

There are placed in Class 4 the much less stringent clauses which provide for the maintenance of former weekly earnings *only in part.*[6] Typical of the provisions in this class is the following:

No employee whose full-time weekly hours for the four weeks ended June 17, 1933 are reduced by the provisions of this code by 20 per cent or less, shall have his or her full-time weekly earnings reduced. No employee whose full-time weekly hours are reduced by the provisions of this code, in excess of 20 per cent, shall have his or her said earnings reduced by more than 50 per cent of the amount calculated by multiplying the reduction in hours in excess of 20 per cent by the hourly rate.

One's first impression is that a wage provision which looks toward the maintenance of former weekly wages sets a high standard. An examination of the chart on page 349, however, induces skepticism. The application of these clauses is chiefly (over four-fifths) in retail distribution, professions and services, wholesale distribution, and finance. Here wages are traditionally paid on a weekly basis and frequently the weekly rate had reached a low level during the depression. Another large application is in ferrous metals (the iron and steel code) where the provision was safeguarded by a proviso that no employer need increase his hourly rates to the point where they are higher than those of a competitor in the same district who has increased his rates 15 per cent. Some of the other applications are in industries that were already working short hours; so that, unless the clause was drawn

[6] As a matter of convenience of classification, there are included (with quite doubtful wisdom) five codes which provide for an increase of hourly rates not to exceed a stated amount. One of these is the large iron and steel code; the others are those for reinforcing material, farm equipment, cordage and twine, and boatbuilding and boat repairing. The last simply calls for an increase of not less than 10 per cent in the hourly rates; the others have much the pattern of the iron and steel code in safeguarding the competitive situation. If these 5 codes were stricken from the group, the total of 2,748,000 employees would fall to 2,264,000.

for a normal "full-time" week, maintenance of "former" weekly wages constituted no serious problem.

This last comment is but one of many illustrations of the pitfalls in phraseology of many of these clauses. Does a given clause purport to maintain *all* former weekly wages or merely those of workers now receiving wages above the minimum? It might make a difference to a given worker. Is the maintenance confined to workers who receive less than a certain amount per week? Does the clause refer to individual workers or to an average of workers in classes of occupations; and, if the latter, is the area covered that of a given plant, a district, or the industry as a whole? In such event, how determine the former weekly wage? Does a clause which does not specifically say "weekly wages" nevertheless have that meaning if there is a further statement that "wages" or "compensation" shall be maintained "notwithstanding any reduction of hours?"[7] These are only a few samples of the difficulties in arriving at the operative meaning.

Definite maintenance of former differentials, standing alone, receives but moderate use. The requirement that former differentials be maintained—without qualification such as "fair," or "equitable," or "so far as practicable," and the like—is termed Class 5 in the table on page 348. The clause may or may not also require the maintenance of hourly rates. It may maintain differentials in relationship with the changed minimum wage or it may maintain differentials only as among the wages above the minimum—two very different things.[8] An example of the

[7] Such a clause is here thus interpreted, but instances are known of resistance to such an interpretation.

[8] It must not be supposed that all the clauses which mention the maintenance of differentials are placed in Class 5. It includes only those in which this maintenance is the matter of primary significance. If it is of secondary significance, the clause is classified elsewhere. For example, maintenance of differentials is frequent in codes that are placed in Class 2 and it appears also in Class 1 codes.

former is found in the lumber and timber products code, as follows: "The existing amounts by which minimum wages in the higher paid classes, up to workers receiving $30.00 per week, exceed minimum wages in the lowest paid classes, shall be maintained." An example of the latter may be taken from the fabricated metal products code:

Equitable adjustments to maintain differentials existing as of May 1, 1933 in all pay schedules of factory employees (and other employees receiving less than $35 per week) above the minimum, shall be made on or before 15 days subsequent to the effective date of this code by any employers who have not heretofore made such adjustments or who have not maintained rates comparable with such equitable adjustments; and the first reports of wages, required to be filed under this code, shall contain all wage increases made since May 1, 1933.

As the chart on page 349 indicates, the major impact of such clauses is exerted through these two codes, with a small amount of aid from other codes in the textile fabrics, food, and graphic arts industries.

"Equitable adjustment" appears in many codes with but modest coverage of employees. The significant word in this group is "equitable"—an "equitable" readjustment is to be made, or "equitable" differentials are to be maintained. Usually, no standard of equity is stated, although in a few instances some attempt at such a statement is made. Are the changes to be equitable in terms of the readjustments already made by a given employer? In terms of an effort partly to maintain weekly earnings? In terms of competitors' conditions? And who is to sit in judgment? Around such issues as these revolved many difficulties of compliance and many causes of labor unrest. The importance of this situation may be sensed by the fact that these classes embrace 197 codes, even if these codes do cover but 11.5 per cent of all employees under codes.

In detail, this group includes Classes 6, 7, 8, and 9 in the table on page 348. Class 6 looks toward the maintenance of "equitable" or "fair" wage *differentials,* usually without setting any standards of fairness. A typical clause runs thus: "Rates of pay in excess of the minimum hereinbefore prescribed shall be equitably adjusted in order to preserve equitable differentials. All such adjustments made since June 16, 1933 shall be reported to the code authority." Class 7 calls for an equitable *adjustment of wage rates* above the minimum without any definition of "equitable" other than is contained in the interpretations that were issued in connection with the President's Reemployment Agreement, as discussed on page 345. Some of these cases probably have the same practical effect as a partial maintenance of weekly wages. Class 8 takes in the codes which order an equitable adjustment with the further statement that there shall be no reduction of hourly rates. Usually there is to be a report made to the code authority and/or the NRA covering the adjustment that is made, and in quite a few cases there is provision for giving the proposal for adjustment the effect of a provision of the code. This latter provision, if carried out, would of course serve to give the force of law to the wages—or the method—approved.[9] Class 9 covers the codes which call merely for "equitable adjustment" without other significant safeguard, except that in some instances a report covering the adjustment is to be made.[10]

[9] An example runs thus: "There shall be an equitable adjustment of all wages above the minimum, and to that end, by July 1, 1934, the code authority shall submit for the approval of the Administrator a proposal for adjustment in wages above the minimum. Upon the approval by the Administrator after such hearing as he may prescribe such proposal shall become binding as a part of this code, provided, however, that in no event shall hourly or weekly rates of pay be reduced."

[10] The automobile code yields this example: "Equitable adjustments in all pay schedules of factory employees above the minimums shall be

Taking all these "equitable adjustment" classes together, the chart on page 349 shows that their main effect is felt in the equipment industries (automobile), with impacts of much smaller moment in a considerable range of industries; including, noticeably, professions and services, textile apparel, wholesale distribution, manufacturing, food, non-metallic products, leather and fur, and rubber.

No positive requirement with respect to adjustment of wages in the higher brackets exists in one-sixth of the codes. These, however, are typically small codes—only three have more than 100,000 employees each—and they cover but 6.6 per cent of the total employees. Class 10 is used for the codes which indicate merely that it shall be the "policy" of the industry to take action looking toward adjustment, or that it shall be done "to the extent practicable," or some equivalent vague statement.[11] Class 11 comprises the codes which make no requirement other than that a report shall be made concerning the action taken on wages above the minimum.[12] Class 12 is the group of 14 codes which contain no provision with respect to wages in the higher brackets.

---

made on or before September 15, 1933 by any employers who have not heretofore made such adjustments, and the first monthly reports of wages required to be filed under this code shall contain all wage increases made since May 1, 1933."

[11] Examples are: "It is the policy of the members of this industry to refrain from reducing the compensation for employment . . . and all . . . shall endeavor to increase the pay of all employees in excess of the minimum wage." Also, "To the extent practicable, the wage rates of employees receiving more than the minimum wage rate shall be equitably adjusted. . . ."

[12] By way of illustration: "Not later than 90 days after the effective date each member of the industry shall report to the Administration through the supervisory agency, hereinafter provided for, the action taken by such employer in adjusting the wage rates for (b) and (c) of this Article IV, but receiving less than $35 per week of regular work period." Machine tool and forging machinery code.

The chart on page 349 shows that the major influence of this group is exerted in the equipment industries (the electrical manufacturing code), with minor influence in five other industry groups. Of these five, the paper codes are the most interesting. Here a definite plan was worked out to give the entire body of labor provisions, including those governing wages in the higher brackets, a consistent and relatively. simple pattern—a unique thing in the code-making process.

THE OPERATIVE PATTERN

It was a basic assumption of the code-making process that maintenance, or rather increase, of the purchasing power of the worker was prerequisite to—not merely attendant upon—recovery. This assumption, it is true, took on more precise substance in the minimum wage area; but it provided at least emotional background in many a hard-fought bargaining struggle to strengthen the purchasing power of the worker in the semi-skilled and skilled ranks. To some varying extent, it found application in the broad meaning and structure of code provisions for wages in the higher brackets; to a very great extent it found application in refinements and subtleties of phraseology.

It was another cardinal tenet of the earlier stages of code formation (and it will be remembered that within nine months two-thirds of the codes covering nine-tenths of the employees had been approved) that "every industry is different"; that the proper procedure was that of hammering and bargaining through for each industry a code which would have the merit of being expressive of the peculiar technology and needs of that industry; that it savored almost of impropriety to regard one code as establishing a precedent for another. True, only within narrow limits does the human mind so operate; but the attitude is worth recording, if only to emphasize the dearth of consciously accepted principles and formulations which might shape the code structure.

If, in addition to these two basic attitudes, allowance is made for the fact that the early patterns for provisions governing wages above the minimum—those of the cotton textile code and the President's Re-employment Agreement—were elusive, not to say evasive, the mind is prepared to find explanations of the course that events actually took. It will contribute to definiteness of treatment if certain major features are given a prominence that is perhaps undue from the point of view of balanced analysis.

The relatively few codes with large numbers of employees naturally determined mainly the patterns of employee coverage. Some 42 codes account for nearly four-fifths (78.4 per cent) of all employees covered. As a matter of pocketbook concern to the workers, these codes are almost synonymous with the higher brackets wage structure pattern. The overpowering statistical influence of these few codes when the count is in terms of employees should be allowed for in the discussion which follows. This statistical influence is well shown by the following table. In this table each of the 42 codes which covers more than 100,000 employees is classified according to the type of higher brackets clause it contains. Since each code is weighted by the number of employees in its industry, the tabulation reveals the position and influence of the respective codes within the special groups.

Higher Brackets Group and Codes	Employees under Code In thousands	As Percentage of Group
Group A. Wage Schedules or Basing Points	**6,112**	**100.0**
(1) Wage schedules or basing points: Construction (provides for collective bargaining on schedules)	2,400	39.3

Higher Brackets Group and Codes	Employees under Code	
	In thousands	As Percentage of Group
Group A, Con.		
Trucking (basing point)	1,200	19.6
Bituminous coal (basing point)	459	7.5
Coat and suit (schedule)	455	7.4
Motion picture (schedule)	290	4.7
Graphic arts (schedule)	275	4.5
Men's clothing (basing points)	150	2.5
Hosiery (schedule)	130	2.1
Motor vehicle parking (basing point)	124	2.0
Petroleum (basing points)	101	1.7
Small codes (36)	529	8.7
Group B. Emphasis on Maintaining Weekly Wages	**10,296**	**100.0**
(2) Maintain, plus other provisions:		
Cotton textile	425	4.1
Small codes (28)	386	3.7
(3) Maintain, no other provision:		
Retail trade	3,454	33.5
Retail food and grocery	563	5.5
Motor vehicle retailing	350	3.4
Bankers	300	2.9
Hotel	291	2.8
Barber shop trade	200	1.9
Scrap iron, non-ferrous scrap metals, etc	180	1.7
Wool textile	151	1.5
Furniture	128	1.2
Wholesale food and grocery	113	1.1
Investment bankers	100	1.0
Needle work in Puerto Rico	100	1.0
Small codes (52)	809	7.9
(4) Partly maintain:		
Restaurant	609	5.9
Wholesaling or distributing trade	460	4.5
Iron and steel	420	4.1
Retail solid fuel	315	3.1
Baking	150	1.5
Bowling and billiard operating trade	136	1.3
Retail rubber tire	100	1.0
Small codes (31)	559	5.4
Group C. Maintain Differentials	**1,620**	**100.0**
(5) Maintain Differentials:		
Lumber and timber	568	35.0
Fabricated metal products	413	25.4
Silk textile	130	8.1
Daily newspaper	106	6.5
Small codes (51)	403	24.9

	Employees under Code	
	In	*As Percentage*
Higher Brackets Group and Codes	thousands	*of Group*
Group D. Equitable Adjustments	**2,539**	**100.0**
(6) Maintain equitable differentials:		
Fishery	180	*7.1*
Small codes (24)	227	*8.9*
(7) Equitable adjustment—PRA interpretation:		
Small codes (11)	41	*1.6*
(8) Equitable adjustment, no reduction in hourly rates:		
Cotton garment	200	*7.9*
Laundry	180	*7.1*
Small codes (118)	558	*22.0*
(9) Equitable adjustment:		
Automobile	447	*17.6*
Boot and shoe	206	*8.0*
Small codes (39)	500	*19.7*
Group E. No Positive Requirement for Change	**1,455**	**100.0**
(10) Policy statement or equivalent:		
Paper and pulp	108	*7.4*
Small codes (62)	434	*29.9*
(11) Report only:		
Electrical manufacturing	329	*22.6*
Small codes (10)	90	*6.2*
(12) No clause:		
Transit	264	*18.1*
Small codes (13)	230	*15.8*

As a matter of historical sequence, the code-making process moved in the direction of less precise standards in this field. Consider in this connection the chart on page 360. (1) Notice that (in terms of numbers of codes) there was a fairly steady decline in the use of detailed wage schedules or basing points. (2) Observe that the maintenance of differentials fell in the second hundred codes to a very minor position and remained there. It was a trouble-making clause; to the extent that it was precise and of operative meaning it invited attention to the traditional relationships of higher to lower wages. (3) On the other hand, it is evident that while there was decline in the use of "no positive requirement for change," there was corresponding increase in the use of the various "equitable" arrangements—and it is difficult to say which of the two is less precise. (4) Finally, although the chart shows an increase in the use of "weekly wage maintenance," it is to be remembered that this includes the *partial* maintenance method. It seems a safe generalization that the tendency was toward increased use of the vague clauses which savored unpleasantly of wishful thinking.

DISTRIBUTION OF HIGHER BRACKETS CLAUSES IN 500
CODES, UNWEIGHTED
(By hundreds of codes, in order of approval)

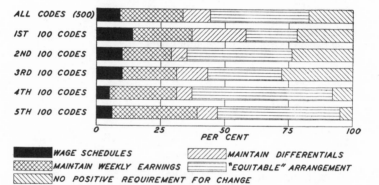

True, these clauses frequently made a gesture that "in no event shall hourly rates be reduced"—but, after all, such reduction was seldom in the realm of possibility with any type of "equitable" adjustment.

Only one group of closely related codes, the paper group, shows a consistent—almost uniform—pattern for the higher brackets clauses. However, the provisions of these codes are largely meaningless from the point of view of the present analysis, for the pattern used is a clause which prescribes a review of wage rates "and such adjustments, if any, made therein as are equitable in the light of all the circumstances." It may well be that this is as much as should be done for wages in the higher brackets; but if so it were wiser, as a matter of law making, to omit the clause entirely.

To say this is not at all to say that good results, from the point of view of the worker, are not possible where such clauses prevail. It depends upon the quality of administration. A "weak" clause well administered may have more effect than a "strong" clause poorly administered.

The technologies and traditions of industry groups did unmistakably play a part. A glance at the chart on page 349 gives ample evidence of this fact. The predominance of a clause looking toward the maintenance of former weekly earnings in the industry groups (retail distribution, professions and services, wholesale distribution, public utilities, and finance) where weekly rates have long been the vogue, and slight use of such a clause in industry groups where other methods of wage payments are customary, are natural developments.[13] The heavy use of this type of clause in textile fabrics does appear a bit strange until the exceptional circumstances of the case are remembered. Indeed, the very fact that it did not spread much to other groups, notwithstanding the early application of the pattern to this manufacturing group, is further evidence of the importance of traditional practices in wage structures.

Practice in collective bargaining also played a part. Reference has already been made to the fact that strong unions and habituation in collective bargaining are fundamentally responsible for the appearance of detailed wage schedules in certain of the industry groups. A similar remark, of somewhat less validity in a few striking cases where hard fighting by an adviser secured results, may be made of the use of one or more basing points for wages

[13] As was explained earlier, the ferrous metals situation is really a case of arbitrary—and doubtful—classification.

in the higher brackets. With respect to both these devices it must be said that they were consciously restricted by NRA policy rulings to industries in which unionization had been carried far. The theory was that unless such devices had been arrived at by collective bargaining, there was no proper sanction for their inclusion. It is doubtful whether, even in the absence of this ruling, these particular devices could have been introduced into the codes of non-union industries. Such industries would have resisted to the last ditch.

The dearth of operative meaning in many of the clauses is unfortunate. It is doubtful whether any other code provisions are as much open to this criticism as are the higher brackets clauses. As has been seen, many of them rest content with vague preachments concerning what is desirable or to be regarded as the "policy" of the industry. However, everything considered, these clauses are better than the typical "equitable" clause. This clause made sizable contribution to labor unrest, and would have made more contribution had not recognition gradually spread that it is largely meaningless and best forgotten. This spreading attitude, while diminishing labor unrest, also diminished respect for the code system as a "law" for the healthful development of industry. The difficulties of the compliance authorities in coping with such vaguely worded clauses are, of course, quite serious.

Nor is this the full story. Law can be effective as an instrument of social control only when words have ascertainable meaning and legal action an objective impact. From such a point of view, what can be said for such phrases as "long-established differential," "former full-time weekly wages," "occupational classes," and the like, unless—as seldom happens—they are carefully defined?

Take, in addition to the illustrations earlier cited, one

further example, the Class 5 clauses which look toward the maintenance of "existing" or "long-standing" differentials. Sometimes the statement is fairly explicit; but in the great majority of cases such questions as these arise: Does this refer to the differentials as they exist in a particular plant, a region, or the entire industry? Precisely what dates or periods are to be taken—a matter of great importance—as the basis of maintenance? Are the definitions and classifications of occupations in the industry or even in a given plant sufficiently clear and sharp to free adjustments from controversy? Are trustworthy records available for use in any adjudication of the problem?

The stark fact stands out that most of these clauses represent poor law draftmanship, poor bases of public administration, poor instruments of industrial relationships. It is, obviously, not a sufficient defense for such inadequacies that in some instances satisfactory agreements had been worked out between various interested groups so that no issues appeared in the public forum; or that in other instances, whether or not on advice of competent counsel or administrators, no substantial issue has been publicly raised although dissatisfaction remains.

There is some evidence that these clauses, when really operative, contributed to unfortunate business conditions. The statement, it will be observed, refers to cases of substantial effectuations of such clauses. In part, these bad conditions arose from varying provisions, and hence varying labor costs, as among competing groups. In part, they arose when given plants had multiple coverage by many conflicting codes—a problem that has caused the Administration many sleepless nights and the business man untold irritation. In part, they arose from certain clauses which resulted in further penalizing any employer who had not cut rates, or cut them but little, during the depression. It is a bit ironical that a law designed to promote fair competition should thus operate to the competitive disadvantage of not a few of the more socially minded employers. With respect to all these, and other similar situations, it can be said only that it is asking too much of human nature to expect it to go along willingly with such a procedure.

Even though intentions may have been of the best, it remains clear that with few exceptions the handling of the clauses governing wages above the minimum was and is inept. In the main, NRA seems to have plunged into legislative and administrative action in this field with few facts for guidance; with few comprehensive or definite policies ever formulated; and with little knowledge of the practical outcome. Innocence of facts, paucity of policy, ignorance of possible outcome—these are serious handicaps in any undertaking, but especially in one of such a complex and far-reaching character as the NRA. If wages above the minimum should be subjected to regulation by the federal government—a question which we may for the moment leave open—it goes without saying that some better means of control is needed than the present code provisions afford.

CHAPTER XIV

HOURS PROVISIONS

Quite understandably, the codes have come to be known as 36-hour codes, less-than-40-hour codes, 40-hour codes, or by some similar designation. This practice, however, should not be allowed to conceal the fact that in nearly every code the so-called basic week is qualified by exceptions—by various types of provisions designed to secure elasticity.

If, for example, a nominal 40-hour code contains a provision that the work week is to be 40 hours averaged over a stated period, but that, in any given week, 48 hours may be worked, it is obvious that elasticity has been provided. Naturally, this elasticity is large or small according to the excess hours permitted, the number of weeks averaged, and other stated conditions. Another example: a nominal 40-hour code may have a provision that, *as a general proposition* (herein called a "general overtime" provision) the basic hours may be exceeded, with or without set limit, provided overtime at a certain rate is paid. Again, a nominal 40-hour week may have extensive provision for peak or seasonal periods during which the maximum hours may rise to some stated amount—this with or without the payment of an overtime rate. Still again, there may be other "excepted periods," such as for emergency maintenance and repairs, for inventory taking, and for other purposes, varying with the requirements of industries and the skill of the code negotiators. Finally, nearly all the codes provide for permanent, not periodic, exceptions of specified classes of employees from the hours provisions of the codes. Such elasticities as these, which appear in many combinations, determine the *real* limitation of weekly hours as contrasted with any *nominal* limitation that may be stated in short-hand terms.

On hours, as on wages, each code is a case by itself. To understand just what limitations, if any, a given code provides, it must be subjected to detailed and careful scrutiny. It will be well to bear this point in mind when proceeding to a discussion of the outstanding patterns of hours provisions. These, it should be stressed, have been formulized for purposes of analysis. The resulting artificiality of logical arrangement must be corrected by first-hand reference to particular codes.

Subject to these qualifications, the purpose of these pages is to see what basic week the codes have set up in American industry; what elasticities have been provided; and what type of employment structure has emerged, as far as hours are concerned.

THE ACTUAL HOURS STRUCTURE

The main motive forces behind the formulation of the hours structure of the codes are clear. Upon the one hand was the desire to spread employment by reducing the work hours, with a secondary desire for short hours in the long run. Upon the other hand was the desire of industry to keep the basic hours from being reduced unduly; and, whatever the basic hours, to provide elasticity sufficient for smooth and efficient operation. These desires, translated into substance in the process of code negotiation, have produced the current complex structure.

An examination of this structure may appropriately begin with an analysis of the nominal or "basic" work week, and then push on to depict the exceptions, qualifications, and elasticities that have been introduced.

THE HOURS CEILING FOR 516 CODES[a]

1. Percentage Distribution of Codes Unweighted by Employees

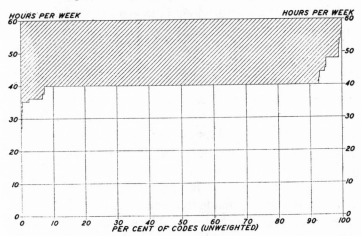

2. Percentage Distribution of Codes Weighted by Employees

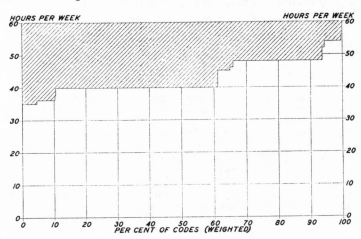

[a] Only one code, that for the fur trapping contractors, does not limit the working hours. The reason given by the NRA is that the industry operates only three months in the year and even then is subject to weather conditions.

The codes have provided a nominal "hours ceiling" over the "wage floor." In an earlier chapter it was developed that the wage floor is in reality a complex of staircases; it is now to be shown that a corresponding complex exists instead of a simple hours ceiling. The nominal ceiling, reflecting the "basic" hours untouched by code elasticities, is shown in the chart on page 367.[1] The upper section portrays this ceiling in terms of numbers of codes. The 40-hour week is emphatically the mode—it is found in 85.5 per cent of the codes; whereas the less-than-40-hour codes and the more-than-40-hour codes each make up only 7.2 per cent. A very different situation appears in the lower section, however, where the measurement is made in terms of the number of employees covered by the codes. Here, the 40-hour codes account for only one-half of the employees—only about 12 per cent more than are found under the more-than-40-hour codes. This changed situation is almost entirely due to long hours in a relatively small number of codes covering large numbers of employees in public utilities, finance, amusements, professions and services, the distribution trades, and the food industries.[2]

[1] The precise significance of these diagrammed ceilings should be kept in mind. They show only the *highest possible* ceiling—a possibility that in a given code may be open to all the employees, and in another code to only a small fraction of them. One code specifically sets the fraction at 10 per cent.

[2] The 44-hour ceiling is considerably influenced by the presence of such codes as motor vehicle retailing with 350,000 employees; motor vehicle storage with 124,000; wholesale food with 113,000; and investment bankers with 100,000. The 45-hour ceiling shows the influence of the fishery code, which has 180,000 employees. The width at 48 hours is attributable to the retail trade code with 3,454,000 employees (this code has several hours provisions but the "ceiling" is 48 hours when only the master code is considered); the trucking code with 1.2 million employees; the retail food code with 563,000 employees; the retail solid fuel code with 315,000 (but the "weight" carried at 48 hours is only 210,000 employees since the 48-hour provision applies only eight months

The nominal ceiling is but vaguely expressive of the really operative ceiling. Obviously, even the nominal ceiling is by no means flat; rather it is a ceiling of various heights and levels. This, however, is a great over-simplification of the actual situation, for each level of the nominal ceiling is stretched up here and there by clauses in the codes which provide for elasticities. A general view of the kinds and numbers of these elasticities may be secured from the accompanying tabulation, which shows the number of times each stated elasticity occurs in the 695 codes, supplements, and divisions now under examination. These elasticities, which appear in all sorts of combinations in the codes, are in the table below treated as four main types: averaging of hours; general overtime (not including overtime for special purposes such as peak period); periods of various sorts during which the basic hours may be exceeded; and permanent, not periodical, exceptions of certain occupational classes from the basic hours.

Averaging provision 113
General overtime provision 174
Excepted periods, all employees:
  Peak and seasonal periods 378
  Emergency repair and maintenance periods . .394
  Other emergency periods 67
Excepted periods, certain groups of employees:
  Repair and maintenance crews 22
  Report and inventory employees 27
  Other classes of employees 319
Permanently excepted occupations:
  Executives and supervisors 683

of the year); and the barber shop code with 200,000 employees. The noticeable jog in the ceiling at 52 hours is due to the bowling and billiard code, which has 136,000 employees. At 54 hours the ceiling is extended by the restaurant code with 609,000 employees, the hotel code with 291,000 employees, and the transit code with 264,000 employees.

Permanently excepted occupations, *Con.:*

Watchmen 587
Outside salesmen 579
Office and clerical 290
Firemen 285
Professional and technical workers 278
Engineers 266
Delivery employees 252
Repair and maintenance crews 212
Shipping and stock 171
Electricians 92
Cleaners and janitors 65
Scarce, skilled, or key workers 32
Continuous process operators 30
Workers receiving more than stated salary .. 20

Elasticity Through Averaging of Hours

As was indicated earlier, elasticity is secured through averaging hours. The device works thus: The hours worked per week *on the average* over a stated number of weeks must not exceed, say, 40; but in any *given* week the hours may be raised to a specified amount. Of course, these excess hours are to be offset by working a lower number of hours than the "basic" maximum in some of the weeks of the period. It is to be noticed that this lower number may be carried down to zero by lay-off or discharge. This is not likely to be done if the averaging period is short, but may be done if the period is long.

Has this device actually produced much elasticity in the hours structure? The crude figures sound impressive, for such a provision appears in 94 codes (113 codes, supplements, and divisions) which cover 4,696,000 employees or 21.3 per cent of the total. However, the mere presence of an elasticity gives no indication of its amount; consideration must also be given to qualifying conditions such as the number of excess hours permitted in a given week, the length of the averaging period, the proportion of the plant workers included under the provision, and the presence or absence of an overtime rate of pay for the excess hours. Since it happens that three-fourths of all the employees under codes with averaging provisions are found under eleven large codes, a tabulation of these codes will indicate in a broad way the averaging pattern, and will provide specific illustrations in connection with an inquiry into the amount of elasticity actually conferred.

ELASTICITY CONFERRED BY AVERAGING PROVISIONS IN MAJOR CODES

Code	Employees Covered (In thousands)	Averaging Period (In weeks)	Possible Increase in Weekly Hours	Overtime Base (In hours)
Trucking............	1,200	4[a]	Unlimited	48 per week
Automobile[b]........	447	52	8	—
Iron and steel.......	420	26	8	—
Bankers............	300	13	Unlimited	—
Graphic arts........	275	13	Unlimited	40 per week, 8 per day[c]
Transit............	264	26	Unlimited	—
Fishery............	180	2	Unlimited	—
Furniture..........	128	26	5	8 per day
Paper and pulp......	108	13	8	8 per day
Petroleum..........	101	2	4	—
Investment bankers..	100	17	4	48 per week

[a] This code permits an average of 54 hours over two weeks but an average of 48 hours over four weeks.

[b] In addition to the averaging provision for factory employees, this code has another for the "supervisory staff and employees engaged in the preparation, care, and maintenance of plant machinery and facilities of and for production." These employees are to average 42 hours per week on an annual basis with no limit for a given week.

[c] In two of the six divisions, only the eight hour per day base is used.

The number of excess hours permitted in a given week is not large. The following table shows the percentage of all codes which permit the specified hour increase in any one week, together with the percentage of all workers covered by codes containing these hour increase provisions. Basic codes are given in the first column, and codes weighted by employees in the second. It will be seen that whether the percentage of basic codes or of employees covered is considered, there is concentration upon two arrangements: (1) an excess of 8 hours and (2) unlimited weekly hours.

2-6 hours	18.1	13.0
8 hours	55.3	31.7
12 hours	2.1	2.0
Unlimited hours	24.5	53.3

Obviously, eight hours per week is not a very large amount of elasticity, even if not attended by other safeguards. Unlimited weekly hours, however, have an ominous sound—until a review of the large codes listed on page 371 shows that in the trucking code unlimited hours are safeguarded by a short averaging period and by overtime; in the graphic arts code by overtime; in the transit code by at least a theoretical limitation of the provisions to 10 per cent of the employees; and in the fishery code by a two-week averaging period. These examples are typical.

Payment of an overtime rate as a check on excess hours is found in almost one-half of the cases, whether the count is in terms of codes or employees affected. The details are as shown in the following percentage table, which lists basic codes first and codes weighted by employees last.

No Overtime Rate	57.4	53.4
Overtime Rate	42.6	46.6
Overtime over the basic week	21.3	35.0
Overtime with some other base	21.3	11.6

It is clear that an overtime rate not only safeguards labor but also acts as a check on the number of hours which will be used by the employer. When the base for the calculation of the overtime hours is the basic week (and this obtains for more than one-third of the employees under codes with averaging provisions), the check is substantial. When the provision does not rest upon the basic week, it usually rests upon an eight-hour day (usually in codes with unlimited days per week), or upon some figure higher than the maximum hours of the basic week or upon the averaging provision. If it be said that these latter two bases constitute no considerable check, it may in answer be pointed out that an examination of the codes affected will show that these weaker standards are, with but a single exception, applied to cases where there is a fairly strict limit set on the excess hours permitted in any given week.

The net of the foregoing examination of the number of excess hours *permitted* under the averaging provisions is either that the number is small; or, if large, that it is usually attended by other safeguards which in practice keep it within narrow bounds.[3]

The length of the averaging period is an important factor in the amount of elasticity conferred. Clearly, an averaging period of a small number of weeks is primarily useful in adjusting the shifts of employees or in handling situations where an operation cannot be closed sharply on a stated hour. Quite different, however, are the periods that run 13, 17, 26, or 52 weeks. As the first column of the following percentage table shows, such periods are provided by almost 74 per cent of the basic codes. As the second column shows, this percentage is reduced to about 63 when the codes are weighted by employees.

2 or 4 weeks	16.0	33.7
5 to 10 weeks	10.6	4.1
13 or 17 weeks	39.4	24.1
6 months or 1 year	34.0	38.2

---

[3] Unfortunately there are exceptions. An extreme illustration is that of the automobile code where certain classes of employees may work unlimited hours in any given week if they do "not exceed 42 hours per week averaged on an annual basis." Obviously, with an averaging period so lengthy there is always the possibility that one group of employees will be worked long hours until the tolerance applicable to them has been absorbed; and this group will then be displaced by other workers, and the process repeated. This possibility is known to have become an actuality in certain circumstances—an actuality probably more irritating and spectacular than otherwise significant.

With such long periods, unless there is sharp limitations of excess hours in a given week or an effective application of an overtime rate, it may readily happen that irregularity of employment will be stimulated by securing through lay-off or discharge the needed average of hours after employees have worked excessive hours for several weeks. Even if this does not happen, unsafeguarded lengthy average periods promote unrest; the employed worker is restless if the circumstances are such as to give a feeling of uncertainty, and the unemployed worker feels that the objectives of the Recovery Act are being frustrated.

Upon the whole and with a few irritating exceptions, the averaging provisions in the codes did not result in deliberate evasions of the basic week; and they did give needed elasticity with sometimes adequate and sometimes inadequate safeguards. The device, however, is not one that lends itself readily to enforcement—concealment is possible, and usually too much time must elapse before the record shows whether or not the basic hours have been violated. Because of this and because of irritation growing out of certain spectacular, even if exceptional, situations, the Administration eventually promulgated a policy which precluded the further inclusion of averaging provisions.

Elasticity Through General Overtime Provisions

In addition to the use of averaging provisions to give elasticity to the basic hours, there is considerable use of a general overtime provision.[4] It has just been seen that this is frequently combined with averaging. It will, accordingly, be appreciated that the data in the following

[4] The word "general" is used to differentiate this situation from the cases where overtime is paid in the excepted periods or to the excepted classes of occupations cited on pp. 369-70.

table include these combination cases, which constitute about 40 per cent of the total. The 174 cases of general overtime cited on page 369 have the following constituent elements, which occur in the indicated number of cases:

Overtime rate:
Time and one-third 84
Time and one-half 81
Other 9
Overtime base:
Less than 40 hours per week 8
8 hours per day 23
40 hours per week, 8 per day 47
40 hours per week 81
Other 15
Maximum week:
Less than 48 hours 20
48 hours or more (with number stated) 50
Unlimited hours 104

It stands out in this table that time and one-half and time and one-third are close rivals and that all other rates are negligible. It also stands out that, although eight hours per day has large usage, the base used in the overtime calculation is typically either 40 hours per week (which gives much daily elasticity unless the code sharply limits daily hours) or 40 hours per week and eight hours per day. These are significant patterns which seem indicative of considerable consensus of opinion.

A highly significant element of a general overtime provision is this: *How much* time shall be permitted? It is noticeable that in 40 per cent of the cases a rigid upper limit is set—48 hours or less—and in about half of these cases there is a further limitation because of the use of an averaging provision.[5] All this spells little elas-

[5] It is perhaps worth repeating that the effect of an averaging provision of the type here under study is that over a period of weeks the hours which may be worked must average less than the maximum hours permitted for any single week.

ticity. In the remaining 60 per cent (104 instances) the hours for any given week are unlimited, and only 18 codes qualify these hours by an averaging provision. Here the elasticity is substantial.[6]

---

[6] Again the influence of a few large codes is noticeable. Eleven codes, as given below, account for four-fifths of all the employees under codes with general overtime provisions.

Code	Employees (In thousands)	Overtime Rate	Overtime Base	Maximum Hours in Any Week
Trucking....	1,200	$1\frac{1}{3}$	48 (week)	Unlimited but not more than an average of 54 hours in 2 weeks or 48 hours in 4 weeks.
Wholesaling..	460	$1\frac{1}{3}$	40 (week)	Unlimited
Fabricated metal products......	413	$1\frac{1}{2}$	40 (week) or 48 until the peak period overtime allowance of 32 hours in 6 months is used up.	Unlimited
Retail solid fuel.......	315	$1\frac{1}{2}$	40–8 (4 months) 48–8 (8 months)	Unlimited
Graphic arts.	275	$1\frac{1}{3}$ or $1\frac{1}{2}$	40–8 sometimes 8 (day)	Unlimited (in one division 48) but not more than average of 40 hours in 13 weeks.
Furniture....	218	$1\frac{1}{2}$	8 (day)	45 hours but not more than an average of 40 in 26 weeks.
Paper and pulp......	108	$1\frac{1}{3}$	8 (day)	48 hours but not more than an average of 40 in 13 weeks.
Newspaper..	106	Indefinite	Indefinite	Unlimited
Retail tire...	100	$1\frac{1}{3}$	48–10	52 hours
Investment bankers...	100	$1\frac{1}{3}$	48 (week) or average of 44 in 17 weeks.	Unlimited
Needle work in Puerto Rico......	100	2	40–8	46 hours but not more than a total of 72 hours overtime in calendar year.

Upon the whole, the amount of elasticity introduced into the hours structure by permitting excess hours on payment of overtime is quite modest. At the most, it applies only to a possible coverage of one-fifth of the employees under the codes; and even within this restricted area its effects are rather strictly limited. It is not easy on rational grounds to account for this situation. In part it doubtless reflects the hostility of certain business elements to overtime rates of pay; in part it reflects a determination to keep hours down and thus spread employment; in part it grows out of a fear of some of the labor group that payment of overtime rates tends to react unfavorably upon basic rates. But after all this has been said, it still remains something of a puzzle why this rather automatic and easily enforced method of securing elasticity was not more popular in the process of code formation.

Elasticity Through Excepted Periods

The table on page 369 shows that various classes of periods were excepted—with various qualifying safeguards—from the basic hours of the codes. Of these excepted periods, the one of substantial significance is the peak or seasonal work period; the others, while attaining large totals in number of times utilized, are minor elasticities in amount, albeit sometimes of pressing character.

The codes frequently provide for elasticity by permitting the basic hours to be exceeded in times of peak or seasonal demand. Indeed this device is found in more than one-half (378) of the 695 codes, supplements, and divisions; and it has approximately the same proportion of coverage of employees. In sheer quantity, this is impressive, but again the real issue is "under what qualifying conditions?" These qualifying conditions and the frequency with which they appear are set forth below:

Weeks in year:
Less than 6 25
6, 8, 10 33
12 138
13-24 60
Indefinite 122

Maximum week permitted:
Less than 48 hours 41
48 hours 274
Unlimited 36
Other 27

Overtime rate:
None (no overtime applicable) 133
Time and one-half 159
Time and one-third 84
Other 2

Overtime base:
None (no overtime applicable) 133
8, 9, 10 hours per day 21
40 hours per week 26
40 hours per week, 8 hours per day 158
Other 40

In these peak periods there is sharp limitation of the maximum hours that may be worked. An analysis of the table shows that in more than four-fifths of the cases the top limit of weekly hours is 48 or less; and in only one-tenth of the cases are the weekly hours unlimited. Nor is this the full extent of the limitation. In more than one-fourth of the total cases the maximum set is further qualified by an averaging provision or by a stated total allowance of hours that may not be exceeded.[7] In other words, while the *principle* of seasonal elasticity is rather fully recognized in the codes, the spread-the-work

[7] For example, a total allowance of 32 hours over basic hours in any six-month period (which obtains in one code) can hardly be characterized as great elasticity.

theory operates sharply to limit the *amount* of this elasticity.

In view of this fundamental limitation, it becomes a matter of minor importance that in almost two-thirds of these situations an overtime rate is applied. However, it is interesting that the overtime patterns which are here applied are quite similar to those utilized in connection with the general overtime provision discussed earlier. Probably too, the factors which limited the use of "general" overtime (see page 377) serve to explain why peak periods were not easily and simply handled by permitting great elasticity on condition of payment of overtime rates.

Again, in view of the sharp limitations placed on excess hours in peak periods, the lengths assigned these periods become more interesting as a matter of code structure than significant for the amount of elasticity secured. The modal period is 12 weeks and it gradually has become "against policy" to have a longer period appear in the codes unless under compelling reasons. The entry in the table of 122 instances of peak periods of indefinite length seems to indicate great elasticities, but this is mainly in the seeming. Quite a few of these entries reflect difficulties of interpretation (and hence arbitrary decisions) with respect to the meaning of certain provisions of the codes. For example, a provision that a given number of *additional* hours (that is, over "basic" hours) is to be permitted "in any three-month period," or equivalent expression, seems to permit no definite statement concerning the number of weeks per year that overtime may be utilized. So also, a provision allowing longer hours in periods of seasonal or peak demand, without express limitation of the number of weeks involved, seems capable of no other classification than "period indefinite."

Clearly, such provisions may or may not mean any considerable amount of elasticity.

To sum up, important to business operations as provision for peak periods undoubtedly is, the code provisions in this field clearly reflect rigid limitation in the interests of spreading the work in a depression period. Under the circumstances, this was but natural. However, it does not follow that such *rigid* limitation in a period of expanding business is in the interests either of recovery or of increased purchasing power; and it seems as certain as can well be that such rigidity will not be able to continue after business revives.

Aside from peak periods, the other excepted periods of the codes do not involve large elasticities. True, one or more of these other periods do appear in most of the codes, and almost 85 per cent of all employees are under codes in which there is some type of excepted period other than the peak or seasonal period.[8] Of these periods, the one most frequently seen is that for emergency maintenance and repairs. It appears 394 times.[9] Since no one can predict in advance the precise elasticities required for emergency repair and maintenance work, this exception is typically for periods of indefinite length, and for unlimited hours weekly and unlimited hours daily within the periods. In a very large proportion of these emergency repair and maintenance cases (85.5 per cent, to be exact), an overtime rate is allowed. As for the base over which the overtime hours is to be calculated, it is typically either a 40-hour week (usually with eight hours per day) or the "regular hours" of the employees affected.

---

[8] The industry group which stands lowest in this particular is the textile apparel group, which in this respect is really in a class by itself.

[9] Notice, too, that repair and maintenance *crews* are in 27 instances excepted *for given periods;* and in 212 instances they are excepted *permanently* as an occupational group.

The expression "regular hours" has in this case a good deal of significance since it is not uncommon for the employees ordinarily utilized in such periods to have normal hours somewhat in excess of the basic week.

Naturally, the elasticity needed to provide for emergency maintenance and repair work is crucial rather than large in amount. Much the same remark may be made of the other excepted periods mentioned on page 369. There are (a) 67 instances of "other emergency periods," and in 38 of these an overtime rate is authorized; (b) 27 instances of exceptions for purposes of making reports or taking inventory, and in 12 of these an overtime rate is applied; (c) 22 instances in which emergency repair and maintenance crews in excepted periods are specifically mentioned, and the overtime rate is applied in 9; and (d) 319 instances in which a number of other classes of employees are excepted to varying extents for various periods (usually brief), and in 157 of these an overtime rate is allowed.

That all this meticulous detail should appear in "law" is difficult to explain save on the ground that the attention of the "law makers" was emotionally centered on rigid hours as the means of spreading work; and the "escape" seized upon to enable industry to operate was detailed provision for all sorts of particular needs. Of course the same goal could have been attained by a single, simple provision which allowed work in excess of the basic hours on payment of an overtime rate. The self-interest of the employer would have kept the excess down to his real needs.

Elasticity Through Excepting Classes of Employees

In addition to elasticities secured by the various types of excepted periods discussed above, practically all the codes provide, with or without limitation of total hours, for the exception of certain classes of employees from the basic hours provisions of the codes—this as a permanent arrangement and not for excepted periods.

Certain of these occupational groups were typically allotted unlimited hours. This was true of executives and supervisors, outside salesmen, and professional and technical workers. Exceptions covering such persons appeared, respectively, 683, 579, and 278 times, with a negligible number of applications of an overtime rate. Here indeed is another area of consensus of opinion; limitation of hours is not appropriate for such workers. In practically all other classes of employees, such exceptions as were made provided a maximum limit to their hours. The watchmen fared least satisfactorily. They were excepted 587 times; no limit to hours was set in 187 cases, while in 302 cases the limit was 56 hours per week or more. Overtime rates fell to their lot only 67 times. As for the rest, the accompanying table shows that out of the code-higgling process a somewhat consistent pattern emerged.

MAXIMUM WEEKLY HOURS PROVISIONS FOR SPECIFIED
EXCEPTED OCCUPATIONS[a]
(As cumulative percentages of 695 codes, supplements, and divisions)

Maximum Weekly Hours	Repair and Maint. Crews	Electricians	Delivery Employees	Firemen	Engineers	Shipping and Stock Employees
Less than 44...	2.8	4.4	2.5	1.9	2.0	7.9
44 or less......	38.9	44.4	27.1	28.7	32.3	53.9
45 or less......	40.8	48.9	31.7	49.1	54.2	61.2
48 or less......	53.1	64.4	72.5	73.6	78.5	80.0
Unlimited.....	46.9	35.6	27.5	26.4	21.5	20.0

[a] The proportion of instances in which overtime rates were provided is as follows: repair and maintenance crews, 54.7 per cent; electricians, 47.8 per cent; delivery employees, 41.3 per cent; firemen, 33.3 per cent; engineers, 34.2 per cent; and shipping and stock employees, 32.2 per cent.

Speaking generally, the tendency was to arrange about a 10 per cent tolerance—a limit of 44 or 45 hours per week.[10] This tendency was modified for certain groups, especially for delivery employees and for those firemen commonly called heat firemen; and it was often overlaid with a pattern of overtime rates paid only for hours worked in excess of the "regular hours" of such employees. None the less a sufficiently homogeneous pattern exists to justify an expectation that, in the light of this experience, a great simplification could be brought about in the code provisions applicable to these workers.

The precise amount of elasticity conferred by all these exceptions of occupational groups from the basic hours cannot at this time be calculated. Indeed, data are lacking for anything more than a few crude sampling estimates in particular industries. Among the factors that must be kept in mind in any attempt to evaluate the situation are these: (1) The number of workers in the excepted group obviously depends upon the technology of the industry or trade. The exception of outside salesmen may in certain instances mean little or nothing; and in other instances it may spell the exception of the majority of the employees. Correspondingly, the facts vary from industry to industry for the other groups. (2) The conditions attendant upon the exception are of the utmost importance and of wide variety. An exception that grants unlimited hours is vastly different from one that extends the hours from 40 to 44; an exception that requires an overtime rate of pay has practical conse-

[10] The number of entries giving unlimited hours seems high until one remembers that in some instances these are unlimited hours for any *single* week but over a stated period of weeks there is an *average* much lower than this maximum, and that there are other types of limitation. And again, overtime payment is frequently applied in "unlimited" cases. Only about an eighth of the instances of unlimited hours had neither averaging nor overtime.

quences quite different from one without an overtime rate, and of course the point at which overtime, if paid, begins, is a significant matter. (3) As among the various codes, much depends upon the number of classes excepted; the pattern is far from uniform even as among related industries. A sampling estimate made recently by the Labor Advisory Board for a score of codes indicates that from 1 per cent to 66 per cent of the total *employees* were affected by occupational exceptions; even this leaves open the extent of the increase in *hours*.

Elasticity by Industry Groups

Thus far, a general view of the "hours ceiling" as fixed by the codes has been secured, as well as a somewhat detailed view of the extent to which various types of elasticity have been introduced into the code hours structure.[11] The more important elasticities (in terms of amount) are those which result from the use of the averaging periods, general overtime, and exceptions made for peak or seasonal periods. The relative use of each of these forms of elasticity in each of the main industry groups is shown by the chart on page 385—and shown in relationship to the basic hours and the number of employees covered.

As a background consideration, it is noticeable that the more-than-40-hour basic week is concentrated in certain industry groups. The bulk of its effects is felt in retail distribution, public utilities, and professions and services; there are minor repercussions in wholesale distribution, food industries, amusements, and finance. So also, the im-

[11] Tables setting forth, in terms of employees covered by the codes, the applications of the hours provisions for each industry group appear in *Tabulation of Labor Provisions in Codes Approved by August 8, 1934,* prepared by Leon C. Marshall and issued in January 1935 by the Research and Planning Division of NRA.

CERTAIN TYPES OF ELASTICITY IN CODES WEIGHTED BY EMPLOYEES

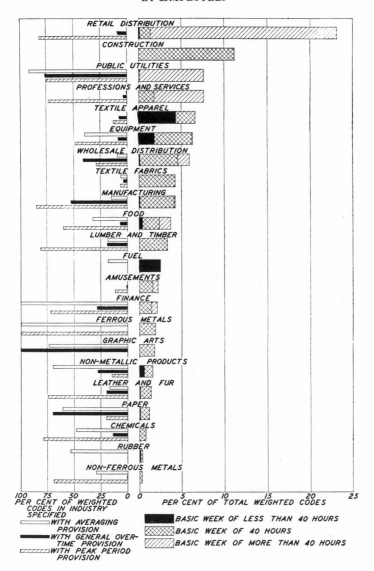

PER CENT OF WEIGHTED CODES IN INDUSTRY SPECIFIED

⎯⎯⎯ WITH AVERAGING PROVISION

▬▬▬ WITH GENERAL OVER-TIME PROVISION

▨▨▨ WITH PEAK PERIOD PROVISION

■ BASIC WEEK OF LESS THAN 40 HOURS

▨ BASIC WEEK OF 40 HOURS

▨ BASIC WEEK OF MORE THAN 40 HOURS

PER CENT OF TOTAL WEIGHTED CODES

pact of the less-than-40-hour basic week is primarily in a small number of industry groupings; textile apparel, fuel, and equipment.[12] Here is seen the influence of powerful labor unions.

It is noticeable, too, that in the two industry groups —textile apparel and fuel—where union influence brought about the less-than-40-hour week, relatively little use is made of the types of elasticity here under analysis. The same influence clearly plays its part in bringing about negligible elasticities in construction and amusements. It will be remembered that union influence brought about either detailed schedules or basing points for wages in the higher brackets in the textile apparel, fuel, construction, and amusement industries. It is worthy of at least passing comment that union influence thus tended to spell rigidity of structure. Union influence, however, does not fully explain the situation in textile fabrics; here is a so-called "sick" industry which by rigid hours and often by machine-hour limitation seeks industrial health.

As for the rest, generalization beyond pointing out the significant role played by a few large codes is not easy. Perhaps this should be expected. Perhaps, in a régime of haste in code formation under conditions of little objective information on employment conditions and employment needs of particular industries, the only patterns that can be expected to emerge are those set by large industry groups, by pressure groups, and by industries of peculiar economic status. Certainly it is a confusing and confused picture that is presented in the chart.

---

[12] The electrical manufacturing code accounts mainly for the equipment situation. Technically, a less-than-40-hour code, actually it contains liberal elasticities without payment of overtime that can be utilized in case of need.

SPECIAL CLAUSES RELATING TO HOURS

In addition to the provisions governing basic hours and exceptions therefrom, as dealt with above, there are in many codes "special clauses" dealing to some extent with hours. The extent of the use made of these special clauses increased greatly as the code-making process continued. In any early code there are few; in some of the later codes the number is considerable. A clause dealing with some aspect of the hours problem would be worked out for a particular industry, and thereafter this clause, or its equivalent, would appear in other codes, with frequency varying according to the technology and customs of the industry, and the interest shown in the problem by some adviser or deputy administrator. The accompanying list presents a summary view of the extent of the use made of special hours clauses in the 695 codes, supplements, and divisions.

State laws to be complied with 547
Excess hours to be reported 152
Employers subject to labor provisions of code . . . 93
Overtime for holidays 89
Lunch interval provisions 69
Special report on hours 69
Hours of work consecutive 66
Number of shifts limited 47
Waiting time counts 39
Geographic or population differential in hours . . 39
Lost-time clause 27
Maximum sharing of work 24
Stretch-out forbidden 21
Night work for women forbidden 20
Regulating start and finish 20
Maximum continuity of employment 18

The provisions which occurred with really great frequency (547 times of the 695) is the one that any state laws which contain requirements more stringent than those set forth in the code shall supersede the code requirements. (See also page 339 for a corresponding provision relating to wages.) A clause of this type, covering not only hours but other conditions of employment, early became "standard" and thereafter appeared frequently. It is the type of clause that a persistent Labor Advisory Board could, without great difficulty, negotiate. It is an interesting speculation whether its frequent utilization spells frequent surrender of some other item as the bargaining proceeded.

The only other special hours clause which is found in a considerable proportion of the codes (152 times of the 695) is the one requiring reports to be made of the number of excess hours worked under the various types of tolerance and exceptions allowed in particular codes. This, it will be observed, is still another limitation, and an annoying one, on elasticity. Its frequent use points again to the fact that the codes were formed in an emotional climate that favored rigidities theoretically designed to spread work. Of similar interest is the provision (found 69 times) calling for a special report on hours. These special reports were supposed to form the basis of further shortening hours if conditions in the industry justified such action, but there are few cases where their effect reached beyond salving a troublesome situation at the time of code formation. It may be pointed out, too, that other special clauses looked toward spreading work. Such were provisions making the employers themselves subject to the hour limitations of the codes (used 93 times), the prohibition of the stretch-out (21 times), and admonitions with respect to the maximum sharing of work (24 times).

Naturally, the different conditions in the various types

of industry and the interest of particular deputies or advisers led to some concentration in the use of these special clauses. Among the situations which strike the eye when the details are examined are the following:

1. The lunch-time provisions, the provisions that hours of work be consecutive, and the provisions that waiting time counts, appear primarily in the wholesale and retail distribution groups.

2. A full half of the provisions regulating the starting and finishing of work are in the textile apparel group.

3. Most of the provisions forbidding night work for women are in the paper codes.

4. The bulk of the provisions limiting the number of shifts fall in textile fabric and textile apparel groups.

5. Almost all the provisions forbidding the stretch-out fall in these same textile fabric and textile apparel groups.

6. Almost half of the provisions calling for a special report on hours appear in the paper group.

As is to be expected, the haste with which code formation was conducted and the paucity of clear expression of policy to guide the process contributed to the lack of balance and consistency in the application of these special clauses. Opinions may differ with respect to the legality or wisdom of having this type of regulation conducted under federal auspices; but, if federal regulation is to be used in this field, there can hardly be two opinions with respect to the desirability of using it with balance and consistency.

As one thinks back over the range of provisions in the codes governing maximum hours, certain matters stand out.

This type of regulation of hours is essentially new in both motive and method. In general, such regulation of hours as has occurred in the past has been designed to protect special types of workers or to prevent sweatshop conditions. This new enterprise has as its main motive recovery from an industrial depression through spreading work and at the same time increasing purchasing power; its secondary motive is that of promoting for the long pull sound business hygiene and fair competition. The method utilized is new in that, for industry as a whole, we have never before attempted significant federal regulation of hours; and of course the code method of regulation is new in both state and federal experience. It is, of course, now too late to raise for any practical purpose the issue whether in both motive and method the field was so uncharted that it was unwise to enter it without prior exploration. It is, however, highly appropriate to examine the consequences of the journey thus far.

In general, the hours structure is intricate and inelastic. There is seeming simplicity in that the 40-hour basic week dominates the scene. The basic week of more than 40 hours is primarily a creature of retail distribution, public utilities, and professions and services—with modest contributions from wholesale distribution, food industries, amusements, and finance. The basic week of less than 40 hours is primarily a creature of the textile apparel and fuel industries.[13] Modest contributions are made by the food and non-metallic products groups; and quite slight contributions by half a dozen other industries. There is seeming elasticity in the multitude of provisions for excepted periods, excepted occupations averaging, and general overtime. But when the structure is examined in detail, and especially when it is studied as an operating situation in related industries, its intricacies and inelasticities bulk large.

[13] It seems to bulk large in the equipment industries; but this, because of certain elasticities in the code primarily responsible, is more a matter of seeming than of reality.

The variation in detail as among the industry groups and even as among the codes within a given industry group is so great that generalization is not easy. It may, however, be said that (always with honorable exceptions) the elasticities that have been conferred do not sufficiently facilitate the smooth operation of business, and many do not sufficiently safeguard the interests of the worker. Inadequate elasticities spell continual incentive to code violation by management; and on the other hand elasticities that do not contain sufficient safeguards or are not capable of being readily understood by the workers tend powerfully to promote labor unrest. Without undertaking at this point to decide the question of whether the NRA program of hour limitations is in general desirable, the conclusion expressed in connection with wage provisions may be reiterated, that if the program is to be satisfactorily administered the present arrangements should be radically overhauled.

CHAPTER XV

CONTINUING ISSUES

The preceding three chapters have been concerned solely with an analysis of the structure of employment conditions under the codes. The scope of the analysis has not extended, except by inference, to the administrative problems involved. Nor has it covered the operative economic consequences in relation to the recovery objective.[1] At this point a brief review of the analysis is expedient. This will be followed by a consideration of continuing problems both of administration and public policy.

STRUCTURAL COMPLEXITIES

In order to facilitate exposition, the earlier discussion has taken up separately the minimum wage structure, the higher brackets structure, and the hours structure. Operatively, of course, these are not separate and distinct; they are inter-woven and interacting parts of the hundreds of separate code structures of employment conditions. Furthermore, these total structures are not abstract entities; they are concrete instruments that are to be administered in the work-a-day business world, and their administration is to be supervised by another complex of governmental and quasi-governmental agencies.

In Chapter XII, it was seen that the minimum wage structure is an outgrowth of a wish to see every worker receive a living wage, and of a vaguely defined idea of the role of wage protection in stimulating business recovery. This outgrowth might have been simple, but it became very complex. In a situation where there was little objective information and less defined policy, there

[1] This subject is dealt with at length in Pt. VI.

were struggles of employers to keep wage costs down, to maintain much of the customary system of wage relationships, and to develop a competent labor force through the use of learners and apprentices. There were countervailing struggles of representatives of workers to push the minimum wage level as high as possible, to bring about a different distribution of income, and to minimize geographic differentials while maintaining occupational differentials. Such struggles, in conjunction with the efforts to expedite code making, resulted in the complex minimum wage structures which are reflected in greatly simplified form in the chart on page 320, Chapter XII. Even as among related industries, there were set varying rates for a single unskilled group; varying minima for two or more groups in a single industry; diverse geographic rate structures; diverse relationships between minimum wage rates and rates in the higher brackets; diverse relationships between the wage structure and the hours structure; diverse kinds and degrees of sub-minimal rates.

In Chapter XIII, it appears that the wage structure in the higher brackets is as complex as the minimum wage structure—often elusively complex. By a process of occasional arbitrary decision and frequent over-simplification, the higher brackets clauses are in that chapter classified in twelve groups although 50 would not have sufficed for realistically detailed treatment. In certain situations, patterns of relationship between these clauses and the other aspects of employment provisions can be pieced out; but these situations are not typical. Of course, this fact matters less than might be supposed; in the main, the clauses have little precise operative meaning that is really enforceable as law. To the extent that this is true, confusion becomes compounded with complexity.

That such a situation should obtain in a matter of such importance illustrates the vagaries of the code-making process. One can sense in the background a desire to increase purchasing power. One can see vividly in the foreground the process of pressure group negotiations in which one party tends to demand specific, even rigid, formulation; while the other fears both high labor costs and any method of leaving the matter to later extra-code determination if that method stimulates collective bargaining with independent unions. In the absence of explicit policy and definite patterns on the part of the Administration, it was to be expected that the final product would be ill fitted to be law.

Chapter XIV reveals a situation of intricacy and complexity in the hours structure similar to that in code wage provisions. With relatively few exceptions, as is shown in the chart on page 385, the basic hours structure of a given industry group is overlaid with a network of excepted periods, averaging provisions, and general overtime provisions. These, designed to permit the elasticity needed for successful business operation—or for what may not be the same, the avoidance of fixed obligations —are in varying amounts and they are molded by varying patterns of controlling conditions. Then too, various occupational classes are exempted in varying degree and under varying conditions from the basic hours. This complex situation, thanks to an atomistic theory of code formation, exists notwithstanding the fact that underlying the complexities and conflicts of detail certain basic patterns and a considerable consensus of judgment can be glimpsed. The detail of regulation is too great to be effective as law which is to be administered, and, where operative, too straitly binding to permit easy adjustment to business operations.

Add to the foregoing the fact that the complex hours structure is of necessity inter-woven with the complex wage structure; add further that related and competing industries operate under varying total employment structures which, if the codes are complied with, mean divergences in cost of operation; and it becomes overwhelmingly clear that the existing complex of employment provision is highly unsatisfactory as a body of law.

ADMINISTRATIVE DIFFICULTIES

Administrative complexities go hand in hand with the complexities of the employment structures. They have arisen from several sources. One fertile source was the early theory that haste should be made in the codification of industry; that vagueness and even contradictions could be rectified by the technical processes of "explanation" of simple matters, by letters from the deputy concerned, more formal "interpretations" by the Administration in the case of more difficult issues, administrative "stays" of provisions demonstrated to be unfortunate, formal "amendments" to rectify basic sins of either omission or commission, and technical "exemptions" of individuals who could successfully plead undue hardship.

The situation is especially troublesome when the code contains instances of phraseology representative of wishful thinking rather than operative implementation; and other instances of phraseology so vague—as was common in the higher wage brackets clauses—that it has no enforceable meaning. The difficulty is multiplied if effort is made to carry the sanctions of law over into fields of control and methods of control for which its genius is not fitted. Add to this the fact that pressure groups are by no means averse to fashioning the instrumentalities here under discussion to serve their particular ends, and the final sum constitutes an unfortunate milieu in which to operate a theory of haste in code formation with later rectification of mistakes.

This, however, is not all. In a new field of social experimentation and control in which customary ways of thinking and acting had no time to emerge—and these, not law, are our chief instruments of social control—there were uncertainty and rapid change in procedures and policies which inevitably increased the complexity and internal strains of the final product. As contributing to the confusion, there must even be mentioned a poor co-ordination of the various governmental agencies (such as the Federal Trade Commission, the Department of Justice, the Agricultural Adjustment Administration, and the National Recovery Administration, to cite only a few) which worked at various interrelated aspects of the common problem. And, it may be added, personnel to cope with these new problems had to be found almost overnight—and where was the personnel that was experienced in the handling of problems of this sort?

One final administrative complexity deserves mention. A code applies to a given industry as that industry is delimited by the definition set forth in the code. In not a few instances, the definitions of different codes have been so drawn that it is a matter of dispute under which code a given plant or process falls. This problem of overlapping definitions becomes a serious matter for purposes of the present discussion if the codes claiming jurisdiction have divergent employment conditions. So also, as the codes have been drawn, a plant producing many products will often find some of its operations under one code, others under another code. This multiple coverage obviously spells serious practical difficulties of operation when the codes have divergent labor requirements—

difficulties which have caused much administrative agony of interpretation and exemption.[2]

PLANS FOR IMPROVEMENT

The officials of the NRA are more vividly aware than any one else of the administrative difficulties which the present complex structure engenders. They have to cope with a continuous stream of perplexing problems. They ponder plans for remedying the situation centering around the concepts of simplification and standardization. Without examining at length the connotations of these terms, it may be said that the primary objectives are (1) to reduce the provisions of codes to precise, administrable operative meaning; (2) to apply uniform types of provisions to competitively interrelated areas of industry; and (3) to achieve elastic forms easily applicable to varying situations.

One of the most widely discussed proposals for simplification is to replace present hours provisions with one in which the basic day or week may be exceeded at will if "time and one-half" wages are paid for all labor over 40 hours per week or 8 hours per day—or whatever hours are thought appropriate—with double wages for a seventh day of work in any week and with longer working hours for special classes of office and technical employees. The particular merit of this proposal is felt to be its elasticity. The deterrent to operating beyond the stated hours is simply the extra wage cost. Proposals for improving minimum wage provisions consist mainly in simplifying the true minimum structure through more precise definition of exceptions and through various other means of attaining clarity and precision.

[2] For discussion of definitions see Chap. VI. For further discussion of administrative problems see Chaps. VIII and IX.

Problems of simplifying provisions for wages above the minimum are more difficult than any others. This is illustrated by a suggested provision—from among several alternative suggestions—under which a worker's current pay for a full-time week must be not less than "he could have earned for the same class of work for the longer full-time week which was normal for that occupation in the establishment as of [a stated pre-code date]," with specific exceptions. Whether applied to individuals as such or generalized by precise occupational description, the provision projects into the future a system inelastically bound to a preceding norm both of occupations and wages.

Proposals for simplifying the structure of wages above the minimum are the storm center of controversy among interested groups. The organized labor groups in general advocate placing in the codes either a detailed schedule of wages arrived at through collective bargaining, or a few "basing points" to check any tendency which may exist to depress wages in the higher brackets toward the level of the minimum wage. Even among labor groups controversy exists over proper means of determining rates. In general, the business groups are opposed to provisions which make wage structures rigid, or impose upon them unwonted relationships of collective bargaining. Some disposition to compromise arises from the desire to have obligations more precisely defined, though in many quarters the present lack of operative meaning is preferred to any alternative increase of precision. A suggestion widely discussed within the NRA rests on the belief that it is inexpedient to write into codes any wage provisions other than minimum rates. Instead, so the suggestion runs, the appropriate course of action is to leave this situation elastic by placing in the codes a clause providing for a real implementation of collective bargaining, carried on in the light of exact information and clear definition of terms. The wages arrived at through this process would not be written into the codes and would not become "law." Out of the many types of proposal which are current none which retain the idea of legal determination of rates can be said to cope successfully with either the technical or controversial elements.

Apart from the attempt to attain more precise operative meaning for labor provisions, attention within the NRA is also being given to the possibilities of making uniform provisions applicable to whole groups of codes in related areas of industry. Thought along this line takes the codes as given, recognizes that their coverage, severally, is not a proper delimitation of areas of regulation of labor conditions, and attempts to remedy the defect by uniformity of terms. It therefore implies a different plane of action than that envisaged by combining and eliminating codes and radically reducing their number, though both objectives might be simultaneously sought.

It is neither possible nor desirable at this point to review the wide variety of suggestions and controversies which are current within the NRA concerning the future of labor provisions. The concern with them is of course a highly appropriate preoccupation for NRA officials. Indeed it is much more than that. Probably there is no exaggeration in saying that a large degree of reform is a minimum condition of the continuance of the NRA as an agency for the regulation of labor conditions. There already exists a serious degree of collapse under numerous codes. Unless the existing inadequacies can be remedied, much more of the complex structure of labor provisions will break down. Some parts will break down because they are non-administrable or lacking in operative meaning; others from the spread of competitive pressures.

A high official of the NRA has drawn up a list of fundamental objectives that should govern the process of attaining simplicity, standardization, and elasticity, as follows:

1. Labor provisions in the codes should be simple, not intricate and complex. Their wording should be clear; there should be a plain, operative meaning; and, in general, the phraseology should be such that the difficulties of administration will be reduced to a minimum.

2. They should not attempt to carry the sanctions of law into areas of control or into methods of control where law cannot operate effectively.

3. They should provide in automatic fashion the elasticity needed by industry for smooth and effective operation. In brief, they should increase the certainty of business operations by placing such control of uncertainties as may be practicable in the hands of management. Requests for individual exemption in order to meet unforeseen contingencies should be largely unnecessary.

4. They should safeguard the interests of labor not only during the process of recovery but also for the long-run pull; and as an element of this safeguarding, they should be designed to promote united action of labor and management. Both on the grounds of spreading employment during a period of depression (if that be accepted as a guiding policy) and on grounds of proper labor standards at any time, a strong incentive should exist against excessive hours; and it will markedly facilitate compliance if this incentive is one which motivates both worker and employer. The semi-automatic device which works most smoothly to these ends is an overtime rate of pay for hours worked in excess of basic hours. The employer will not increase his labor costs unless his need is substantial; the worker has a strong incentive to collect the overtime pay authorized by the law.

5. They should run in such patterns, as applied to related industries, as to promote comparable competitive conditions; and they should reduce to the minimum difficulties arising from overlapping definitions of codes and from multiple coverage of codes.

This statement of objectives recognizes that unless the methods of altering labor provisions are used with a clear sense of guiding patterns, the result can easily be increased complexity and confusion. It recognizes also that law which proceeds on the assumed need and propriety of an elaborate scheme of lawful exemption of individuals is a clumsy, even dangerous, tool. Regarded as the thoughts of responsible administrative officials this is all very sensible.

But the total meaning of the statement, it should be noted, is that the pattern of labor provisions should be almost entirely different from what it is. In strictly administrative terms the question which it raises is whether the procedures of the NRA are adapted to the approximation of the objectives stated.

Many officials are hopeful that the oppressive and irritating character of the present provisions has served to break down the separatism of the code-making process, to an extent where simplification and standardization can be put in motion on a voluntary basis. Taken up piecemeal, code by code, many situations are without doubt capable of improvement. The general situation is not, however, capable of rapid rectification.

Elimination of weaknesses on a large scale sounds more feasible than it actually is. In practice, vested rights are soon claimed; amendments on a particular issue are not freely offered if there is fear that such a proposal will open up consideration of other aspects of the code. The mills of a huge organization in which pressure groups must be consulted at every turn grind slow, whether or not they grind exceeding fine. Moreover, were labor provisions opened up for general re-examination, even with plans for simplification and standardization in hand, the situation might well explode into bits of contrary opinion and interest.

The well-intentioned plans of NRA officials for administrative improvement are backed by little definitive ability to change the situation materially in any reasonably short span of time. What they preside over is law applying to a large number of delicate and unstable employer-employee situations. The NRA can cause any or all of these situations to collapse. But it has small power to move rapidly toward bringing them into line with general dictates of administrative efficacy, no matter what the degree of good will applied. This is of course on the assumption that wide and general use will not be made of authoritative power to change the terms of codes by executive fiat—a reasonable assumption in view both of past NRA history and of the political risks involved.

To the poor prospects of moving rapidly in the direction of simplicity under existing procedures need to be brought certain elements of administrative experience which were discussed at length in Chapters VIII and IX. There is sufficient evidence to permit confident assertion that code agencies, except in exceptional cases, are unlikely to provide impartial and efficient administration of labor rules. Nor is the NRA now equipped to provide such administration. Administrative implementation involves the necessity of inspection and policing. For even a much simpler body of rules than those existing, this would involve a great expansion of federal organization, unless state governments were to take over the duties. In the making of any plans for the future of federal labor law the question of how far the government wishes to go in new administrative paths will be an important consideration.

The long run is the time span in which one must consider the really fundamental questions. The hope for improvement in the long run is the principal hope that now remains. In long-run terms, it is possible to entertain a reasonable anticipation of considerable improvements, measured from the present unsatisfactory situation. Unless under a new set of standards and procedures, the prospects would depend very much upon personalities. Intelligence and energy, working through reformed procedures, could make some progress. But it would be equally possible and much easier, rather than to move toward simplicity, to introduce greater complexity through the multiplication of exemptions. In any case, when the long-time view is introduced into the picture, such procedures as the NRA has used offer a very bad choice of means for effecting a permanent system of labor legislation. Yet as a going concern the NRA might, unless thought is taken, be permitted to project its pattern indefinitely into the future. It becomes necessary therefore to state clearly what the issues of public policy are.

ISSUES OF PUBLIC POLICY

The NRA has produced an elaborate body of wage and hour legislation under the codes. But the government has developed no permanent policy on wage and hour legislation. A government bureau (acting of course within its emergency commission) continues to make and remake the body of such law. This is a very anomalous situation, and not one which ought to be continued very far into the future.

The origins of this situation of course lie in the exigencies of the spring of 1933. The development of code law reflected the purpose to spread available work and to halt what was regarded as a "destructive" disintegration of the wage structure. The manner in which this situation was met through the procedures of the NRA does not commend itself either as a careful readjustment of economic relationships in the interests of recovery nor as a system of protective labor legislation to be permanently maintained. What now stands upon the books is a body of rules which, as has been demonstrated, is unsatisfactory technically as law, incapable of effective administration, and unoriented as to economic policy.

The precise problem now before the country is that of establishing a permanent federal policy on labor legislation. This involves Congressional determination of the areas of control within which it is thought appropriate for the federal government to operate. The problem presents itself in a series of more specific issues.

The first issue is whether the United States government proposes to maintain a system of minimum wage legislation. The second is whether it proposes to regulate the whole wage structure by rules covering higher than minimum wage rates. The third is whether it proposes to engage in those detailed forms of regulation now represented by the so-called "special clauses" of codes, covering such detailed matters as methods of wage payment and classification of employees. The fourth is whether it proposes to engage in a permanent program of limitation of hours of work. The fifth is what the policy shall be toward collective bargaining.[3]

It is within the limited area of the reasonably feasible that the questions of principle have to be decided. No single and simple set of criteria is available to guide de-

[3] Problems relating to industrial relations and collective bargaining are discussed in Chap. XIX.

cision. Each item in a proposed program can be examined according to strictly economic analysis, with reference to the effects upon the creation and distribution of wealth. Each can be examined with reference to whether it falls within responsibilities which the federal government ought to assume for protecting citizens in their capacity as wage earners. Each can be examined with reference to the changes which it will entail in the characteristic scope of the operations of the federal government. There is no wholly common denominator between these economic, ethical, and political questions. The considerations differ in qualitative character, and cannot be accurately weighed against one another in quantitative terms. No easy road therefore exists to the goal of definite public policy.

What is insisted upon here is that the issues, as presented above, have not been faced in the United States. Action has taken place on an emergency basis. But, in terms of permanent policy, the issues have not been the subject of public discussion. They have not engaged the serious attention of Congress. They have not been seriously canvassed at the NRA. They represent issues of public policy for which there exists no appropriate avenue of determination except legislative action.

In view of the uncanvassed state of the issues, it would be presumptuous, not to say foolhardy, to attempt to outline here a program of labor legislation for the United States. Such an attempt would also go far beyond the defined scope of the present volume. But the issues have to be brought into focus in order to give exact statement of the considerations bearing upon the future of the NRA.

In a canvassing of the issues of public policy, the NRA can contribute a mass of factual information upon labor conditions. The importance of this is very great. It can also contribute a variegated body of experience concerning the attempt to apply many types of control under diverse circumstances. Less than justice would be done were it not also stated here that under the labor provisions many things have been done in detail which may be considered highly desirable from the point of view of a social interest in the welfare of workers. Moreover there has been a striking educational process at work covering the facts and problems of working conditions and constituting a preparation for the crystallization of national policy. And finally, in various detailed situations, there have emerged constructive patterns of action which illustrate feasible lines of development, so that choices of policy are now possible in the light of somewhat tested concrete proposals.

Whatever education and experience the NRA may contribute to future guidance, there remains the necessity, however, of saying that it does not, as now constituted, provide a legislative policy nor a pattern of labor provisions appropriate for future maintenance and development. And, whatever items of permanent policy are decided upon, if any, the NRA and code agencies, as now constituted, are not to be recommended as an appropriate administrative system.

A danger exists that the present pattern of labor rules and the present procedure for making them will harden into permanent form merely through Congressional inertia. It would be much easier to let the NRA take its course than to come to a decision on the questions of principle involved and to adjust action thereto. If the former were to happen, as has been pointed out, some technical improvement of code provisions would be possible, with correlative easing of the administrative difficulties. This is merely a possibility, not a certainty. Meantime, the government would continue indefinitely to provide the country with the unedifying spectacle of a mass of federal law as honored in the breach as in the observance. The most pressing need is to root out unsatisfactory forms of labor law and ways of making such law before they become set in fixed patterns, simultaneously with the introduction of such forms and means as are determined upon in line with the dictates of permanent policy.

In strictly practical terms the process will not be easy or pleasant, either economically or politically. Business activities have been adjusted to the present rules, where operative, and vested interests have been created therein. The interested parties, both labor and business, are organized and articulate. But they are unlikely to become less so as time goes on.

One consideration now seems most paralyzing to constructive action concerning the future of the code labor provisions. This is the fear—entertained by many officials, workers, and others, including business men— that abandonment, or even essential change, of NRA powers over the making and administration of labor rules would disturb business operations, precipitate a collapse of wages, and undo the work spreading which has been accomplished. Fear of change, not approval of the *status quo* of labor provisions, is the most conservative influence in the situation. This is not an entirely idle fear, though opinions may reasonably differ concerning the degree of disturbance entailed. In any case, if the fear is permitted to estop constructive action, it serves merely as the easy defense for failure of ingenuity. The exact problem before Congress *is* that of defining a policy on labor legislation and following it with the minimum of disturbance.

The difficulties of effecting the change are made much greater by the organic character of codes, in which are comprehended not only the complex of labor rules, but also the trade practice rules and forms of collective market control. It is highly improbable that appropriate policy can be applied to these several matters through the present procedures of the NRA and the present devices of the code system. The particular problem to which legislative ingenuity would need to be applied, after the determination of policy, would be that of salvage and administrative reconstruction.

If the government decides to embark upon a permanent program of legislation on wages or hours or both, highly technical questions will arise in connection with the delimitation of scope and the devising of appropriate administrative organization. While it is desirable that the rules of law be as simple and as uniformly applicable as possible, there is little possibility of devising rules with operative significance, on minimum wages for example, which could be applied with complete uniformity on a national scale without excessively disturbing economic consequences. Carrying out a national policy on labor legislation would therefore undoubtedly require extensive delegation of quasi-legislative powers to administrative agencies. This fact emphasizes the necessity that Congress utilize the most competent technical advice, both in stating the principles to guide administrative action, and in devising forms of organization and procedure which would guarantee continuity of policy and impartial administration. There is no dearth of experience in this country of bringing technical competence to bear upon the framing of legislation, nor in devising the means for performing complex administrative functions. No one in the government has yet, however, initiated the essential preliminary moves in any form that is currently helpful in providing a new approach to the problems at issue.

Since any permanent program of labor legislation, if initiated, would presumably center on the maintenance of minimum standards and continuity of livelihood, its relationship, in principle and in administration, with other possible legislation covering social insurance and industrial relations would need to be carefully worked out. Conversely such a program would have no generic relationship with further legislation and administrative agencies concerned with general trade practices. It can of course be expected that special legislation on labor standards and trade practices would be closely related in the case of industries which for special reasons the government decided to place under close federal regulation. In any case the consideration of a permanent program of federal labor legislation cannot properly be subordinated to the fact that the NRA is operating as a going concern in the field.

PART IV

THE NRA AND INDUSTRIAL RELATIONS

CHAPTER XVI
THE GOAL OF "UNITED ACTION"

It would be imputing to the framers of the NIRA and to the enacting Congress more logical consistency than they themselves would claim, to find in the Recovery Act the outlines of a clearly conceived labor policy or of a theory of industrial relations. Like most of our social-economic legislation, the NIRA was the product of improvisation and compromise. Moreover the act was an emergency measure, hammered out in a rush, and intended to get immediate results.[1] Nevertheless the labor provisions of the act present a more or less coherent system centering around several major ideas.

The new federal labor policy which the National Industrial Recovery Act outlined as essential for the achievement of its twofold objective of recovery and reconstruction rests on three major principles: (1) The establishment of minimum wages, maximum hours, and good working conditions as standards of "fair competition"; (2) the creation of legal safeguards for labor organization and collective bargaining; and (3) the maintenance of industrial peace or what is termed, in the declaration of public policy, "the united action of labor and management."

In Part III we discussed the code provisions on wages, hours, and other working conditions as related to the purposes of the act. In this section of our study, we are concerned primarily with the other aspects of labor policy, namely collective bargaining, labor organization, and labor-management relations.

[1] For the background of the NIRA see Chap. I.

413

The major question which this part of our study posits is: What influence has the effectuation of the Recovery Act had upon employer-employee relations in American industry? This query resolves itself into two parts: (1) What was the NIRA—the Recovery Act—intended to accomplish? (2) What did the NRA—the machinery for administering the act—actually accomplish? Whether what was intended or what was done helped or hindered the process of recovery is of incidental importance from our point of view. What interests us here is the extent to which the work of the NRA in trying to put into effect the labor policies of the NIRA has tended to re-shape American labor relations, and the significance of the changes which it has wrought in the status of labor.

In other words, the emphasis in this section is not so much on recovery as on reconstruction. A change in the character of industrial relations will no doubt, indirectly and in the long run, influence wage rates and working hours. But the influence is environmental, and operates through a shift in the balance of bargaining power. True, we cannot leave the recovery problem entirely out of account. Any policies intended to strengthen labor's bargaining power, while a campaign for re-employment is on, must react on the results of that campaign. But the fact remains that the controversies aroused by the attempt to carry out the labor policies of the NRA have been animated by fears and hopes, not of what was temporary in character, but of deep and lasting changes, intended to reconstruct the economic and legal foundations of industrial relations in the United States.

UNITED ACTION AND COLLECTIVE BARGAINING

The Recovery Act was based on the theory that the quickest and surest way of recovery from the depression was to increase mass purchasing power by raising wage rates. It was further assumed that to shorten the work week, while increasing wages, would stimulate re-employment. It was also thought that prosperity based on higher wages and shorter hours would be an enduring prosperity. At this point, as at many others, the objective of recovery merged with that of reconstruction.

For the success of such a program, the "united action of labor and management" was desirable. If employers and employees could get together and settle amicably issues of wages and hours, there would be little or no danger of strikes, lockouts, or other drags upon re-employment. "United action" was thus necessary to help put men back to work and to keep them there, once re-employed. As for its wider implications, "united action" was a *sine qua non* for the reconstruction of the economic order.

But the sponsors of the Recovery Act were aware that, against the background of industrial relations in the United States, "united action" was hindered by traditional biases and fears on the part of both employers and employees, and by radically divergent views on the issues raised by the organized labor movement. It was therefore declared to be the policy of Congress "to induce and maintain united action of labor and management *under adequate governmental sanctions and supervision.*" If this meant anything, it meant that the government was to become an arbiter in matters of labor policy and was to promote methods and patterns of industrial relations which it regarded as sound bases for "united action."

The *method* which the act indicated as a basis for industrial relations was that of collective bargaining.[2] Few

[2] Conclusions based on a study of Congressional hearings and debates. For further discussion, see pp. 423-24.

express statements were made by the authors of the NIRA or by Congress on the relation of collective bargaining to the purposes of the act. But in the light of the discussions which accompanied the passage of the act and of current ideas on the subject, the main considerations in the matter were fairly clear. Collective bargaining, by promoting greater equality of bargaining power, would presumably enable workers to secure higher wage rates than if they bargained individually. As the government seemingly was not ready to engage in fixing wage schedules for all occupations and trades,[3] the codes could be expected to augment the wages of unskilled workers earning the lowest rates of pay. But even assuming that codes of fair competition were expected to set forth minimum wage scales for semi-skilled and skilled workers, it was arguable that these groups of workers would be able to secure better conditions if they were organized for collective bargaining than if they were not.

But if collective bargaining could be regarded as a means of effectuating the purposes of the NIRA with reference to wages and working conditions, was it also likely to promote the united action of labor and management? To this question many have answered with a decisive "no." It has been argued that the insertion in the Recovery Act of Section 7(a) with its guarantee of the right to organize and bargain collectively was bound to encourage among trade unions a state of mind conducive to strikes. It was bound also to antagonize employers and thus, instead of inducing peace, accentuate the elements of conflict in industrial relations. From this point of view, the guarantee of collective bargaining in the NIRA was an ill-considered effort at reconstruction which was in contradiction to the aims of recovery. For to the extent

[3] This is evident from Section 7(c) of the NIRA. See p. 421.

to which Section 7(a) was calculated to stir up labor disputes, it could not but operate against the success of re-employment. It is further argued from the same point of view that it would have been wiser to postpone such reconstructive experiments and to limit the contents of the act to such provisions alone as were likely to stimulate immediate re-employment.

The point of view just outlined seems untenable for two main reasons. In the first place, it draws a line between recovery and reconstruction much too sharp to be altogether in accord with the spirit of the NIRA. The two objectives are merged, not only in the labor provisions of the act, but also in the provisions affecting fair trade practices. The concept of "fair competition," the suspension of the anti-trust laws, and the idea of establishing codes for the self-regulation of industry are presumably steps towards a new and "reformed" industrial set-up; they are measures with long-range implications and purposes. There is just as large, if not a larger, element of reconstruction in these provisions of the act as in Section 7(a).

Second, and more to the point, had the Recovery Act been passed without some such guarantee of rights as is contained in Section 7(a), it would probably have become a source of increasing labor unrest. The promises of the New Deal had created a tense, fervent, and expectant state of mind among American wage earners. In view of the special encouragement given in the act to self-organization by employers, all labor, and especially organized labor, would have been put into an ugly, resentful mood, if not given equivalent rights and opportunities. Thus, even assuming that it would have been politically possible to pass the NIRA without its provisions on collective bargaining, to do so would soon have proved a boomerang for the cause of "united action" and industrial peace.

Politically and logically, the three labor objectives of the NIRA—the raising of wage rates and working standards; the guarantee of the right to organize and bargain collectively; and the promotion of united action in labor-management relations—were all of a piece and interdependent. Whatever one thinks of the validity of these objectives for recovery or reconstruction, one must recognize their logical connection in analyzing the developments to which they gave rise.

PROVISIONS FOR IMPLEMENTATION

Although the Recovery Act was largely an enabling act, it laid down several provisions which bear upon the specific implementation of its general labor principles. From this point of view three sections of the act are of special importance—Section 3, Section 4(a), and Section 7.

Section 3 of the NIRA is a new extension and application of the method of protective labor legislation. Under Section 3(a), the President of the United States is empowered to approve a code of fair competition upon the application of "one or more trade or industrial associations or groups"; provided, that "the President may, as a condition of his approval of any such code, impose such conditions . . . for the protection of consumers, competitors, *employees*, and others . . . as the President in his discretion deems necessary to effectuate the policy herein declared." Under Section 3 (b), after approval by the President, the provisions of such code, including the labor provisions, "shall be the standards of fair competition for such trade or industry or subdivision thereof," and any violation of such standard shall be deemed an "unfair method of competition" within the meaning of the Federal Trade Commission Act. Further, Section 3(d) sets forth specified conditions⁴ under which the President, "after such public notice or hearing as he shall specify," is authorized to "prescribe and approve" codes of fair competition, these to have the same effect as a code approved under Section 3(a).

Taken in its entirety, Section 3 is conceived without reference to the *form* of bargaining, collective or individual, which may help to determine the labor standards of an industry. It invests the President with power to impose on all employers in an industry potentially subject to a code specific labor standards regarded as essential to fair competition. For although the employers have the right to draft their own proposals for submission to the President, the President may insist upon the inclusion of any standards deemed necessary to protect the employees. When prescribing a code, the President enjoys the same discretionary powers. In brief, Section 3 implies that the executive branch of the government, guided by its concern for the public interest, will establish requisite labor standards, without regard to the kind of bargaining which prevails between employers and employees.

A method for implementing collective bargaining is first introduced in Section 4(a) of the NIRA. This section authorizes the President to "enter into agreements with, and to approve voluntary agreements between and among, persons engaged in a trade or industry, *labor organizations*, and trade or industrial organizations, associations, or groups, relating to any trade or industry,

⁴ "Upon his own motion," "if complaint is made to the President that abuses inimical to the public interest and contrary to the policy herein declared are prevalent in any trade or industry or subdivision thereof," or "if no code of fair competition therefor has been approved by the President."

if in his judgment such agreements will aid in effectuating the policy of this title." . . . Under the authority of this section, the President has the power to approve labor provisions mutually agreed to between labor organizations and employers. In other words, a voluntary collective bargain, if approved by the President, would enjoy the sanctions of the act. This presupposes circumstances under which it might be more desirable to determine labor standards by collective bargaining than by the ordinary procedures of code making.

The most comprehensive implementation of the policy of the NIRA is contained in Section 7. The now famous clause (a) of Section 7 contains the provisions which became during 1933-35 the center of so much controversy. According to this clause, every "code of fair competition, agreement, and license approved, prescribed, or issued under this title" must contain the following provisions:

(1) That employees shall have the right to organize and bargain collectively through representatives of their own choosing, and shall be free from the interference, restraint, or coercion of employers of labor, or their agents, in the designation of such representatives or in self-organization or in other concerted activities for the purpose of collective bargaining or other mutual aid or protection;

(2) That no employee and no one seeking employment shall be required as a condition of employment to join any company union or to refrain from joining, organizing, or assisting a labor organization of his own choosing; and

(3) That employers shall comply with the maximum hours of labor, minimum rates of pay, and other conditions of employment approved or prescribed by the President.

Clause (b) of Section 7, which has attracted less attention, but which has been put to considerable use under the construction and bituminous coal codes, defines a fairly specific procedure for applying methods of collective bargaining to the determination of labor standards. Under this clause, the President is instructed to afford, "so far as practicable . . . every opportunity to employers and employees in any trade or industry or subdivision thereof with respect to which the conditions referred to in clauses (1) and (2) of sub-section (a) prevail, to establish by mutual agreement, the standards as to the maximum hours of labor, minimum rates of pay, and such other conditions of employment as may be necessary . . . to effectuate the policy of this title." The standards established in such agreements, "when approved by the President," shall have "the same effect as a code of fair competition approved by the President under sub-section (a) of Section 3."

Clause (c) of Section 7 is in some ways an elaboration of the method specified in Section 3(d), except that it is limited to exceptional situations in which labor standards alone have to be imposed, presumably upon a recalcitrant industry which refuses to subject itself to a code. Under this clause, when no mutual agreement has been approved by the President, "he may investigate the labor practices, policies, wages, hours of labor, and conditions of employment in such trade or industry or subdivision thereof." Upon the basis of these investigations and after such hearings as he finds advisable, the President is authorized "to prescribe a limited code of fair competition fixing such maximum hours of labor, minimum rates of pay, and other conditions of employment . . . as he finds to be necessary to effectuate the policy of this title." Such a limited code of labor provisions "shall have the same effect as a code of fair competition." In establishing labor standards pursuant to this procedure, the President "may differentiate according to experience and skill of the employees affected and according to the locality of employment; but no attempt shall be made to introduce any classification according to the nature of the work involved which might tend to set a maximum as well as a minimum wage."

In brief, Section 7(a) creates rights for employees and obligations for employers, that is, sets forth the legal conditions under which collective bargaining and "united action of labor and management" will become possible. Section 7(b) defines as an alternative to code making, a procedure whereby labor standards may be established by collective bargaining, and supplies a method for conveying statutory sanction to the terms of a collective labor contract. Section 7(c), finally, outlines a procedure whereby the President may, if necessary, impose labor standards of fair competition on industries and trades where no standards would otherwise be established.

To sum up, there are three methods by which the NIRA proposed to implement the objective of "united action of labor and management." (1) the government is empowered to prescribe or impose, through code-making procedure, the labor provisions which shall constitute standards of fair competition. (2), legal conditions are created such that workers may be free to organize for collective bargaining through representatives of their own choosing without "interference, coercion and restraint" on the part of their employers. (3), provision is made for the establishment of labor standards, when convenient and practicable, by direct collective bargaining rather than by code-making procedure. Basically, although the act provides for the immediate determination of labor standards with or without the assistance of collective bargaining, we may say that it has in view the potential establishment of collective bargaining relationships throughout codified industry.

THE FORM OF LABOR ORGANIZATION

Assuming that the NIRA contemplates industrial relationships based on collective bargaining, what forms of labor organization, if any, did it point to? Two forms of labor organization had emerged in the United States by 1933—the trade union and the company union. Did the act favor the one or the other? And if the act could be interpreted to favor trade unions, what attitude did it take on the forms and methods of unionism, such as the right to strike, the closed shop, industrial or craft unionism, and similar problems?

It is easier to say what the act did not propose to accomplish than to say what it did aim at positively along these lines. All that can be said on the basis of Congressional hearings, debates, and other evidence may be summarized in the following propositions:

First, the act does not require workers to belong to trade unions or to any other form of labor organization. All the act confers upon workers is freedom to join, organize, and assist labor organizations if they so desire. At the same time, the act restrains employers from interfering with such freedom.

Second, the act does not require the compulsory substitution of collective for individual bargaining. Workers *may* organize and bargain collectively with their employers. The act probably invalidates an individual contract calling for lower wages and longer hours than those set forth in a code. But the same principle would apply to a collective contract calling for less favorable labor conditions than those laid down in a code.

Third, the act does not outlaw the company union as such. All that it says on the subject is that no employer may require membership in a company union as a condition of employment.

Fourth, the act does not make the trade union the exclusive instrumentality for collective bargaining. No doubt it was the intent of Congress to make the way easier for trade unions and harder for company unions. But nothing was put in the act to justify claims by trade unions to be the exclusive spokesmen of the workers.

These are negative statements. But the act contains no more than that. It left the task of determining the form, methods, and agencies of collective bargaining to the administrative agencies which were to make the act a living thing.

CHAPTER XVII

COLLECTIVE BARGAINING UNDER THE CODES

It was to be expected that the application of the NIRA would give rise to a struggle between employers and employees for the interpretation of its labor provisions and for the determination of the specific labor standards to be established in codes. What the NRA tried to do and actually did, must thus be viewed not only in the light of the intent of the act, but also against the background of contending forces..

In Part III, the work of the NRA in formulating code labor provisions during 1933-34 was surveyed. These provisions represent, in a way, the major part of the NRA's performance in relation to labor. On the basis of that survey, conclusions were drawn as to the changes wrought in the wage and hour structure of American industry, and in the competitive interrelations of various industries as affected by labor standards. In Part VI an analysis is also made of the effects of code wage and hour provisions on cost-price relationships and their influence on the drive towards recovery.

In the present section, we intend to review the NRA's performance in applying the provisions of the NIRA which bear on collective bargaining and on industrial relations. In considering this problem we must remember that the NRA acted in a threefold capacity: (1) it was a code-making mechanism; (2) it was an administrative agency supervising the administration and enforcement of codes; and (3) it assumed the task of interpreting the provisions of the act and of the codes.

As the NRA performed, or tried to perform, these three functions with regard to labor, three major questions were raised. First, to what extent was collective bargaining actually applied in the making of codes, and what effects did collective bargaining have on the character of code labor provisions? Second, to what extent were methods of collective bargaining embodied in the machinery devised for administering and enforcing code labor provisions and for composing the controversies arising out of these provisions? And third, how did the NRA construe the intent and interpret the meaning of Section 7(a)?

COLLECTIVE BARGAINING IN THE MAKING OF CODES

Between June 16, 1933 and March 1, 1935, the NRA turned out 550 "basic" and 225 "supplementary" codes of fair competition applying to as many separate trades and industries. Our question in this chapter is: In what sense and to what extent can the labor provisions of these codes be said to have been the product of collective bargaining? How did the various procedures adopted in the making of different codes affect the results?

For the purpose of our analysis, it is convenient to distinguish between two main kinds of code-making procedures: (1) the "normal," based largely on the provisions in Section 3 of the Recovery Act;[1] and (2) the "special," deriving its sanctions from Section 7 of the act.[2] These two procedures differed radically in so far as the labor provisions were concerned, and this fact must be clearly grasped for an understanding of the comparative results.

[1] See Chap. XVI, pp. 418-19.
[2] See Chap. XVI, pp. 420-22.

Indirect Representative Bargaining

When the NIRA was first enacted, many trade unionists hoped that, before promulgating the labor standards of an industry, the NRA would request the employers and the employees engaged therein to confer and to execute a collective agreement. These trade unionists were soon disillusioned. During the very first day of the NRA, the Administrator ruled that it was not necessary for code labor standards proposed by employers in any industry to be the outcome of collective negotiations between employers and organized employees. The privilege of formulating and presenting labor standards, in the first instance, was to be the exclusive prerogative of the employers. The factor determining approval, rejection, or amendment by the NRA would be the specific contents of the labor provisions, not the nature of their origin.[3]

In the "normal" code procedure, one of the factors determining the NRA's action on particular codes was the advice rendered by the Labor Advisory Board. To each deputy or assistant administrator charged with the conduct of some particular code, the Labor Advisory Board assigned one or more advisers from its own technical staff, supplemented as a rule by some trade union officer chosen for the occasion by the Board. These advisers participated in the negotiations preceding the public hearings, brought the labor point of view to the attention of the deputy or assistant administrator, supplied the members of the Labor Board with data and evaluations for recommendations to the Administrator, stated labor's case for or against specific code provisions at the public hearings, and took part in the negotiations which

[3] See *NRA Bulletin No. 2*, p. 2.

followed public hearings and at which the final adjustments were made. In brief, the Labor Advisory Board worked on the assumption that it was its duty to express and protect labor interests throughout the progress of code-making negotiations between the employers and the government. This duty it sought to fulfill to the extent permitted by the NRA's loose administrative procedures and by the speed of code making.

The ability of the Labor Advisory Board to perform its functions was at all times conditioned by the fact that the NRA code-making process was a matter of higgling and haggling, of give and take, and of a continuous search for formulae of accommodation and compromise. Between the labor standards proposed by employers and the labor standards that the NRA might regard as desirable, there was ordinarily a considerable area for bargaining. During the course of negotiations within this area, the employers might threaten to withdraw their code; the government might threaten to impose a code; organized labor might hint at the possibility of strikes unless the code came up to certain expectations. Within this area of bargaining, the Labor Advisory Board sought (1) to influence the NRA to stand behind labor standards such as a 30-hour week, classified wage scales, elimination as far as possible of regional wage differentials, generous minimum rates of pay, equal labor representation on code authorities and; (2) to prevent the code labor provisions finally drafted from falling too far in the direction of proposals favored by the employers, such as excessive averaging of the maximum work week, liberal exceptions and exemptions, low basic minimum rates of pay, multiplication of regional differentials, and qualifications of the right to collective bargaining.

The composition of the Labor Advisory Board was

presumably such as to enable the Board to represent the interests of labor in the code-making process. Its membership consisted of trade union officers and leaders[4] or of persons believed to be in sympathy with the aims and methods of organized labor.[5] True, as code followed code, and as the issues of industrial relations became acute, there developed a widening gap between the A. F. of L. union leaders, on the one hand, and the chairman of the Board, on the other. Nevertheless, the Labor Advisory Board could be regarded as the spokesman within the NRA of the organized labor movement in the United States; and more narrowly, as the spokesman of the A. F. of L. and its affiliated unions.

Whether or not the NRA's normal process of code making, in which labor was represented by the Labor Advisory Board, constituted a method of establishing labor standards by true collective bargaining, has been a subject of much dispute.[6] The controversy resolves itself to a considerable extent into a question of definitions. The NRA code-making procedure was certainly not collective bargaining in the sense in which the term has long been used by students of the labor movement and is understood today by trade unionists. Nor was the procedure "collective bargaining" in the more general sense of the term; that is, a process of making collective agreements through direct negotiations between an employer

[4] William Green, president of the American Federation of Labor; John Lewis, president of the United Mine Workers of America; George Berry, president of the Printing Pressmen's Union; Sidney Hillman, president of the Amalgamated Clothing Workers of America, and others.

[5] Such as Father Francis J. Haas and Dr. Leo Wolman, the chairman.

[6] Dr. Wolman claimed that the procedure pursued by the NRA applied in spirit and in fact the principles of collective bargaining. William Green denied that labor participated directly in the drafting of code labor provisions. These points of view were put forth at the Code Authorities' Conference in March 1934. See *United States News*, Mar. 16, 1934, Vol. 2, No. 11 (statements by Dr. Wolman, p. 12, and by Mr. Green, p. 21).

or employers, on the one side, and some *labor organization*, on the other.

To coin a new term, the procedure which the NRA hammered out may be described as *"indirect representative bargaining."* In accordance with this procedure, labor proposals are first formulated by organized employer groups; these proposals are then submitted to an administrative agency of the government; final standards are laid down after a process of higgling and haggling in which labor representatives, officially designated, try to influence the result by giving advice to and exerting pressure upon the official administrative agency which possesses the power of final decision. This procedure, clearly distinct from all accepted forms of collective bargaining, represents a novel departure in American industrial relations. What we have, in effect, is a series of negotiations between employers and an administrative agency of the government. The subject matter of these negotiations is not a collective agreement between organized labor and organized industry, but the terms of a covenant among employers alone. Once granted executive approval and promulgated as a code, the terms of the covenant have binding force on all members of the industry or trade, regardless of individual failure to assent thereto.

Direct Collective Bargaining

In a handful of codes, the labor provisions were determined largely by direct collective bargaining between trade unions and employers. Two classes of such codes may be distinguished, although the lines of demarcation are not altogether distinct; (1) the regional agreements formally executed in accordance with Section 7(b)—for example, the Appalachian Agreement supplemental to the bituminous coal code, and the numerous area agreements between building trades unions and employers, which were supplemental to the construction code; and (2) codes whose labor provisions in whole or in part incorporated terms of an agreement previously made between a union and employers—such as the coat and suit, dress manufacturing, men's clothing, legitimate theater, and a few other codes.

For a clear understanding of what this procedure involved it will be convenient to describe briefly the making of the agreements in the coal, building, and clothing industries.

The Appalachian Agreement. No code in the history of the NRA gave rise to more struggle, more perplexities, and more procedural crises than did the bituminous coal code. Bituminous coal was not only one of the chronically "sick industries"; it was also a house divided against itself on the score of industrial relations. In the Central Competitive Field (Illinois, Indiana, Michigan, etc.) collective bargaining between the coal operators and the United Mine Workers of America was a long-established and accepted fact. It was a fairly simple task, therefore, to incorporate into the code, without directly invoking Section 7(b), the labor standards already established by district agreements between the operators and the unions. But the United Mine Workers, despite a long and bitter struggle, had never been able before 1933 to establish itself in the great Appalachian producing district, where the operators were inspired by an intense anti-union feeling. It would have been impossible, in view of the objectives of fair competition, to require the Central Competitive Field producers to pay a trade union scale of wages, but to allow the Appalachian producers at the same time to pay a scale of wages in the determination of which collective bargaining had no part. The problem then arose: Assuming that certain regional differentials would have to be written into the code, was it possible to reduce the extent of these differentials by prevailing upon the Appalachian operators to recognize the union and to enter into a collective agreement with it?

The problem was solved in part thanks to the astonishingly successful organizational drive launched by the union in the Appalachian area as soon as Section 7(a) was enacted. Realizing that they were facing a *fait accompli*, the Appalachian operators finally agreed to deal with the union. On September 18, 1933, the U.M.W.A. and various groups of operators, proceeding in accordance with Section 7(b), negotiated what came to be known as the Appalachian Agreement. This was approved by the President on September 21, 1933, and was renewed with certain modifications on March 29, 1934.

As finally incorporated into the bituminous coal code, Schedule A set forth basic minimum wage rates per day and per hour by districts. For the Central Competitive districts, Schedule A set the wage rates already in force by virtue of pre-existing union contracts; for the Appalachian districts, Schedule A set the wage rates provided for in the newly negotiated agreement.[7]

There remained, however, a few major producing districts—for example, western Kentucky (District H) and Alabama, Georgia, and Southern Tennessee (District J), which the union had failed to organize effectively. Its failure to do this was reflected in the regional differentials permitted by Schedule A.[8] Unable to exert

[7] It should be noted, however, that miners are ordinarily paid by tonnage. It is a delicate problem in collective bargaining to adjust tonnage to daily or hourly rates.

[8] For instance, the minimum rates per day for inside skilled labor were $5.00 for Illinois (District E); $4.60 for Pennsylvania, Ohio, Michigan

direct pressure on employers in Districts H and J, the union, acting jointly with the operators who subscribed to the Appalachian Agreement, sought to move the NRA into action. On March 31, 1934 the NRA fell into line by promulgating amendments to Schedule A.[9] At the same time, the maximum work week in all districts was shortened from 40 hours per week, or 8 hours per day, to 35 hours per week, or 7 hours per day.

The amendment of March 31 aroused violent protest on the part of the operators in the non-unionized districts. Their protest was successful to the point of inducing the NRA to amend the wage schedule on April 22, 1934 in their favor.[10] However, still angered at what they regarded as a plot of the union and the union operators to force higher labor costs upon them, the western Kentucky mine owners initiated proceedings to restrain the NRA from enforcing the new wage schedules. These proceedings had not yet, by March 1935, reached the United States Supreme Court.

Area agreements in the building trade. The difficulties in formulating the construction code[11] were similar to those of the bituminous coal code; the industry was a house divided against itself on the score of industrial relations. In one section of the industry, the building

lower peninsula, West Virginia panhandle (District A); $4.20 for southern West Virginia, eastern Kentucky, West Virginia upper Potomac, Maryland, Virginia, northern Tennessee (District C); $4.00 for District H; and $3.00 for District J.

[9] In District A the rate was raised to $5.00 uniform with Illinois; in District C the rate went up to $4.60; most important was the fixing of a uniform rate of $4.60 for Districts H and J.

[10] The rate in District C remained fixed at $4.60; the western Kentucky minimum was set at the same level; in District J the minimum was allowed to drop back to $3.80, except for certain counties in Tennessee (set apart as District J-1) where $4.24 was prescribed.

[11] A full story of the making of the code may be found in *Report of the Proceedings of the 28th Annual Convention of the Building Trades Department, A. F. of L.*, pp. 58-82 (San Francisco, October 1934).

trades, the unions were powerful, the employers accustomed to bargaining collectively, and the closed shop a recognized custom. The other section of the industry, heavy "open" construction, was largely non-unionized and the employers were among the most ardent "open shoppers."

To prevent the non-union employers in the industry from "capturing" the code-making and the code-administering machinery, the building trade unions formulated a series of demands; namely, that separate codes be drafted for the building trades and for the open construction divisions of the industry, that the code prescribe not only minimum wage rates for unskilled labor but also classified wage schedules for semi-skilled and skilled occupations, and that organized labor be granted adequate representation on the basic code authority. Although the unions were not strong enough to gain their demands, they were able to delay the promulgation of the code for months and obtained in the end important concessions.

As finally approved on January 31, 1934, the construction code was a patch-work of compromises. (1), The provisions of the code were to apply to the industry as a whole but the various divisions of the industry—for example, elevator manufacturing, railway construction, road building, plumbing installation, plastering—were permitted to organize divisional code authorities and to govern themselves separately by specific provisions which were to have precedence over the general code provisions in case of conflict. Thus, although one code governed the entire industry, the trade unions were safeguarded against the danger that their systems of collective bargaining would be upset in the event that the employers in the non-unionized section of the industry gained control over the basic code authority. (2) Membership on the construction code authority, the basic authority, was to be confined to representatives of enumerated employer organizations which sponsored the code. But no such restrictions were laid down for membership in the divisional code authorities, leaving the door open for labor representation in some of the building trades where the unions were most firmly established. Provision was made for the establishment of a National Construction Planning and Adjustment Board, vested with arbitrational powers over all disputes concerning wages, hours, and conditions of employment which were voluntarily submitted to it. The Board was to be constituted of 21 persons, ten of whom were to be selected by the Labor Advisory Board of the NRA from nominations by the constructio nlabor organizations, subject to the approval of the Administrator. (3) A minimum wage rate of 40 cents per hour was fixed, but it was expressly laid down that this rate "shall not be construed as establishing a minimum rate of pay for other than common or unskilled labor" and "shall not be construed to authorize reductions in existing rates of pay." A maximum work week of 40 hours was provided, though under certain conditions 48 hours might be authorized.

The basic minima were to have force, however, only in the event that labor standards determined by mutual agreement between employers and employees were not applicable to the division and locality. The procedure for arriving at such mutual agreements, defined in Article 3, Section 1, of the code, was in essence the technique by which the unions and employers in the building trades traditionally executed their collective agreements; that is, it provided for separate agreements

covering the performance of a single function such as
bricklaying, plumbing, carpentry, electrical work, and
so forth, within the limits of a single area—for example,
New York City, Philadelphia, Detroit. Such area agreements, after approval by the President in accordance with
Section 7(b) of the act, were to be binding as code labor
standards upon all employers whether parties to the
agreement or not. To help in putting the area agreements
into effect, the Administrator was instructed to establish
for each division of the industry one or more boards authorized to investigate complaints of "unfair competition" and to report to the Administrator with a view to
enforcement. These boards were to have two employee
representatives, two employer representatives, and an
impartial chairman.

The building trades unions were not slow in taking
advantage of Article 3, Section 1, of the code. By January 7, 1935, 213 such agreements had been submitted to
the NRA, of which ten had already been approved by
the President; the rest were slowly moving through the
administrative machinery preliminary to approval.[12] As
one might have expected, these proposed area agreements have been confined to the well-organized crafts
within the building trades, such as masonry, painting,
decorating, paper-hanging, and electrical work. They
have also been confined in application to metropolitan
areas such as New York, Philadelphia, Chicago, Denver,
and St. Paul, where the unions are most powerful. In
brief, Article 3, Section 1, of the code has served to re-
enforce the existing balance of power between capital
and labor in the building trades.

The codes in the needle trades. Several of the needle
trades codes exemplify the process of determining labor

[12] See *NRA Release No. 9516,* Jan. 7, 1935.

standards by collective bargaining through trade unions. The most important of these are the codes which apply to men's clothing, the coat and suit trade, and dress manufacturing. We shall consider here only the one mentioned last, which is typical of the entire group.

The drafting of the dress manufacturing code was beset by difficulties. The industry has a complex system of producing and distributing its commodities, as explained in the preface to the code. There are the jobbers and wholesalers who are concerned only with styles, with prices of piece goods, and with distribution; there are the inside manufacturers who make garments from their own materials on their own premises and sell directly to retailers; there are the contractors who complete the manufacture of garments cut on the premises of a jobber or manufacturer; and there are the sub-manufacturers who produce directly for a jobber or a manufacturer from materials and trimmings furnished by the latter. This complex organization, prior to the code, made for friction between employers and employees; the friction was accentuated by the unequal degree of unionization in Eastern and Western markets, and by the migration of shops from New York City to the cheaper labor markets of small towns in New Jersey, Pennsylvania, and Connecticut.

Perhaps the principal factor in forcing through the code in its final form was the series of strikes conducted by the International Ladies' Garment Workers' Union among the smaller non-union shops in New York City, Chicago, Cleveland, St. Louis, and elsewhere; and the extraordinary rapidity with which the union was able to organize the workers in the small towns in New Jersey, Pennsylvania, and Connecticut. Practically all of the strikes were successful. They ended, as a rule, in collective agreements granting union recognition and setting a union scale of wages. Thanks to this success, the I. L. G. W. U. and the group of union manufacturers gained ascendency in the making of the code for the industry. A five-day work week was established up to a maximum of 35 hours per week. Elaborate wage scales, classified by occupational groups, were set forth: two for the City of New York (low-priced and high-priced garments); two at lower levels for the eastern metropolitan area outside of New York City—that is, Philadelphia, Boston, and Baltimore; two also at lower levels for the eastern area outside of the principal markets—that is, the out of town labor markets; two at still lower levels for the western area—that is, all parts of the country other than New England, New York, Pennsylvania, New Jersey, Delaware, and Maryland. These wage scales established guaranteed minimum rates per hour or per week, regardless of whether compensation was on a time rate, piece-work rate, or other basis.

The code authority was constituted on the management side largely of union manufacturers and provided for direct representation of labor by union representatives. The code authority was authorized, among other things, to issue NRA labels to be attached to manufactured garments, registration numbers for this purpose being assigned to the various manufacturers; to determine the distinction between "high-priced" and "low-priced" garments, a distinction bearing directly on wage scales; to obtain from employers periodic reports on wages, hours of labor, conditions of employment, and other matters of interest to the industry.

Finally, the code sought to eliminate the major difficulty which had prevented the union from enforcing uniform labor standards throughout the industry; namely, the system whereby jobbers and manufacturers contracted out their work, in whole or in part, to contractors and sub-manufacturers, who underbid one another. All manufacturers and/or jobbers, it was provided, "who cause their garments to be made by contractors shall adhere to the payment of rates for such production in an amount sufficient to pay the employees the wages and earnings provided in this code and in addition a reasonable payment to the contractors to cover overhead." A number of other provisions gave the code authority power to regulate the relationships between manufacturers and contractors so as to assure the maintenance of the code labor provisions in all shops.

The Contrast in Results

In the labor provisions of the codes we find marked differences, attributable in large part to the particular procedures followed in their formulation. We shall summarize briefly these differences in view of the light they throw on the relation of method to content.

The outstanding feature of the "special" codes in which direct collective bargaining was followed is that they ordinarily prescribe, not only minimum wage rates for common labor but minimum wage scales by craft and other occupational groupings. This they do either directly, as in the needle trades codes, or indirectly by means of regional agreements, in accordance with Section 7(b). The "normal" codes, in contrast, provide, as a rule, basic minimum rates only. When such codes do concern themselves with workers who earn super-minimum wages, they usually recite some variation of the ambiguous "equitable adjustment" formula. The minimum rates in the "normal" codes are hedged in by differentials of all sorts—differentials by region, by sex, by type of product. Such differentials apparently bear but little relation to variations in skill and productivity. They seemingly perpetuate the accidental and haphazard system of wage differentials which had grown up long before the Recovery Act.[13] True, the "special" procedure codes also contain regional differentials, but to a more moderate extent. These differentials reflect the variations of the union's bargaining strength in different areas.

Another important difference is that the "normal" procedure codes are full of possibilities for avoiding the minimum wage rates. They abound in clauses intended to exempt and except many labor groups: "apprentices," "learners," the "occupationally handicapped," and so forth. The terms, as a rule, are loosely defined and ambiguous, thus removing much of the legal force which the minimum wage rates might otherwise exert. The "special" procedure codes, on the contrary, are largely free from provisions of this character. As a problem in administrative adjudication, it would be much easier to determine in the case of a "special procedure" code than in that of a "normal" one, whether or not the employer was complying with the code wage requirements.

At first glance, the differences between the "special" and "normal" codes with respect to maximum hours do not appear to be important. The general run of "normal" codes provide for a 40-hour working week; a number of the "special" codes dip down below this figure to 36 and even 35 hours per week. Examined more closely, however, the differences swell out in magnitude. The maximum length of the work week in the "special" codes is clearly defined; exceptions are rigidly restricted; no allowance is ordinarily made for averaging the maximum over a period of weeks or months. In the "normal" codes,

[13] See especially the regional differentials in the iron and steel, petroleum, paper, pulp, and the lumber codes. Compare Chap. XII.

on the contrary, it is extremely difficult, as a rule, to discover just how long the maximum work week is supposed to be; exceptions and exemptions abound; seasonal and emergency variations are permitted; the maximum allows for averaging over a period of weeks and months. It would be a relatively simple problem to decide whether or not an employer subject to a "special" code was violating its provisions on hours; to determine that under the "normal" code provisions would call for complex and drawn out computations.

Another important difference is in the provisions for labor representation on the code authority. True, not all the "special" codes expressly provide for labor representation on the code authority; for example, no such provisions are to be found in the construction or in the bituminous coal codes. But in the needle trade and the legitimate theater codes express provision is made for the representation of organized labor; either the trade union is named, as in the legitimate theater and in the coat and suit code, or the Labor Advisory Board is empowered to name labor representatives, as in the men's clothing code. In the "normal" codes, in contrast, with one or two exceptions, the code authority is set up so as not to allow for direct labor representation.[14]

[14] The contrast in labor provisions between the two main types of codes can best be illustrated by a detailed comparison of these provisions. In view of the limitations of space, we cannot here enter into such an analysis. We refer the reader to Pt. III, in which wage and hour provisions are discussed, and to the various tables and charts which classify these provisions by industry groups. Briefly, we may also indicate that the "special" codes form but a tiny portion of the NRA code total. Not over a score of codes may be said to have been formulated in accordance with the practice of direct collective bargaining. The more important of these codes are: men's clothing; coat and suit; dress manufacturing; legitimate theater; bituminous coal (in part only); construction (in part only); hosiery (in part); various printing trade codes (in part); a few other garment and textile and amusement trade codes. All others are the product of what we have called the "normal" procedure.

Summary

We have distinguished between two principal groups of codes so far as concerns the making of their labor provisions. The first group of codes contains labor provisions which were originally drafted by employers, without trade union participation, and then modified in the process of indirect bargaining under NRA auspices. The second group of codes contains labor provisions which resulted from direct bargaining between trade unions and employers, the contents of the bargain being submitted to the NRA for approval. The first group of codes we find in industries, which, prior to the NRA, had been unorganized on the labor side. The second group of codes is in industries where, prior to the NRA, trade unions were fairly well organized and where collective bargaining was an established tradition.

It cannot be doubted that the Labor Advisory Board had a real voice, even if small, in determining labor standards in most, if not all, the "normal" NRA codes. On the whole, however, the LAB was ineffective. The theory of the NRA and its practice were in wide divergence on this point as on many others. The NRA was moved by the desire of pushing codes through the administrative mill as rapidly as possible. In the great majority of codes, resistance by employers was a much more important factor to reckon with than the possible resistance of labor, and for obvious reasons. For a variety of causes which we need not here examine, the American trade unions, prior to the Recovery Act, had succeeded in organizing but small segments of industry: the building trades, the printing trades, railroad transportation, the needle trades, various skilled occupations among the metal trades, and so forth. In short, despite the assistance of the Labor Advisory Board which scrupulously performed the allotted task of advising, criticising, evaluating, and protesting, the workers in most industries were unable to exert much direct pressure upon their employers. For this reason they were also unable to exert much pressure upon the NRA; for the NRA was highly sensitive to outside forces. In other words, the continuous effort of the NRA to adjust itself to the balance of power in capital-labor relations reflected itself in the code labor provisions which were finally approved. In most cases, therefore, the Labor Advisory Board could not accomplish much more than rendering advice and striking an attitude. True, the Board's persistent intervention into the code-making process served to bring about many minor modifications of proposed labor provisions, and to establish limits beyond which the NRA could not yield without running the risk that organized labor might withdraw its co-operation in carrying out the objectives of the act. Only in the unionized industries was the Labor Advisory Board able to shape labor provisions and to reinforce collective bargaining in accordance with the desires of the labor groups; and even here, the Board's capacity was at all times dependent upon the amount of direct pressure which the trade unions in these industries were willing and able to exert against the employers.

So far, then, as concerned the making of code labor provisions, the NRA may be said to have accomplished four things. In the first place, it established a novel procedure of "indirect representative bargaining" by which labor standards might be set. In most industries, this procedure changed somewhat the balance of bargaining power in favor of labor, though it would be difficult to argue that there was any approximate equality of bargaining power between the Labor Advisory Board and the employers' associations which submitted the various codes.

Second, the NRA helped to give a new legal status to the collective bargain. Collective labor agreements, prior to the Recovery Act, were binding, if at all, upon the signatory parties alone. From the legal point of view, they had to be enforced by suits running in terms of the law of private contracts. Under the NRA, these contracts could now be incorporated into codes, either directly or as supplementary regional codes in accordance with Section 7(b). Thus the terms of the collective bargain could assume the force of law. They could become lawfully binding standards of fair competition which might be enforced against employers not signatory thereto. Their enforcement was no longer a matter of the law of private contracts alone, but also a matter of statute law. The government thus laid the foundations for the development of a new and special system of industrial law.

Third, in a few industries where the trade unions had sufficient strength to profit by Section 7(a), the NRA was able to expand the area of trade union influence and to re-enforce the principle of direct collective bargaining.

Fourth, by developing the "normal" and "special" technique for establishing labor standards, code by code, the NRA served as an administrative agency for the enactment of protective labor legislation.

COLLECTIVE BARGAINING ARRANGEMENTS IN CODE ADMINISTRATION

In pursuing the code-making procedures described above, the NRA took important steps toward the potential reshaping of American industrial relations. But these were first steps only. As is well known, industrial relations depend not only on the existence of collective contracts and on the manner of their making, but also on the methods used for composing and adjudicating the individual and collective grievances of the workers, whether covered by a collective agreement or not. In the United States, prior to the NRA, this phase of industrial relations was less developed than in most other western countries, showing besides great variations from industry to industry. Some of the unionized industries, especially clothing, mining, transportation, and printing, had elaborate systems—local, regional, and national— for the adjustment of disputes arising under collective agreements. In a few other industries, where no collective agreements were in force, employee representation plans, "company unions," provided some means whereby the complaints of individual workers as well as the more general questions of shop life could be examined through joint conference machinery. By and large, however, there was wanting in American industries an orderly procedure for considering labor complaints or labor disputes; such matters were usually handled, as an incidental part of their daily tasks, by foremen, corporate officials, or managing owners.

It was, therefore, of considerable importance for the future development of industrial relations in the United States whether or not the NRA would establish adequate machinery for administering the labor provisions of codes; and whether or not such machinery, if established, would be based upon any particular scheme of collective bargaining. During the first months of frantic code-making, the NRA did not seem much alive to this problem. Excepting the cotton textile and bituminous coal codes, none of the early codes expressly provided for a method of handling labor complaints or labor disputes based on the declared objective of "united action" between labor and management.

But as codes gave rise to a widening wave of strikes and as attention shifted from code making to code administration, the NRA was forced to turn its attention to this issue. After struggling for some time with diverse schemes and projects, the NRA finally evolved the policy of distinguishing between labor complaints and labor disputes. A brief summary of the evolution of this policy is necessary for an understanding of the present situation.

Evolution of Policy

The first code approved by the NRA, the cotton textile code, provided[15] for the establishment of a National Cotton Textile Industrial Relations Board, supplemented by state boards and by mill committees created *ex post facto* upon the occasion of particular disputes in particular plants. It was, perhaps, the NRA's original idea that every code should be equipped with a labor board. Code making went slowly, however; the PRA program had to be extemporized; and a strike wave gathered momentum. On August 5, 1933, therefore, upon the joint recommendation of the Industrial Advisory Board and the Labor Advisory Board, the President created the National Labor Board. Under the influence of its chairman, Senator Robert F. Wagner, the NLB soon began to assert its independence of the NRA and to function as an agency for the adjustment of all labor disputes and for the interpretation and enforcement of Section 7(a). Before long, the NRA and the NLB were in conflict on many issues. In this struggle the NLB seemed for a while to be the victor. The NRA gave up, for the time being, the idea of establishing industrial relations boards code by code.

[15] Section 17, promulgated on Aug. 8, 1933 as an amendment to the code approved July 9, 1933.

Nevertheless, various committees of the NRA, official and informal, continued to struggle with the problem. We find evidences of an emerging policy on the administration of labor relations in *NRA Bulletin No. 7*, a "Manual for the Adjustment of Complaints," issued in January, 1934. This bulletin addressed itself both to state directors of the NRA compliance system and to code authorities.[16] The bulletin drew a distinction between labor complaints and labor disputes. A labor complaint was defined as an allegation that some employer was violating the code provisions on wages, hours, and other working conditions. A labor dispute was defined as a controversy, ordinarily expressing itself in a strike or threat of a strike, arising out of the collective bargaining requirements of Section 7(a). Labor complaints, according to the bulletin, were to be handled by the state directors of compliance, except in industries in which adequate adjustment machinery was attached to the code authority. The procedure for setting up such machinery, that is a labor complaints' committee, was described as follows:

An approved organization of such a committee would be one having an equal number of representatives of employers and employees, who would choose an additional member as chairman. The representatives of the employers may be appointed by the code authority subject to the disapproval of NRA. The representatives of the employees should be chosen in such manner that all employees in the industry may be represented as fairly as possible. A possible method of selection may be appointment by the President (or by the Administrator, in industries of less than 50,000 employees) upon the recommendation of the Labor Advisory Board of NRA. Any other organization agreed upon by the employees and employers in the industry may be approved by the NRA. The committee should be small enough

---

[16] For details of organization, see Chaps. IV, VII-IX.

to function actively and its members, as far as possible, should be persons who are free to give the committee as much time as its work may require. The committee should have a legal adviser and an executive secretary who will be charged with responsibility for all routine correspondence and records. The Administration member of the code authority will be a member of the committee without vote but with a veto, subject to review by NRA, and will be responsible to NRA for the proper functioning of the committee. The committee may set up divisional, regional, or local agencies. The committee and its divisional, regional, and local industrial adjustment agencies may be organized to function for only certain of the divisions of the industry or regions of the country, leaving the other divisions or regions to governmental agencies.[17]

Between January and March, 1934, the National Labor Board was gaining influence. But by the end of March the situation changed. The NLB lost prestige because of its failure to achieve an adjustment of the threatened automobile strike. At the same time, the President's automobile settlement of March 25, 1934 provided for the establishment by the NRA of an Automobile Labor Board, thus throwing the NRA into the industrial relations problems of one of the principal codified industries.

The Administrator of the NRA was quick in trying to follow up this advantage. On March 29 he issued Administrative Order X-12 calling for the establishment of industrial relations boards as well as labor complaints committees in every codified industry. The order remained a dead letter for several reasons. The Labor Advisory Board blocked the promotion of such committees because it feared that, if they were set up in non-organized industries under the dominance of code authorities composed exclusively of employers, company unions would be promoted. As for the code authorities, many

[17] *Bulletin No. 7*, p. 24.

of them were struggling through their first organizational stages at the time when the committee idea was most vigorously pushed by the NRA. Of those code authorities which were already fairly well organized, some were cool to the idea of labor compliance through joint conference committees, while others were so heavily burdened with problems arising out of the "fair trade" provisions as to have little energy for the "labor" provisions. Furthermore, the condition essential to joint conference procedure—complete labor self-organization running parallel to complete management self-organization—was wanting.

In any case, continued labor unrest and the imminence of a general strike in the steel industry forced the passage of Public Resolution No. 44,[18] under which the President established, independently of the NRA, the National Labor Relations Board and a series of special boards for separate industries. By July 1934, the NRA had definitely lost out in its attempt to exercise primary authority over the collective bargaining aspect of industrial relations. This new state of affairs was recognized by the issuance of Administrative Order X-69 of July 29, 1934. In this order the NRA abandoned the idea of establishing an industrial relations board for each code. It was announced, (1) that the NLRB would be consulted before any industrial relations board would be set up. (2) The order urged the advisability of, but did not require, the immediate establishment of labor complaints committees under codes. (3) The order advanced the idea it might be more practicable to group together codes in related industries for the purpose of creating labor complaints committees. (4) The order accepted the idea that primary

[18] Passed June 16, 1934, approved by the President June 19, 1934.

authority over labor disputes was vested in the National Labor Relations Board.[19]

These various shifts in NRA policy on labor relations explain why the present administrative set-up is far from orderly or logical. In a few codes provision is made for labor complaints committees; a few codes are equipped with industrial relations boards; the vast majority of codes are without either device. In practice, if not in the-.ory, no clear or strict lines of demarcation are drawn between the work of labor complaints committees and of industral relations boards. This confusion must be kept in mind when reading the following analysis, which probably gives the impression of greater systematic structure than exists in fact.

Labor Complaints Committees

For the reasons indicated above, the NRA was unable to advance far during 1933-34 in attaching labor complaints committees to the code authorities. Also because the situation changes continuously, no definite picture of these committees under the NRA can be presented. The review which follows is an incomplete sketch of conditions in March 1935.

Actively functioning committees are to be found in the codes for the men's clothing industry, dress manufacturing, and the coat and suit trade. Less effective, perhaps, is the committee operating under the cotton garment code. In the first three industries mentioned, all fairly well organized on the labor side, the pre-existing machinery for the adjustment of grievances was carried over into the code. The labor complaints committees in these codes merely gave an NRA administrative pattern to institutions that had already struck deep roots in the industries concerned.

[19] See pp. 475-77.

Another group of labor complaints committees is to be found in some of the codes which apply to the printing trades, such as engraving, electrotyping, lithographic printing, and commercial relief printing. These committees also operate under conditions similar to those present in the needle trades. In the large cities at least, the printing trades unions are firmly established and have considerable power. Collective agreements are common throughout the industry, and elaborate machinery for the adjustment of grievances under these agreements antedate the NRA.

Outside the needle and printing trades, it is difficult to discover many functioning labor complaints committees in the strict sense of the term.[20] The construction code provides for the establishment of labor complaints boards (independent of any code authority) with jurisdiction over complaints arising out of the area agreements under Section 7(b). But the making of such area agreements has barely commenced; it is still too early to say how many of these agreements will be promulgated; how these agreements will work; and how adequately the proposed boards can function. For all practical purposes, we may say that labor complaints committees are a reality only in a very few industries where, prior to the NRA, trade unionism was an established institution, and where the technique of adjusting complaints arising out of collective agreements was highly developed.[21]

Labor complaints committees, even where effective, are restricted in function to the investigation of alleged violations of code labor provisions, and to the adjustment of such difficulties between workers and employers.

[20] Except for the arrangements under the burlesque theatrical, brewing labor, shipbuilding, cigar manufacturing, and importing codes.

[21] Arrangements formerly existing under the lumber, rubber, cleaning and dyeing codes are now defunct.

They have no disciplinary powers. To enforce their find-ings and recommendations, labor complaints commit-tees must turn to the NRA's Compliance Division, either directly or through the intervention of the code author-ity. When they turn to the Compliance Division, they take recourse to mills which grind very slow and not very fine. By the beginning of 1935, the machinery of the Compliance Division was jammed by the accumu-lation of thousands of labor complaints, the overwhelm-ing majority of which had arisen under codes having no labor complaints committees. Because of this, the effec-tiveness of any labor complaints committee must de-pend primarily not upon the Compliance Division, but upon the degree of trade union pressure in the partic-ular codified industry.

Industrial Relations Boards

Where labor complaints committees profess to be concerned with the employers' observance of code stand-ards on wages, hours, and other working conditions, industrial relations boards have as their purpose the ef-fectuation within a given industry of the collective bar-gaining requirements of the Recovery Act. In the ter-minology of the NRA, the jurisdiction of industrial relations boards is supposed to extend over labor "dis-putes" rather than over labor "complaints." In prac-tice, however, most of the boards established under NRA codes seem to deal with labor complaints as well as labor disputes; many of the committees with dis-putes as well as complaints. We shall here consider the boards in their capacity of adjusting labor complaints only, leaving the examination of their other functions to a later section.[22] It should be kept in mind that we are

[22] See pp. 480-82.

considering here only the NRA code boards. The "joint resolution" boards, and the Petroleum Labor Policy Board are treated in a later section.

The industrial relations boards under NRA codes,[23] like the labor complaints committees, are uniformly of the joint conference type; a given number of employer representatives, an equal number of employee representatives, plus an impartial chairman. In practically all cases, the labor representatives are chosen from the trade union or trade unions active in the industry.[24] Their organization and methods of operation differ. Some of the boards merge into pre-existent joint conference machinery developed in the industry by the trade unions or supplement such machinery; other boards create new machinery from the ground up. As examples of the former, we may cite the bituminous coal labor boards,[25] the newspaper industrial relations board,[26] and the labor boards contemplated by the construction code. As examples of the latter, we may cite the first system of cotton textile labor boards now abolished,[27] and the automobile labor board.[28] The types of complaints with which these various boards deal, or are expected to deal, vary with the nature of the industry, the provisions of the respective codes, and the prevailing character of industrial relations. Thus, the regional labor boards under the construction code would be expected to deal with controversies arising out of the application of area agreements

[23] For list of these boards, see p. 454.
[24] An exception was the first national cotton textile board where the labor representative was the president of the printing pressmen's union.
[25] See the bituminous coal code, Art. 7, Sec. 5.
[26] See daily newspaper publishing code, Art. 6, Sec. 5.
[27] Cotton textile code, Sec. 17, as amended on July 10, 1934. A silk-wool textile board, now abolished, also functioned for a time.
[28] Based on the President's automobile settlement of Mar. 25, 1934, incorporated into the automobile code by executive order on Jan. 31, 1935.

under Section 7(b). The divisional bituminous coal labor boards concern themselves largely with grievances over wage and hour provisions of the code. The automobile labor board devotes a considerable part of its time to adjudicating complaints of improper, that is discriminatory, discharges and lay-offs. The first cotton textile board sought, as one of its principal activities, to adjust speed-up and "stretch-out" complaints.

The NRA's Compliance Division

Of some 400 approved codes examined as of June 10, 1934, only 45 contained express provisions, specific or general, for the establishment of a labor complaints committee and/or an industrial relations board.[29] The number of committees and boards supposedly functioning as of March 1, 1935 was 23.[30] The total number of workers covered by these functioning committees and boards may be estimated at about 2.5 million out of a

[29] For list, see p. 455. Later estimates indicate that about 70 codes out of 775 contained such express provisions, direct or indirect.

[30] Staff members of the Labor Advisory Board and of the NLRB have supplied the following information on NRA labor complaints committees and/or industrial relations boards as of Mar. 1, 1935. (All boards independent of the NRA have been excluded.)

Industrial Relations Boards (some also deal with labor complaints): Automobile Labor Board; Bituminous Coal, Divisional Labor Boards and National Board; Construction National Planning and Adjustment Board; Daily Newspaper Industrial Board; Household Goods Storage and Moving Trade Industrial Relations Board; Trucking Industrial Relations Board.

Industries having labor complaints committees (some of which also deal with labor disputes): Infants' and children's wear; commercial relief printing Zone No. 16; cotton garment; dress manufacturing; men's neckwear; cigar manufacturing.

Industries having boards or committees not definitely classifiable in either of the foregoing groups: National lithographic printing; electrotyping and stereotyping; photo-engraving; textile print roller engraving; coat and suit; shipbuilding and ship repairing; printing ink manufacturing; importing.

Bipartisan code authorities set up to handle labor complaints and/or disputes: Brewing labor; burlesque theatrical; men's clothing.

Code	Sections
Cotton textile	Sched. A, p. 23
Wall paper	Amend. 1, 11, 6
Bituminous coal	7, 4–5
Cleaning and dyeing	6, 3(b), and Amend.
Motion picture	4, C, 6(b)
Domestic freight forwarding	6, 7(F)
Refractories	4, 7
Rolling steel door	5, 8
Rubber tire manufacturing	2, 3(e)
Electrotyping and stereotyping	7
Photo-engraving	8
Picture moulding and frame	6, 10
Rope and allied products	7, 8
Furniture and floor wax and polish	7
Porcelain breakfast furniture assembling	7, 6
Construction	8
Paper disc milk and bottle cap	9, 2
Food dish and pulp and paper plate	9, 2
Ornamental molding carving and turning	6, 9(c)
Foundry equipment	6, 2(a)
Trucking	6
Steam heating equipment	4, 4(c)
Beauty and barber shop machine equipment	6, 7(g)
Graphic arts	2, 24
Daily newspaper publishing	6, 5
Sample card	9, 2
Fibre can and tube	4, 2
Wrecking and salvage	3, 2
Textile print roller and engraving	6
Tapioca dry products	6, 9
Coal dock industry	3, 12(e)
Printing ink manufacturing	6
Machinery and allied products	6, 6(d)
Burlesque theatrical	5, 1(c) and 4
Men's neckwear	5, 8(j)
Expanding and special paper	9, 2
Shoe rebuilding	6, 6(d)
Infant's and children's wear	7, 8(j)
Air valve	6, 5(c)
Household goods storage	5, 13
Boat building and repairing	11
Undergarment and negligee	Ex. Order No. 408-5
Bank and security vault	5, 7
Commercial fixture	5, 4
Petroleum	6, 4(f)

[a] NRA Research and Planning Division, Post-Code Analysis Unit, "Organization of Code Authorities as Provided in 400 Approved Codes," *Serial No. 48A.* June 10, 1934.

total of over 20 million covered by all the approved codes.

Labor complaints under the majority of codes are thus handled neither by complaints committees nor by industrial relations boards. They are subject to the investigation, adjustment, and enforcement procedure established by the compliance agencies of the NRA. The organization, powers, and procedures of these bodies, as well as their general place in the NRA scheme, have been considered elsewhere.[31] We are concerned here with their labor activities alone; more particularly, with how they handle labor complaints.

With regard to labor complaints arising under the overwhelming majority of the codes, investigation, adjustment, and part of the enforcement have to be accomplished by the NRA compliance agencies. The main body of this work is done through the NRA state compliance officers, leaving only a residue of unadjusted cases to be handled by the regional offices and the Compliance Division. The complaint—in short, an allegation that some employer is violating his code on wages, hours, or other working conditions—may emanate from a trade union on behalf of a worker or workers; or it may be initiated by an individual worker directly and on his own behalf. In either case, the procedure is logically independent of the extent to which, if at all, the workers in that industry are self-organized for collective bargaining. On the policing side, it might be argued, reports of violations will be more readily and thoroughly forthcoming in industries where the workers are organized than in industries where they are not. But the compliance agencies do not engage in policing, that is, in periodic, systematic, and thoroughgoing inspection of establishments subject to the various codes. They start

[31] See Chaps. IV, IX.

out to perform their functions only after some outside agency—say, a trade union—or some outside person— say, the worker affected—reports an alleged violation. The job thereafter is to inquire into the validity of the complaint; to bring about a settlement, if necessary and possible. Should the employer refuse to make the necessary adjustments, enforcement measures may be taken through removal of the Blue Eagle and by proceedings in the federal courts or before the Federal Trade Commission.

As for the few codes which are equipped with apparatus empowered to deal with labor complaints, the work of investigating and adjusting, in the first instance, is performed by the labor complaint committee or the industrial relations board. If no proper adjustments can be made, these agents may pass on cases to state compliance offices. They transmit a finding of fact—the employer has violated particular code requirements on wages or hours—and recommend such disciplinary measures as may be pertinent. This finding of fact need not be accepted as final, nor the recommendations as conclusive. Before proceeding to enforcement, the compliance officers will ordinarily wish to conduct their own investigations and to explore further the possibilities of voluntary settlements. Thus, even in those industries where collective bargaining arrangements for the application and enforcement of code labor provisions have been set up, the truly authoritative instruments are governmental agencies, not labor complaints committees or industrial relations boards.

When we consider the application and enforcement of Section 7(a)'s collective bargaining requirements— that is, labor disputes—the story becomes a little more complex. It involves, on the one hand, a system of industrial relations boards, some of them attached to the NRA, others independent of it; and, on the other hand, the NRA Compliance Division. With respect to disputes of this character, the Compliance Division's powers are limited, for the most part, to discipline. It becomes concerned with the disputes only after receiving a recommendation from such a board—say the National Labor Relations Board—that an employer be deprived of his Blue Eagle. The Compliance Division may act upon or refuse to act upon the recommendation, as it sees fit. But it cannot, if the dispute passes through the hands of a joint resolution board,[32] intervene actively in the settlement thereof or attempt to go behind the Board's findings of facts.

Labor Representation on Code Authorities

Regardless of their specific content, the labor provisions of the ordinary NRA code must depend for effective enforcement in reality upon the administrative efficiency of the code authority. Each code authority, with reference to its own code, functions as the unit cell of "industrial self-government."

In the belief that "industrial self-government" must be based on the co-operation of all elements in industry, and because of its stake in labor standards, organized labor has carried on a persistent campaign in favor of labor representation, preferably equal labor representation, on all code authorities. The A. F. of L. and the Labor Advisory Board which spoke for it, demanded that all code authorities include, as full voting members, representatives of the trade union or trade unions directly concerned, in order, so it was argued, that organized labor might watch over the enforcement of the labor provisions and the collective bargaining requirements. With

[32] See pp. 478-79.

few exceptions, the employer associations which sponsored the various codes were opposed to this demand. They insisted that code authorities were agencies for the government of industry, a function which was the exclusive prerogative of employers.

In this matter as in others, the NRA hastened to adjust itself to the balance of capital-labor power in the various codified industries. As a result, organized labor secured code authority representation only in very few codes. Most of these were in industries where trade unions were not only fairly strong but also had made common cause for many years, with a dominant group of union employers against other groups of anti-union employers. As for general principles, the Labor Advisory Board, despite persistent pressure, made almost no headway. The NRA yielded no further than to recognize in theory the principle that labor advisers should be attached to the staffs of the Administration members of the various code authorities.

Early in January 1935, of the 775 approved basic and supplementary codes in operation, it would seem that no more than 26 allow for labor representation on the code authority.[33] In four cases the trade unions had sufficient bargaining strength so that the codes specifi-

[33] From materials made available by the Research and Planning Division of the NRA and the Labor Advisory Board it was possible to classify the 26 codes which give actual or potential labor representation on the code authority as follows:

Clothing codes: Coat and suit; dress manufacturing; men's clothing; millinery; blouse and skirt; leather and wool knit glove; ladies' handbag; infant's and children's wear; cotton cloth glove; men's neckwear; cotton garment; hosiery; light sewing, except garments; pleating, stitching, etc.; hat manufacturing.

Amusement codes: Legitimate theater; burlesque theatrical; radio broadcasting; motion picture; motion picture laboratory.

Miscellaneous codes: Bituminous coal; brewing labor; transit; refractories; Nottingham lace curtain; Schiffli hand machine embroidery.

A more detailed analysis will be found in "Labor and Employer Repre-

cally provide that a given number of labor members, chosen by specified labor organizations, shall sit on the the code authority.[34] In twelve cases, the codes provide that a given number of labor members shall be chosen upon nomination by the Labor Advisory Board.[35] In the remaining cases, either some other method of choosing the labor representatives is specified,[36] or else the union brought pressure to bear upon the NRA with the result that a trade union officer was chosen as one of the Administration members.[37]

Organized labor, although it conducted a prolonged campaign toward that end, was unable to force the NRA into accepting the general principle that at least one of the Administration members on all code authorities, where no other provision for labor representation was made, should be a trade union officer. True the Administration members may in theory have labor advisers attached to their staffs. But the Administration members are themselves restricted in function and in authority (as a rule they are without vote). Their labor advisers, if any were named, would be still more restricted in function and authority. It can hardly be argued that such advisers are capable of playing an effective part in the machinery of code administration.[38]

To the extent that labor representation on code au-

sentation on Code Authorities as Provided in 21 Codes," *Social and Economic Reconstruction in the United States*, International Labour Office, Geneva, 1934, p. 218.

[34] Coat and suit; legitimate theater; dress manufacturing; and Nottingham lace curtain codes.

[35] For example, men's clothing; hosiery; blouse and skirt; radio broadcasting; and cotton garment codes.

[36] For example, refractories and transit codes.

[37] For example, bituminous coal code.

[38] See Chap. VIII, pp. 212-13, for the attitude of the Labor Advisory Board on the matter.

thorities may be regarded as a method for effectuating "united action" of labor and management, the NRA has been slow and reluctant to make use of that device. To be sure, the NRA has not laid it down as a general rule that organized labor must be excluded from code authorities. But the NRA's general practice has been to include labor members on code authorities only where compelled to do so by the pressure of external forces. By pursuing this attitude, the NRA has blocked organized labor's efforts to participate, fully and authoritatively, in the administrative devices essential to effectuating labor's ideal of "industrial self-government."

INTERPRETING SECTION 7(A)

Both in formulating codes and in administering them, the NRA found itself confronted at all times with the question: Was it interpreting the provisions of the Recovery Act in accordance with the inherent purpose of the statute and the intent of Congress? Because of the conflicting attitudes of employers and organized labor this question was especially urgent in relation to the collective bargaining provisions of Section 7. The NRA was thus forced from time to time to make declarations on the meaning and methods of collective bargaining implied in Section 7(a), declarations which influenced public opinion and affected the development of industrial relations. We shall now review briefly these declarations, (1) to complete the picture of how, if at all, the NRA reshaped industrial relations, and (2), to clarify the developments which resulted in the evolution of the labor relations boards considered in a later section.

When we speak of the interpretation of Section 7(a) by the NRA, we have in mind primarily the series of statements, joint and individual, issued especially during the first ten months of the NRA by General Hugh S. Johnson, the Administrator, and by Donald R. Richberg, the General Counsel. The governmental policy laid down in these statements with regard to Section 7(a) may be characterized as that of "perfect neutrality."[39] The government, according to this view, was to stand aside from the struggle between labor and management. It was neither the duty of the government to promote the self-organization of workers for the purpose of collective bargaining, nor to take sides for or against any particular form of labor organization. The government's sole function was to secure "fair play" as between the two contending agencies, the trade unions, and the company unions.

It was the duty of the government to safeguard individual workers against "interference, coercion and restraint." No employer should be permitted to discharge a worker, lay him off, or otherwise discriminate against him because of his membership or activity in any labor organization. No employer should be permitted to require, as a condition of employment, that any worker join a company union or refrain from joining a labor union.

But this did not mean that the government must see to it that employers did not devise company union plans or that they should extend exclusive recognition to any one labor organization which represented a majority of the workers. The character of "recognition" and the execution of collective contracts were matters for negotiations between the employer and the representatives of his employees. The statute assured the workers "free-

---

[39] The summary presented here is based on the statements which will be found in NRA releases and in the daily press. See particularly the Johnson-Richberg joint statement of Feb. 3, 1934, *New York Times*, Feb. 4, 1934.

dom" in the designation of representatives for collective bargaining. In a particular plant, the workers might unanimously choose a single set of representatives; or the majority might choose one set, and the minority another; or a number of separate sets of representatives might be chosen by several groups. The employer's obligations under the law were equal towards the representatives of all groups. The will of the majority could not be permitted to suppress the will of the minority or minorities.

There was also no necessary conflict, under the law, between the trade union and the company union. Both might exist side by side among the same labor groups. The employer was obliged to treat with both on an equal and impartial basis, regardless of which represented the majority or minority group. The trade union representatives could claim to speak and negotiate on behalf only of the workers who belonged to the trade union; the company union representatives, similarly, on behalf only of their own members. Messrs. Johnson and Richberg thus introduced the concept of plurality in labor representation for collective bargaining within one and the same labor unit. This concept, to be workable, had to be connected with the ideas of "proportional representation" and "works councils."[40] In any given establishment, there would be a single agency authorized to conclude a collective contract on behalf of the totality of the workers. That agency could be termed a "works council." But the "works council" must provide a vehicle of expression for the representatives of majority and minority groups among the workers. This meant that the works council would have to be constituted of members chosen on a proportional basis from among the various representatives.

[40] The necessary connection was furnished by the President's automobile settlement of Mar. 25, 1934. *New York Times*, Mar. 26, 1934.

The Johnson-Richberg interpretations of Section 7(a) aimed not only to make room for minority representation, but also to maintain the right of workers who so preferred to bargain individually. Although the law gave the workers freedom to act in groups and to choose representatives for collective bargaining, it did not, according to Johnson and Richberg, deprive the individual worker of the right to reject any and all systems of collective bargaining, nor did it give organized workers the right to force their particular brand of collective bargaining upon an unwilling worker. In stating these doctrines, Messrs. Johnson and Richberg took pains to maintain that the terms "closed and open shop" should be excluded from the vocabulary of the NRA. One might be justified, however, in drawing the conclusion from their statements that they tended to regard the closed shop as opposed to public policy and out of harmony with Section 7 of the Recovery Act.[41]

So far as concerns the main purpose of collective bargaining—namely, the making of collective agreements—the Johnson-Richberg statements were entirely negative. They stressed the idea that neither management nor labor representatives were obliged to assent to any specific set of proposals. The employer, in particular, was not required to conclude a contract of any kind. He had fulfilled his obligations under the law if he manifested his readiness to confer and negotiate with any and all employee representatives.

[41] See particularly the "interpretation" which Messrs. Johnson and Richberg sought to put into the bituminous coal code. The President ordered this interpretation excluded because it might lead to "confusion or misunderstanding," but took pains to say he did not necessarily disapprove of the joint statement. The statement is appended to early texts of the code as Schedule B. An almost identical statement was broadcast by the Administrator, Aug. 23, 1933. See *NRA Release No. 463*.

Whatever their legal soundness, the Johnson-Rich-berg interpretations of Section 7(a) had the practical effect of placing the NRA on the side of anti-union employers in their struggle against the trade unions. Was this consistent with the intent of Congress in enacting Section 7(a)? Certainly there is no evidence that Congress intended to outlaw the company union or to authorize the trade union as the exclusive instrumentality of collective bargaining. But there is evidence that Section 7(a) was intended to remove pre-existent legal obstacles to the growth of the trade union movement and to put new obstructions in the path of company unions.[42] In so far as this was true, the Johnson-Richberg statements served to block the full effectuation of the purposes presumably inherent in the Recovery Act.

It can thus be readily understood why organized labor became indignant at the NRA's attempts to interpret the statute; and why first the Administrator and later the General Counsel became embroiled in a series of struggles with the A. F. of L. and its affiliated unions. From organized labor's point of view, the NRA proved derelict in its duties. It fostered the self-organization of employers for collective action, while trying to be "neutral" towards labor organization. The NRA thus threw its weight against labor in the balance of bargaining power between capital and labor. From their own point of view, however, the Administrator and General Counsel were merely striving to put into effect the express instructions of the act. The act was definite in permitting employers to join together for their own collective ends. It was also definite in conveying certain immunities to

[42] Lewis L. Lorwin and Arthur Wubnig, *Section 7(a), Labor Boards and Collective Bargaining*, to be published in 1935, Chap. II.

workers and imposing certain disabilities upon employers. But the act nowhere expressly directed the government to pursue a policy of favoring or promoting a semiofficial, or quasi-public trade union movement.

THE SYSTEM OF LABOR BOARDS

From the very beginning, the process of putting the Recovery Act into effect was accompanied by labor unrest, later intensified by the difficulties of code administration and by the NRA declarations on Section 7(a). From June 1933 through the year 1934, the country was swept by a series of strike waves comparable in intensity, if not in scope, to the labor unrest of 1919. This movement was due in part to the short-lived "inflation scare" boom of the summer of 1933; but in larger measure to the psychological effects of Section 7(a) which stirred the unions into new life and at the same time gave a new impetus to the organization of "company unions."[43]

The NRA, overwhelmed by the deluge of early codes, was unprepared to deal with labor disputes during the summer of 1933. The result, as we have indicated, was the establishment of the National Labor Board. It would seem that the sponsors of the Board had in mind a temporary tribunal, with jurisdiction limited to controversies arising under the PRA, pending the formation of industrial relations boards under the different codes.[44] If this was their idea, the National Labor Board soon transcended it. Within a short time, the Board built up a nation-wide system of regional boards which displaced the local compliance boards of the NRA in the tasks of handling labor disputes. Almost from the start, the Board advanced beyond its assigned task of mediating

[43] For details, see Chap. XVIII.
[44] See President's statement, Aug. 5, 1933. *New York Times*, Aug. 6, 1933.

disputes to the role of a quasi-judicial tribunal interpreting Section 7(a). The Board soon began to hand down a series of rulings on the essence and methods of collective bargaining.[45]

Before long, it became clear that the National Labor Board was interpreting Section 7(a) in a spirit opposed to that of the NRA. The Labor Board also found that it could not rely on the NRA for overcoming the resistance of employers to its rulings, as was shown in the Weirton, Budd, Harriman, and several other famous cases. The Labor Board tried to solve the problem by obtaining from the President executive orders which extended its jurisdiction and powers and regularized the procedure for enforcement.[46]

Meanwhile the NRA had not ceased entirely its efforts to equip some if not all of the codes with industrial relations boards. At the same time, there was established under the petroleum code, cut loose from the NRA and assigned to the Petroleum Administration, the Petroleum Labor Policy Board. As a result, three types of boards were soon functioning: (1) the National Labor Board system; (2) a few NRA code boards; and (3) the Petroleum Labor Policy Board.

In the conflict between the NRA and the National Labor Board, the latter, for a while, had the upper hand. Determined to strengthen the position of the Board, Senator Wagner, on March 1, 1934, introduced into Congress his Labor Disputes bill,[47] which if enacted would have excluded the NRA from any and all part in the adjustment of labor disputes and the interpretation

[45] For a statistical summary of the work of the NLB and its regional boards, see *NRA Release No. 6295*, July 7, 1934.

[46] Executive Orders Nos. 6511, 6580, and 6612-A, dated Dec. 16, 1933, Feb. 1, 1934, and Feb. 23, 1934.

[47] 73 Cong. 2 sess., S. 2926.

of Section 7(a). The bill specified certain "unfair labor practices" which were designed to put "company unions" out of business, and proposed the establishment of a statutory National Labor Board with powers similar to those of the Federal Trade Commission.[48]

The Labor Disputes bill never came to a vote in Congress, although the Senate Labor Committee reported it out favorably in an amended version. By the end of March, in connection with the threatened automobile strike, the Labor Board lost prestige and influence, and the NRA was again in the ascendant as the official spokesman on industrial relations policy. But the NRA's success was short-lived. Those friendly to trade unionism distrusted the NRA labor policies, and they succeeded in blocking the Administrator's efforts to equip each code with its own industrial relations board.

As a compromise between the various forces and under the pressure of a new wave of strikes, Congress on June 16, 1934, passed Public Resolution No. 44[49] which empowered the President to establish, independently of the NRA, a system of labor boards vested with full and exclusive authority to adjudicate in controversies over Section 7(a). On July 9, 1934 the National Labor Relations Board, established "in connection with," though not subject to, the administrative authority of the Department of Labor, began to function as the successor to the National Labor Board. The NLRB was not only authorized to investigate labor disputes, to hold hearings on Section 7(a) violations, to conduct elections of employee representatives, but was also vested with power to study the structure and operation of all existing·labor

[48] On Feb. 21, 1935, Senator Wagner reintroduced a substantially similar measure under the title of the Labor Relations bill, 74 Cong. 1 Sess., S. 1958.
[49] 48 Stat. L. 1183.

boards and to recommend the creation of regional labor relations boards and/or of "special labor boards for particular industries vested with the powers that the President is authorized to confer by Public Resolution. No. 44."[50] A basis was thus laid on which the NLRB might develop an integrated system of labor boards.[51]

During the summer and fall of 1934, the President created three additional "joint resolution" boards, the National Longshoremen's Labor Board, the National Steel Labor Relations Board, and the Textile Labor Relations Board.[52] The Steel Labor Board was set up in opposition to proposals from the NRA and from the Iron and Steel Institute that there should be established an NRA code tribunal on the model of the Automobile Labor Board. The establishment of the Steel Board thus served to drive home the point that the NRA would henceforth be excluded as a major factor in the creation of an integrated labor board system. This was further illustrated, following the settlement of the nation-wide textile strike, by the abolition of the old boards in the cotton textile, wool and silk industries which were replaced by the Textile Labor Relations Board.

By February 1935, there was in operation a system of labor boards which fell into four groups: (1) the National Labor Relations Board with its subordinate regional boards; (2) the other joint resolutions boards; (3) the Petroleum Labor Policy Board; and (4) various NRA code boards. The principal accomplishment of these boards, from the point of view of industrial rela-

[50] See Executive Order No. 6763, June 29, 1934 providing for the establishment of the NLRB.

[51] But this basis disappeared for practical purposes when the President instructed the NLRB not to interfere with the work of NRA code labor boards. See the *New York Times*, Jan. 23, 1935.

[52] Executive Order Nos. 6748, 6751, and 6858 of June 26 and 28 and Sept. 26, 1934.

tions, was their work in clarifying the meaning and intent of Section 7(a) and in establishing methods whereby the united action of labor and management might be achieved. From this point of view, the most important contributions were made by the National Labor Board, and by the National Labor Relations Board. We shall, therefore, consider these boards at greater length than the others.

The National Labor Board and Section 7(a)

Soon after its creation, the National Labor Board assumed a quasi-judicial role, that is, the administrative adjudication of Section 7(a) cases. Before long, the Board had constructed a ground-work of principles and rules embodying a specific theory of collective bargaining, which was to give substance to Section 7(a). Although the NLB was abolished in July 1934, its theory of Section 7(a) continued to exercise influence and underlies the work of most of the boards in existence today.

The specific features of the NLB's interpretation of the statute were conditioned by the character of the cases brought before it for administrative adjudication. As a rule, these cases involved strike situations, caused by employers' resistance to trade union claims for "recognition." As a rule, also, such trade union demands were complicated by the existence of company unions, newly brought into being by employers, which contested the outside union's claims to be the authorized representative of the employees for purposes of collective bargaining. In many cases as well, trade union members complained that they had been discharged or laid off or refused reinstatement after a strike because of their organizing activities. In brief, the background against which the NLB worked out its doctrines was one of high tension in industrial relations; of a nation-wide organizational campaign by the trade unions under the stimulus of Section 7(a); of a counter-offensive by employers who set up employee representation plans in many of the major codified industries, notably, automobile manufacturing and iron and steel; of confusion and turmoil with regard to the identity and authority of employee representatives within the meaning of the statute; and of general labor unrest manifesting itself in turbulent strikes throughout the country.

Against this background, the National Labor Board was compelled to lay down, above all, a set of principles which would enable the workers to designate the representatives of their own choice for collective bargaining. The Board's basic idea was that the workers were "free men" and the employer should in no way interpose obstacles to the expression of their choice. It was for the workers, and for them alone, to say whether they wished to be represented by individuals or by a labor organization, by "fellow employees" or by outsiders, by a trade union or by a company union. In so far as the determination of the representatives was concerned, the employer must keep his "hands off." His part in collective bargaining began only after the freely chosen representatives had been properly identified and duly authorized.

Two issues were thus raised: (1) How could the identity of the freely chosen representatives be established? (2) Once their identity was established, what authority might the representatives thus chosen properly claim?

The most difficult problems of representation arose in cases where a company union, functioning side by side with a trade union, contested the latter's claim to speak on behalf of the employees. The National Labor Board did not proceed on the assumption that the company union *per se* was an unlawful instrumentality for collective bargaining. But it rejected the contention of employers that participation by the workers in selecting representatives under an employee representation plan was equivalent to affirmation by the workers that they preferred such scheme to any other type of self-organization. The workers, the Board held, must be permitted to say for themselves whether or not they wished to carry on their collective bargaining through the company union plan; whether or not they chose the company union form of self-organization in preference to the trade union form.

This reasoning eventuated in the principle that where representation was at issue, it must be determined by means of an election. The principle of ordering and conducting elections, under its own auspices, was the key to the NLB's theory of Section 7(a). The elections which the NLB called for from time to time permitted the workers to choose, (1) between representation by an outside or inside union; and/or (2) between representation by a given labor organization and no scheme of collective bargaining at all. The former type of election was typical; the latter exceptional.[53]

The election device was obviously inspired by the concept that democratic ideals of representative self-government should be applied to industrial relations. In accordance with American versions of these ideals, the Board also favored the principle of majority rule. The Board held that the labor organization chosen by

[53] For a statistical analysis of National Labor Board elections, see Emily Clark Brown, "Selection of Employee Representatives," *Monthly Labor Review*, Vol. 40, No. 1, pp. 1-18. In all, 183 elections were held, involving 546 separate industrial units. Trade unions won 74.7 per cent of the elections and polled 69.4 per cent of the votes. Employee representation plans won 23.1 per cent of the elections, and polled 28.5 per cent of the votes. In the remaining cases, no representation was chosen.

the majority of the workers within a collective bargaining unit was entitled to bargain collectively on behalf of all the workers comprised in it. The Board rejected the principle of proportional representation because that principle had never established itself in American political life and because collective bargaining traditionally meant that one and only one labor organization should negotiate a contract on behalf of a given group of workers.

Once elected, the representatives of the employees, whether individuals or a labor organization, had definite rights. They could claim the right of "recognition"; that is, the employer must regard either the individuals or the labor organization in its collective capacity as vested with exclusive authority to negotiate collective agreements on behalf of the workers concerned.

As for collective bargaining, the Board emphasized over and over again that its aim was the making and maintaining of collective agreements. This does not mean that the employer, on his part, and the labor representatives, on their part, are bound to accept any specific terms that are presented by the other party to the negotiations, or that they are bound to assent to the proposals advanced by an outsider who intervenes in order to compose differences. It means, in the opinion of the Board, that both parties to collective bargaining are required to "exert every reasonable effort" to conclude an agreement. It means that both parties must enter the negotiations with a "will to agree"; that they must negotiate in good faith; that they must manifest an intent to enter into a bilateral contract on the assumption that it is not impossible to bridge differences on specific terms—that is wages, hours, and other working conditions. The contract may be written or oral; preferably it should be in writing. If a trade union has been chosen as the repre-. sentative of the employees, it is entitled to ask that it be permitted to sign the contract in its quasi-corporate capacity.

The National Labor Board also developed specific principles bearing upon alleged cases of discriminatory discharge for union membership or activities. According to the Board, the right of hiring and firing was modified by the statute in one and only one essential respect: the employer was disabled from exercising this right, if, in exercising it, he was animated by an anti-union bias. The only valid reasons for discharging, laying off, or otherwise disciplining a worker were the worker's service record, his behavior, and the exigencies of business. To discharge, lay off, or otherwise discipline a worker because of his union connections was unlawful.

To sum up, the interpretation of Section 7(a) developed by the National Labor Board ran as follows: The workers should be entirely free in the choice of their representatives for collective bargaining; they should be free to choose individuals or labor organizations; if controversy arose, it should be settled by an election of employee representatives, majority rule governing; the representatives, whoever they were, were entitled to claim and receive recognition; the representatives elected by the majority were exclusively authorized to bargain collectively on behalf of the totality of the workers; collective bargaining meant the exertion of every reasonable effort in good faith and with a will to agree to make and maintain collective agreements; and the employer must refrain from discrimination against his employees for their union activities.[54]

[54] See Decisions of the National Labor Board, Pt. I (August 1933-March 1934); Pt. II (April-August 1934). For a summary statement,

The National Labor Board thus read into Section 7(a) a series of obligations binding upon employers. The specific content which the Board put into its interpretations was largely conditioned, to repeat, by the type of labor disputes with which it had to deal. The typical strike which came before the Board for adjustment was not a strike for higher wages, shorter hours, or other improved working conditions. It was a strike for "union recognition," and against "company unionism." Company unions were pitted against trade unions on a far-flung industrial front because where the trade unions took Section 7(a) as a mandate to organize the unorganized, the anti-union employers took the statute as a permission to entrench themselves behind employee representation plans. The Board was thus constrained to evolve an interpretation of Section 7(a) in terms of the principles underlying the theory and practice of collective bargaining. It was rarely called upon to evolve an interpretation of the statute in terms of the specific contents of collective bargains.

The National Labor Relations Board

The National Labor Relations Board inherited from its predecessor a fairly complete theory of Section 7(a). For the most part, the decisions of the NLRB merely reaffirm, more systematically and more compactly, the principles which the NLB worked out under the stress and strain of eleven months of labor disputes.[55]

It remains true, nevertheless, that the NLRB has carried the theory of Section 7(a) beyond the point where the NLB had left it. Without going to the extreme of

see *National Labor Board Principles with Applicable Cases*, NLRB, Aug. 21, 1934.

[55] See Decisions of the NLRB (July-December 1934). For a summary statement, see *Sixth Monthly Report of the NLRB*, pp. 3-5.

ruling that the company union is *per se* unlawful, the NLRB has held that where a company union could be shown to be dominated by the employer, it might be disqualified—dis-established from functioning as an instrumentality of collective bargaining. The Board has also held that an employer might be required to desist from contributing to the financial support of an employee representation plan. At the same time, the NLRB has affirmed the idea that a company union, no matter how employer dominated, is entitled to a place on the ballot, if, as, and when a controversy about representation makes an election expedient. The process by which a company union has come into being and the methods by which it has been maintained in existence, are from this point of view immaterial; the important thing is that the workers should be permitted a genuinely free choice in the selection of the agency through which they desire to exercise their rights of collective bargaining.

The NLRB has not only enunciated, like the NLB before it, the principle of majority rule; it has also attempted to clarify the question of the area within which majority rule should hold. In other words, the Board has attacked the question of what units, plant or departmental, might properly be regarded as units for collective bargaining. We need not enter into details because the NLRB has treated the question on the merits of specific cases. The NLRB has also held in effect, if not in so many words, that Section 7(a) does not invalidate closed shop agreements between a *bona fide* labor organization and an employer. In general, the NRLB may be said to have treated the question of the closed shop more frankly and with fewer reservations than did the NLB—and has stated its conclusions with greater emphasis.

The doctrines of the NLRB, like those of the NLB,

have been concerned with procedural forms of collective bargaining rather than with the specific contents of collective bargains. This is due to the fact that the NLRB not only inherited the theories of the NLB but also had to face much the same problems: company union versus trade union; determined employer resistance against the basic doctrines of elections, majority rule, negotiations in good faith, and the final making of a collective agreement.

The NLRB has had a smoother career than the NLB for several reasons. First, while the NLB was constituted of partisan interests—an equal number of employee and employer representatives, plus an impartial chairman— the NLRB is constituted of three impartial experts. Second, by the time the NLRB swung into action the strike outburst of 1933-34 had spent much of its force. Third, much of the NLB's energies had been spent in jurisdictional struggles with the NRA. But with the establishment of the NLRB the NRA retreated from the field of labor disputes and ceased to issue what professed to be authoritative interpretations of Section 7(a). Fourth, the NLB had struggled in vain to extend its sphere of influence over iron and steel, automobile manufacturing, and other major industries. Public Resolution No. 44 saved the NLRB from spending its energies in similar struggles; for the President, relying on the resolution, created special boards for the steel and textile industries.

The Petroleum Labor Policy Board

Dissociated both from the NRA and NLRB, and attached instead to the Petroleum Administration, is the Petroleum Labor Policy Board. Within its own sphere of influence, the Petroleum Board—the PLPB—engages, among other activities, in the administrative adjudication of Section 7(a) cases. Within its limited area, the Petroleum Labor Policy Board speaks with a more authoritative voice than almost any other labor board. Each decision in which it sets forth the meaning of the statute is formally approved by the Petroleum Administrator, who is the Secretary of the Interior, and enjoys the force of an administrative ruling backed up by the sanctions which are at the disposal of the Administrator.

Taken by and large, the PLPB's interpretation of Section 7(a) has been identical with that developed first by the NLB and later by the NLRB: free choice between representation by company unions or trade unions; elections, if necessary, to express the choice; majority rule; one and only one labor organization entitled to claim the authority of a representative within the meaning of the statute; the making and maintaining of collective agreements; disability of the employer to engage in discriminatory practices. One procedural refinement is worthy of attention. If necessary, the PLPB calls for an election; but, if the parties involved are willing to waive an election, the PLPB proceeds to determine the right of a trade union to claim representative powers by making comparisons between payroll records and the names signed to the petition asking that the union be certified as representative. Having determined the identity of the authorized representatives, whether by payroll comparisons or by an election, the PLPB proceeds to issue an appropriate certification.

The Joint Resolution Boards

Of the various boards (other than the NLRB) established from time to time under Public Resolution No. 44, the National Longshoremen's Labor Board may be dismissed with a mere mention. Its task was clear and specific: to adjust the Pacific Coast longshoremen's strike. Having adjusted the dispute and having handed down its arbitrational award, the Longshoremen's Board fulfilled its only important function.

Not until the end of 1934, six months after it began to function, did the National Steel Labor Relations Board begin to hand down formal decisions wherein there was incorporated a definite theory of Section 7(a). These decisions were of a twofold character: (1) The Board called for collective bargaining elections at which the workers might choose between trade union and company union representation, and (2) the Board adjudicated upon complaints of discriminatory discharge and lay-off. Prior to this time, the Steel Board had long been engaged, without success, in trying to work out an agreement between the employers, who stood by their employee representation plans, and the A. F. of L. trade unions, which demanded elections.

As for the Textile Labor Relations Board (cotton, silk, wool, and other related textile industries), it had its hands full for many months in seeking to clean up the débris of the nation-wide textile strike and in putting into effect some of the recommendations of the Winant Commission. The textile strike was followed by what the A. F. of L. union maintained was an epidemic of discriminatory discharges. The result was to overwhelm the Textile Board with discrimination complaints, on many of which, voluntary adjustment proving impossible, it was constrained to rule.

On the whole, we may say, the Steel and Textile Boards have refrained from ambitious efforts to interpret Section 7(a). They have left this function to the NLRB, whose doctrines were presumably to be followed by all the joint resolution boards.

The NRA Code Boards

The original Cotton Textile Board occupied itself with the adjustment of labor complaints, with investigations into speed-up and stretch-out charges, with the mediation and arbitration of strikes, and with encouraging the development of mill committees to handle local controversies. The Board's failure or refusal to strike out along the doctrinal lines pursued by the National Labor Board was a principal factor in arousing the resentment of the A. F. of L. union against it. This led, in the end, to the collapse of NRA's pioneer experiment in industrial relations boards.

The Automobile Labor Board has also refrained from attempting to impose upon the industry a theory of Section 7(a) similar to that developed by the NLB, the NLRB, and the PLPB. Instead, the Board has issued a series of rules and regulations designed to govern (1) the conduct of negotiations between employers and employee representatives; (2) discharges, lay-offs, and rehirings; (3) the election of works councils on the basis of proportional representation. The Board has relied on the terms of the President's automobile strike settlement of March 25, 1934. Resentful toward the Board's attitude and procedures, the A. F. of L. unions have broken off all relations with it and are seeking to replace it, if possible, by a joint resolution board. The Board meanwhile has gone ahead with its program of establishing works councils, independent of company and trade unions alike, and sponsored by the government.

The several divisional bituminous coal labor boards have addressed themselves largely to the interpretation of Section 7(a). The results so far are somewhat paradoxical. On the one hand, the boards have come out for the free choice of employee representatives, majority rule, the execution of collective agreements, and union recognition, at least in cases where anti-union employers refused to recognize the United Mine Workers of America. On the other hand, the most important of the boards (with jurisdiction over Illinois) has denied the right of choosing representatives for collective bargaining by means of elections to workers involved in the dual union conflict between the U.M.W.A. and the Progressive Miners of America, an independent outside labor organization. The board has held that where either union enjoyed collective contracts antedating Section 7(a), no election was required until the contract had expired. In most of these cases, the P.M.A. constituted the complainant, who petitioned for the election, and the U.M.W.A. the defendant, who contended for the sanctity of contracts in the face of Section 7(a). In its only major decision up to the end of 1934, the National Bituminous Coal Labor Board affirmed a divisional board ruling that the P.M.A. was not entitled to an election in the Peabody properties. The labor board system in the soft coal industry may be said to constitute a working arrangement between the U.M.W.A. and the employers, limiting, in part, the right to strike, and providing, in effect, for a degree of compulsory arbitration. The U.M.W.A. has thus captured control of the code machinery for industrial relations, and uses this machinery both to prevent employers from violating Section 7(a) and to shut out contending labor unions from the benefits of the statute.

The Newspaper Industrial Board has gone through the motions of exercising its powers, but with no perceptible success, because the Board has almost invariably deadlocked—the four employer members on one side, and the four employee members on the other. As for the

National Construction Planning and Adjustment Board, it has been inactive because of the continuing depression in the building trades and because of strife within the A. F. of L. Building Trades Department. Little can be ascertained regarding the activities of the remaining NRA code boards; some of them, in all likelihood, exist only on paper.

The Problem of Enforcement

If the various labor boards, particularly the NLB and the NLRB, had succeeded in putting their interpretation of Section 7(a) into practical effect, they would have wrought profound changes over a wide range of American industrial relations. But the quasi-judicial work of the boards had but little practical effect. For this the inadequacy of the enforcement machinery was in large measure to blame.

In the matter of collective bargaining, organized labor had everything to gain and little to lose by relying upon the principles put forth by the NLB and the NLRB. The unions saw that by winning elections they could drive ahead toward "recognition." On the other hand, if they lost elections, nothing more serious would result than the maintenance of the *status quo*. The boards had little trouble, therefore, in getting the trade unions to accept their doctrines.

The efforts of the NLB and the NLRB to put their interpretation of the statute into effect were blocked by the attitude of anti-union employers. Such employers refused (1) to permit the boards to conduct elections of employee representatives;[56] (2) to accept the principle

[56] Some of the outstanding cases were: Weirton Steel and E. G. Budd Manufacturing, under the National Labor Board; Firestone Rubber and the Goodrich Rubber, under the National Labor Relations Board; Carnegie Steel Company, under the National Steel Labor Relations Board.

of majority rule;[57] (3) to enter in good faith into collective negotiations with employee representatives for the purpose of making a collective contract;[58] and (4) to reinstate workers whom the Boards found to be victims of "discrimination."[59] It was not merely a question of individual employers, acting singly, but of an organized campaign of non-compliance in which entire industries acted in concert, supported by their trade associations and by the leading employer organizations. This resistance the employers justified by arguing that the ideas evolved by the NLB and the NLRB were a deviation from traditional legal doctrines and would lead to a forced unionization of all industry.

Face to face with employer non-compliance, the Boards could resort to one or both of two alternative forms of discipline. They could recommend to the NRA's Compliance Division that the employer be deprived of his Blue Eagle. They could refer the case to the Department of Justice, urging that appropriate legal proceedings be initiated. The effectiveness of the first form of discipline depended on the readiness of the Compliance Division to co-operate and on the degree to which a given employer might be hurt by being deprived of his Blue Eagle. To withhold or withdraw the Blue Eagle from a recalcitrant employer was tantamount to inviting the general public to engage in a boycott of his merchandise. Failure to obtain or to retain a Blue Eagle might

---

[57] It was partly the fear of the consequences of majority rule which caused the automobile manufacturers to reject the NLB's effort to adjust the threatened strike in March 1934. The NLRB's affirmation of majority rule, for the first time, in the Houde case, led to defiance of the Board's authority, and necessitated proceedings in the federal courts.

[58] The most spectacular case under the NLB was that of the Harriman Hosiery Mills in Tennessee; a similar issue was involved in the Houde case handled by the NLRB.

[59] Complaints of discriminatory discharges formed the bulk of the cases upon which both the NLB and the NLRB had to rule.

also lead to certain legal disabilities, such as inability to bid on government contracts. The effectiveness of the second form of discipline depended on the readiness of the Department of Justice to institute proceedings; on the kind of relief sought; and on the willingness of the courts to grant such relief.

The difficulty of establishing an effective *modus oper-andi* with the NRA's Compliance Division was one of the principal factors which rendered the NLB largely ineffective. A provisional working arrangement was finally established[60] and four Blue Eagles were removed, two of which were later restored. By this time, however, the NLB was nearing its end. The National Labor Relations Board has faced the same problem with regard to the NRA Compliance Division. Under the executive order of June 30, 1934, the Compliance Division is bound to accept the NLRB's fact findings as final and conclusive; but is not obliged to act upon the Board's recommendations. In practice, the logical impasse has been resolved by an arrangement according to which the Compliance Division agrees to act upon the Board's recommendations in "normal" cases, while the Board recognizes the Compliance Division's ultimate power of discretion.[61]

[60] The NLB was established Aug. 5, 1933 but not until Feb. 23, 1934 did the President issue an executive order defining the relationships between the Board and the Compliance Division. Prior to this order, the Compliance Division took the attitude as shown in the Budd case, that it was free to investigate, adjust, and adjudicate any controversy submitted to it by the Board and that it was not bound by the conclusions and opinions of the Board. In brief, the Compliance Division refused to remove Blue Eagles merely upon the request of the Board.

[61] This arrangement led to difficulties in the Jennings discharge case, in which the NRA opposed the exercise by the NLRB of jurisdiction over a case which might have been routed through the Newspaper Industrial Board. From July 9, 1934 to Jan. 9, 1935, of 36 cases transmitted to it by the NLRB, the Compliance Division removed 24 Blue Eagles; 12 cases were still pending at the end of the period. *Sixth Monthly Report of the NLRB*, p. 1.

It has also proved difficult, first for the NLB and later for the NLRB, to establish smooth working arrangements with the Department of Justice. Where the Boards saw a clear-cut violation of the statute, the Department of Justice foresaw difficulties in building up a conclusive case. As a consequence, the Department was much more reluctant to prosecute than the Boards were to initiate prosecutions. How slow, cumbersome, and ineffective the procedure proved to be is shown by the record. By the end of 1934, the tide of alleged employer non-compliance had been mounting higher, day by day, for almost a year and a half. During all this time the Department of Justice had initiated proceedings in two cases in all, neither of which was concluded, that is, brought before the United States Supreme Court.[62]

Fear of losing the Blue Eagle was by no means a motive sufficient to drive recalcitrant employers into compliance with Labor Board decisions. It was not altogether certain, to begin with, that the Blue Eagle would be taken away; and the actual loss of Blue Eagles, once NRA's "cracking down" phase had passed, did not seem to matter much. Indeed, as time went on, the anti-union employers became more aggressive and began to carry the attack to the Labor Boards. Thus, the National Association of Manufacturers advised all employers to fight the NLRB's version of majority rule (as set forth in the Houde decision) by resorting to the federal courts. Having issued election orders in the rubber and tire industry

[62] (1) The Weirton suit, begun upon the urgings of the NLB, which occasioned a ruling by Federal Judge Nields on Feb. 27, 1935 that Section 7(a) was unconstitutional and that the company union in question was not unlawfully imposed. This suit had dragged through the courts for more than a year. (2) The Houde suit, begun upon the urgings of the NLRB. The Weirton case was the only one referred to the Department of Justice by the NLB. Up to Jan. 9, 1935, the NLRB had referred 21 cases to the Department of Justice. See *Sixth Monthly Report of the NLRB*, p. 1.

cases, the NLRB was at once dragged into the federal courts. Having issued election orders in Carnegie Steel and in other cases, the Steel Labor Board was also dragged into the federal courts.[63]

Under circumstances like these, it was useless to look for quick and vigorous enforcement. The typical situation was a prolonged and tortuous process. One *cause célèbre*—Weirton, Budd, Harriman, National Lock, Houde, Goodrich, Firestone, Jennings—followed another in quick succession. In the process, first the NLB and then the NLRB became voices crying in the wilderness of non-compliance.[64]

In effect, then, the Labor Boards were compelled to depend for enforcement of their rulings on the force of public opinion. To judge by the increasing vigor with which anti-union employers pushed their resistance as time went on, it would follow either that the Boards failed to awaken public opinion or else that public opinion was not a factor of sufficient strength to accomplish the purpose. After the first outburst of NRA excitement, public enthusiasm for the objectives of the act subsided considerably. Also, public opinion was bound to be confused by the multitude of conflicting voices: the NRA versus the NLB; General Johnson versus Senator Wagner; Donald R. Richberg versus the NLRB; Public Resolution No. 44 versus the automobile strike settlement; and so on.

Basic to the inability of both the NLB and the NLRB to enforce their rulings on Section 7(a) was the reluc-

[63] In the former case, the suit against the Board was brought by the employers. In the latter case, the suits against the Board were brought, at least technically, by the employee representation plans. In 7 of the 86 cases decided by the NLRB up to Jan. 9, 1935, actions were brought to enjoin enforcement of the decisions. The same, p. 1.

[64] For a statement by the NLRB of its importance on the enforcement side, see the same, p. 7.

tance of the Administration to face the fundamental issue raised by the statute, namely the part to be played by trade unions in American industry. To encourage vigorous enforcement of Section 7(a) as interpreted by the two Labor Boards would have precipitated an industrial battle to the finish between trade unions and anti-union employers. These consequences the Administration was not ready to face, partly because of the possible effects on re-employment and recovery, partly because of the long-range implications of collective bargaining through trade unions upon the economic structure.

CHAPTER XVIII

CHANGES IN THE POSITION OF
TRADE UNIONISM

In the preceding chapter we made references to the ways in which the NRA was affected in its labor policies by the activities of trade unions and how it in turn influenced these activities. To complete our picture of developments in industrial relations under the NIRA, we must now consider more fully what took place in the organized labor movement during 1933-34. What new trends were released by Section 7(a)? What were the results?

By March 1933, trade unionism in the United States had reached the lowest point in two decades in membership, financial resources, and morale. Four years of depression had aggravated the internal and external difficulties of the trade unions inside and outside the American Federation of Labor. It was being seriously debated whether or not all trade unions were on their "deathbed," soon to pass from the economic scene.[1] Today, 20 months later, the trade unions are on the upward grade again in numbers, resources, and self-assertiveness, and are clamoring for co-equal status with management in the developing scheme of "industrial self-government."

This striking change in the outlook for trade unionism may be regarded as one of the major effects of the Recovery Act. It can be ascribed more particularly to the forces released by Section 7 of the statute. It is, therefore, of special interest to examine the specific influences

[1] See Lewis L. Lorwin, *The American Federation of Labor*, pp. 451-55.

which the NIRA and the NRA have had upon trade unionism. What changes have taken place in the membership, structure, and functions of the trade unions? What new problems have been placed before them? How have the unions met these problems? To what extent have the unions been given a new orientation which may shape the course of the labor movement in the near future?

SETTING THE SCENE

Before the Industrial Recovery Act was many days old, it became evident that Section 7(a) was operating as a potent factor in stimulating trade union growth and expansion. An organizing fever spread through the ranks of American labor recalling in scope and intensity the greatest labor organizing periods of the past.[2] The new stirrings in the world of organized labor could be explained in part by the economic stimulus of the "business boomlet" of May-July 1933 and of anticipated inflation. Far more important was the psychological effect of Section 7(a). The fear of employers which had long kept workers from joining trade unions was for the time being overcome. Paid trade union organizers, as well as voluntary self-appointed ones, not only emphasized the new freedom to organize, but asserted that the NIRA required the organization of both employers and workers to carry on collective negotiations under codes of fair competition. The point was also made that since the act was temporary, it was necessary to act quickly in order to build up strong labor organizations against the day when the act would expire.

During July, August, and September 1933 organizing activities throughout the country were intense, often quite spontaneous. This movement was accompanied by

[2] 1829-34; 1885-87; 1899-1902; 1910-12; 1919-20.

a rising wave of strikes, for the most part in the textile, mining, and clothing industries, although many other industries were also affected. Some of these strikes were strategic maneuvers undertaken by the unions to influence the formulation of the labor provisions of the codes in their respective industries. Others were primarily strikes for union "recognition."

From November 1933 to March 1934 the strike movement subsided somewhat and union growth went forward at a slower rate. This paralleled to some extent a recession during the same period in industrial activity. But the scene was being set for greater labor unrest in the future. During the first phases of the NRA, anti-union employers were somewhat uncertain as to just what the NRA meant to do about labor organization. But after a brief interval these employers concluded that the field was open to them to fight the unions if they could. Hastily, but systematically, the anti-union employers began to form employee representation plans and to discharge workers, so it was complained, for trade union activity. By the fall of 1933 "company unionism" had assumed the character of a nation-wide counter offensive against trade unionism. The result was that trade union organizers found themselves blocked because many of the old psychological difficulties of organizing the unorganized made themselves felt again.

At the same time, officers of the A. F. of L. and trade union leaders were coming to rely more and more, for the purpose of gaining "recognition," upon the machinery of the National Recovery Administration and of the National Labor Board. The struggle of the trade unions against company unions was transferred from plants, mines, and mills to the Department of Commerce building, where officials of the NRA and members of the NLB held hearings and executive sessions in the strenuous effort to find some formula that would assure the "united action of management and labor." The trade unions became increasingly enmeshed in the administrative machinery of the NRA and of the NLB, spent much time in efforts to obtain industrial relations boards and labor representation on code authorities, and only slowly discovered that their success in such efforts depended on their power to use organized external pressure.

A new wave of strikes and a new upswing of union organizing began in March 1934, reaching a peak in the summer months. There was a new element in the situation which differentiated the movement of 1934 from that of a year before. By the spring of 1934, the labor groups had lost some of their earlier faith in the NRA and even in the NLB as agencies that might be helpful to their cause. There was a growing resentment in labor ranks against continued unemployment, inadequate weekly earnings, increasing discrimination on the part of employers against union workers, and the growth of company unions. The new temper made itself felt in a change of leadership in some unions, in greater pressure upon the older leadership for more aggressive action, and in an outburst of labor militancy. Union development was thus carried along not by faith in the rights granted by Section 7(a), but by a somewhat defiant determination to make the law, as interpreted by the A. F. of L., a reality through the force of organized and direct action. The last explosion of this movement was the nation-wide textile strike in the fall of 1934, after which the movement began to subside.[3]

The total effect of these various factors and movements up to the end of 1934 was a considerable increase

[3] For complete statistical details on the strike movement during 1933-34, see "Industrial Disputes," *Monthly Labor Review*, vols. 37-40.

in trade union membership and activity. But different unions had varying shares in the total result. To get a true picture of the growth of American trade unionism during 1933-34 it is necessary to consider separately three main groups of trade unions: (1) the international unions already in existence and affiliated with the American Federation of Labor; (2) the so-called federal labor unions adhering directly to the A. F. of L.; and (3) the independent unions outside the A. F. of L.

THE GROWTH OF THE A. F. OF L.

Between the summer of 1933 and the winter of 1934-35, the A. F. of L. added about 1 million paid-up members to its ranks. The average paid-up membership for the fiscal year 1933 was 2,126,796; as of August 1934, paid-up membership totalled 2,823,750.[4] By January 1935 the total may reasonably be estimated at or near 3 million. If we allow for non-dues-paying members as well, and if we adjust for the peculiar manner in which many of the international unions compute their per capita taxes, we may safely estimate the total A. F. of L. membership, at the end of 1934, at not less than 3.5 million and nearer 4 million.[5]

In any case, the A. F. of L. more than recouped, during 1933-34, the losses of the depression years. The achievement was substantial, although the final result fell far short of the average paid-up membership of 1919-20, and came nowhere near the claims put forward in the early summer of 1933 that the A. F. of L. would shortly have 10 million workers.

In seeking to analyze the membership increase in

---

[4] See *Proceedings of the 54th Annual Convention of the A. F. of L.*, 1934, p. 41.
[5] For a discussion of the character of A. F. of L. membership figures, see Lorwin, *The American Federation of Labor*, pp. 302-05.

greater detail, we restrict ourselves to figures of voting strength at the 1934 convention of the A. F. of L. This means that we have to deal with a membership increase (computed on a dues-paying basis averaged over the fiscal year) of about 500,000 workers.[6] Three factors were responsible for this increase: (1) the addition of one new large international union; (2) the rapid rise in the membership of some 35 of the 109 international unions of the A. F. of L.; and (3) the spectacular increase in membership of newly formed federal and local unions under the direct supervision of the A. F. of L.

The International Unions

Long outside of the A. F. of L., the Amalgamated Clothing Workers of America joined it at the 1933 convention, following an adjustment of protracted jurisdictional difficulties with the United Garment Workers' Union. This reconciliation was due to the recognition on the part of the leaders of the Amalgamated that it was necessary for them to make their peace with A. F. of L. in order to play any significant part on the NRA stage. Thus, as an indirect result of the NRA, the Amalgamated Clothing Workers contributed to the A. F. of L. over 80,000 members who were effectively organized and committed to progressive policies. Among the international unions affiliated with the A. F. of L. before 1933, the most spectacular increase in membership—125,000 workers[7]—was shown by the International Ladies' Gar-

---

[6] The average membership for the fiscal year 1933 was, as indicated above, 2,126,796. The average membership for the fiscal year 1934 was 2,608,011. See *Report of the Executive Council*, 1934, p. 8.

[7] It cannot be doubted that the United Mine Workers' membership must have increased by at least 250,000; but the voting strength in 1934 was the same as in 1933, that is 3,000 votes, indicating a total membership in each year of 300,000 workers. The 1933 figure is undoubtedly a gross over-estimate; the 1934 figure is probably an understatement.

ment Workers' Union. The United Textile Workers of America added almost 25,000 workers to its rolls. Thus, three unions exercising jurisdiction over the clothing and textile trades accounted for a membership increase of approximately 230,000—almost half of the total increase.

Substantial increases in membership were made by two unions in the transportation trades.[8] The remainder of the increased membership was scattered in a variety of trades.[9] All told, about 35 international unions out of a total of 109 accounted for a membership increase of about 455,000 out of the total increase of 500,000. As for the remaining international unions, some reported negligible increases;[10] a few reported no change whatever; and the

[8] The International Longshoremen's Association gained over 10,000 new members, and the International Brotherhood of Teamsters added almost 25,000 dues-paying members to its rolls.

[9] Thus, the International Brotherhood of Electrical Workers gained about 37,000; the International Association of Machinists, about 17,000; International Union of Brewery Workmen, close to 10,000; the Hotel and Restaurant Employees' Union, some 15,000 members. The International Mine Mill and Smelter Workers raised its membership from 1,300 to 11,600—a gain of 10,300; the International Oil Field Gas Well and Refinery Workers, from 300 to 12,500; the International Jewelry Workers, from 800 to 4,900; the International Tobacco Workers, from 2,600 to 8,300; International Coopers, from 700 to 2,500; International Metal Polishers, from 1,400 to 3,500; Brotherhood of Papermakers, from 2,300 to 11,500; International Leather Workers, from 800 to 3,000; Federation of Government Employees, from 4,000 to 8,300; Brick and Clay Workers, from 100 to 1,400. Other appreciable increases were reported as follows: Journeymen Barbers, 7,300; Boot and Shoe Workers, 5,800; Bridge and Structural Iron Workers, 6,000; Hatters, Cap and Millinery Workers, 6,400; Meat Cutters and Butcher Workmen, 8,400. Smaller increases were reported as follows: Bakery and Confectionery Workers, 2,200; International Bookbinders, 1,200; Building Service Employees, 1,200; International Fire Fighters, 1,700; Foundry Employees, 1,500; Flint Glass Workers, 2,500; Glove Workers, 2,900; Maintenance of Way Employees, 3,400; International Molders, 2,800; Pulp and Sulphite Workers, 1,900; American Federation of Teachers, 1,500.

[10] The Amalgamated Iron, Steel and Tin Workers reported a gain

rest reported decreases. In the latter two groups were most of the important building trades and printing trades unions.

The Federal Labor Unions

In August 1932 the number of federal and local unions affiliated directly with the A. F. of L. had fallen to 307—the lowest figure since 1899—with a total membership of 11,368.[11] During the twelve months ending August 31, 1933, the Federation issued 386 new charters to federal and local unions, of which number 340 were issued during July and August 1933, the two months immediately following the passage of the Recovery Act. The phenomenal advance continued during 1933-34. During the year ended August 31, 1934 the A. F. of L. issued 1,196 charters to new federal and local unions, and reported, at the end of the fiscal period, a total of 1,788 such unions with an average membership for the year of 89,093. Between the summer of 1933 and the autumn of 1934, the number of workers organized in these unions increased by at least 80,000. This represents the peak in the history of these unions in the A. F. of L., compared with 1,286 locals and 86,784 members in 1920, the previous period of greatest union expansion.[12]

Another important feature of the situation was the

---

of only 900 members. But the evidence seems to point to an increase of many thousands. The Amalgamated would seem to be one of the A. F. of L. unions which prefer to understate membership rather than pay heavy per capita taxes.

[11] In addition to national and international unions the American Federation of Labor issues charters to two kinds of organization; (1) local trade unions and (2) federal labor unions. Seven workers in any locality in the same trade may form a local trade union. If that many workers in the same trade are not available, seven workers in different trades may form a federal labor union.

[12] See *Proceedings of the 54th Annual Convention of the A. F. of L.,* 1934, pp. 6-7; also Lorwin, *The American Federation of Labor,* p. 488.

spread of the federal unions into the hitherto unorganized mass production industries. An entirely new development was the organization of national councils
among such federal unions. Most successful perhaps of
all drives into industries previously unorganized was that
against the rubber tire and rubber manufacturing industry. When it began in the early summer of 1933, only
2,500 workers in the Akron district were organized. In the
fall of 1934 the A. F. of L. estimated that "there were
from 60,000 to 70,000 union members in the district, the
vast majority of whom were rubber workers." Not all of
these newly organized workers belonged to federal or
local unions; a substantial number belonged to some of
the international unions. However, federal plant unions
had been set up and were more or less active in almost
all of the important manufacturing units of the rubber
tire and rubber industry. Some 75 unions were operating
in these plants, and were joined in a National Council
of Rubber Workers.[13]

Gains were also made in the automobile manufacturing industry. In June 1933 there was not one union of
automobile workers affiliated with the A. F. of L. By
the autumn of 1934, 104 federal labor unions had been
established; and first steps toward organization had been
taken in most of the important and many of the minor
plants. The total number of workers in these unions was
estimated at between 25 and 50 thousand, and a national
council had been organized.[14]

In the entire aluminum manufacturing industry there
was in July 1933 only one local union. By the autumn
of 1934 every aluminum plant in the country, with one
exception, had been organized into federal labor unions;

[13] See *Report of the Executive Council,* 1934, pp. 18-20.

[14] The same, pp. 20-22.

and in the case of that one exception, organizational work was going forward. As a result of the year's drive, there were in the industry 20 federal unions representing some 15,000 workers, with a National Council at the head.[15]

The federal unions in the rubber, aluminum, and automobile manufacturing industries showed the greatest progress during 1933-34; but there were gains among other groups of workers. Lumber and sawmill workers had, by the autumn of 1934, 130 unions, representing an estimated 15 per cent of eligible wage earners. In the coke and gas industry, more than 50 labor unions directly affiliated with the A. F. of L. were set up during the period in question. In the cement industry, by the fall of 1934, some 30 federal unions, most of them set up during the past year, were functioning. Advances were made also among flour, feed, and cereal workers, in the electrical manufacturing industry (particularly among radio manufacturing workers), in the cleaning and dyeing trade, among office workers, cannery workers, agricultural workers, gasoline filling station attendants, wholesale establishment employees, theater ushers, chemical workers, aeronautical manufacturing workers, and several other groups.[16]

ORGANIZING THE "GREAT CAMPAIGN"

We may describe the period 1933-34, with respect to the organizational activity carried on by the A. F. of L. and its constituent unions, as the period of the "Great Campaign." The unions went out during this period with unusual zeal and energy to direct and utilize the new interest in organization aroused among workers by the NIRA. As a result, the problems of organizing became

[15] The same, pp. 21-22.
[16] All the data given above are summarized from the *Report of the Executive Council*, 1934, pp. 24-37.

even more important for the A. F. of L. than they had been before the NIRA.

In general, traditional policies and practices were pursued in this organizing campaign. As a central body the A. F. of L. devoted most of its energies to the formation of directly affiliated federal and local labor unions in the mass production industries. The specialized workers in the crafts and trades were left to the devices of the international unions. Some co-ordination was effected through the departments, the central labor unions, and the state federations.

As a central body the A. F. of L. continued to carry on its organizational work through the usual system of volunteer and paid organizers. But more energy was manifested. Although the number of volunteer organizers remained about the same, the number of full-time organizers was increased from 33 in 1933 to 55 in 1934. Expenditures for organizational activities increased more than threefold: from $100,301 in 1932-33 to $323,874 in 1933-34.[17] At the same time, it is important to note that the A. F. of L. paid out only $1,084 to federal labor unions for defense purposes during 1933-34, although the contributions of federal labor unions and local trade unions to their defense fund totalled $133,615.31.[18]

Some attempts were made by the A. F. of L. to give central direction to the organizing campaign of the autonomous internationals. In January 1934 the Executive Council called a conference of affiliated unions to consider the common problems of organization under the new conditions created by the Recovery Act. Three principal recommendations were put forward:

[17] *Proceedings of the 54th Annual Convention of the A. F. of L.,* 1934, p. 14.
[18] *Report of the Executive Council,* 1934, p. 5.

(1) That A. F. of L. organizers and union officers should arrange conferences in order to promote harmony in organizing work and to avoid friction arising out of overlapping jurisdictional claims, particularly between the international and the federal unions;

(2) That periodic meetings should be held at which methods of organization and programs for planning would be discussed, and

(3) That mass meetings should be arranged throughout the country; these mass meetings to be addressed by A. F. of L. officers and by A. F. of L. speakers specially trained for that purpose.[19]

Very little seems to have been accomplished, in a concrete way, toward putting these recommendations into effect. A. F. of L. organizers were scrupulous not to transgress clearly defined jurisdictional lines in forming new federal labor unions. This they did, however, not so much through conferences with international union officers, as by instructions from Washington headquarters. Such instructions were due to pressure put upon the A. F. of L. by the officers of international unions, jealous, as ever, of the rights staked out in their respective charters. As to periodic and mass meetings, what was accomplished was done informally.

At the 1934 convention, the Executive Council was instructed "at the earliest possible date" to inaugurate, manage, promote, and conduct a campaign for organization in the iron and steel industry.[20] To do so would call for co-ordination of the work of the Amalgamated Association of Iron, Steel, and Tin Workers, of a large number of other internationals, and of the A. F. of L. Metal Trades Department. It was not yet apparent, by the beginning of 1935, that the Executive Council had acted concretely on these instructions.

[19] The same, p. 17.
[20] *Proceedings of the 54th Annual Convention*, pp. 586-87.

As in past years, so also during 1933-34, the A. F. of L. failed to devote any considerable energy to the special training of new organizers. Direction of the work remained in the hands of the Secretary, Mr. Frank Morrison, who was burdened with many other duties as well. Some progress was achieved along the lines of preparing new literature for organizational purposes. Thus the A. F. of L. issued reprints of the Recovery Act with the section bearing on labor italicized. President Green issued, from time to time, open letters explaining the codes of their respective industries to the automobile workers, the rubber workers, the cleaners and dyers. In other open letters the composition and powers of the Labor Board system were set forth, and the necessity of police duty by labor unions was stressed. Oil workers and filling station men were sent summaries of important decisions bearing on collective bargaining, which had been handed down by the Petroleum Labor Policy Board. A series of sample trade agreements were prepared for the instruction of new unions which might be engaged in drafting collective contracts. The *American Federationist* printed a number of articles describing the progress of organization in the various mass production industries.

On the basis of the record, it can hardly be said that the A. F. of L. mapped out a carefully planned program of organization which it proceeded to execute according to schedule. There was a good deal of talk concerning the need for such planning. But the characteristic procedure was to assign some specific organizer to a specific industry, and then to leave matters in his hands. This procedure throws the burden of thought, not upon working out a carefully conceived plan of attack, but on choosing the right man for the right job. Fortunately for the

A. F. of L., during the early months of the Recovery Act the organizers found groups of workers who were for the time being highly receptive to the trade union idea.

The A. F. of L. officers themselves spent much of their time and energy in attendance upon the vast administrative machinery of the NRA and the Labor Boards. Quite as wholeheartedly as during the war period, the A. F. of L. accepted the idea of a "partnership" with management and government. To bring about union recognition, the A. F. of L. leaned heavily upon the Labor Boards and upon the compliance apparatus of the NRA. In accordance with this policy the A. F. of L., as a central body, refrained from encouraging strike actions. Rather than run the risk of an automobile strike in March 1934, the A. F. of L. assented to settlement terms which, in the sequel, proved a setback to the further progress of the federal labor unions in the industry. When the aluminum workers finally walked out in the late summer of 1934, A. F. of L. representatives hastened to bring about a quick settlement which accomplished little besides maintaining the *status quo*. A. F. of L. pressure also served to hold back strikes, for which "rank and file" groups were pressing in the steel and rubber industries. In part, this reluctance by the A. F. of L. to sanction strikes may be explained by the persistence of unfavorable economic conditions, not to speak of the fear that the new organizations might be wrecked by rushing into hasty action. Important, however, was the belief that the A. F. of L. might gain more by peaceful co-operation in carrying out the purposes of the Recovery Act than by militant action.

We cannot consider here in detail the organizational campaigns conducted by the various international unions separately. A number of unions did very little. Such were the printing trades unions, which came through the depression with membership and morale more or less intact, owing to the skilled character of the trades and to their solidly established systems of benefits. Other unions, operating in industries where the codification process contributed nothing toward re-employment, were too much weighed down by the depression to engage in organizational campaigns. Such were the unions in the building trades—the A. F. of L.'s largest and most important single bloc. Many of the other craft unions, recalling the mushroom growth and catastrophic decline during the period 1919-1922, moved cautiously in the fear of enrolling too many low-paid, semi-skilled workers, not likely to be capable of paying dues regularly, and likely, at the same time, to become a burden on the benefit system. Still other unions, sluggish and set in old habits of thought, were incapable of devising tactics and weapons to cope with the new order of things.

A small number of unions were capable, however, of rising to the occasion and of profiting to the full by the psychological forces which Section 7(a) had released. The two principal needle trades unions, the International Ladies' Garment Workers and the Amalgamated Clothing Workers, were among the foremost in this group. The I.L.G.W.U., driving ahead at a phenomenal pace, not only re-established its hold over the dressmaking division, but also took big steps forward to organize the "out of town" open-shop areas of the ladies' garment trade. The A.C.W.A. similarly conducted a strenuous and on the whole successful drive to organize the unorganized segments of the men's clothing industry, principally outside of New York. In both cases it was found that groups of workers previously believed immune to trade union propaganda had, in fact, become first-rate union material. Both unions made full use of the strike, both to win recognition and to further their demands for concessions in code making.

Equally energetic and successful were the United Mine Workers of America.[21] Breaking through barriers long believed to be insurmountable, the United Mine Workers rounded up thousands upon thousands of workers in the anti-union parts of Kentucky and West Virginia. Trade unionism, as a going concern, was established in Logan and Mingo counties (West Virginia) and in Bell and Harlan counties (Kentucky). Against the resistance of the iron and steel companies, the U.M.W.A. organized thousands of workers in the "captive" mines of western Pennsylvania; in this case, not peacefully, but by force of a determined and violent strike. Out in the Central Competitive Field, where the U.M.W.A. had been for years slowly falling apart since the expiration of the Jacksonville agreement, membership and morale were regained, and the U.M.W.A. took the upper hand in its life and death struggle with the dual union, the Progressive Miners of America. By mass meetings in coal towns and by "motorcades" bearing the gospel of trade unionism from town to town, the U.M.W.A. gained 135,000 members during three weeks of June 1933. By the end of August 1933, the union claimed a total membership of 600,000—five-sixths of this claimed total being in the bituminous coal division. This came close to the 1920 claimed total of 650,000 members.[22]

In brief, the year 1933-34 was a fruitful period for

[21] We are concerned exclusively with the bituminous coal division, for the anthracite industry had not, by March 1935, come under a code.

[22] The rapid organizational advance of the United Textile Workers of America should also be mentioned. For the first time in its history, the U.T.W.A. was able to grasp a foothold in the cotton textile mills of the South. In the early fall of 1934, the U.T.W.A. was able to call a nation-wide textile strike, the force of which was felt particularly in the South.

those A. F. of L. unions which were sufficiently aggressive to reap quickly the benefits of Section 7(a). While the social idealism of the New Deal was still fresh, many of the old fears of, and prejudice against, unionism on the part of workers, were dissolved. After the company union counter-offensive picked up momentum, the situation began to change. Affairs settled down into a stubborn battle between the two sides. Organization became a more difficult and complex job, for which the A. F. of L. devised no new methods.

TRADE UNIONS OUTSIDE THE A. F. OF L.

We need not concern ourselves in this study with the most important group of American trade unions outside the A. F. of L., the four Railroad Brotherhoods. The fortunes of the "Big Four" during 1933-34, and to a large extent also the fortunes of the A. F. of L. railroad unions among the shop crafts, the clerks, and the maintenance of way employees, were determined, not by the Recovery Act but by the Emergency Transportation Act of 1933 and the Railway Labor Act as amended in 1934.

The Railroad Brotherhoods excluded, there remain two groups of unions which demand attention: (1) the left-wing, so called "Communist" unions, affiliated with the Trade Union Unity League, and (2) other unions independent of the A. F. of L., usually to the "left" of the A. F. of L. in social outlook, although in varying degrees.

The Unions of the Trade Union Unity League

In the view of the Trade Union Unity League the Recovery Act was merely another "capitalist" scheme to depress the living standards of the workers, to limit the right to strike, and to prepare the mind of the nation for an imperialist war. Starting from this base, the T.U.U.L. denied that the wage earners' interest could be protected in the NRA code-making and code-administering process, or that their statutory rights would be protected by independent labor boards. Accordingly, the T.U.U.L. unions were hardly in a position to profit from the psychological effects of Section 7(a) upon the worker's attitude toward collective bargaining.

Only a few of the unions of the T.U.U.L. were sufficiently strong in their respective trades to be able to maintain their position under the new conditions. The outstanding example was the Industrial Fur Workers' Union, connected with the Needle Trades Workers' Industrial Union. Dominant in the New York City fur market for some years, the Industrial Fur Workers Union was able to hold its own against the International Fur Workers affiliated with the A. F. of L., and to maintain its collective contracts. But the Industrial Fur Workers' Union was unable to make headway in the out of town markets. As to the branches of the Needle Trades Workers Industrial Union other than fur, they were overwhelmed by the advance of the A. F. of L. unions.

Spasmodic, though fervent, efforts were made by the Marine Workers' Industrial Union. This union played a part in the Pacific Coast dock strike far out of proportion to its numbers. The union also tried to gain "recognition" in the Eastern Seaboard cities. But the results were negligible. The International Longshoremen's Association and the International Seamen's Union, both affiliated with the A. F. of L., emerged the dominant organizations on the Pacific Coast, while in the Eastern Seaboard cities the former finally negotiated, in the fall of 1934, a collective agreement with the shipping companies.

Except for these two unions, and for the National Furniture Worker's Industrial Union, which also displayed activity, the elements of the T.U.U.L. dropped out of the picture during the "Great Campaign" of 1933-1934. Thus, the National Miners' Union was buried under the avalanche of the United Mine Workers, and the National Textile Workers' Union disintegrated as a result of the advance of the United Textile Workers. The Metal Workers' Industrial Union, after some early flurries in the iron and steel industries, vanished from the scene.

No reliable data on the membership of the T.U.U.L. unions are available. There is no doubt, however, that the membership, never over 25,000, declined between 1933 and 1934. It would also seem that, as a result of their experience in 1933-34, the T.U.U.L. leaders have reverted from the policy of dual unionism to their former policy of "boring from within."

Other Independent Unions

Outside the T.U.U.L. there were three principal industries in which independent trade unions—what the A. F. of L. calls "dual unions"—were formed during 1933-34. These industries were coal mining, boot and shoe manufacturing, and automobile manufacturing.

Unions in coal mines. In Illinois, the Progressive Miners of America continued its factional struggle against the United Mine Workers of America. But the P.M.A. lost ground continually. Owing to its participation in the bituminous coal labor boards, the United Mine Workers captured control of the administrative machinery to strengthen its own position. When the P.M.A. presented to Divisional Board No. 2 the demand that elections be held to determine the identity of the representative labor organization in the Peabody coal mines, they received the answer that contract rights were inviolate and took precedence over the rights of free choice created by Section 7(a).[23]

In the Pennsylvania anthracite fields, the United Anthracite Miners of Pennsylvania, a "rump" union, challenged the U.M.W.A. in a conflict marked by violent strikes. It could not, however, dislodge the U.M.W.A. from the position which it held by virtue of long-established contractual relationships with the operators.

Unions in the boot and shoe industry. As a strong and powerful competitor of the A. F. of L.'s Boot and Shoe Workers' Union, particularly in the New England manufacturing centers, there emerged during 1933-34 the United Shoe and Leather Workers' Union. This union is a merger of independent labor organizations, and professes to be more militant and more progressive than the Boot and Shoe Workers' Union; but it rejects the communist-led T.U.U.L., and is much more concerned with problems of collective bargaining than the propaganda of "revolutionary class consciousness." The U.S.L.W.U. conducted a major strike in Haverhill, Massachusetts, during the spring of 1934. The membership of the U.S.L.W.U. is probably as large as that of its A. F. of L. competitor—about 20,000.

Unions in automobile manufacturing. The strongest independent union which emerged largely owing to Section 7(a) is the Mechanics Educational Society of America. This is an organization of tool and die makers and affiliated machinists—highly skilled craftsmen—

---

[23] The Peabody decision was upheld by the National Bituminous Coal Labor Board; the National Labor Board, to which the matter was later referred, refused to interfere. The P.M.A. was repulsed in its efforts to get relief in the federal courts on the argument that private parties could not, under the Recovery Act, invoke the sanctions thereof.

some of whom are employed in job shops, others in the automobile manufacturing plants. The M.E.S.A. claims a membership of 25,000 workers, a large part of whom are concentrated in four Detroit locals. Other locals function in Pontiac and Flint, Michigan; in Cleveland, Toledo, Youngstown, and Salem, Ohio; and in Brooklyn, New York. By its vigorous organizational drive and by using militant tactics with success, the M.E.S.A. has shut out, for the time being, the International Association of Machinists of the A. F. of L. from the automobile industry. There has been talk from time to time that the M.E.S.A. was about to devote its energies to organizing the production employees in the manufacturing plants, and thus go into competition with the A. F. of L. federal labor unions. Nothing, however, has been accomplished along these lines.

The M.E.S.A. was for a while powerful and vigorous. It unites highly skilled craftsmen, essential to the production of the new annual models. The moving spirit of the M.E.S.A. is its general secretary, Matthew Smith, who was active for 16 years in the shop steward movement in England, and who has sought to contrive the M.E.S.A. along similar lines. If the A. F. of L. proves capable of setting up an autonomous automobile workers' international along industrial lines, and if the jurisdictional claims of the International Association of Machinists can be overcome, it is possible that the M.E.S.A. might join as an independent unit with a status comparable to that of the American Federation of Hosiery Workers in the United Textile Workers of America.

The other independent unions in the automobile industries are of a fugitive and transient character. It is impossible to keep track of them or even to say whether some of them—for example, the Society of Designing Engineers and the Chamber of Labor—are still active. Here and there the I.W.W. has popped up again in the industry. Other left-wing organizations, equally feeble, have made their appearance. Strife within the A. F. of L.'s National Council of Automobile Workers' Unions has led to a number of schisms and splits, the most important of which resulted in the establishment of the Associated Automobile Workers of America.[24]

VERTICAL VS. HORIZONTAL UNIONS

For several years prior to the NIRA, the American Federation of Labor struggled in vain with the problem of industrial versus craft, or vertical versus horizontal unions. The problem, which is as old as American trade unionism, became a challenge to the A. F. of L. between 1924 and 1929 in view of the increasing importance of the mass production industries. Several attempts by the A. F. of L. to organize the automobile, steel, and other mass industries broke down largely because of craft methods of organization.[25]

Almost as soon as the NRA began making codes of fair competition, the question of the structural basis of American labor unions assumed importance. In the public hearings on some of the earlier codes in unionized industries, officials of the NRA were confused and annoyed by the multiplicity of craft organizations, each of which pressed demands for a special group of workers without regard

[24] The automobile industry is notable for the establishment, by virtue of Automobile Labor Board elections, of "works councils" which are neither trade nor company unions in the established sense of these terms. The works councils may be described as plant unions; representatives are elected on the basis of proportional representation.

[25] See Lorwin, *The American Federation of Labor*, Chap. X.

to the other labor groups in the industry. The difficult problems of wage rates, wage differentials, and other labor provisions were complicated by the strategic maneuvers of the craft groups which were concerned with their own special conditions, not with the structure and needs of the industry as a whole. As a result, the claim of the A. F. of L. that Section 7(a) implied collective bargaining through trade unions was met by the counterclaim that, in the basic American industries, it was impossible to fit the craft union to the needs either of management or of the workers.

To some extent, the difficulties of craft unionism were accentuated by the procedure of the NRA itself. Its hasty and unsystematic promotion of codes resulted in drawing artificial lines between trades and in creating numerous "industries" which were even more narrow than the crafts delimited by labor unions. The NRA's inability to define an industry and to delimit with strict logic the practical frontiers of American industries gave organized labor the feeling that after all its craft structure had a pragmatic sanction and was better than the haphazard structure of hundreds of unrelated codes. But whatever labor's attitude in the matter, employers and many of the NRA officials responsible for the making of codes continued to stress the impossibility of incorporating craft unionism into the scheme of a codified American industry.

The effects of the code-making process were soon reinforced by the growth of federal labor unions in the mass production industries. As the organizing campaign spread to the automobile, rubber, aluminum, and other industries, the craft unions became apprehensive that their jurisdictional claims to the respective groups of skilled workers involved would be disregarded by the new federal organizations. At the same time, the federal groups demanded as the *sine qua non* of success a clear and unequivocal mandate to organize all the workers in these industries on an industry-wide basis.

The A. F. of L. became directly involved in these conflicts as a result of its own efforts at organizing. As the Federation sent out organizers to push the formation of federal unions as well as to help its international unions, it invariably found that the two kinds of unions got into each other's way. An organizer of the A. F. of L. would hold mass meetings for all workers at some hitherto unorganized plants, enroll members and send in for a federal charter. At this point, after weeks of effort, the local officers of some international union would appear and claim men of their craft who were in the new union. The federal union would be unwilling to give them up, or the men to go. Appeal would be taken to Washington, which under the constitution of the A. F. of L. had to sustain the international union. The new federal union might lose so many members to various craft unions as to be unable to continue, while the men taken over sometimes dropped out, because dues were higher in the craft union, or for other reasons. To make the confusion worse, the older unions resented what they felt to be the intrusion of A. F. of L. organizers into their fields.

For several months after the passage of the NIRA, the issue of vertical versus horizontal unionism was a topic of heated discussion in the A. F. of L. Although the arguments were not altogether new, they may be briefly summarized here as a means of elucidating the nature of the issue. The craft unionists stress the cohesive power of craft and the value of craftsmanship as a basis of associative action. The craft union, they say, brings together workers who are most intimately related in the process of production and whose common interest in wage rates and working conditions is most vital. The craft union is national in scope and can thus help to equalize labor costs and labor conditions throughout a trade. The federal union, on the contrary, is a hybrid; it brings to-gether a miscellaneous lot of workers whose interests are diverse; it is usually confined to one plant and cannot act on a national scale; because of its composition, it cannot develop either financial or fighting strength. It can thus be of little help to the unskilled worker and it is of no use to the skilled mechanic. For example, how is a skilled machinist to hold membership in anything but a craft union when he may work one month in an automobile factory, the next in a radio or refrigerator plant? Craft in the labor world, in this view, is the equivalent of management in the business world. The workers who have craftsmanship are usually the only ones capable of developing leadership and managerial aptitude. As a matter of fact, even the large industrial unions are managed, carried, and driven forward by the craft nucleus in them. From this point of view, the craft unions are the basic and permanent organizations; the federal unions are important only as nuclei for national craft and trade unions.

Those favoring vertical or industrial unionism point out that the craft union is too narrow in scope, too selfish in outlook, and too limited in its resources to serve the needs of labor in modern industry. The independence of craft groups, under the horizontal form of organiza-tion, makes it impossible to obtain efficient co-operation among the workers of a whole industry on any program of action. One union, prepared to press the employer for demands, is estopped from doing so because other unions refuse to go along. Because of its narrow outlook, the craft union hinders the growth of a large sense of solidarity among workers and obstructs the development of a consciousness of class interests which is essential for a vigorous and influential labor movement. Above all, the idea of craft has but little meaning for the mass of the workers in modern industry; they think of themselves rather as attached to an industry or a plant. Nor can craft organization be applied, even with the best will, to mass production industries, where the workers, if craft organization were pressed, would often come under a dozen or two unions. In such industries, craft lines cannot be drawn, and the workers there cannot be organized except into industrial unions.

The industrial unionists do not regard the federal union as an effective form of labor organization. Restricted to a single locality and often to a single plant, the federal union cannot develop a program for an industry. Under the constitution of the A. F. of L. the federal unions have no powers of action, being dependent on the decisions of the Executive Council. Nevertheless, the industrial unionists within the A. F. of L. have favored the federal union in the mass production industries as a first and provisional step towards the industrial form of organization, as the nuclei of the vertical unions of the future.

Under the impact of the developments described above, the A. F. of L. was forced to consider the question of union structure at its first convention under the NRA, held in Washington, D.C., in October 1933. The craft unions in the A. F. of L. made no secret of their intention to oppose the progress of industrial unions. Several resolutions on the subject were presented. One asked for complete recognition of existing craft lines. Another suggested that the question of jurisdiction should rest for a year. A third called for a strategy board of seven to map out plans for strengthening united action by the crafts, "and at the same time for extending organization into those industries in which the present form of organization has obviously not been successful." The committee on resolutions presented a majority and a minority report. The matter was not allowed to come to a vote in the convention but was referred without discussion to a special conference of the national and international unions soon to be called. The convention ordered the Brewery Workers' Union, traditionally industrial in form, to give up its truckmen, engineers, and firemen to their craft unions; and the Amalgamated Clothing Workers of America, in order to gain admission to the Federation, had to make certain concessions to various craft groups.

Thus the 1933 convention, in spite of efforts on the part of some of its delegates, made no changes in policy or methods. The A. F. of L. structure was unchanged and the traditional adherence to craft unionism maintained.

The action of the 1933 convention in referring decision on the matter of federal unions to a later meeting was a serious hindrance to the organizing work of the Federation. Was the effort to be made to enroll as many as possible in federal unions, leaving the jurisdiction question, if it arose, to be settled later on? Or was the organizer to avoid taking in any men from a given plant who were eligible to membership in an international union? If the latter, in many cases he could hardly hope to organize a plant. Could he promise a group that, joining together, they would be allowed to continue as a group? Owing to this uncertainty, applications for new federal charters dropped precipitously.

The anticipated meeting of representatives of the national and international unions with the Executive Council of the A. F. of L. was held in Washington January 23-25, 1934. It had before it a resolution of four points, prepared at a conference held on January 23 by delegates from over 90 federal unions. This resolution demanded: (1) That federal charters again be issued and "aggressively continued" in mass production industries; (2) that federal unions be neither separated nor segregated into craft unions, but be held intact on industrial lines; (3) that a bureau be established within the A. F. of L. to aid the formation of industrial unions; and (4) "that where a sufficient number of federal unions to form a national association applies for a national charter, it be immediately granted by the A. F. of L. executive council."

These demands were far too radical for the A. F. of L. meeting. It made, however, a somewhat liberal answer, possibly more liberal than would have been made if the federal unions had not hinted that, in the event their demands were denied, they might affiliate themselves outside the A. F. of L. The principal decision of the conference may be summarized as follows:

1. That organizing work proceed with increased vigor; that the fullest latitude be exercised by the Executive Council in the granting of charters; that wherever a temporary infraction of the rights of National and International Unions might be involved, the Executive Council should adjust such difficulties in the spirit of taking full advantage of the immediate situation and with the ultimate recognition of the rights of all concerned;

2. That conferences be arranged by the Executive Council between organizers and officers of all unions in certain centers, to create harmony and lessen friction "due to varying financial requirements";

3. That periodic conferences be called, of representatives of departments and divisions within the A. F. of L. to plan means of organizing;

4. That the A. F. of L. officers arrange for mass meetings throughout the land.[26]

The federal unions were not satisfied with the plan of the January conference. They feared that it would enable the Executive Council to divide them up. As a matter of fact, the A. F. of L. was slow in putting the decisions of the January conference into effect. No large local conferences and no departmental meetings were called. But owing to favorable conditions on the labor front, organizing proceeded and the number of charters granted to federal unions steadily increased during 1934.

As the federal unions made progress, some of the crafts were alarmed, and William Green was forced to reassure them by sending out to the general and federal organizers a letter of instruction to respect the jurisdictional rights of the national and international unions. Organizers were to organize only those workers ineligible to membership in the craft unions. And when doubt arose, a conference was to be held, to resolve it. In general, organizers were supposed to avoid trouble by avoiding craftsmen, rather than to take them in and deal with the difficulties later on.

Thus the A. F. of L. tried with considerable energy to take its stand where it had stood before. But the problem would not stay put. Despite official opposition, federal unions in several industries took steps to form larger associations. The unions in the rubber industry formed a national organization, and officers were elected, but the A. F. of L. managed to prevent further action toward full autonomy. The radio workers and the aluminum

[26] See *Report of the Executive Council,* 1934, pp. 16-17.

workers started organizing national councils. Similar developments took place in the fields of electrical equipment, food, and airplane manufacturing, and a combination of federal locals in the automobile industry was effectuated.

The A. F. of L. frowned upon the efforts of the federal unions to secure quick and full autonomy, not only because of the pressure of the craft unions, but for two other reasons. One was the financial weakness of these locals;[27] the other, their lack of experienced leadership. At the same time the A. F. of L. had to allow for the possibility that the federal unions might become resentful and try to organize on a national basis outside the A. F. of L. Such attempts had been made several times in the past, and there was talk of such a move again in the early months of 1934.

In view of these developments, the Executive Council of the A. F. of L. placed the problem before the 1934 convention of the Federation. The interest in the issue was shown by the fact that fourteen different resolutions on the subject were introduced at the convention. In the course of the discussion there were presented the usual arguments for the complete reorganization of the A. F. of L. on the basis of industrial unionism. Yielding little if any ground, the craft unionists defended their position, although they manifested a more than ordinary concern for the status of labor in the unorganized mass production industries. The committee on resolutions which reported on the question recommended a course of action which was presented as a compromise between

[27] The A. F. of L. has been accused of preventing the consolidation of federal unions because the latter are a larger source of income to it than internationals would be. See Lorwin, *The American Federation of Labor*, Chap. XII.

the extremes. In view of their importance, we quote the significant sections of this report, which read as follows:

During recent years there have developed new methods. This has brought about a change in the nature of the work performed by millions of workers in industries which it has been most difficult or impossible to organize into craft unions. . . .

The American Federation of Labor is desirous of meeting this demand [for organization]. We consider it our duty to formulate policies which will fully protect the jurisdictional rights of all trade unions organized upon craft lines and afford every opportunity for development and accession of those workers engaged upon work over which these organizations exercise jurisdiction. Experience has shown that craft organization is most effective in protecting the welfare and advancing the interests of workers where the nature of the industry is such that the lines of demarcation between crafts are distinguishable.

However, it is also realized that in many of the industries in which thousands of workers are employed, a new condition exists requiring organization upon a different basis to be most effective.

To meet this new condition the Executive Council is directed to issue charters for national or international unions in the automotive, cement, aluminum, and such other mass production and miscellaneous industries as in the judgment of the Executive Council may be necessary to meet the situation.

That in order to protect and safeguard the members of such national and international unions as are chartered, the American Federation of Labor shall for a provisional period direct the policies, administer the business, and designate the administrative and financial officers of such newly organized unions.[28]

The approval of this recommendation was hailed by many as a signal victory for the advocates of vertical unionism. In fact, however, it did not extend the powers of the Executive Council, nor did it materially alter the policy of the Federation. Nevertheless, it was an im-

[28] *Proceedings of the 54th Annual Convention of the American Federation of Labor*, 1934, pp. 586-87.

portant step in that, for the first time since 1920, the Federation officially recognized that the special character of the mass production industries might justify an industrial basis of organization. At the same time, with its usual caution, the Federation was careful to hold on to traditional functions and powers. It assumed a special protectorate over the national unions which might thereafter be formed in the mass production industries.

The convention of 1934 authorized the Executive Council of the A. F. of L. to conduct organizing campaigns in the mass industries. During the months since the convention very little, if anything, has been done along these lines. This is explained in part by lack of Federation funds, partly by unfavorable industrial conditions. Just so long as no unions on a national basis are organized in the mass production industries, the issue of vertical unionism can be of little practical value. The existing internationals are not interested in pressing this issue. Moreover as long as the federal labor unions fail to increase their present strength, they cannot exercise substantial pressure within the A. F. of L.

Thus, the sum total of the developments in union structure during the past 20 months is not very large. What has taken place is resuscitation of the vertical-horizontal issue in new forms. The formation of the federal unions has provided a nucleus from which increasing pressures for changes in the structure of the A. F. of L. may later come. But to date the structural changes in American unionism have been few and slight.

CHANGES IN FUNCTIONS AND POLICY
Code making and code administration have necessitated changes in the methods and policies of trade unions. Time has been too short for these changes to become pronounced, but their tendency is clear.

An important change has been the recognition by the trade unions of the need for economic research. When the first codes were being formulated, it became at once clear that most of the international unions and the A. F. of L. as a whole were unprepared to argue their cases at the public code hearings on the basis of statistical or economic data pertaining to their respective industries. Some of the more aggressive unions, especially in the clothing industries, made haste to engage expert assistance for the formulation of the labor provisions in the codes for their industries. The A. F. of L. also began organizing a research staff in order to aid those unions which were unable, financially or otherwise, to defend their own cases at the public hearings.

It was thought that this function would be gradually enlarged, and that the A. F. of L. might develop an effective research department which would serve its affiliated unions. But in this, as in other matters, the A. F. of L. has been moving slowly, partly on account of lack of funds, partly on account of the jealousies of the international unions, which prefer to keep as many functions as possible under their own jurisdiction. Some of the bigger unions have strengthened their research departments and thus have made fewer calls on the A. F. of L. for aid.

It has been said that in time the trade unions will rely more and more on the Division of Research and Planning in the NRA for data on which code labor provisions will have to be based. Undoubtedly, the A. F. of L. must depend for basic data on this Division, on the Labor Advisory Board, and on the Department of Labor. But as long as code labor provisions are determined by a process of bargaining, the interpretation of data will have to be made independently by the different groups engaged in the process of bargaining. From this point of view, the separate unions and the A. F. of L. are likely to find it necessary to have their own research staff.

We have already indicated how the process of collective bargaining has been modified by the NRA and the various labor boards.[29] The making of collective agreements, which is the primary and major function of trade unions, is becoming a quasi-public function. The government is either taking part in the making of these agreements or is assisting the trade unions to do so. Many of the trade union mechanisms built up in the past for the purposes of collective bargaining are being incorporated into the code machinery, thus gaining a semi-public status. The collective bargain itself is assuming a legal status which it did not have before the Recovery Act.

Closely related to these changes in collective bargaining are the changes which are taking place in trade union strategy. True, the trade unions have insisted upon the maintenance of the right to strike without any qualifications. Many unions have carried on strikes during 1933-34, as described above.[30] The A. F. of L. has also, in accordance with its traditional stand on this issue, opposed all suggestions for compulsory arbitration.

Nevertheless, there has been a noticeable change in the character and nature of the strike. Industrial relations under the NRA have been determined not by employer-employee dealings alone, but by government intervention as well. Thus the problem for labor, organized and unorganized, has been not only to coerce employers into the acceptance of labor terms, but also to induce the government to support those labor demands. As a result, strikes have assumed, to a consider-

[29] See Chapter XVII.
[30] See pp. 489-92.

able extent, the character of demonstrations with a view to exercising pressure upon the government and its agencies. In the strikes which have been carried on, the question of endurance or of financial preparation for a long drawn out contest between employers and workers has ceased to be as important as it once was. The more important question is how to stage a quick and dramatic demonstration of labor unrest, with a view to forcing the government into favorable action.[31]

A significant trend in trade union policy under the NRA has been the emphasis upon a recognized status in the management of industry, through representation on code authorities. True, demands of a similar general character were made by trade unions after the World War, but such demands were little more than abstract declarations. Since the passage of the Recovery Act, however, these abstract demands have assumed more concrete substance. If industry is to be "self-governed" by code authorities there is a concrete administrative basis for the workers' claim to share in such self-government.

Whether or not the general changes indicated above will induce the A. F. of L. to take a greater interest in starting a labor party has been a subject of much debate. So far, the answer would seem to be in the negative. The A. F. of L. is proceeding on the belief that co-operation with the government and with industry in general is the most promising policy for organized labor. Such co-operation, however, does not preclude bargaining with the powers that be for the terms of support. The trend is for the A. F. of L. to become an opposition group within the Administration.

[31] If the change in strike strategy continues, it is likely to have important effects on trade union finances. The latter are likely to be profoundly affected also by the new developments in social insurance.

Other important changes have taken place since 1932 in the social outlook and economic program of American trade unionism. The A. F. of L. has abandoned some of its old ideas, such as opposition to unemployment insurance. But these changes cannot be imputed specifically to the NIRA or the NRA. They are part of the total effect of the New Deal.

THE STRUGGLE AGAINST THE COMPANY UNION

The changes described in the preceding sections have no doubt increased the strength and influence of the American Federation of Labor. Since 1933, the A. F. of L. has assumed an importance in the economic and social life of the nation which it enjoyed only once before—during the World War. This growing influence has been seriously threatened, however, by the development of "company unionism" as a nation-wide movement. During 1933-34 company unions, in the form of employee representation plans, experienced a growth even more remarkable than that of the trade unions. The growth was directed and conducted by "open-shop" employers, as part of a deliberate counter-offensive against the "Great Campaign" of the A. F. of L., in the belief that Section 7(a) did not exclude company unions as agencies for collective bargaining. The movement of 1933-34 was far more extensive and organized than that of 1919-22 when the employee representation scheme first came to be widely used by employers as an offset against the trade union.

Some idea of the development of company unions is given by the studies of the National Industrial Conference Board.[32] From its 1933 sample studies, the Board

[32] National Industrial Conference Board, *Individual and Collective Bargaining under the NIRA; A Statistical Study of Present Practices*, Nov. 1933; also *Conference Board Service Letter*, Dec. 30, 1934.

concluded that "individual bargaining has not in any way been eliminated by Section 7(a)," and "that employee representation plans have expanded greatly both in number of companies affected and particularly in number of employees covered."[33] The 1934 sample studies would seem to indicate that, like the 1933 figures, close to 50 per cent of the workers in manufacturing and mining were covered by employee representation plans.[34] But these figures probably reflect a bias due to the character of the plants covered and are not representative of American industry as a whole. It is difficult to make an entirely satisfactory estimate, but it is not unlikely that the membership of company unions, which was estimated at 1.3 millions at the end of 1932,[35] was between 2.5 and 3 millions at the end of 1934.

A significant feature of the company union movement during 1933-34 was its concentration in three mass pro-

[33] *Individual and Collective Bargaining*, 1933, p. 30. The study covered 3,314 companies, which at the time employed a total of 2,585,740 employees, estimated at 27 per cent of the total labor force in manufacturing and mining. Of these workers, 45 per cent, or 1,165,294, were employed by establishments where some plan for dealing with the management through an employee representation organization was in force; 45.7 per cent of the workers dealt with their employers on the basis of individual bargaining relationships; only 9.3 per cent bargained collectively by means of trade union arrangements. Prior to the enactment of Section 7(a), only 365,937 workers employed by the establishments in question had been covered by company union schemes. The increase therefore amounted to 800,000 workers. The study showed further that about 61.3 per cent of the company union plans then operative were put into operation subsequent to the passage of the Recovery Act. See *Individual and Collective Bargaining*, pp. 16, 18-20, 22, 24, and 26.

[34] Of 3,975,683 workers in manufacturing, mining, public utilities, and railroads covered by the studies of the N.I.C.B., 1,769,921 or 44.5 per cent dealt with their employers through employee representation in 1934 as against 904,279 or 22.8 per cent who dealt through trade unions. *Conference Board Service Letter*, Dec. 30, 1934, p. 95.

[35] See *Employee Representation and Collective Bargaining, a Report to the Business Advisory and Planning Council for the Department of Commerce*, 1934, p. 2.

duction industries where, prior to the Recovery Act, individual bargaining relationships prevailed; namely, iron and steel, automobile manufacturing, and the manufacture of rubber products. By the end of 1934 there was hardly an important establishment in these three industries where an employee representation plan was not in force, the most important exceptions being the Ford properties in automobile manufacturing.[36] Company unionism was also strengthened in some industries, such as petroleum refineries and power and light plants, where it had been established for many years before the Recovery Act.

In many of the large plants in the iron and steel and automobile manufacturing industries, employee representation schemes were recast during 1933-34 so as to liberalize their provisions. Thus, the more rigid limitations upon the right to vote or hold office under such plans, based on age, length of service, and service record were either abolished or made less restrictive; also the declared functions of such plans were enlarged. Nevertheless, it remains true that employee representation plans in most plants bear the impress of management influence and are not fashioned for the specific purpose of carrying on group bargaining about the terms of employment. At best, employee representation plans constitute a device (1) for adjusting employee grievances due to the effects of employment conditions established by management, and (2) for enlisting the worker's loyalty to the establishment in which he is employed.

American trade unions since 1922 have regarded the company union as the chief obstacle to their growth. It

---

[36] The later emergence of "works councils" in automobile manufacturing makes it likely that the company union plans will be dropped or at least radically modified.

was the hope of many trade union leaders that Section 7(a) would put an end to company unions. It is one of the ironies of history that Section 7(a), presumably intended to enlarge the legal opportunities for independent labor self-organization, should have thrown the obstacle of company unionism more directly and ominously than ever before across the path of the A. F. of L.

CHAPTER XIX

SUMMARY AND OUTLOOK

In the preceding chapters we described and attempted to evaluate some of the major shifts and changes in industrial relations attributable to the effectuation of the labor provisions of the Recovery Act. Before discussing the problems of and the outlook for the immediate future, it will be helpful to recapitulate the main results.

REVIEW OF DEVELOPMENTS

The principal developments in industrial relations between June 1933 and March 1935 due to the Recovery Act may be summarized as follows:

1. The NRA as a code-making and code administering agency evolved a new method for enacting protective labor legislation on a nation-wide basis, industry by industry. The incorporation of labor standards into codes of fair competition may, if the code device is perpetuated, serve as a substitute for or as a supplement to statutes enacted by Congress and by the several state legislatures. Regarded as protective labor legislation, the code requirements on wages and hours are, in large measure, indeterminate, and administratively difficult to construe and to enforce.

2. Two procedures whereby code labor standards may be formulated have been evolved: First, there is the "normal" procedure according to which proposals emanating from employer groups pass through the mill of administrative criticism, amendment and redrafting. This procedure we have termed "indirect representative bargaining." Second, there is the "special" procedure of

527

"direct collective bargaining" under which employers and trade unions get together, either to draft code labor standards or to conclude agreements pursuant to Section 7(b). This procedure tends to vest collective agreements with the force of law.

3. The independent labor boards, acting as quasi-judicial tribunals developing a "common law" of Section 7(a), represent the emergence of a new governmental machinery for introducing a uniform pattern of collective bargaining throughout codified industry. The underlying principles of this "common law" are: free elections of representatives, majority rule, exertion of reasonable efforts to make and maintain agreements, and restraint upon discriminatory discharges. The efforts of the boards to put these principles into practical effect ran up against resistance by anti-union employers.

4. Neither the NRA agencies with reference to labor "complaints" nor the labor boards with reference to labor "disputes" have been able to work out an adequate system of enforcement and compliance. The two disciplinary agencies, the Compliance Division of the NRA and the Department of Justice, have proved insufficient for the purpose. Blue Eagle removals and federal court proceedings alike have so far failed to secure thoroughgoing compliance with the wage and hour provisions of the codes or with the "common law" of Section 7(a).

5. Organized labor took the stand that the term "industrial self-government" should be interpreted to include labor representation, preferably equal representation, on code authorities. The NRA did not accept the trade union view on this matter. Only a handful of trade unions, and these functioning in industries fairly well organized on the labor side, were able to secure direct representation on code authorities.

6. A few trade unions solidified their position and conducted successful campaigns in what was once "open-shop" territory, and thus gained in membership and power. The trade unions secured a provisional foothold, but little more, in several of the basic mass production industries. Membership in the A. F. of L. organizations increased by more than a million workers. The number of wage earners working under trade union collective agreements also increased considerably. The A. F. of L. was forced to reconsider its established program on industrial versus craft unionism and to make important changes in some of its traditional policies and methods.

7. A few unions were able to incorporate into and to adapt to the administrative machinery of the codes pre-existent mechanisms for dealing with labor grievances and complaints. By gaining influence in the use of this administrative machinery, these trade unions obtained a strategic advantage over and against anti-union employers and dual union movements. The NRA made little progress, however, in the general direction of equipping all codes with labor adjustment apparatus.

8. The company union movement went ahead even more rapidly than trade unionism. The result has been to block the A. F. of L. for the time being. But the movement has another aspect as well. As a result of the establishment of company unions in industries and plants where individual bargaining prevailed before, hundreds of thousands of American workers have been familiarized, for the first time, with the ideas of collective action and self-organization. Many employee representation plans have been made more desirable from the workers' point of view. Furthermore, the trade union-company union conflict has focused public attention upon the larger issues of labor organization.

9. Inspired with the vision of "partnership" among labor, management, and government, the trade unions have come to rely upon the NRA and the labor boards more than upon "direct action." The result has been to involve the trade unions in the beginnings of a nation-wide network of governmental agencies for the determination of labor standards and the adjustment of labor disputes. The result is likely to be a trend towards compulsory arbitration, both in industries where trade unions are firmly entrenched, and where they are getting started. The trade unions are moving in the direction of greater responsibility to the government and of a semi-public status.

10. Industrial peace has been disturbed during the past two years by successive nation-wide strike waves. The principal factor in most strikes has been union "recognition," the attempt by organized labor to redeem what it regards as the inherent pledge of Section 7(a). Another important motive behind strikes has been that of exerting external pressure upon the NRA to treat trade unions as principals in the code-making process. A third factor has been the desire to implement the codes with adequate machinery for the application and enforcement of collective bargaining and other labor requirements. The ordinary motivating causes of strikes—grievances over wages and hours—have also been at work.[1]

On the basis of these developments we may say that the effectuation of the Recovery Act, in so far as labor relations are concerned, has been a bundle of missed op-

---

[1] Typical of the union "recognition" strike was the Reading hosiery walkout. Typical of strikes aimed at the code-making process were the needle trade walkouts. Resentment against the then existent adjustment apparatus was one of the causes of the nation-wide textile walkout.

portunities, doubtful compromises, and unpremeditated achievements: missed opportunities in that the government failed to grasp the chance of formulating a clear policy on collective bargaining; doubtful compromises in that the government, so far as it did act on policies, adapted them to the pressure of external forces; unpremeditated achievements in that few persons could have foreseen the skill with which some trade unions would be able to turn Section 7 to their advantage, and the vigor with which employers in many of the major industries would push the company union movement.

Although the actual results achieved by the NRA have been small compared to the expectations it raised, potentially the NRA and related agencies have acted as a challenge to the *status quo* in industrial relations. It is this challenge and its implications which have made of the NRA and of the labor boards a focus of agitation and turmoil in employer-employee relationships.

LABOR RELATIONS AND ECONOMIC POLICY

Industrial relations are only part of a general labor policy. We have centered our attention in preceding sections on the procedures and techniques of industrial relations, because of the dominant part which these have played in the impact of the Recovery Act upon wage earners and employers. To find an answer to the problems involved in the *method* of industrial relations is the first step towards a peaceful and orderly determination of *labor standards,* that is, wages, hours, and other working conditions. And it is labor standards which constitute the substance of a labor policy.

It is not within our province here to pass judgment upon the practical elements or theoretical bases of any general labor policy which the federal government should pursue. The problems involved cover a much wider area than the NRA. Their discussion in detail would necessitate a consideration of all the policies of the New Deal in so far as they affect wage-earning groups.

Brief comment, however, is called for here on three points in order to indicate the larger setting in which the analysis of this chapter must be viewed. First, a general labor policy may be regarded as the sum total of specific policies with regard to wages, hours, economic security, apprenticeship, hiring and firing, and so forth. The present legislative tendency is to enact separate measures on each of these problems without regard to their interrelations. Because of political considerations that may be an inevitable procedure. But it is neither the best nor the most logical way of developing a coherent labor policy, in view of the unity of the wage earner's problems in modern society. The opposite method—that of carrying out a unified system of labor measures—may not be immediately feasible, but it would be well for our governmental agencies, especially the United States Department of Labor, to aim at developing such a procedure in the long run. This might be accomplished in part by establishing in the Department a labor policy co-ordinating division which would make the study of an integrated legislative program its main task.

Second, the pattern of industrial relations exerts a profound influence upon the content of labor standards. Any attempt to maintain a definite wage and hour structure under the NRA or under any other system of government supervision will necessitate an answer to such questions as: How far should the traditional methods of individual bargaining remain undisturbed? Within what limits can "indirect representative bargaining" be effective for achieving improvements in labor standards? Shall the government promote direct collective bargaining as the basis of employer-employee relations?

Third, neither the contents of labor standards nor the patterns of industrial relations can be considered apart from the government's general economic policy. The method of determining employment relationships by collective bargaining involves taking a stand on the larger aspects of the national economy. For if one believes that the best economic results can be obtained by making our national economy as free and flexible as possible, one must regard collective agreements, which fix labor standards on a group basis and for long periods of time, as a cause of undesirable rigidity. On the other hand, collective contracts may be regarded as one of the methods for slowing down the processes of economic change and for achieving a higher degree of stability and balance in the economic system. Here it is evident that we plunge into the general issue of free competitive markets versus programs of economic control.

Whether the tendency is to be toward a greater freedom and flexibility in the economic system, or toward greater collective action and agreement, is a matter open to any degree of discussion. We shall not enter into such a discussion here. What is pertinent here is the bearing of our study on the issues involved. The NRA exemplifies one effort to improve industrial relations primarily through the use of associative action under government supervision. Our analysis shows that the NRA has proved an unsatisfactory mould for shaping a comprehensive policy on industrial relations. It is certainly incapable of becoming a vehicle for a complete labor policy. Our general conclusion is that it is advisable to lift the job of formulating and maintaining a general labor policy out of the NRA and to entrust it to such special agencies as may be called for by the requirements of the public interests.

It is important to realize clearly the issues and problems which must be faced if a general program of associative action under government supervision is to continue in force. We shall review here some of the more basic problems which have been brought to the fore by the Recovery Act itself, as presented in the industrial relations section of our study.

ISSUES INHERENT IN SECTION 7

Section 7 of the Recovery Act is uncertain in purpose, vague in content, and ambiguous in language. To these attributes of the law can be traced much of the shifting and a good part of the "muddling through" that have characterized the federal government's labor policies since the summer of 1933.

Upon close analysis, however, Section 7 is seen to contain the possibilities of three distinct approaches to the problem of industrial relations: First, Section 7(a) suggests the approach of giving workers "safeguarded free choice" in the designation of representatives empowered to bargain collectively on their behalf. Second, Section 7(b) suggests the approach of establishing labor standards by collective agreement between employers and trade unions, such agreements when approved by the President to have the force of a code. Third, Section 7(c) suggests the approach of setting wages, hours, and other working standards by Presidential action in industries where mutual agreements are not made.

Section 7, taken as a whole, raises the highly controversial issue of collective bargaining as a method of shaping industrial relations. The merits of this method have been and remain a subject of dispute. Collective bargaining has been defended as a means of reducing pre-existent "inequalities in bargaining power" between employers and their individual employees and as a technique of "stabilizing" employment relations. It has been assailed because it presumably gives "monopoly" powers to labor organizations and increases the "rigidity" of an economic mechanism which, it is claimed, is already much too rigid for the public welfare.

The major issue of collective versus individual bargaining will not be discussed here in view of the attention which the NRA has focused upon the forms and procedures of collective bargaining itself. Advocates of trade unionism and of company unionism both have found arguments in Section 7(a) to support their respective causes. On the one hand are those who would interpret the term collective bargaining in its traditional meaning as a system whereby independent labor organizations and employers meet to negotiate collective agreements, fixing wages, hours, and other conditions of employment applicable to all the wage earners of some single plant or department, or of some craft or industry. On the other hand are those who claim that the various employee representation plans—"company unions"—are a more modern form of collective bargaining and more conducive to a co-operative relationship between the workers and management.

In view of the central place which this issue holds in the discussion of labor relations under Section 7(a), it may be well to state briefly the contentions of the two sides.

The advocates of company unions make five points against trade unions which may be summarized as follows: First, trade unions, because of their usual craft structure, cannot develop the worker's loyalty to a particular plant. Also, jurisdictional squabbles are bound to arise. Second, trade unions, both craft and industrial, are directed by professional leaders who must cause disturbances in order to hold their followers. Also, trade unions interfere with plant discipline by demanding the right to visit shops; to watch over working conditions; to enforce union rules; to limit the power of "hiring and firing." Third, trade unions are managed by outsiders who do not appreciate the needs and difficulties of particular employers. Fourth, trade unions drain the wage earner's purse by levying dues and assessments. Fifth, trade unions are controlled by cliques and engage in "machine politics."

In constructive support of the company union, its protagonists contend that it is the only form of collective bargaining agency capable of protecting the worker's true interests. In detail they argue as follows: the company union, which covers all the workers in an establishment, has a structure adapted to the industrial organization of business. The company union is flexible in procedures and methods. It cultivates friendly relations between workers and management, and gives all employees a voice in shaping the labor policy of their plant. It is not burdensome to the workers because it collects no dues and is financed by the employer.

The advocates of trade unions make five points against company unions which may be summarized as follows: First, company unions are a sham and subterfuge, organized by employers for no other reason than to ward off trade unions, and with no sincere purpose of promoting the worker's interests. Second, even when sincere in motivation, the company union cannot function as a vehicle of genuine collective bargaining, for it is dominated and financed by the employer. Subject at all times to transfer or discharge, the employee representatives are incapable of acting as "free" men. Third, the company union cannot adequately protect the workers or greatly improve their wages, hours, and other working conditions. Fellow employee representatives are hardly likely to develop into trained and efficient negotiators or to acquire the statistical and other data necessary for negotiating with the employer. Limited in their knowledge to a single plant, the representatives cannot appreciate labor conditions in the industry as a whole. Fourth, the company union is at bottom a subtle form of coercion by which the management tries to keep the workers docile and obedient. Fifth, at its best the company union bespeaks a form of paternalism out of step with democratic traditions and ideals. Would any group of employers have faith in a trade association organized and financed by their competitors and rivals?

It is therefore contended by its protagonists that the trade union is the only agency which can truly protect the worker's interests. It is their own organization, which they can mould and use as they think best for their own good. Devoted to the making of collective agreements, it is served by leaders who are expert in their functions and loyal to their constituents—an advantage not outweighed by occasional abuses.

The issues as stated above have become so acute under the NRA that further discussion is justified.

Safeguarded Free Choice

Without comprehending too clearly just what it implied, Congress wrote into the Recovery Act the principle that workers, in order to bargain collectively, should be free to designate representatives of their own choice.[2] In interpreting the statute, the National Labor Board and the National Labor Relations Board laid the foundations of what may be called a "common law" of collective bargaining. The principles laid down by the boards tend to set up a definite type of collective bargaining. The NLB-NLRB interpretation of Section 7(a) calls for employee referendums in order to ascertain the free will of the workers: By what set of representatives do they wish to have their collective bargain executed? This interpretation calls for majority rule as a device to identify such representatives and to empower them to negotiate a wage and hour agreement on behalf of the totality of workers. The interpretation stresses the duty of employers and employees to exert every reasonable effort to make and maintain agreements, because the bilateral contract, as the end result, is what gives meaning to collective bargaining. The interpretation also implies that the government cannot allow employer dominated organizations—"company unions" in the invidious sense —to shut out independent labor organizations.

The Labor Board's interpretation of Section 7(a) is based on considerations which we have discussed elsewhere.[3] Briefly summarized, the considerations presented by the NLB and the NLRB run as follows: The aim of collective bargaining is a collective agreement on the terms of employment. An agreement will be more equitable if both parties bargain through their own representatives freely chosen. If there is a difference of opinion as to

[2] For a discussion of Congressional intent, see Paul F. Brissenden, "Genesis and Import of the Collective Bargaining Provisions of the Recovery Act," *Economic Essays in Honor of W. C. Mitchell*, 1935, Chap. II.

[3] See Lewis L. Lorwin and Arthur Wubnig, *Section 7(a), Labor Boards and Collective Bargaining*. To be published in 1935.

who the representatives of any group of workers are, the best way to settle the issue is by an election, the method of democracy. To be free, elections must be carried on under proper conditions; namely, outside the plant, after working hours, and so forth. If the workers split their votes, then the representatives obtaining a majority of the votes should bargain for all the workers; this is majority rule—the basic principle of democracy. Majority rule in collective bargaining is justified by experience, which proves that collective bargaining is nullified in practice wherever the workers are divided. Majority rule is also necessitated by the fact that labor standards cannot be properly set for all the workers of a plant, craft, or industry, if different sets of representatives bargain at the same time with the same employer. Finally, company unions, in the invidious sense of the term, turn collective bargaining into a sham, for where the employer dominates a labor organization which he imposes on his employees, he negates the idea of free choice and sits on both sides of the conference table. Such, in effect, is the manner in which the boards have construed the statute.

Senator Wagner's Labor Relations bill of 1935 (the successor to his Labor Disputes bill of 1934) seeks in effect to project the NLB-NLRB interpretation of Section 7(a) into the law of the land.[4] At the same time, the bill seeks to endow the NLRB with more adequate enforcement powers than it now possesses. Because of its frank and outspoken point of view, the Labor Relations bill has served to precipitate the highly controversial issue of trade versus company unionism into the arena

[4] For the text of the 1935 measure, see 74 Cong. 1 sess., S.1958; for the proposed text of the 1934 measure, see 73 Cong. 2. sess., S.2926; for the text as reported out by the Senate Committee on Education and Labor, see 73 Cong. 2 sess., S.2926 (rep. 1184).

of public discussion. Trade unions and sympathizers with the organized labor movement have rallied to the support of the measure; employer associations and spokesmen of employee representation plans have come forward to oppose it.[5]

The merits of the dispute aside, one fundamental point is clear. The NLB and the NLRB have filled the somewhat amorphous outlines of Section 7(a) with a clear and specific content. If the type of collective bargaining aimed at by the NLB-NLRB interpretation of the statute is what Congress wishes to encourage, then Section 7(a) ought to be replaced by frank and outspoken legislation which would affirm, in explicit detail, the principles which the two boards have sought to read into the existing law.

Legal Status of Collective Agreements

Prior to the Recovery Act, it was by no means certain in American law whether collective agreements should be regarded as real contracts or as mere "memoranda of usage." It was by no means a clearly established principle that the terms of such agreements were binding upon the parties subscribing thereto.[6] Section 7(b), therefore, was a tremendous leap in a new direction. For it implied that terms of bilateral contracts between representative labor and employer groups, when approved by the President, shall have the same force as the provisions of a code;

[5] The arguments for and against the 1934 measure (Labor Disputes bill) are contained in 73 Cong. 2 sess., Hearings before Senate Committee on Education and Labor, on S.2926. The arguments for and against the 1935 measure (Labor Relations bill) are contained in 74 Cong. 1 sess., Hearings before Senate Committee on Education and Labor, on S.1958.

[6] For a discussion of the question, see Ralph F. Fuchs, "Collective Labor Agreements in American Law," *St. Louis Law Review*, Vol. 10, No. 1, pp. 1-33. This article does not carry the discussion down beyond 1924. But the legal status of collective agreement was not much clearer in 1933 than it was at the time the article was written.

shall be enforceable, in other words, against all members of an industry or trade regardless of individual failure to assent.

That Congress was aware of the implications of Section 7(b) is hardly likely. In the minds of those who prepared the bill, Section 7(b) was to serve to handle NRA wage and hour problems in a few areas of American industry where collective bargaining was already highly developed: for example, the building, printing, and needle trades and coal mining.[7] And in the sequel, as we have seen, Section 7(b) was actually applied to an extremely narrow range of codified industries.

There is no logical tie-in between Section 7(b) and Section 7(a). The mere fact that a government might see fit to stimulate the growth of collective bargaining agencies by safeguarding free choice does not of itself require the government to invest the collective agreements which result with the force of law. The logical tie-in is between Section 7(b) and Section 7(c) as alternative methods of putting a "bottom" to wages and a "ceiling" to hours. Where Section 7(c) supposes that the investigatory agencies of the government are capable of fixing wages and hours which are socially desirable, Section 7(b) supposes that, subject to governmental approval of the terms agreed on, collective bargaining, in industries and trades accustomed to it, can be used for the purpose.

Those who oppose collective bargaining as a method for determining wages and hours necessarily reject also the principle implied in Section 7(b). To confer legal force on the terms of collective agreements and to extend these terms to non-signatory parties, they assert, would re-enforce the monopoly power of trade unions. Some

[7] Based on an interview with Mr. Richberg.

representatives of employer groups have argued, however, that if labor organizations are to be vested with special rights in regard to collective bargaining, they should accept corresponding duties, such as legal responsibility for their agents and for the enforcement of agreements.

Those who advocate collective bargaining are not agreed on the issues raised by Section 7(b). Some would support the intent of the statute, because, they argue, all employers in the same industry or trade would then be compelled to compete at the same level of "living wages" and "labor costs." Others are doubtful about such a policy because, they argue, labor organizations would then become subject to excessive government control.

At present it would seem premature for Congress to enact legislation on the legal status of collective agreements. The subject is one which calls for careful thought on underlying economic premises, for an exact weighing of fundamental social values, and for a comprehensive survey of experience in other countries, such as the Scandinavian nations and some of the British dominions. However, if Congress should see fit to push further the principles embodied in Section 7(b), it would have a positive duty to see that any agreement approved was consistent with good public policy.

The question of Section 7(b)'s future is also dependent on how far the government pursues its present program of establishing minimum wages and maximum hours, whether by means of codes or otherwise. This brings us to the issues raised by Section 7(c).

Government Fixing of Minimum Labor Standards

Experience, both at home and abroad, suggests that a government which engages in fixing minimum wages and maximum hours may be guided by four main purposes:

1. To "safeguard" unorganized workers, who because their own bargaining power is "inadequate," are likely to suffer from "exploitation" by "anti-social" employers or "parasitic" industries.

2. To establish wage scales at such a level that those wage earners who have employment are assured of an income adequate for the purposes of a "living wage."

3. To promote "fair competition" by establishing a "floor" for wages and a "ceiling" for hours, thus helping to equalize labor costs.

4. To stimulate the revival phases of the business cycle, upon the theory that the depression phases persist because "mass purchasing power" is inadequate.

Behind each of the purposes thus stated there exist many assumptions which would require the most careful analysis before they were to be considered the basis for action. No such analysis being attempted here, there is no intent to indicate the desirability or undesirability of action along these lines. The general questions involved in a policy of government fixing of minimum wages and maximum hours, and some of the more general issues such as "purchasing power" and "fair competition" are discussed elsewhere in this book.[8] We are concerned here only with the relation of such a policy to collective bargaining.

We may reasonably suppose that if the government stands firmly behind "safeguarded free choice," independent labor organizations in the United States will gradually be extended to new groups of workers and collective agreements will become more numerous. It is also safe to assume, however, that for some time to come there will remain large areas of industry in which independent labor organizations will be unable to establish them-

[8] See Pts. III, V, and VI.

selves, partly because of resistance by employers, partly because of the workers' psychology. If, within these areas, a policy of setting minimum standards by government agencies will continue, problems will be created as a result of the differentials in standards established by government agencies, on the one hand, and through collective agreements, on the other. That such a condition is likely to develop is suggested not only by the logic of the case, but by the experience with codes formed by "indirect representative" and "direct collective" bargaining respectively.[9]

IMPLEMENTATION FOR DISPUTES AND COMPLAINTS

In devising mechanisms for dealing with labor complaints and labor disputes, it would be judicious to distinguish between conflicts over "rights" and conflicts over "interests."

The distinction is a familiar concept to most European students of industrial relations. A conflict over "rights" relates to some contract right or right at law: for example, the provisions of a minimum wage law, the terms of a collective agreement, or the labor standards prescribed by a code. The problem is one of the judicial determination of the obligations imposed on employers and employees. A conflict over "interests" relates to a struggle for setting the terms and conditions of employment. It may be illustrated by the process of negotiating collective agreements between employers and labor organizations and by the making of code labor provisions. The basic problem here is one of so guiding the course of negotiations as to bring about a settlement on terms consistent with the public welfare. The specific questions are: What hours? what wages? and the like.

[9] Chap. XVII.

Mechanisms for handling conflicts over "rights" should be separated, as far as practicable, from those devised for settling conflicts over "interests." The mechanisms for determining "rights" perform judicial and policing functions. Judicial issues arise because of alleged non-observance; policing is required to assure the observance of labor standards clearly set forth in federal or state enactments, in code provisions, or in collective agreements. The mechanisms for determining "interests" perform a facilitative function. The task is to hasten the establishment, by mutual agreement, of such standards on wages, hours, and working conditions as are consonant with the public interest.

The tense emotions aroused by the "strike waves" under the NRA are reflected in the demand of employers' associations for laws in favor of compulsory arbitration and waiting periods during which strikes would be illegal. These demands are made, as a rule, without careful consideration of the premises on which such legislation is based and of the possible consequences. For the government to engage in compulsory arbitration means that the government must fix wage rates in all situations where strikes occur or threaten to occur. This leads toward a state of affairs whereunder all wage scales are potentially subject to determination by the government. Whether or not either policy—that of compulsory arbitration or that of government fixing of wage rates— is desirable, the advocates of the one must be willing to accept the other.

A certain amount of open conflict between employers and employees would seem to be inevitable, no matter what means of avoidance are pursued. No democratic country has as yet succeeded in devising machinery for eliminating all strikes, or, for that matter, major strikes alone. Neither the elaborate adjustment devices developed in Germany between 1920 and 1930, nor the compulsory arbitration systems of New Zealand and Australia, nor the waiting period requirements of Canadian law, nor the flexible arrangements of industrial courts, joint boards, and works councils in Great Britain have put an end to strikes and lockouts. There is no reason to suppose that where other democratic countries have failed, the United States can succeed.

Further, the maintenance of industrial peace does not depend primarily upon the presence or absence of boards, commissions, courts, and bureaus devoted to that purpose. Surely all such devices are helpful. At bottom, however, labor unrest results from a complex of employment, economic, social, and psychological conditions. These include the worker's ability to earn an adequate livelihood; the duration, extent, and intensity of the labor exacted from him; the security of his employment; the continuity of his income; his status on the job; his opportunities for promotion and advancement; the grating of his ego against the ego of the "boss" or "foreman." By setting up boards, commissions, courts, and bureaus, the government merely devises mechanical ways and means for reducing the area of potential conflict, and for mitigating the violence of disputes which do break out from time to time.

GOVERNMENTAL RECOGNITION OF TRADE UNIONS

Governmental recognition of trade unions as the exclusive agencies authorized to speak on behalf of all wage earners has been advocated, expressly or by implication, by the American Federation of Labor.

Adherence to such a policy assumes that no type of labor organization other than the trade union is qualified to perform the functions which collective bargaining requires. Those who make this assumption rest their argument, for the most part, upon the traditional occupation of the field of collective bargaining by trade unions.

It is easy to understand why trade unions should be eager for the privilege of exclusive recognition as collective bargaining agencies. If thus recognized by the government, the trade unions would find their organizational tasks considerably simplified, and would probably gain enormously in membership, resources, and pressure power. The trade unions, it is likely, would become a truly co-equal factor with management in the governance of industrial relations.

Despite the apparent simplicity of the idea, the policy of granting to trade unions alone, recognition as instrumentalities of collective bargaining raises questions which its advocates and sponsors generally refuse to face. Possessing quasi-official power, enjoying quasi-official status, the trade unions would have to submit to a considerable degree of governmental supervision and regulation. As an offset to the privileges of exclusive governmental recognition, there would be the burdens of a semi-official status. It is doubtful whether those who sponsor the granting of the privileges would be ready to accept the correlative burdens.[10]

From the point of view of public interest, at least two important objections may be raised against the proposal to recognize trade unions exclusively as agencies of collective bargaining. First, the government is far from adequately equipped to exercise the amount and the kind of direct control which would be required of it. Second,

[10] For a discussion of the probabilities that a semi-official trade union movement may emerge in the United States, see Lewis L. Lorwin, "The Challenge to Organized Labor," *Current History Magazine*, Sept. 1933.

for our government to take over the regulation of an official trade union movement might readily lead toward patterns of control incompatible with the ideals of American democracy.

CONCLUSION

Whether or not the NRA is continued, the federal government will be confronted by all of the issues discussed above. The extent to which these issues should be dealt with by separate statutes; the extent to which the several issues might be combined for statutory enactment —these are problems, not of labor policy, but of legislative technique. In any event, whatever new measures are enacted should be separated from the Recovery Act in whatever form the latter may be renewed or extended, so as to give the federal labor policies an independent foundation in law.